Walter Besant

The City of Refuge

Walter Besant

The City of Refuge

ISBN/EAN: 9783744713221

Printed in Europe, USA, Canada, Australia, Japan

Cover: Foto ©Lupo / pixelio.de

More available books at **www.hansebooks.com**

THE MAN CARRIED A LARGE BASKET. [p. 103.

THE CITY OF REFUGE

BY

WALTER BESANT

AUTHOR OF
'ALL SORTS AND CONDITIONS OF MEN,' 'CHILDREN OF GIBEON,'
'THE MASTER CRAFTSMAN,' ETC.

A NEW EDITION
WITH A FRONTISPIECE BY F. S. WILSON

LONDON
CHATTO & WINDUS
1897

PREFACE

As I have received certain questions and heard certain irresponsible criticisms concerning alleged rapidity of production, based on the appearance of the 'City of Refuge' only a few months after that of the 'Master Craftsman,' I think it is necessary to explain that the former was written for serial publication in the *Pall Mall Magazine* for last year, 1895, and in accordance with that arrangement the story occupied me during the greater part of the year 1894; that it was not found convenient to carry out the original intention, and that the serial publication was therefore deferred until the present year, viz., from April to October. Again, if the matter concerns anybody, I might mention that it would be to me, and I believe to everybody, utterly impossible to write two novels at the same time.

Certain alterations and additions to the story as it appeared in the Magazine may perhaps be noted by any reader who first saw it in serial form.

W. B.

UNITED UNIVERSITY CLUB,
September, 1896.

CONTENTS

PROLOGUE.

	PAGE
WHO SHALL RID ME?	1

BOOK I.
THE HOUSE OF MEDITATION.

CHAPTER
I.	THE MASTER	21
II.	THE MONASTIC HABIT	30
III.	RESTORATION AND MEDITATION	41
IV.	LABORARE EST ORARE	56
V.	A WARNING AND A PROMISE	68
VI.	'NOT TO-DAY'	76
VII.	A SECOND AND A THIRD MESSAGE	89

BOOK II.
AFTER FIVE WEEKS.

I.	STRAWBERRIES! FINE STRAWBERRIES!	101
II.	VOICES IN THE NIGHT	112
III.	ON THE VERANDAH	125

CONTENTS

CHAPTER		PAGE
IV.	SINGLE ATTACHMENTS	137
V.	AN EXPLANATION	147
VI.	LADY OSTERLEY'S ARRIVAL	154
VII.	PROPOS D'AMOUR	162
VIII.	CRITICISM	168
IX.	REVOLT	179
X.	FLIGHT	189
XI.	MARRIAGE FOR ELEVATION	198
XII.	REVOLUTION	213
XIII.	WHAT IS HER NAME?	225
XIV.	HUSBAND AND WIFE	240
XV.	BACK AGAIN	257
XVI.	THE MASTER ABDICATES	271
XVII.	THE ORDEAL BY CARDS	285
XVIII.	FREEDOM	303

THE CITY OF REFUGE

PROLOGUE.

WHO SHALL RID ME?

'GILBERT! At last!'

She had been leaning forward, her hands clasped over her knees, staring straight before her; her eyes were angry and hard—there were black rings round them; her face was pale; her look was set; and her lips were drawn as one who suffers physical pain.

On the floor there rolled about a child of a year and a half. The nurse, who had brought in the boy, thinking to distract her mistress in this mysterious trouble, stood watching at the door, for the mother seemed not even to know that the child was there. Great, indeed, must be the trouble when even the child could remain unnoticed.

She sprang to her feet with a cry. 'At last!' she repeated, and gave her visitor both hands—nay, she seized him by both hands—the action was like the despairing clutch of one who is drowning, one over whom the waves are sinking for the last time. 'Gilbert! You have come!'

Then the nurse, who was an intelligent young person, stepped forward and carried off the child. Mr. Gilbert had come home. Everybody knew that whatever was wrong would be set right when Mr. Gilbert came home. This belief, which was universal, is almost enough by itself to explain Mr. Gilbert.

'I reached home the day before yesterday. I received your note this morning. I came on to town at once. Now, my dear Dorabyn——'

She threw up her arms. 'Oh! I must tell someone, or I shall go mad.'

'Tell me, then, as much or as little as you please. What you said in your note is the most wonderful thing, the most incredible thing——'

'Use up all the adjectives in the language, and you will not find one that is adequate. My husband, as I told you, is actually, literally, and irretrievably ruined: nay, what I did not write, he is disgraced, degraded—among those few who know—sent out of the country.'

'Disgraced? Sir Charles?' Gilbert gasped with bewilderment. 'But—but—how?' Because, you see, a man may go very far indeed before all these things happen to him—ruin, disgrace, exile. Many doors may be closed to the wicked man; but this is a world of various standards: many others still remain open to him—doors of other wicked men's houses: the world is full of wicked men. What could Sir Charles Osterley have done so miraculously wicked as to bring all these things upon his head?

Yet the face of the woman showed that she was not exaggerating. Never had Gilbert seen that face, which he knew very well indeed, in all its moods, betray such a tumult of emotions. She was, to begin with, the proudest, coldest woman outwardly, in all England: too proud to betray the least sign of weakness at any possible or conceivable disaster. But her pride was broken down in the presence of disaster inconceivable, impossible, irretrievable; one that would be felt by the children and the grandchildren to the third and fourth generation, unless—which seemed impossible—something could still be done.

'I sent for you, Gilbert. You are my oldest friend—at such a moment as this you seem to be my only friend.'

Gilbert was one of those very rare creatures who have received the gift of making every woman—except the shrew, the termagant, the envious, the evil speaker, the liar, the slanderer, and the Devil—his close and personal friend in a very surprising manner and in an incredibly brief space of time. I know not how the thing is done; of all the gifts and graces bestowed upon man it is the most enviable: in my own experience I have known but two or three men who possess this gift. Mere cleverness will not command that power; by no accomplishments, arts, intellect, or worldly success can any man acquire it: one must be born with it; women, in fact, are not generally so very greatly moved by superiority of intellect or accomplishments, or success, things which they regard either as means of making money, like an office in the City; or as so many parlour tricks, like playing the zither. It is a gift of the gods; it is a heaven-descended power. Gilbert had it; there is no more to be said about it. With Lady Osterley, however, he was a really old friend—a friend of youth: they were of the same age; they grew up together; as a boy he received all her confidences. When all the world fell in love with her for her beauty, which was cold, and for her moneybags, which were heavy, Gilbert did not. He remained her friend and continued to receive her confidences.

And now, what had happened?

'How, my dear Dorabyn?' Gilbert repeated. 'I read in the paper——' he had the *Times* rolled up in his hand. He opened it and read: '"The announcement made in another column of the resignation and retirement into private life of Sir Charles Osterley will surprise most of our readers, and cause great regret on both sides of the House. That the nation should lose at so early an age the services of a statesman who has already acquired the confidence of his countrymen for probity, clearness of head, and a masterly grip of the problems of the day, is nothing less than a national disaster."'

'"National disaster,"' Dorabyn repeated. 'Go on, Gilbert: "national disaster." Is there more?'

'Yes, there is more. "It is understood that the decision arrived at by Sir Charles is final. Long though his life may be spared, there is no hope, it is said, that he will ever be able to return to the field of politics. This surrender of a career is not, we understand, suddenly forced upon Sir Charles. He has had it in contemplation for some time, though hitherto he has been able to entertain some hope that his symptoms would take a favourable turn. That hope has now been abandoned. While the country regrets, on its own account, to lose the services of this young statesman, we must not forget the sympathies which we must extend to Sir Charles on the loss of most that he prized——"'

'"Most that he prized,"' Lady Osterley repeated bitterly.

'"We must not forget what this blow means to a man in his position——"'

'Ah!' said Lady Osterley, 'if only the writer knew what it really does mean to him! But I should like to hear what he thinks it means.'

'"Loss of place; loss of power; loss of those higher offices—even the highest—which would probably have fallen to him in due time; loss of rank, if he desired higher rank——"'

'He desired everything, Gilbert—everything. I hope that he will buy a copy of this paper. It should be pleasant reading.'

'"These are grievous losses,"' Gilbert went on reading: '"it requires great philosophy or great resignation to lose these things just as they seemed within reach. But there is more. It is the laudable ambition of every statesman to occupy a page in history: for this young statesman, cut off, so to speak, at the outset, there is no such place possible. And again, it is reasonable to suppose that every statesman looks forward with hope to the passing of broad and wide measures, conducive to the public welfare. The nobler part of such a man survives in the services, the harvest-bearing services, which in his lifetime he is privileged to render to his country. All these things and more have been lost by Sir Charles Osterley.'

'You have read enough,' said the wife: 'I hope that he will read it too, and that the words may become to him a scourge of scorpions. Oh! Gilbert, I am becoming like a railing fishwife. But you will calm me. Oh, my dear Gilbert!—she laid her sisterly head upon his shoulder—' you have come home in my direst need. You will tell me what to do.'

'Well—but there is nothing in this paper about degradation.'

'Yet the man is degraded. First of all, he is not stricken with any disease at all—he is quite well and strong. Next, he will go abroad immediately, because he must. Thirdly, he will never dare to return again. Give me a minute or two—to recover—Gilbert.' She walked to the window and looked out. Then she turned. 'You are looking well. That is the photograph of my boy: did you know I had a boy?' She went on saying things conventional, without meaning, as if speaking unconsciously. Then she left the window and fell into silence, standing on the hearthrug, gazing into the fire.

A tall and handsome woman; something reginal in her appearance; a woman born for authority and high place. Her neck looked as if diamonds would grace it; her dark hair looked as if it wanted the gleam of a coronet; upon her shoulders lay the queenly drapery of costly lace. In ancient days she would have been a queen or a countess by right of her beauty; for, of course, none but one of the conquering race could produce a woman so victorious. In later—say Tudor—times, Dorabyn, as the Lady Imperia or as the Lady

Gloriana, would have led after her an ever-lengthening chain of captive lovers: they would have fought for her; they would have written poetry about the sunlight in her eyes and the tangles of her hair and the blinding splendour of her face. In the restricted manner possible for a self-governed age, which does not understand flames and darts and raptures and swoonings, which is comparatively passionless, Dorabyn could only follow the example of Lady Imperia at a distance. She had many admirers: all the men admired her; some dared to make love to her, but were speedily dismissed; she was gracious always, as becomes a gentlewoman, but she did not invite the wooing of the casual youth of the period. And as to marriage she had her own ideas. 'I understand very well,' she wrote in one of her letters to Gilbert, 'that marriage is a partnership in which the man must have the nominal command; the woman's is the second place. This must always be the case, in spite of the advanced woman, unless man becomes a contemptible creature. I will accept the second place when I can find a lover whom I can obey without losing my esteem. He will be a man whom I must respect for many qualities—intellect in the first place. And I should like him to be a man whom the world has already learned to respect.'

Presently there came along such a man: he was young; he was in the House; he had already made something of a name; he was a man of practical affairs; he could make the driest subject interesting in a speech; he was a man of family; he was a handsome man. He had also the reputation of being a proud and reserved man. The marriage was arranged at a time when Gilbert was travelling about the world. Six months after the marriage Sir Charles Osterley's party came in, and he was made Under Secretary for the Fisheries—a very good beginning on the official ladder.

And it was upon such a woman as this, holding such

a position, with such prospects, that disgrace of the most horrible kind, shame unspeakable, the ruin of ambition, the loss of social position, and, worse still, a blight upon the whole life of her boy, had fallen. Nothing more terrible, as you shall see immediately, could have happened.

As for Gilbert Maryon, for whom Lady Osterley sent, he was neither her brother, nor her cousin, nor her lover. He was the son of her guardian, and they were brought up together. And because Gilbert was strong and brave and always helped her along when she was a girl, and always looked up to her and thought for her, she believed in him more than sisters believe in brothers, or maidens believe in lovers: she told him everything; and when they were separated she wrote to him about everything.

The kind of confidential attachment—neither friendship nor love, but an exalted form of the former—which sometimes exists between two persons not of the same sex may be a most delightful thing for both shepherd and nymph, provided that it does not degenerate into the less exalted passion. It is an education for a girl, because she will not willingly suffer anything mean or base to enter into her letters or her words. She must rise to the situation: the height to which she rises is measured by the mental stature of the man. Now, Gilbert was taller than most men; therefore Dorabyn became a girl of higher standards than content many of her sisters.

Such a confidential attachment may be, in fact, more satisfying than love, because the girl gets all the sympathy that she needs for herself. In too many cases the lover regards his mistress mainly as the giver of sympathy, not the recipient: he talks to her entirely about himself, and expects her to listen. Now, Gilbert Maryon asked for nothing for himself; he gave all that he had to give, which was an amazing store of sympathy, interest, and counsel, to the girl, and wanted nothing in return. As for love, why, of course—but not in that way.

As for Gilbert, Lady Osterley's confidential friend, he was, to look at, the ordinary young man of this generation, which is a handsome, athletic generation; he was not quite the ordinary young man, because he was possessed of large brains: he took a First in something or other; then, which is also not common, he had a moderate fortune, and belonged to a respectable family. He also had good manners, a kindly disposition, and a pleasant voice. Like many young men of fortune, he travelled: he shot big game; he spent a summer among Eskimo; he climbed the Andes; he learned that Eton, Trinity, the West End, and the country house are not everything; and he acquired that attractive kind of contempt for things in general, especially things connected with money-getting, which men who roam and ramble and have plenty of money for themselves do easily acquire. Nobody, you see, despises money-getting quite so much as the young man of generous instincts who is born rich.

Now, you have heard that Gilbert made every woman his friend. Yet, so far, his name had never been associated with that of any woman. You know the story of Petit Jehan de Saintré: how the continual contemplation of the perfections of his mistress made him blind to every other woman; his case, we are told, though I find it hard to believe, was common in that day. It is now uncommon, yet not impossible.

Gilbert's ideal woman grew up in his mind out of those letters. He found in the world plenty of charming women, but not that woman. Dorabyn herself was not that woman. He fell, in fact, into the danger connected with ideals: he found no one like unto his ideal. Not that he was always looking out for his ideal, or yearning for it. Not at all. Only that smaller women did not attract him. The thing is exactly like acquiring a taste for the very finest claret: an inferior vintage ceases to please, yet the lower creation laps it up with avidity. Give me, however, an honest liking for such wine as I can afford to buy. Give me the power of worshipping such a woman as I can expect to win. And since, fortunately, women do not grow really more noble or finer as they go up the ladder of rank, the latter petition must be referred to the mental and moral limitations of the lover. Put it in another form. In order to ensure happiness, which is contentment, let us not be too much in advance of our friends or our income.

'Now,' said Gilbert, when Dorabyn had been silent for two minutes, 'tell me what you really mean.'

He sat down, and leaning against the arm of his chair he showed the ear and the side face of the listener. To look at her with full face might make things more difficult.

'Tell me,' he repeated, in his gentle and persuasive voice, 'all that you choose to tell.'

'It seems so dreadful that no one warned me. Some one must have known.'

'I wish I had been at home, Dorabyn—though I knew nothing.'

'Do you think a man can go on for ever doing things without being found out?'

'I don't know. Some men do. I never heard anything about Sir Charles. At the same time I did not know him; we belonged to different sets. For my own part, I have very little sympathy with the parliamentary hand. The party politician, always angling for more votes, does not interest me.'

'You know everybody. Do you think that anyone suspects—things about Sir Charles?'

'What should anyone suspect? I assure you no one, so far as I know, suspects anything at all in Sir Charles except that he is ambitious. What should a traveller like me know of the scandals, if there are any, of the day?'

'Then, Gilbert,' she sat upright and forced herself to

speak plainly, yet could not bring herself to a simple statement of fact, 'could you believe that this man who looks so superior—this man with the cold eyes and the proud face and the austere voice—is nothing better than—oh!—all that we read about?'

'One can believe anything about any man, if the thing is proved.'

'It seemed to promise so well. There was everything. He was the most promising man of the time; he was good in conversation; he was a handsome man—I care something about that: it is true, he did not make violent love; but he was well bred and quiet over it— which was a change, after some of them. And his people were pleasant. Why did no one tell me?'

'First, I repeat, no one knew anything at all against him. Next, everybody thought that ambition entered into that marriage. Perhaps, if a woman marries for ambition she has less right than other women to look into the past life.'

'Perhaps you thought I was marrying for position.'

'Well, Dorabyn, you wrote to me fully at the time— I got your letter, I remember, in British Columbia— and you allowed me to believe that love had very little to do with it.'

'Love had nothing at all to do with it, Gilbert,' she confessed. 'I did marry him entirely for ambition. I thought I should like to be the wife of a great statesman. It is a very fine position indeed—far better than any coronet can give. But I did think I could respect him. And now you see the end of my noble ambition.'

'I shall see it, I dare say, presently.'

'Then you will tell me what I shall do, Gilbert. Because I do not know. My letters!' she went on. 'My letters! Oh! what things I have said to you. Gilbert, you are my father confessor. I wonder if any woman ever took any man so completely into her confidence.'

'It seems as if I know you so well, Dorabyn, that I know beforehand all that you will do under any given circumstance. It would always be the best and the wisest thing to do.'

She walked again to the window and looked out: the rain was falling on the asphalte of a London road in South Kensington. She turned and took up one trifle after another on the table: when one is mentally perturbed these trifles seem to bring relief; people in great trouble always talk of things irrelevant, or occupy their minds for a moment with a trifle. I read, once, of a murderer who, on being arrested, pleasantly took up a shell from the mantelshelf and called attention to the singular beauty of its colouring. It was a relief from the terrible tension of his mind, you see. Gilbert sat in the same attitude, not moving—still with the side face.

'You were married,' Gilbert reminded her quietly.

'Yes. Yes, I was married. I was going to be proud of him. Proud! Oh! Heavens! Things began directly upon our marriage.'

'What things?'

'You shall hear. The honeymoon was tedious, and we came back to town after a week or two. Then Things began. Oh! it was line upon line, and precept upon precept. The first blow fell the day after our return. His solicitor called. You must know that we have never had any vulgar quarrels. Charles was not that kind of man. Everything has been most politely managed by an aged, bland, respectable old gentleman. Never was a woman led into the Valley of Humiliation more politely. Nobody could be more polite, more religiously polite, than this old solicitor. I always think of him as an Archbishop.'

'Well?'

'The first thing he broke to me—oh! with the utmost kindness, and as if it was an unexpected, sudden disaster, which nobody could understand—was that Sir

Charles had already gone through the whole of his property. He had married me simply for my fortune: this was a pleasing discovery for a woman who thought something of herself. Well, I had enough to carry on the house, and it didn't seem to matter very much. Speculation on the Stock Exchange, this dear old man called it. I accepted the statement. As my husband was going to be Prime Minister some day, I accepted it without a murmur.'

'I fear it pains you to tell me these things, Dorabyn.'

'Not so much as to brood over them in silence. The second blow fell when the Archbishop called again. He came to tell me, with sympathy most profound, that my husband had lost a large sum of money—many thousand pounds—which must be paid for him, in order to escape dishonour. Stock Exchange, he sweetly called it, again. When I refused to listen to any talk about Stock Exchange debts, he confessed that it was a gambling debt. And then the whole thing came out. The old man warned me plainly that one of two things would certainly happen. Either I should ruin myself in paying Charles's gambling debts, or he would fail to pay them and be expelled from his clubs, which would be social extinction. He has been, all the time, in spite of his austerity and his hard looks, a gambler *acharné:* there is a club to which he belongs where there is an inner circle: they play constantly; they play very high; they never talk about their play.'

'You paid that money?'

'He was going to become Prime Minister. One would give a great deal to become the wife of the Premier. Yes, I paid it. But as he had married me for my money I let him understand that henceforth he would get nothing but the money. So we parted, yet he remained under this roof. Was that right?'

'It seems right. Did you have to give more money?'

'Yes. Much more money. My once large fortune, Gilbert, has been seriously impaired. The man is insatiable: he would drink up all the money in the world. I made up my mind, at last, that even to become the wife of the Premier one might pay too high a price. And besides, there was the boy to consider. I sent him word by the Archbishop that I would not give him another penny. That message, I suppose, was the cause of what has happened.'

'Yes?'

'I let the child go out just now because I could not bear to think that, even at his tender age, he should hear this terrible and shameful thing.'

She could not, still, bear to tell it; she kept approaching the thing—talking about it—going away from it.

'It is the final blow,' she went on, once more fencing with it. 'It is, I do believe, the most terrible thing that has ever happened to any woman. Gambler or not, I could still take pride in his success. I could endure even to be ruined if it were not for the boy. Many most honourable men have ruined their wives at the green table. Even then I could still be proud of him for his eloquence and his intellect. But this—this—oh! who can bear it?—who can bear it?' She wrung her hands —her cheek was hot and flushed—there were no tears in her eyes. 'Who can bear such a blow, Gilbert?'

'Again, Dorabyn, do not pain yourself to tell me.'

'I tell you it is worse to be silent with it. And nobody knows except you and me and the man to whom it happened. Oh! let me try to tell it exactly as it happened. It was two or three days ago—I don't know when. He sat down to play at this club with his gambling friends. He had no money at all; there was nothing at his bank; to play at all was worse than madness; yet he played. He knew that I would give him no more money; he could not possibly pay the smallest loss; he knew that, for the sake of the boy, I was inflexible. Yet he played. And he lost. When they left off he had lost over three thousand pounds.'

'Yes—over three thousand pounds.'

'Next day he paid his debts in full, as a man of honour must.'

'His cheques were refused?'

'Not at all: the cheques were honoured. Because, you see, a letter with a cheque for £3,500 had that morning been received at his bank; and the cheque was for the account of Sir Charles Osterley.'

'Well?'

'The cheque and the letter purported to come from my cousin, Lord Richborough.'

'And they did not?'

'No. They were forgeries. My husband forged them.'

'But—Good Heavens! Was he stark, staring mad?'

'I suppose that he reasoned this way: "No one will know who forged the cheque and sent the letter. I will say that I know nothing about it. My wife will give back the money to her cousin." But I don't know how he reasoned. A gambler is a madman.'

'Was the fact proved?'

'Yes. Beyond the possibility of any doubt. The handwriting was his—it was impossible to doubt this; there was the fact that, a day or two before, he had sent for his bank-book, so that he knew there was nothing to his credit; and yet that morning he drew cheques for over three thousand pounds. And the forged cheque was torn out of his own book; for Lord Richborough and he had the same bank. The thing was quite simple as soon as the handwriting of the letter was discovered.'

'Well?'

'My cousin called upon him, and charged him point-blank with the fact. At first he expressed astonishment. Then my cousin explained the evidence of the case. And then he confessed.'

'Confessed? Good Heavens!' Gilbert was no longer listening with an impassive side face, like a father confessor; he was sitting upright in his chair facing the unhappy woman, with amazement written all over him. 'He confessed?'

'My cousin anticipated this confession, and he had made up his mind what to do. He said that he would honour the cheque, so as to save a scandal: this he would do for my sake; but on conditions. Sir Charles must go away and kill himself as the price of silence. He pointed out that in this way Charles's honour, and my honour, and my son's honour would be preserved, and no one would ever know the real reason of the suicide. Would you believe it? He refused! Coward!—Coward!—Coward!' She wrung her hands passionately.

'Coward!' Gilbert echoed.

'Then my cousin, again for my sake, gave him another choice. If he would, that very day, resign everything—his post, his political career, his seat, his clubs—and leave the country never to return, he would not prosecute. He left the wretched man to find his own excuses; for his own part he promised—for my sake —silence. If he refused this offer he would be prosecuted in a court of justice.'

'A dreadful alternative. And then?'

'He accepted. He went out of that room. Oh! Gilbert, much as I loathe and hate the man, I cannot bear to think of it; he went out of that room, I was told, with—what shall I say?—the white despair of a man disgraced stamped upon his face. I try not to remember his agony at that moment, for fear of pitying the man. My cousin, who brought me the story, told me that the sight made him tremble. The tears came into his eyes while he told me. Oh, the horror of it! Oh, the shame of it! Gilbert! Think of it! He went out fallen—changed from a gentleman into a detected rogue, with the full knowledge of what detection meant to a man in his position! Oh! think of it—think of it! How could he?'

'Indeed—how could he?' What more could Gilbert

say? There are no words of consolation in such a case as this. Nothing can console.

'In the morning—yesterday morning—his solicitor came—the Archbishop. He assumed a face of deep sympathy: I had no doubt heard from Sir Charles of this sudden breakdown — "long threatened, dear Madam, long expected, borne with fortitude." I wonder how much he knows of the story. Sir Charles, he said, was ordered, as his only chance, to go abroad immediately. As he said nothing, not even by way of keeping up appearances, of my going to see the man, I take it that he knows, or suspects, a good deal. But he will not talk. Meantime, on the subject of money. It was for no gambling debt, he explained, that he asked for money; but when a man smitten by sudden sickness—this old Pecksniff never even smiled—is told that his one chance is to go abroad, why, he must have some money to go with. "I do not say," he admitted, "that my client has behaved well; however, forgiveness is the act of a Christian; he must have money, and perhaps under all the circumstances"—I think he guesses pretty well what they are—"it will be best for you to give him what he wants." So I gave him a cheque for £500, with the firm assurance that nothing in the world would ever induce me to give him any more; that he might starve—and so on. I spare you the rest, Gilbert. Then I heard that you were at home, and I wrote to you. And you have come. There, Gilbert! you know all—and a very pretty whole it makes.'

'Yes,' he said: 'this is the most miserable business I have ever heard. My poor Dorabyn! But the man has gone out of your sight. That is something.'

'But not out of my life. Oh, Gilbert—help me to drive him out of my life. All the world is told that Sir Charles has been sent away hastily—smitten with some sudden disease. That fiction will have to be kept up, I suppose, till people begin to forget him.'

'People forget very easily nowadays. In a week it will be as if Sir Charles had never existed.'

'How can I go about—meet my friends—with this guilty knowledge?'

'Not guilty, Dorabyn.'

'Shameful knowledge, then. I am a wife, but not a wife; a widow whose husband is still living: my husband is a guilty and shameful wretch of whom all the world speaks well. Why am I not abroad with him in his illness? Why have I deserted him?'

'Where is he now?'

'I don't know. He must go to America, I believe. Gone to take another name in some place where his face is not known. He can never come back here again. He could never bear to face that story. Meanwhile, I remain——'

'Yes.'

He used the word as indicating reflection.

'I remain. Do you understand what that means? He goes away, stricken down by disease, followed by the sympathy of the world. I—his stony-hearted wife, the only one who does not feel for him—remain.'

'Yes.'

'Another thing. He vanishes. He wanders about the world. Whether he lives or dies I know not. I shall never know, for he will be too proud—he has that one quality left of his birth and education—to tell anyone who he is. I am therefore bound to him, perhaps, for more than his life; for years after he may have gone to gamble and to commit forgeries in the other world.'

'Yes.'

'Still another thing. On every side there are difficulties. There are his own people: he has any number of people. They will all be wanting to know every day where he is, how he is. Good Heavens! There is his mother, there is his sister: they must never know—any more than my boy. And there are my own people as well. Of course they will want to know what it all means—where he is and how he is. And his political friends, they have already begun to send letters and messages: his private secretary came this morning, and the newspaper people are besieging the house. Good Heavens, Gilbert! I believe I shall go mad with it all.'

'You would not call a few of his friends together and let them understand in general terms something of the truth?'

'No—no—NO!' she cried vehemently. 'No one must ever suspect. My boy must grow up to respect his father, whom all the world respected, as well as his mother, who cruelly suffered him to go away alone—perhaps to die.'

'Perhaps to die. Dorabyn—if he were to die!'

'He will not. He is too strong.'

'If you were to go to your country house and fall ill—shock to nerves—and remain ill——'

'No. They would all run down to see me.'

'You might send round a paragraph to the effect that Sir Charles had mysteriously disappeared——'

'He would most certainly be discovered.'

'Then, Dorabyn, there seems only one thing to do. Go and live abroad—or travel abroad where English people do not resort.'

Dorabyn broke down. She sank into a chair and burst into tears.

'Oh!' she cried, 'there is nothing but continual deception! And the thing so hopeless!'

'Nay, after a year or two you can return. You can tell his people that you have had to separate from him.'

'But there is the boy. What am I to say to him?'

'We might advertise the death of the man.'

'And he would be seen the next day in the streets of Paris. Oh, Gilbert, cannot even you help me? I have always thought you were so clever and so strong.'

'If you were free from this man.' Gilbert rose slowly—his face was very troubled: he bent over the weeping woman, and his eyes became humid—he could have wept with her. It was terrible to see this queenly woman broken down with shame that seemed hopeless, except on one chance.

When the valiant knight of old rode out to deliver the helpless maiden from monsters, giants, dragons, and loathly worms, it was not because he was in love with that maiden. Not at all. Occasionally, it is true, love came after rescue; but not always, nor, indeed, as a rule.

Gilbert was not in love with this *belle Dame*—not at all: but she was his sister and his friend; she was in sore trouble; and only one thing could help her.

There was in Gilbert something of the knight errant: he might become on occasion like the noble-hearted hidalgo, Don Quixote; he could rise to the height of throwing away his own life, even for a woman whom he did not love in earthly fashion: the power of throwing away one's life seldom survives the age of one-and-twenty, in the world of society. But Gilbert was a traveller; in the lonely woods and mountains, among simple folk, the ancient virtues still survive: that is one way of explaining what follows.

'If you were free from this man,' he repeated. 'If you were free from him! You cannot get a divorce from him. There is only one. . . . Why'—his face cleared; he smiled; he looked cheerful and confident again—'of course!' he added. 'Dorabyn—dear Dorabyn—a little patience; and Courage! You *shall* be free. A little patience. I will set you free.'

He stooped down and kissed her bowed head. Then without a word more he walked out of the room.

Had Lady Osterley looked up she would have been struck with the resemblance of Gilbert Maryon to the gallant youth Perseus when he started off on that adventure of his, the rescue of Andromeda. She might, perhaps, have reflected, at the same time, that there was but one way, in both cases, by which that freedom was to be effected. Only one way. But this she did not, at the time, understand.

It was with somewhat lightened heart—did Gilbert ever fail?—that Dorabyn packed up her things, and, with her maid, her nurse and her boy, went abroad—to join, they said, her interesting husband.

* * * * *

Extract from the *Morning Post* :—

'The circumstances which have caused the resignation of Sir Charles Osterley are still partly unexplained. It appears that he is not acting by the advice of the learned practitioner who has the care of his household, either in town or the country, nor does that gentleman know anything of the case. He has never been consulted by Sir Charles, who, according to those who knew him, always seemed to enjoy the best of health. The fact, however, remains that Sir Charles has been ordered abroad immediately: it is now certain that he was suddenly taken ill while on a visit: the case was so urgent that on a partial recovery he was hurried away under charge of a medical man without even going home; nor did her Ladyship, who was at the time out of London, know what had happened till he was gone. The shock proved almost too much for her. She is quite unable to see anyone. It is understood that she will at once join him. Sir Charles is reported to have shown some signs of improvement, but very little hope is entertained of a speedy or a permanent recovery. His physicians have not thought fit to inform the world as to the precise nature of the attack; but the rumour is persistent as to disorder of the brain. We fear that Sir Charles Osterley is lost to politics and to the House of Commons. Meanwhile, we believe that a house has been taken for him in the South of France. We venture, as political enemies, to hope that the time will come when we may again measure swords with an antagonist so worthy—so courteous—and so honourable.'

BOOK I.

THE HOUSE OF MEDITATION

CHAPTER I.

THE MASTER.

'You desire, you say, to stay with us,' said the Master. 'Are you merely anxious to study our Community? You can only stay with us in obedience to our common Rule. Do you understand what that is?'

'Not very well.'

The new comer, or novice, was none other than Gilbert, and the Community was seised or possessed of a house and land in the State of New York.

'Why do you come here, young man? Are you disappointed with Outside? We have such among us who come, bruised and broken, to find, if they can, peace and calm. Have you, perhaps, committed some crime? We have some who come to us, thus disgraced, to recover self-respect beneath this roof. Do you come in the pay of some newspaper, to pry into our lives and make "copy" out of things sacred to us? Some do that, also, pretending other reasons.'

'It is not for any such reason that I come here. I am neither disappointed in ambition, for I have none; nor am I a criminal; nor am I a journalist. I would stay here for a while: receive me as a paying boarder if you will.'

'I would rather that you came for Elevation. It is for Elevation that the Community exists. It is for

Elevation that we have left Outside. Well, you may stay with us; but if you stay you must work like us for your living: we take no money. You look like an honest man. Stay as long as you please on that condition. You will find refreshment for your soul in our simple life if you choose to take it. Perhaps you will remain with us altogether if you lose the recollection of Outside.'

'By "Outside" you mean, I take it, the world? Well, I thank you for your permission. I will obey your Rule of Work, and I will stay.'

The place was a large and very ugly hall, built of wood, bare and plain, with not the least attempt at decoration. The roof was open, showing the rafters; the walls were painted a bright yellow; there were three large square windows on each side. These windows were provided with green blinds as a protection against the sun; the blinds were partly drawn down. Along one end stood a low platform raised about twelve inches; a pianoforte stood in the corner of the platform. The body of the room was occupied by three parallel rows of narrow tables, along which were common wooden benches; the tables were bare; the room was empty. This was the refectory, the common room, the calefactory, the chapter-house, the cloister, all in one, of the Community.

The Master sat at the end of the middle table in an armchair: he was the only member of the Society who was allowed a chair; the new comer stood before him looking, it must be confessed, ill at ease, on account of a certain difficulty in explaining his motives for craving admission.

The Master was an old man, probably past seventy years, but still tall and erect. His long white hair hung down upon his shoulders, and his long white beard flowed over his chest. In appearance he was truly patriarchal. His face was handsome still; his features not yet, despite his age, exaggerated by the graving tool

of time: it was like the face that they used to show in
the so-called spirit photographs, which always represented a long face, rather a handsome face, yet a weak
face, a conventional face, supposed by believers to represent great possibilities of intellect: a high square forehead, straight eyebrows, a long straight nose and an air
of self-satisfaction. The Master's eyes, however, were
his most remarkable feature: they were large and
limpid, of a soft dark blue; they were full of light;
sometimes the light was soft and steady, kindly and
benevolent; sometimes it glowed and burned like a
flame: it waxed and waned according to his mood.
They were the eyes of the Prophet—Mohammed himself, I am sure, had such eyes—though his were black
and perhaps almond shaped. They were also the eyes
of the Visionary, the Crank, who thinks himself en-
trusted with a message never before delivered to an
expectant world.

' Whatever your motive,' the Master went on, ' whatever your history, you are welcome. Here you will
receive the Discipline of Labour, the Discipline of
Silence, the Discipline of the Simple Life. Here you
will be freed from care, from ambition, from jealousy
envy, strife: all that stands between yourself and the
Higher Life shall fall away and vanish.'

Gilbert opened his lips as if he would like to inquire
further into the Higher Life, but changed his mind.

'What other rules are there,' he asked, ' besides the
Rule of Work?'

'There are no vows of admission. If you desire to
go, you can go. Some have grown tired of our discipline, or they have longed again for the outer world,
and so have left us. As for our rules, they are only
such as are necessary in a Community; designed for
order and for the carrying out of our principles. Take
down that card' (he pointed to a large card hanging on
the wall). Gilbert obeyed, and read the rules.

' 5.30, Rise and dress; 6 to 8, Fatigue; 8, Restoration;

9—12.30, Fatigue; 1, Restoration; Afternoon, Rest and Recreation; 6, Restoration; 7, Meditation; 9, Repose.'

'Fatigue? Restoration?' asked Gilbert.

'Fatigue is work, which is necessary for the health of the body. Restoration is food. Outside, it is called breakfast, dinner, or supper.'

'Is this all the Rule?'

'This,' said the Master, 'is our life: we work together; we take Restoration together; we take Recreation as we choose; we meditate.'

'You meditate?'

'Meditation, of which you know nothing as yet, is the handmaid of the Higher Life. Meditation has for ages past formed a part of the Higher Life among the Orientals. It is our especial service to the Western world that we have restored the Rite of Meditation. You do not yet, of course—how should you?—understand what this means. Young man, if you stay here, like the rest of us you will presently find that our evening Meditation crowns the day and glorifies it. Wait: wait till you, too, can fall into Meditation when you please. To return. There are no vows, yet we must obey each other; we live in common, yet there is no need to share our property, because we want no property: most of us have none. I do not ask you whether you are rich or poor; we live by our labour: rich or poor, you must live by your labour; rich or poor, you will live with us, fare as we fare, dress as we dress; give to all and receive from all.'

Said the novice tentatively, 'It is your scheme that each should work for the other; give to him, and receive from him?'

'Remember that man is always alone, although with a companion at his side,' continued the Master, not replying. 'Every individual soul is in space, alone, with nothing but itself, rising higher or sinking lower. The loneliness of the soul demands frequent Meditation: that means absolute absorption; but for purposes of work, or even of Recreation, we want association; so we live together. We do not encourage, at any time, not even in the hours of Recreation, idle talk; and we do not encourage too much interest in our work—that is to say, we must not make work the chief subject of our thoughts. Work must be a servant, not a master. Many of us, I have found, are hindered by their devotion to work, especially when it is artistic work. I teach that work once done should be put away and forgotten.'

'I suppose,' said the inquirer, 'reading and writing belong to the afternoon?'

'No. We never read at all. We have no books. We have been uplifted into the understanding that all reading is foolishness. What should we read? History? What is it but a record of man's iniquities and cruelties? Science? It is the mind groping after things which, when they are discovered, are made the engines of more iniquities. Man is not one whit the better for any discovery of science. Poetry? It is at best a quickener of emotion—some Communities use it in the singing of hymns. At its best it may help to Elevation; at its worst it fills the soul with damnable witcheries. Novels? They are for the most part idolatrous offerings to Love, of whom they make a god—yea, and far above all other gods. With us Love takes the place which nature intended for it, and no more. What else should we read? There is Theology. It is the worship of the Word. We want no Theology here. Or there is Philosophy. We have already all we want.'

'How can one live without reading? It is like breathing: one *must* read.'

The Master laid a hand on the visitor's arm. 'You are new among us,' he said. 'You bring with you the habits of the world. In order to calm your ever-present disease of restlessness you must be for ever reading or writing when you are not talking. You begin by thirsting after books as a drunkard thirsts after strong drink. Your restlessness demands the usual sedative. Presently, if you stay here long enough, the disease will vanish; you will gradually become, like myself, absolutely calm.' His eyes began to be filled with light; his rich, persuasive voice began to swell like an organ, crescendo. 'Your mind will float like a vessel on a calm sea; you will altogether forget Outside; you will soar upwards, free from earthly ambitions, free from human passions; you will have no hopes, no fears, and no attachments to this earth; one by one the ropes will break which now connect you with Outside. To you, as it has long been to me, this House will become the whole universe. To you, as to me, the unhappy beings who struggle and suffer Outside will cease to exist. But you must first forget the Past.'

'But this Meditation?' he asked.

'The power of abstraction does not arrive all at once, or readily. But there are helps. Some of the younger members dance. You look astonished? Dancing has always proved a stimulus to Meditation. For myself, I know not by experience how dancing affects one.'

'In the chapel?'

'We have no chapel; we have no collective prayers, praise, singing or preaching. We do not keep any days, seasons, feasts or fasts. Remember that our Rule is no new thing. We have been here twenty years. It has proved salutary to many. Doubt not that it will give you the peace and calm which perhaps you want.'

'Peace and calm,' the visitor repeated, with doubt or misgiving in his eye. He had not come to this place in search of either.

'In our Community,' continued the Master, 'there is no working for private profit, no desire for gain; there are no offices to be filled, no ambitions to be gratified. Think. With the abolition of wealth and ambition vanish half the temptations of the world. With anxiety about the future, with the fear of want, vanish half the hindrances of life. And then there is the passion of love.'

'Of love, repeated the listener.
'Think of the happiness of living without love.'
'Ah!' said the novice, but doubtfully.
'We do not advocate that exclusive friendship called love; each soul should feel that it stands alone; we do not foster the passion of love in this house; single attachments we discountenance: yet if man or woman wish to marry, we suffer it, but after warnings. With the greater part nothing binds a man to the earth more than the love of wife and children. Here, at least, you will be spared the temptation that assails the young continually Outside. But you must first forget the Past.'

Gilbert sat down on the bench opposite to the Master. 'You are,' he said, 'more serious than I understood. I thought that this was a Community principally for the purpose of following the common life—a kind of co-operative brotherhood.'

'To Outside it is little more. To us—how much more! My son, you are, as yet, perfectly ignorant. But fear not: you will learn. And first, you will have to learn the elementary lesson, that there is nothing in the whole world to desire—nothing worthy of any man's efforts—except Elevation.'

He rose—a tall and stately figure—and, as he stood over his disciple, Authority fell upon his face and upon his figure, and upon his garments. As much Authority wrapped him round as if he had been in lawn sleeves and silk instead of an old tweed jacket and a flannel shirt. And his dark blue eyes kindled, and his voice rose.

'We have been created—we know not when. Man, who will have no ending, never had a beginning. Let me speak to you a little. I am old, and I have meditated much; I know a great deal that you cannot know, and many things that I cannot explain to you—you would not understand.'

His voice was full and musical; if it rose but a little

it became sonorous; if it fell it was like the rolling of an organ softly played. Never had Gilbert heard so wonderful a voice. It held him—just as the music of an organ will seize and hold the soul and sway it this way and that as the musician wills. The words that he spoke, as you read them on this cold printed page, mean little. As they were spoken they were words which the soul could not choose but receive—words not to be questioned; words of new wisdom; a new revelation.

'We pass from life to life,' he went on; 'from age to age, from æon to æon, through all the countless years. We never die; we cannot die; death is but a short sleep—there is no time in death—and birth is but a renewal of the former life; through all the births man's soul mounts—mounts—mounts; or falls—falls—falls. Oh! We who stand upon the higher levels, where you will soon join us—we can look around and behold heights invisible to those below; nay, we can even look above—through the veil—beyond the veil, and have glimpses, and see visions. How can I tell you what we see? How can I express the things which the mind of man cannot conceive nor his words paint? How can I repeat the things that no voices say to us?' His eyes suddenly flamed—they became balls of fire—he gazed outwards as one who hath a vision. 'Voices invite us, hands press ours, fingers beckon us into the next world—the next step in our ascent. Believe me, it will be a far, far nobler, a far, far lovelier world, than this; everything that we have here we shall have there, but far, far more perfect. For even in the highest heaven itself the things will be those that we have here, but made perfect inconceivably. There are others in this house beside myself to whom the voices come; these are those who lead the perfect life. Yet this next world itself is but a stepping-stone to the next. Oh, happy, happy brother!' he took the novice by the hand, 'you have left Outside. Do not seek to go back to it; find peace and rest amongst us.'

The voice, the eyes of the man moved Gilbert more than the words. His brain reeled; he would have lost command of himself, but for a thought which returned to him—the disturbing thought which stood between his soul and the influence of this magnetic voice—he remembered the reason why he found himself in that house.

The words, to repeat, mean little. It would be easy to scoff at them: one might ask where the speaker found all this wonderful knowledge; but the words were spoken with so much authority, with a voice so rich and sonorous, with such magnetism in his eyes, that the newly-arrived brother, who expected nothing but a commonplace religious quackery, was moved to the depths. Yet he was a man of West-End London, a man of the world, a man of society.

The preacher ceased; he sat down; the Authority went out of his face; the light went out of his eyes; he was again a clean, nice-looking old man, with white hair and dark blue eyes—a gentle-looking person, probably a favourite with old ladies at the tea-table—dressed in a rather shabby tweed jacket, with a black felt hat on the bench beside him. Then he spoke in quite a different voice:

'You come to us, Gilbert Maryon, for some reason or other—I know not what; but I perceive clearly that it is not the desire of the Higher Life. Nor is it the desire to escape the consequences of crime—a thing which has brought us pretended converts. I perceive also that you are an Englishman, apparently of better station than many that you will find here; you are further, as is apparent from your manner, one of education and refinement. You will find some things among us that you will not understand, or perhaps approve: do not mock at these things, even in your heart; do not laugh at us, even secretly. Say to yourself, "Such-and-such are their ideals; in some unknown way these things are found helpful by the Community; I will wait." Promise me so much, Gilbert.'

'I will promise so much, at least. You have greatly moved me. I expected nothing like it——'

'Enough. Now, it is already past five o'clock. I will send one of your new sisters to take you round the house and show you the workshops. You will choose your own work. And your sister will show you your room. And, my brother, you must resolve at once, and from this moment, to forget the Past.'

CHAPTER II.

THE MONASTIC HABIT.

GILBERT sat down and waited while the Master went off to find that sister. 'This,' he said, 'is a very remarkable Community; I must see something of it before I complete the job. If the Prophet knew why I have come here!' He felt horribly guilty, because, of a truth, it was not at all the kind of job to suit the House. Yet it had to be done somehow, and that speedily. I suppose he won't know me; if he does, I must settle it at once. I don't think he knows me; I have never seen him, and I don't think he has ever seen me. Yet he is here and I am here, and Dorabyn must be set free.' He took a letter from his pocket-book and opened it. 'There can be no mistake possible; he put the fact into words plain and clear; the information is certain—he is in this house. A pretty reason, truly, I could give the Prophet for joining this Community of men who are rising to other worlds!'

He read the letter over again for the tenth time. It was from a private detective of New York.

'I am pleased to report that I have at last discovered the hiding-place of the man you want. He has changed his name so often and has worked with so much secrecy that it has been extremely difficult to trace him; I have only done so by following up from place to place the mischief which he and his company have caused.

'What I have learned is this. He came over in April, 1893, under the name of Charles Lee. Whether this was an assumed name or a true name I cannot tell; nor have any inquiries in Scotland Yard been answered satisfactorily. He does not seem known to the London detectives. He went first of all to a French hotel of doubtful reputation; and he was received in certain gambling clubs, where he seems to have lost a considerable sum of money in a very short time. Presumably it was all he had, because he was next seen in the streets of New York in a destitute and miserable condition. This was changed, however, before long; for we find him again in a first-class hotel, living as an English gentleman of fortune. The explanation is simple: the men among whom he lost his money—a ring of sharpers—wanted a confederate whose manners and appearance would command more confidence than their own; he joined them. He has been with them ever since. They travel about—but singly, not together: they never own each other. They go from town to town; sometimes they pretend to rook the rich Englishman, in order to disarm suspicion. Always the rich Englishman is drawn into the gambling den, and loses money; then the men of the place have a turn or two with him, and the luck miraculously turns. They appear to have done very well. At Chicago, in the summer of 1893, they made quite a pile, and lived on the best of everything all the time. They added to their gaming certain operations of a "long-firm" character. What broke up the gang was the death of a young Mexican at one of their haunts. I do not know the particulars. Mr. "Charles Lee" was present, certainly; but very little is said about it, and nothing gets into the papers. The ring is broken up and dispersed; the police are picking up the members here and there. As for your man, he has found a hiding-place where they are least likely to look for him. It is in a quiet Community of Cranks—one of the many Communities which have been tried in this country. They admit anybody who conforms to their Rule; they are only a small body; they are said to be quite harmless; they live about four miles from the city of Aldermanbury, N.Y. There your man is at present hiding; he will stay there, if he is wise, a long time.

'I learn further from my informant, who was one of them, that "Charles Lee" is the ablest as well as the best-mannered man in the gang. It is he who devises new combinations and novel methods. He is a devil for ingenuity and ruthlessness. His only weakness is that he goes mad over gambling. They let him play as much as he pleases, but he is always made to play with one of the gang. For the rest, he is full of resource and always devising new schemes—a most dangerous man. He would do well, I repeat, to stay where he is as long as he can.'

'Well,' said Gilbert, folding up the letter, 'I am here, and he is here. Dorabyn, the day of your redemption draweth nigh. He is here, and I am here, and—he shall fight me. It shall be a duel to the death.'

He sighed with relief; he replaced the pocket-book, and he returned to the consideration of the House.

'One expected,' if we may put his thoughts into words, 'to find on the religious side of the Fraternity a smug and self-satisfied sectarianism. One thought the Master would have been something like a Primitive Methodist minister, but more narrow and more cocksure; instead of that, one finds a Prophet with eloquence, persuasion and nobility. He has interesting views; he has constructed an entirely new scheme of the universe and of humanity; and he apparently enjoys a private revelation of his own. On the practical side one expected there would be futility and pretence: on the other hand, there is solid work. What the Master actually teaches in matters of doctrine will be ascertained in good time; at present it appears that they have no creed, no articles, no chapel, no services. It is a religious house without any religion! As for myself, I am ashamed, thinking of my mission. The reason of my coming is not in the least the elevation of my soul, as the Master hopes. It is—what? Justice or revenge? I know not. As for the Rule, there is none; or, if any, it is comprised in the simple law, "Thou shalt do no reading." No chapel, no religious services, no sacred books, no preaching—a religion, therefore, without doctrines; everybody to believe what he pleases; no priest, no mysteries, no——'

At this point Gilbert's speculations were disturbed. The disturbing influence was a girl, who came into the hall with the evident intention of speaking with him. She was quite young—not more than nineteen or twenty; she was bare-headed, but carried her hat in her hand. Gilbert sprang to his feet. Good heavens! was this a sister of the Community? Were all the sisters like this girl? Was he, in sober reality, in a paradise peopled with veritable angels? Because, you see, this girl possessed a face which few artists could ever imagine, invent, or find—a face of such purity, holiness and unworldly beauty, with so much tranquillity in it, so much virginal sweetness in it, so much innocence in it, that she might have been standing behind the Master and whispering in his ear while he discoursed upon the voices and the unspeakable glories of his vision. Such a face as Dante saw in Beatrice, such a face as Petrarch saw in Laura—such a face was that which met this new brother of the House. The features of her face were perfectly regular; her head was shapely, her hair fine—and it would have been abundant too, had it not been ruthlessly cut short just below the ears; her eyes were gray, touched with blue, and very, very serious: her face was composed and grave; her mouth was set. It was an oval face, a Greek face, with a somewhat low forehead.

3

Her stature was tall, and her figure slight. This was a girl born in the House: she had never been outside it; she had never even spoken with anyone out of the Community; she had never heard anyone laugh; she knew nothing of the outer world, except that it mostly belonged to quite the lower levels; she had an unbounded belief in the Master and in the Community; and she lived for the greater part of her time in a world of dreams.

'Brother Gilbert,' she began, with a pretty, maidenly blush, 'the Master has sent me to look after you.'

'It is very kind of the Master—and of you.'

'I generally receive new comers to the House. My name is Cicely.'

'My Sister Cicely,' he repeated gravely. 'There is no tie more delightful than the brotherly and sisterly bond. I hope I shall prove worthy of it.'

The appearance of this interesting maiden was another reason why the completion of the business in hand must be made to wait for a day or two.

'You are an Englishman, the Master said. My father was English, too. I hope you will stay. I think you look as if you could rise. Some who come here go away again very quickly.'

'Oh!' the latest comer repeated. 'It is good of you to say so. They go away. Why do they come? Why does anybody come here?'

'I don't know. Sometimes they come crying and weeping—they are the sisters; they cry for the wickedness they have left Outside. Sometimes they are bad people, who come here to repent. You will find it a beautiful place for repentance—but I hope, Brother Gilbert, that you are not that kind. We have had burglars here.'

'I have not done anything, Cicely, I assure you—not even a burglary.'

'Then you begin at once, like me, on the higher levels. I have never been in the world at all, so that I never had the opportunity of doing anything. Otherwise I might have been a burglar too.'

'Very likely indeed,' Gilbert replied, with a little laugh. 'At least——' he remembered the very serious views of the Prophet, and was ashamed of laughing. 'That is—I mean—well—I shall be pleased to fall in with the customs of the House. And you can tell me who the members are—all of them?'

'Yes. But it is nearly half-past five: Restoration bell will soon ring, and you are not even dressed yet.'

He was surprised at this objection. He had not expected such refinements in a monastery.

'Do you dress for Restoration here, then?'

She looked puzzled. 'I mean,' she said, 'that you have not yet put on the dress of the House.'

'Oh! but I haven't got the dress of the House.'

'I will show you presently where you can get one.'

'Oh!' He now observed that she wore a curious kind of uniform. 'Is that the sisters' dress?'

'Of course it is.'

She was such a very lovely, dainty and ethereal maiden that she even rose superior to her costume. The full dreadfulness of the dress did not burst upon him all at once—such a thing requires time; it grows upon one; its ugliness cannot be realized by the human imagination at the first aspect. There are enormities in ugliness as there are enormities in figures, fortunes, distances, which have to be slowly approached and gradually appreciated. The sisters of that Community were clad in a uniform profoundly ugly. I cannot believe that the Master, black and dark as is that prophetic soul as regards art and æsthetics, could possibly have invented it. Respect for the memory of his mother would have forbidden him to invent such a dress. Alas! even respect for their mothers could not restrain the sisters of the Community from inventing this dress. And they designed it, treacherously and wickedly, of set purpose to make (but no one can) a lovely woman unattractive; and (which any one can do) a plain woman hideous.

One is ashamed to write down the details. However, if it must be done—the dress consisted of a bodice, made of some gray stuff, and of a short, scanty skirt of the same material; the skirt reached just below the knee, and then there became visible loose trousers, also of the same material and also short. Stout boots completed the costume at that end. At the other the hair was cut below the ears and pulled back. There was no bright ribbon either for hair or for throat. One small, very small concession to feminine vanity was, that the sisters were allowed to wear a brooch and to exercise their own taste in choosing it. It is astonishing that a brooch was allowed at all when a common safety-pin would have answered equally well. The scantiness and the brevity of the skirts forbade any sense of drapery: you cannot get folds, or curves, or any grace of falling drapery with only three feet in length to work upon.

'A truly wonderful face,' Gilbert observed. 'It must indeed be sweet not to be spoiled by such a hideous dress. Poor child!'

He shouldered his portmanteau and followed his new sister. She led him out of the hall into the grounds of the House. This monastery did not follow the usual disposition of a Benedictine house. There was in it neither cloister, nor cloister garth, nor chapel, nor scriptorium, nor misericordia, nor library, nor chapter-house. There was no beauty in the buildings; no picturesque effect in the grouping or in the gardens. The House consisted simply of the central hall, with a gaunt, wooden erection of four stories at either end. These contained the sleeping-rooms for the members; those of the women at one end, and those of the men at the other. Nothing could be simpler than these buildings, or more hideous than the square structures of wood painted a dull yellow; there were no creepers over the wall to relieve the monotony; there were no flower-beds along the wall; the houses rose gaunt and hideous out of the bare ground. Along the side of the hall, which had a porch in the middle, ran a deep verandah, and at the back of the verandah was a low bench with a sloping back.

In front of the House stretched a broad lawn, not too carefully kept, but still a pleasant breadth of green; a few flower-beds were set at the edges; a shrubbery or two at the corners; the flowers were chiefly roses and lilies—in the month of May both roses and lilies are beginning to put forth blossoms. On the grass a small party were playing croquet, but languidly, perhaps because the sun, now sloping westward, was still hot; perhaps because they took little interest in the game. Along the back of the lawn was planted a fine avenue of shade trees, limes and elms; under these trees were benches. On one side of the lawn was a vast garden full of flowers, acres of flowers; not planted singly, as in a private garden, where each rose bush is an object of solicitude, but in patches and squares; here a square of roses and there a square of lilies, and so forth— evidently a flower farm. On the other side stretched an equally large garden planted with strawberries, raspberries, and all berries that grow for the delectation of man, with the vegetables which correct his carnivoracity and keep him gentle—evidently a kitchen garden.

All this, with the orchard, the pasture-land, the coppice for firewood, the cornfield and the rest of the fraternity farm, Gilbert discovered gradually, not at that first view from the porch.

On the other side of the House were the offices— kitchen, scullery, pantry, dairy—a huge place; evidently a dairy which made great quantities of butter and cheese and cream; some women were at work still, for one cannot clear off dairy work every day by twelve o'clock; there were also the farm buildings—barns, yards, sheds, implements and machines; pig-sties, cattle-pens, turkeys, geese, ducks, and fowls; beehives, ponds, ricks—everything. And all well kept and in order. The Community knew how to farm, if they could do nothing more. One can farm, we may remark, without books.

Besides the farm there were workshops. These were now closed. Gilbert looked into the windows. There was the carpenter's shop, the blacksmith's shop, the shoemaker's shop, and so on. The Community, therefore, made everything that they could for themselves.

He remembered the words of the sage: 'We must not think too much about work. It is man's servant, not his master.' It was the true monkish idea of work. One must labour, not to produce fine work, artistic work, not as if good work is an end in itself, but in order to subjugate the body. For this purpose, a walk over a ploughed field, an hour's exercise with a spade, the digging of a hole in order to fill it up again, is sufficient and laudable. But since people must eat, why not utilize the labour and make it productive? Nothing, therefore, can be more highly recommended for monastic purposes than a farm, an orchard, and a garden. In the Carthusian Order every monk had his own garden to himself. The Master knew what was wanted when he provided the House with a farm.

The place was very quiet. There was no sound of voices, yet women were at work in the kitchens and in the dairy. Did even the women refrain from conversation?

'This,' said Cicely, opening the door of a large wooden barn, 'is the wardrobe. If you will go in there, you will find all you want. I will wait for you.'

'Strange,' Gilbert thought, as he looked round the shelves in the wardrobe. 'This is the practical side of the monastery. Even a monk must have a place to keep his things. Did the Eremites in the desert have shelves where they kept their Eremitic things? Was St. Francis particular about the folds of his gray gown? Was there a Monmouth Street in the Solitudes?"

He reserved further speculation on this point, and proceeded to select the robes of the Order. In a few minutes he emerged in his new costume, which was simply a suit of gray tweed, useful for working purposes. He carried the habits of Outside rolled up in his portmanteau.

'Now,' he said, 'I have taken the vows, and been received, and I wear the robes. They are convenient, if not beautiful. What next, O my sister?'

'Now I will take you to your room.'

She led the way to the men's wing, and ran lightly up the stairs to the top of the house. There was a narrow passage on each floor, with doors standing open on either side. On the third floor the girl walked along the passage to the very end. 'Number forty-one,' she said: 'that is your room. Do not forget the number.'

Gilbert found himself in a little room about ten feet square. It was simply furnished with a small camp-bed, one chair, a washing-basin with taps for letting in and letting off water, a towel, two or three pegs on the wall for hanging clothes, and a small cupboard with shelves. No carpet; no curtain; no blind; a single gas-jet without any glass. The lower part of the window was painted over, so as to avoid the necessity of a blind. There was no lock or bolt on the door. On the wall was hanging a card with the words, 'Make your bed. Sweep out your room. Brush your boots.'

'Humph!' he said; 'it is small—it is like a cell; yet a monk has no reason to complain of his cell.'

'They are all exactly alike,' said the girl. 'Ours in the other building are just the same. What can one want more?'

'Am I to give up my money and watch and things?'

'Give them up? Why? They are of no use to you or to anybody else. You may throw them away if you like. We have no use for money among ourselves.'

'I think I will keep them. No one knows of what use they may be some time or other.'

She began to turn over the things which he laid on the chest of drawers. 'Let me look at them. What a pretty ring! Is that your coat-of-arms? I have my father's coat-of-arms, and a box full of rings and jewels and things that belonged to my mother. I keep them all because they were hers. Some of us have things which we keep—some have nothing. We do as we please. Some of them say that rings are a hindrance, but I don't think they matter.'

'Not much, especially if you never wear them.'

'The brother who sleeps next to you keeps things in a box. He is a bad man.'

She spoke like a child who reckons up a king in history as a bad king or a good king, without further discrimination. To the child, as to Cicely, all wickedness is alike.

'You look like a good man,' she said. 'If you are, perhaps we may meet in the Hour of Meditation. We often talk of meeting each other in upward flights; but I have never met with anybody yet except my dead parents.'

Gilbert listened, and marvelled. The girl gazed upon him, not boldly, but with clear and candid look. 'You are not like any of them,' she said. 'Your eyes are different. You look good. I like your face and your voice. But there is a burden upon your soul. I do not know what kind of burden. Shake it off, Brother Gilbert, and try to meet me in the Hour of Meditation.' She laid her hand upon his arm. 'Shake it off, I pray you. Leave it behind you. Forget the Past—forget the Past!'

Always the same refrain. He must forget the Past. How can a man forget the Past?

He evaded the point. There was a burden. Most

likely the girl thought he had 'done something' Outside. The burden he bore was not, however, that which she meant or could understand. He returned to the other man, the bad man, the man of the next room.

'About the man who is bad. How do you know that he is bad?'

'One can tell by looking at him. Besides, he does not try to improve. He lives in the Past always. We have no Past. It is all present and future. Presently he will grow tired of us and go away.'

'What is the name of this bad man?'

'Charles—Brother Charles. He is an Englishman, like you.'

'Charles! Charles! Is his name Charles Lee?'

'I do not know anybody's name. I dare say he had some name Outside. He has only been here a few weeks.'

'Next to me! He sleeps next to me! It must be the man.'

'What do you mean?' For he changed colour, and showed signs of excitement.

'Nothing. I may, perhaps—who knows?—be the humble means of making this bad man feel sorry for certain things. He sleeps next to me.' Gilbert looked into the next cell. It was exactly like his own; a portmanteau, also like his own, stood in one corner. 'Good!' he said: 'we shall perhaps find opportunities of conversation.'

CHAPTER III.

RESTORATION AND MEDITATION.

AT that moment Cling—clang—clash—broke out the most discordant bell possible to imagine—certainly the worst bell even in this wide world of bad bells.

'Good Lord!' cried Gilbert, 'what instrument of torture is that?'

'It is our bell. It rings for Restoration—at eight o'clock and one o'clock and six o'clock. And it wakes us up in the morning.'

'I can well believe that,' said Gilbert. 'This bell would wake the Seven Sleepers.'

'Let us go in to Restoration, then. Your place will be next to me—I have you on one side, and the other Englishman——'

'Him of the badness?'

'Yes—on the other side.'

'Oh, I shall have to meet him—sit opposite to him at Restoration—three times a day, shall I? Curious! For how many days, I wonder!'

The three long, narrow tables, which were the principal furniture of the hall, were now spread with tablecloths, not too white, for it was near the end of the week, and laid with dishes and plates. The Fraternity—brethren and sisters—were all assembled in their places; they filled the benches, and were in number about a hundred and twenty. There was no grace or formality of any kind—never was a monastery more free from rules, not even the famous House of Thelema, on the Loire. Each one as he arrived took his seat, seized knife and fork, and without further ceremony began to eat and to drink with zeal. Already, though the bell had only just stopped, there was audible from all parts of the hall the musical tinkle of knife and plate.

On the platform one of the Community played the piano. By his long fair hair, by his blue eyes, by his beard, by his glasses, he proclaimed himself a German. He played extremely well: soft, pleasant music, that dropped upon the ears with soothing, not stimulating, effect; he improvised, he played continuously: it was the pleasing custom of the House to take this soft music with evening Restoration, by way of preparing the mind for what followed after.

'This is my place,' said the girl, taking the end of

the middle table nearest the door. 'Sit here, Brother
Gilbert, on my right. This is Brother Charles, the
only other Englishman in the House.'

Gilbert started. He ought to have known what to
expect; but the thing startled him. Imagine, in a
Community full of country people, rustics, sitting down
to a rude and coarse supper of pork and steaks and
other such preparations, the arrival of a guest with the
manners and appearance of an aristocrat of the finest
and most finished and most exclusive. In such a case
one feels that it is not always dress that makes the man.
This man—this Brother Charles—was dressed like all
the rest in the gray tweed : the difference lay in his
face and his manner. All the West End was recalled
by that face and by that manner.

He came in last of all : he looked round the room
coldly, as a French noble would look upon the *canaille*,
as if they did not exist; his appearance, his manner,
were those of the ideal duke; he bowed slightly to
Cicely, as one would acknowledge the presence of a
woman who is just not one's servant; and he stared in
the customary insolently fixed gaze upon the new-comer.
Then he took his seat and contemplated the steak in
front of him doubtfully.

'Brother Charles,' said Cicely, 'this is Brother Gilbert
—our new-comer.'

The man bowed slightly, but said nothing. Gilbert
changed colour. The time had come, then, and the
man. Before him sat the man whom he had hunted
for two years. There he was—Sir Charles Osterley,
Baronet, late M.P., and sometime Under-Secretary of
State for the Fisheries. You have heard that Gilbert
had never met the man before he had left the world in
order to join the devil. But he had heard of him, and
he knew the photographs and portraits of him: a dark
man, tall, slight and spare of figure, pale, clean shaven,
careful of dress, reserved in manner, said to be serious
in his views. The man before him was tall, slight and

spare, clean shaven, pale, looking serious and self-contained : so far there was no change in him. As Gilbert looked, however, Brother Charles lifted his face. Then the swift, suspicious glance showed that there had been change: it was the look of the hunted man, hiding in this home of Crankery, where no one was likely to find him, asking himself with sinking heart what a second Englishman wanted in the place. It was also the look of the hawk, relentless. With the prophetic power which often accompanies a full knowledge of the circumstances, Gilbert understood that searching look of inquiry and suspicion; and the hunted look; and the look of the hawk. 'They are fine eyes,' he thought, ' keen eyes : they should be beautiful eyes; but . . .' He felt his breast pocket. ' I have your portrait in my pocket, Sir Charles Osterley,' but this he did not say. ' When it was taken you were supposed to be a gentleman of England. Now you are undoubtedly a child of the Devil.'

Then Brother Charles spoke, courteously this time, but coldly. He had quite preserved the old manner. In fact, it was his principal asset.

'This is an agreeable surprise,' he said. ' One does not often meet with a countryman in so secluded a spot. Have you been long in the States?'

'About two years,' Gilbert replied.

'Ah! I have been here so long that I have left off counting the years : my name is Lee—Charles Lee.'

'Mine is Maryon—Gilbert Maryon.'

'Maryon,' the other repeated—' Maryon. I have heard the name. You have the appearance of a gentleman.'

A dubious compliment. Perhaps he meant to be insolent.

'Why should I not have that appearance? You yourself. . . .' But remembering things, he did not finish the sentence.

'I mean only that it is unusual in this House, so far as I have discovered.' He spoke coldly, with the manner of one who converses with a secretary—that is, he spoke as a master.

'My father was an English gentleman,' said Cicely, 'but we must not talk of such distinctions in this House. Here we are all alike; we have nothing to think about but Elevation. Otherwise we have no business here.'

She looked from one Englishman to the other, comparing and wondering. One, she knew, was a bad man: the other, she was certain, was a good man. Yet they were both gentlemen.

Brother Charles politely bowed his head, with just the least, almost imperceptible, sneer upon his lips, such as any courtly devil might show on being invited to Elevation. Then he lapsed into silence.

The supper was plentiful, but coarse; the dishes illustrated the observation of Brother Charles as to the rank and station of the Brotherhood. There was pork and beans—a favourite dish: Gilbert presently remarked that it was exhibited at every-day Restoration, morning, noon, and evening; there were steaks, but not exactly the kind of steak which one can command in the City of London: a tougher and thinner variety of the delicacy; and there was pie—pie open, pie cross, and pie covered—that is to say, pie in all its branches; an abundance of pie. Everything was put on the table at the same time, and there were no waiters. Between the dishes there were teapots and coffee-pots and jugs of iced water. It never entered into the head of any brother or sister that one could possibly hanker after whisky: of wine, probably not one in the room, except the two Englishmen, had ever heard.

Gilbert looked round the hall, studying the faces of his new friends. Alas! he could not disguise from himself the fact that they looked common — very common. They were all feeding like cattle; with avidity, seriousness, and silence. There was neither speech nor language among them. But, he reflected, if you were to take all the members of the House of Lords and dress them in a uniform of gray tweed, and then attire their consorts and their sisters and their daughters in the most hideous costume ever designed, and, lastly, cut off the feminine locks, you would produce a common appearance, even among those exalted beings. But lofty thoughts, sacred thoughts, Meditation on things too high for speech, ought to produce their effect upon the face: they should stamp it, they should refine it, however rugged may be the first modelling. Except on the faces of the Master and of Cicely, he could see no sign of any such refining: the faces were common —mostly vacuous, dull and common. Just now, however, they were universally lit up by eagerness after food.

They had already, as has been said, begun to break bread. Now, there is one test which never fails: it is a touchstone, it is the spear of Ithuriel. Gilbert observed by application of this test, which is that of table manners, that the Community belonged apparently, one and all, to what we call in this country quite the lower middle class.

Well, one cannot expect an ideal Community such as this to attract the rich and the luxurious. They would want such a house to be directed by an Archbishop of lenient disposition, and to contain none but themselves, with a fine cellar and good cigars. Among these people of the lower middle class there would be gifts and graces, no doubt, as yet unrevealed and unsuspected. The girl who had taken him to his room, Sister Cicely, was, he observed with satisfaction, an exception. She possessed, apparently, the refinement of a gentlewoman; her father, she said, was an English gentleman: she knew how to sit, how to walk, how to speak, and how to approach the necessary subject of food. Gilbert was never insensible to an interesting person of the other sex: he began to talk to her.

'Is there,' he asked, 'a rule of silence, that no one speaks?'

'No,' she replied. 'There is no rule of any kind in the House, except that we must above all things respect Meditation.'

'Come,' Gilbert objected; 'you cannot meditate while you are eating. Pork and beans cannot possibly go with Meditation.'

She shook her head.

'You know nothing as yet, Brother Gilbert. You have come from a world where there is no Meditation.'

'May I talk with you, Cicely, or are you meditating?'

'You may talk with me if you like, but not so loud, so as to disturb the others; they may be composing their minds by silence after Restoration. You may go away if you like, but if you stay here you will very soon understand that you must not talk. Nothing disturbs the mind so much.'

'I remember the name of Maryon,' Brother Charles said after a long pause. 'I have heard of people named Maryon, but at present I do not connect the name with any person or family.'

Gilbert had given his own name boldly. He thought that Dorabyn's husband must have heard of him. He forgot, however, that it was immediately after the honeymoon of a week that the future Premier had begun his depredations on his wife's property; and that the pair had then virtually separated. Gilbert's name, in fact, had never been mentioned between them.

'I suppose,' he replied, 'that my name is known well enough among my friends. Outside my own circle I see no reason why it should be known. I have never, for instance, distinguished myself in any way. Have you?'

The man winced visibly, and again shot a glance of suspicion across the table. In this frank-faced young Englishman he could see nothing to warrant any suspicion. Yet, what was he doing in this place?

Gilbert turned to consider his neighbour on his left. This, as he learned afterwards, was a certain Brother

Silas, a young man of thirty or so. He was evidently a countryman, a rustic of the American type, which is not at all the English type; he belonged to the farming class, and was a man of Maine; his powers of working through Restoration were prodigious: he uttered no words; when he wanted anything he just reached across his neighbours and helped himself; he drank tea with his pork and beans, and coffee with his pie; his table manners wanted polish; when he desisted for a moment and raised his head Gilbert observed that his features were naturally hard, but that his soft and dreamy eyes took away the rugged look. In the course of a day or two Gilbert learned to classify the Fraternity. There was the soft and dreamy eye which belonged to most; there was the restless, unsatisfied eye which belonged to some; there was the eye of sadness as for an unburied and unforgotten Past, which was also found among them; and there was the wolfish eye, which belonged to Brother Charles and to nobody else.

Restoration ended, everyone rose—not to say grace, but to reverse himself. They now sat with their backs to the tables, and they all assumed the same position; they folded their hands; they inclined their heads slightly backward—a position necessary unless they wished to gaze in each other's faces; the men stretched out their feet. Then half a dozen of the sisters, including Cicely—a duty taken in turn—carried out the dishes and cleared the tables and rolled up the tablecloths. Some of the men lit the petroleum lamps which hung against the wall. The musician ceased and silence fell upon the place. Brother Charles leaned across the table.

'One is not obliged to stay,' he whispered. 'I always go outside when the foolishness begins. Come out and let us talk of London.'

'I shall stay here,' Gilbert replied coldly.

Brother Charles rose and went out, and came back no more. And then the Master came walking softly down the lines of white faces turned upward to the light of the lamps. He stood beside Gilbert and spoke in a kind of murmur.

'It is the hour of Meditation. It is the hour which sanctifies the day.'

In these days everybody travels; everybody has seen everything, from nautch girls to dervishes. But Gilbert had never seen, or imagined, or heard of, or read of, anything more remarkable and wonderful than the thing which followed.

The bell rang, just one note and no more, like the last note of the Angelus; the musician at the piano began to play again, more softly, more dreamily.

Then, suddenly, upon the faces there fell, as it were, a veil; it wasn't really a veil, it was the sudden withdrawal from nearly every face of all the life and expression that lay in it. The life went out of it; the face became vacuous; it became rigid; the people seemed all to be dead, to be suddenly killed; their open eyes saw nothing; through their parted lips there passed no breath.

'Good heavens!' cried the new-comer. 'What are they doing now?'

'They meditate.'

'Meditate? They are all fallen into trance!'

'You have read, doubtless, or heard, of miraculous trances and raptures of saints in days gone by. You have perhaps scoffed at them. It is the fashion of the day to disbelieve what we cannot understand. But even the wisest man of science understands nothing; he only states a physical law and calls it a cause. Scoff no more at these stories. Here you behold a whole company of a hundred and more who can, at will, fall into this miraculous trance. There they sit, and there, unknown to each other and to you, they see visions, hear voices, and receive instruction.'

'You hear voices?' he repeated, incredulous.

'It is our miracle—our own—a special and a wonderful

4

gift, bestowed upon this Community alone. It is impossible to doubt the blessing that rests upon us. You too will presently fall under the holy influence. As for me, I have reached to the level of the life above, the next life. I converse with the people whom I am soon to join. I see them with spiritual eyes. Is not this a great and wonderful gift? But, to obtain it, you must first forget the Past.'

'It is indeed most wonderful.' Gilbert felt himself half ready to fall into the same trance.

The Master laid his hand upon the newly-joined brother's shoulder. 'Join us,' he said. 'Cease to think of the Past which belongs to the world and to ambition. Fix your thoughts upon the path that lies before. Forget the Past; it is full of shadows: learn the realities of life.'

So saying, he left him and walked back to his place at the head of the central table, where he occupied a wooden armchair. As he sat down, immediately there fell upon his face the white, fixed, vacuous look of trance. Gilbert looked about him. Not all the faces, he now perceived, wore this look of fixed vacuity; in a few there were signs of imperfect wakefulness. Not all of them, then, possessed this strange power completely. As for himself, Gilbert felt like a sleepy man who cannot sleep for thinking of things. He was very near unto trance. His thoughts were wandering beyond control. He was back in his London chambers; he was listening to Dorabyn's wretched story; he was hunting down the man whom he had caught at last; he was wondering, not what he should do, but how he should do it—and when. He knew very well indeed what had to be done. He had sworn to give Dorabyn her freedom. In what way? There is but one way in such a case as this. Gilbert knew very well what had to be done. Now that the time for doing it drew near he felt no hesitations and no fears; he was no longer anxious, but he was naturally excited, and the villainous eyes of the man— the seal upon his front—only strengthened his purpose.

Such reflections, however, interfered with the conditions of mental repose necessary for trance. So, like the sleepy man who cannot sleep, he only grew more restless every moment.

He got up and walked softly along the lines of sleepers; he peered into their faces: they moved not nor took the least notice; the open eyes did not blink though he passed his hand over them; the partly-wakeful ones only shut their eyes impatiently.

As he passed along he became aware that they all resembled each other. You know that if you regard a flock of sheep collectively you say that they are all alike; when you take them individually you find that they are all different. Yet your first impression was right, because they all have the same face with little variations. So, if a man dwells in a monastery he presently assumes the monastic face, whatever that may be. These people all had the same face, collectively. Individually they exhibited the ordinary variations: there was the oval face, the round face, the square face, and the long face; there were the faces of the horse, the lion, the snake, the fox, the hog, the crocodile and the lamb. Somehow, no doubt because of the trance, Gilbert failed to find the spiritual face. Yet the Master, before he dropped into his rapture, had that face. The face of the Community, corresponding to the face of the flock, was, Gilbert had already observed, a common face. Now, a man may wear any expression he pleases; he may be as ugly as he pleases—no one will blame him; but he must not look common; and the collective face was undoubtedly of the common type.

The German musician went on playing; he played as if he were himself in a trance. His face, too, was fixed; he played louder and more inspiring music: a march; a war song; a hymn of triumph.

Then one of the brothers—one of those with the wakeful eyes—arose and stepped upon the platform; one of the sisters followed; then another brother and another sister, till there were ten or a dozen of them. They stood in silence; not laughing or smiling; in awkward and clumsy attitudes. They spoke not, nor smiled; they were perfectly grave. They took places in a procession two by two, and bending forward with outstretched hands, an attitude as ungraceful as could be well imagined, they began a kind of rhythmic walk round; not that boisterous, cheerful, self-asserting walk round that used to be seen in the burlesques of thirty years ago, but a meek, shuffling, shambling tramp, whose only recommendation was that it was true to time.

'This is the exercise mentioned by the Master,' observed Gilbert. 'A man can lift his soul by means of music; a little more of that man's playing would carry me out of myself; but to tramp with heavy boots round and round a stage . . . perhaps I shall do it in a day or two.'

The music grew louder and faster; the tramp of the feet grew noisier; but the faces of those who danced or tramped remained the same—white in the lamplight, silent, expectant. They were dancing themselves into a condition of complete trance. One by one they dropped out and fell back into their seats, and the light went out of their open eyes.

A most astonishing dance. Gilbert looked to see the performers fall into some kind of ecstasy and whirl round like the dancing dervishes whom he had seen at Damascus. No, the dance was sufficient in itself, dull and monotonous as it was. Presently the last man left off tramping round and stepped off the platform.

Then the musician changed his time. Heavens! he was playing one of Strauss's most delightful waltzes—a thing which made the senses swim, partly with the recollection of it, partly with the suggestion of it. All that love contains of joy and rapture was in that waltz. He knew it well, and the world to which it belonged came back to him with a rush. And it seemed only natural and a thing to be expected when the girl Cicely

sprang upon the platform and began to dance all by
herself. Nobody saw her; nobody looked at her,
except Gilbert; and of his presence she seemed un-
aware. She danced, being self-taught, with neither
model to copy nor master to teach nor audience to
applaud, a kind of skirt-dance without the long skirts.
She had taken off her heavy boots, and was in slippers.
The sight of her dancing was like the cool shadow of a
great rock, like a long draught to a thirsty throat, like
smooth water after a storm. It was a marvel and a
delight to mark the exquisite grace of this girl's
gestures, the free carriage of her arms, the suppleness of
her limbs, the flexible movements of her figure, the
ordered movement of her feet. Where had she learned
it? She had that ineffable charm of the born dancer,
who, with every step, seems to express some thought
suggested by the music; she surrendered herself to the
music; she obeyed it; she followed it.

'This,' said Gilbert, 'is the most truly wonderful thing
of any. And not one turns his head to look at her!'

That, however, was not wonderful, because in this
kind of trance you may fire a cannon beside the patient,
or you may cut him into small pieces with blunt knives,
but you will not awaken him. So none of these sleepers
had the least knowledge of the music or the dancing.

Next, the one-man audience observed that this
danseuse was dancing entirely for herself. You know
the threefold smile of the professional—that on her
entrance, that with which she vanishes, and the fixed
smile with which she performs. Imagine a dancer without any smile at all, utterly unconscious of her audience:
such was this dancer.

Suddenly she threw up her arms, and, with a cry—an
exultant cry—she whirled round with swiftly twinkling
feet—faster, faster, faster.

'It's splendid!' said the audience, longing to applaud.

Then she stopped suddenly, and, lightly stepping off
the stage, took her seat, and became instantly entranced.

The musician stopped, and there was silence; and in this goodly company of a hundred and more this stranger was the only one not in the trance which the Master called Meditation.

'What are they thinking about?' he asked. 'They can't all hear voices and see visions. Perhaps the girl heard voices while she danced. She is a heaven-sent genius; she is inspired. With that lovely face, with that divinely-graceful step, surely, surely, if there were any voices to be heard, she would hear them. But what a dress! what a dress!'

If you come to think about it, we have, as the Master said, lost the power of Meditation. No living European can concentrate his gaze and his thoughts upon his great toe and continue in abstracted Meditation for days or years together. Formerly we had recluses who thus meditated, lost to the outer world; they had to, or they would have been unhappy in the long winter days and nights when no one came to see them. We had hermits, too, but they were more sociable. The Carthusian, neither hermit nor anchorite, meditated a good deal. Nowadays, however, no one meditates at all—unless it be a novelist over a plot or a mathematician over a problem. We call it Meditation when we sit with a pen in hand, or when we walk alone, or when we are reading: we fix our thoughts elsewhere, while the eye, unheeded, runs mechanically over the page. I once knew a boy who meditated much because he had to go to church much; his Meditations began and ended with the sermon. Gilbert, however, had never in his life set himself to meditate, and he wondered, very naturally, what the thing might mean.

All kinds of questions might be asked about this trance. Did they carry on this kind of thing every night? Did they really advance themselves, elevate their souls in this wonderful way? Did they really get visions, hear voices, see things, while they were in trance? Would this one-man audience, without any volition on his part, become, if he stayed long enough, a performer with the rest—perhaps to tramp round with the grace and agility of a rhinoceros?

All in silence: there was no sound at all; no one coughed; no one breathed; there was no scraping of a restless foot. The rows of white faces turned up to the light of the petroleum lamps were as still and motionless as the dead—only one man of them all left alive, only one to count the dead; the place seemed a tomb. Gilbert felt as if he must fly from it into the open air under the stars. To be sitting in the company of a hundred dead men and women, yourself alive, is terrible. Still he stayed on, looking for the return to life.

It was about seven when they 'went off.' At nine the Master moved, sat up, stood up, and the light of life came back to his face and eyes. At the same moment all the rest with one consent sat up and breathed again. Then they rose, and, without the formalities of wishing each other good-night—'twas a House without any manners—they separated into two companies of men and women, and so filed out of the hall by the two doors which led respectively to the men's and the women's wing. Gilbert held back; he was left alone with the Master.

'You have seen,' said the latter, 'the way in which we spend our evenings. To-morrow you yourself will, perhaps, feel the gracious influence of the place. Sometimes there are exercises; perhaps there have been some to-night.'

'There was dancing. Did you not hear or see, then?'

'I neither hear nor see; I am carried out of myself. Remember, we are each for himself. What everyone does, he does for himself. The soul is absolutely alone in the world. If any wants to dance, let him—it is for himself. As in a march some walk and some run, some ride, some lag behind, some are driven, some press on in front, so in this House, some possess, like myself, the gift of voluntary trance, and some must stir the sluggish soul. But, Brother Gilbert, forget the Past.'

So the Master passed out, and Gilbert sought his cell. The gas was alight in every room, and there was the sound as of the taking off of boots; the brothers were all going to bed.

But the room next to his own—that of Brother Charles—was dark and empty. Where was Brother Charles?

Gilbert was excited by the adventures of the day; he rolled about unable to sleep. It was about two in the morning when he heard footsteps on the stairs—soft footsteps. They came along the corridor; they passed his room; they stopped at the next room—that of Brother Charles. He sat up and listened. To-morrow —nay, that day—the ordeal by battle should decide. He smiled to think of it: he had no fear. Meantime, what mischief had that saintly brother been about, that he should get up to his room four hours after the rest of the college? Would the gate porter take down his name? Would the Dean send for him? Would he be gated or rusticated before the duello? He fell asleep again before he found an answer to these questions, and dreamed of the dancing-girl.

CHAPTER IV.

LABORARE EST ORARE.

AT half past five in the morning the Bell Terrible awoke and began to clash and clang with such discordancies that every man, woman, child, and pig, sprang headlong out of bed, as if obedience would quiet it. Gilbert, who in dreams was in the neighbourhood of St. James's, returned with violent haste to the House of Meditation, and remembered suddenly not only where he was, but also why he was there. And his eyes saw red.

There was no shrinking or hesitation in Gilbert's mind. He intended, with all seriousness, to rid the earth of a man in order to bring freedom to a woman. This he would do out of the great reverence and worship which he entertained for this woman. Yet one must not, even in such a cause as this, commit common and brutal murder. Therefore there might be either the duel until one is killed—nobody calls that murder—after the good old fashion, or there might be the duel after the Western fashion, in which each man goes armed with the understanding that each may fire at sight. What would the Master say to such an arrangement? There was another method still—but Gilbert put this aside. How if the man refused the duello? One cannot always compel another to become a target. Well! the police were looking for him. There was a long list of crimes. If one were driven to the thing—it was not a pretty thing—there might be submitted a plain offer, an alternative—either arrest and trial on many charges, imprisonment, probably for life; or the simple duel unto death, with the equal risk for both men. Which?

Gilbert dropped his revolver into his breast-pocket. He had to deal with an unknown quantity; things might be rushed upon him: the man evidently suspected him. He would wait, if possible, for a day or two, and see more of this Community.

The decision was like a reprieve. His eyes ceased to see red; he remembered the duties of the House; he made his bed, brushed his boots, swept out his room, and went downstairs and into the open. In the clear, strong light of the early morning—the sunrise in May is not so early there as here—he observed how beautifully the House, so hideous in itself, was situated. Behind it stretched the Berkshire hills, a lovely range covered with woods; a broad and shallow stream, clear, bright, and evidently filled with fish, ran winding through the estate; cornfields, meadows, orchards, coppice, covered the ground; only the ugly buildings—the workshops and sheds and farm buildings, the engine-room—all the places, which in England would have been venerable and beautiful with thatch and ivy and gables and windows, marred the scene. Already the tramp of heavy boots on the stairs showed that most of the men were up and going out to work. They were moving slowly and singly, not in pairs, towards the workshops. He was to work for his living as well. What work would he be expected to do?

Not knowing what to do or where to apply, he repaired, as one of the unemployed, to the hall. There he saw the Master sitting at the end of the table, quite alone, with books—the account-books of the House—spread out before him. Even in a monastery these must be kept—the hard, practical, matter-of-fact books of expenditure and receipt. The House, like every other place, was run as a matter of business. It had to pay expenses. I suppose that it was a shock to the recluse, when he entered his hermitage and took possession, to learn that, after all, it had to pay expenses. Living costs at least so much, however much one may macerate. And even the hermit has got, somehow, from somebody, to get that amount as a minimum in cash or in kind.

Gilbert stood before the Master like a schoolboy waiting for a task.

The Master looked up. The prophetic light was gone. He was engaged in the daily task of ascertaining that both ends met. It was a prosperous Community; there was even a margin. But there were branches which did not pay; and these irritated the Master. This occupation robbed him of his dignity: he now looked like an old clerk, say, in a country brewery, where the clerks are not expected to wear black cloth coats; he seemed to be one who had done nothing all his life but add up figures.

'You want work, do you?' he said irritably. 'It's more than some of them seem to want, then. I hope you mean to work, Brother Gilbert; you can't meditate all day long. It's against the spirit of the House. And it isn't fair on the others.'

'I understood yesterday that work is to be a servant and not a master.'

'Certainly. But while you work, remember that you are not at play. You work partly to subdue and fatigue the body, partly to occupy the mind, partly—which some seem to forget—to keep the House going. Well! what can you do? You have the look of a gentleman.' Certainly the Master looked and spoke with greater dignity as a Prophet. 'Well, I suppose you can do nothing except go out with a gun to kill God's creatures. That is all the English gentleman of my time could do.'

'I do not know any trade, to be sure; but you have a large garden. I think I might be of some use in the garden. Or, if not in the garden, I believe I understand something about horses.'

'Oh! You are a gardener?'

Gilbert did not set him right. Why should he? The Master had been so long out of the world that he had forgotten most things.

'Well, I'm glad to hear it. The other Englishman here—Brother Charles—who was also a gentleman once, and is now—something else, whatever he is, cannot do anything at all. I was brought up to the turnery trade myself, before I became a preacher in the Baptist connection where I first found light. Whenever I do any work now I always go back to the old trade. I was a good worker once—very good. Very well, you shall go into the garden. I am glad to find that you are not a gentleman. We don't want fine gentlemen here. Yet you've just the same manner as my good and worthy friend, Cicely's father, who was my earliest disciple. And he was a gentleman. You might have been too proud for the Community. My dear friend and brother, in spite of his faith, found it difficult to remember that we are all equal here.'

'I will try to remember the equality.'

'As for me,' the Master continued; 'it is my daily work to keep the accounts. I am too old to need Fatigue. We've got a farm and a garden and workshops: we grow and make all we want, except our tea and coffee and a few other things; we sell everything that is over to get these simple luxuries—which are really necessaries. The body, you see, must be kept satisfied and in good temper—if possible without pain—while the soul inhabits it. Those who practise austerities and privations become mere slaves to a tortured body. Pain is a hindrance. They think it is a help; the more they suffer the better they think themselves. We cultivate painlessness. So that we work in order to exercise the body; yet work, as I told you last night, must be a servant, not a master. And temptation comes in there, as well, because one may fall into the habit of slovenly work, or one may become lazy. And we have to live by our work.'

Gilbert sat down beside him.

'Tell me more,' he said, 'about the House—how you live and how you get on.'

The Master pushed away his books with alacrity and leaned back in his chair, folding his hands, as becomes one who is going to tell a story. And Authority returned to him.

'It is pleasant,' he said, 'to remember how we have grown and from what we have sprung. I told you that I was in the turnery trade, at first, in Clerkenwell; little as you would think it now. I got conviction and entered the ministry—a Baptist connection it was—and I had a call. There I received the light——'

'How did it come?'

'As light always comes, with a sudden flash. Of course they wouldn't have me any longer. I wanted to convert the service of song and prayer and preaching into Meditation; they could not understand Meditation —so I had to go. Then I made the acquaintance of those two shining ones, Cicely's parents'—he cast his eyes upwards as if he saw them. Doubtless he did see them. 'They joined me, and we came here to lead by ourselves the Life of Meditation.'

'So that was how you began.'

'That was twenty years ago. I had just those two disciples, Cicely's parents. Her father bought the land. He had brought over enough money for that; the rest he left behind for anybody to take who chose. We put up a log hut and we began. . . .' He paused. 'Ah! That beginning!'

'You suffered privations?'

'We had no money: we had a hard struggle—my two disciples, man and wife—and I: we cleared the ground, we grew things, we lived on bread and potatoes with a little bacon; I went back to my turnery; he made traps and such notions and peddled them. Then the baby came. That is the girl Cicely—my daughter, as I call her. The mother died—I think the hard life killed her; but the baby thrived. And her father died, but only four or five years ago. In Meditation I can see them both, every day: I converse with them, I share their happiness, I am mounting with them side by side. Otherwise I should desire to go hence and be no more seen.' The strange light that they used to call Enthusiasm returned to his eyes, and continued there. 'We got on,' he continued. 'Everything began to prosper with us. The blessing of increase lay upon our fields and our gardens like the sunshine of this beautiful land. Our little homestead grew; we attracted people, the report and fame of us went about the world; here was a Community aiming solely at the Perfect Life, refusing to take money except for their needs, living in equality, despising the toys of Outside; in such a country as this, where the people are naturally inclined to religion, and yet are prone to fall into money-getting, the example is wholesome; and in a country like this of political equality, such a Community is sure to attract.

'So they came: they were curious at first, not being able to understand the contempt of wealth; but some remained. You are curious; you want to be pleased with us; but there are things which you do not understand. Wait in patience for a little. Our people are free to depart, but they remain. Nowhere else have they the same freedom from care. Some of us have been city clerks, hard-worked and badly paid, always in anxiety about the daily bread; here we have no such anxiety. Some have been tormented while in the world by ambition and disappointment, here there are no ambitions: some by injury and wrong'—Gilbert changed colour—'here there are no such emotions Some have fallen into habits of vice, drunkenness, gambling, and I know not what; here there are no temptations. You have yourself doubtless found some of these hindrances in the world.'

'Truly.'

'Well, everybody works at something; there is a town three or four miles away which takes all we have to sell; we have a name for honesty and good work; people who buy our jam don't get glucose and they don't get parsnips. A good name for thorough honesty is worth something, I can tell you.'

'I suppose so.'

'We have no rent to pay, no wages, no partners, no servants; we only have to keep ourselves. I have calculated that if every one earned—over and above what we consume for ourselves—two dollars and a half every week, we should manage very well. But it is difficult to get this average of work out of them. Some of them, if they could, would be for ever meditating. We do not want money—I desire never to see money in the House. What we cannot exchange we put into a bank and exchange from that place.'

The Master in his simplicity could not understand that having money in a bank was exactly the same thing as having it in the House.

LABORARE EST ORARE 63

'Have you any money, young man?'

'Yes: that is, there may be a little, somewhere.' He coloured slightly, being a young man of great possessions.

'Leave it there. Never ask after it—let it go. That is what my first disciples did. They just left their money behind them.'

'I thought of offering a gift of money to the House,' said Gilbert. 'I fear, however, that it would not be accepted.'

'It would not. Go, instead, and work. Young man, there is something, I know not, standing between you and the gate of the Upward Path. Until that obstacle is removed I fear that Meditation will be impossible for you. Go now and work.'

He sighed, drew the books down again; obviously resisted a powerful temptation to meditate; and became again the clerk and accountant.

Outside, work was now going on in full swing. Gilbert looked into the workshops, where a great number of industries were carried on, the most important appearing to be the turning of chair legs. There were, however, many other trades: there were dressmakers, sempstresses, shoemakers, saddlers, carpenters, upholsterers, bookbinders, decorators, turners, cabinet-makers; and others. Some of them worked listlessly, even sitting beside their work, with hanging hands and eyes far away; they were the spirits who would fain pass their whole time in the trance which they called Meditation; others worked steadily, after the manner of good and trained workmen; others, again, worked by fits and starts, feverishly; these were the restless, unsatisfied souls, those who had to dance in order to invite the sleep of Meditation.

No one spoke to his neighbour; there was the whirr of the engine from the engine-room; there was the sound of the work itself; there was the click of the tools; but there was no voice. No one spoke. It was like a Carthusian House, save that there was no Rule. If you think of it, to those who never read, who have no connection with the outer world; to whom there comes no news of the outer world; who have no longer brothers or sisters, parents, or enemies, or friends; who try to bury and forget the Past; who use no form of prayer and have no litanies to chant and no services to attend; to whom one day is like another, save that one may be cold and one may be hot; to these people there is nothing to talk about. Why should they talk? In a Benedictine monastery there are the ambitions and the offices of the house; here there are no offices and no ambitions.

Nobody appeared to notice him: one expects, in such a house, a flocking of the members to the newcomer, if only to congratulate him upon his arrival or to ask why he has come, or what news he brings from the outer world, or if it is true, as reported, that the devil is dead. There was no notice taken of him at all.

He left the workshops and looked round the farmyard, and was enabled to understand why his neighbour, Brother Silas, suggested that occupation at supper. He repaired to the scene of his labours. He was to be a gardener.

Of all human occupations gardening is by far the most interesting. The gardener not only cultivates the soil, making it produce delicious peaches, strawberries, plums and pears, apples and quinces; radishes and cabbages; roses and lilies; corn and barley; but he also cultivates many most useful human faculties—such as patience, self-sacrifice, observation, perseverance, memory, forethought and many other things. It is not without meaning that Adam is said to have been a gardener. For my own part, I have never been able to understand why kings and the great ones of the earth, who have often become watchmakers, carpenters, cabinet-makers, chemists, poets and painters, have never become gardeners They always have a garden of their own—yea, a back garden and a front garden; they have every opportunity of self-improvement by means of the garden; yet so far as we have got in history the kings and the great ones of the earth have neglected that opportunity.

The gardens covered a large area; there were flower-farms, kitchen-farms, and fruit-farms. It was the month of May, when things are growing and blossoming, and ripening fast. The splendid sun of America warmed the buds and flowers through and through; it never fails; our own summers grow cold and wet for twenty years on end; but in the States the summer sun fails not, any more than the winter ice and snow. In the gardens were employed a good many of the members, men and women. Like the men in the workshops, they spoke not at all to each other.

With a hoe in his hand, which he held as one who never brandished that instrument before, Brother Charles stood over a piece of ground. Now and then he stuck his hoe into the earth; for the most part he gazed at his work with a kind of loathing. Never was disgust written upon human face more plainly.

Not far from him the girl Cicely was at work among the rose-bushes. Presently she drew nearer to the man with the hoe. Now, he was exactly the opposite of Bunyan's man with the muck-rake; for Bunyan's friend raked with zeal with his eyes cast down, but this man did not rake at all—he looked upwards and sidewards and forwards and backwards, and every way but downwards. Had there been an angel hovering over him with a crown of gold he would certainly have seen that angel and would have proposed a game of *écarté*, with that crown as the stake.

'Brother Charles,' said Cicely firmly, 'that is not the way to handle a hoe. See—I will show you. I am sure you can learn if you choose. If you do not like gardening there are many other things to do. You can go into the farm-yard.'

'No, no—I like gardening.'

'You are doing nothing at all to-day; you did nothing yesterday. If you go on idling, the Committee will criticise you. It is a dreadful thing for the Committee to criticise you. You never remain at the hour of Meditation. Perhaps they would not so much mind that, for a time; but we cannot keep with us a man who will not work and does not wish to meditate.'

'Perhaps it is because I am restless.'

'Perhaps. You are always thinking over your Past. Can you not forget it? It is a terrible Past, I know—I can see so much in your face. Will you always be tied and bound by your Past?'

The man dropped his eyes. 'Never mind my Past,' he said huskily.

'There is the Present—here. And the Future—where you please.'

'Where I please,' he echoed. 'Yes, where I please.'

'Why do you stay with us?'

'For Elevation, I suppose,' he replied, with an ugly sneer; 'like the rest.'

'It will be difficult,' thought Gilbert, looking on, 'to persuade this man to adopt an honourable and happy despatch.'

Cicely left him and turned to meet Gilbert.

'You are going to work in the garden?' she said, with a smile of welcome on her sweet and serious face.

If she had looked ethereal in her dance last night, she was even more lovely among the flowers in the morning sunshine. How came this flower here among these common vegetables?

'Oh! I am so pleased,' she went on simply. 'You will work with me. Perhaps I can help you a little, because you are strange to us. And no work, I always think, is half so good for us in this Community as gardening. We are out every day under the sky, and among the things that grow and blossom for us, we have no temptation to think of the past. Sometimes the hours pass and I feel as if it had been one long Meditation.'

'Without any dancing?'

'You saw me last night? Dancing helps me.'

'Oh! but you dance most beautifully. Who taught you?'

'No one. I have always danced. But I cannot dance with the others. To-night if you try to meditate you will not be able to see me dancing. If it is any hindrance to you I will not dance.'

'I would much rather see you dance than go off into Meditation.'

'Brother Gilbert'—she laid her hand upon his arm, not timidly, nor yet boldly, but without any hesitation or any blushes—'do not speak of our Meditation until you understand it. I should like you to remain with us. You remind me, somehow, of my father: you speak like him, with the same soft voice—he had a very sweet voice; and you look like him, thoughtful, with deep eyes—only yours are troubled.'

'I am glad to be like your father, Cicely.'

'Yes. But you have not attained to his heights.' She withdrew her hand, and over her face there fell something of the strange, rapt, far-off look which Gilbert had observed in the Master. 'He has risen so high—so high—whither I cannot reach. My mother is with him. They come down to meet me every day and talk to me.'

'Cicely!' cried Gilbert, 'come back to earth. Tell me,' he said, after a pause, 'are there many people in this House like you and the Master? Do you all see visions and have dreams?'

'I do not know. We live every one for himself. Only the Master talks to me. Sometimes I know what he sees and where he goes. For my own part, at Meditation time I sit with my father and my mother and they speak to me. I will ask them to help you, if you will try.'

'If I will try,' Gilbert repeated dubiously.

'As yet you cannot, because your mind is darkened. You are thinking of something gloomy; it fills your soul with sadness; yet you are not a bad man. Not like that other'—she looked at the man with the hoe— 'his soul is black through and through. Yours is full of gleams.'

'You are a witch, Cicely.'

'Put it from you, Gilbert. Forget the Past. Leave bad people and bad things behind. Let your soul lie open to the light.'

She spoke like the Master, because he was the only one who ever talked with her.

'No, Cicely,' Gilbert answered his own question, 'there can be no others in the House like yourself.' He thought of their voracity at supper, of their stupid silence, of their shuffling, ungraceful dance, of their vacuous faces. 'If these people were like you, Cicely, if they had your mind, they would no longer remain in silence; they would be constrained to talk, if it were only to tell their thoughts to each other, like the birds who cannot choose but sing.'

CHAPTER V.

A WARNING AND A PROMISE.

GILBERT took off his coat—the regulation coat—and set to work. 'I must earn,' he said, 'my board, which is three square meals a day—pork and beans, and steak and coffee—and two dollars and a half a week over and above—say, about seven dollars a week in all. This means zeal.'

The work set before him was of the lightest possible kind—a little weeding and clearing; nothing could be lighter. Yet unaccustomed stooping made the shoulders ache; he was fain to straighten himself and from time to time look about him. Cicely was going about among her roses, her face always set with a serious responsibility, as if she were doing something especially sacred, such as decorating the altar—she who had never seen an altar—or making beautiful for the next day's service the pillars of the church—she who had never seen a church or any pillars of a church. She showed no signs of wishing to continue the conversation; in fact, she had learned one lesson at least in the House of Silence—not to give utterance to vain repetitions. In this respect the fashion of the world is so very different. We not only repeat vainly, but we cannot do anything, persuade anybody, or breathe the simplest truth without vain repetitions: they are a necessity. Formerly, the Sage, when he had anything to say, came forth with importance, and, after commanding silence, said, once for all, what he had to say; then he went in again and waited for the next message. In these days he has to say what he is charged to say a dozen times over—first, in a monthly magazine; at the first delivery of the message no one listens. He then says it again, in another form; at the second delivery people are irritated. He then says it a third time; then they begin to call him names and to throw stones at him, because novelty frightens and irritates them. Perhaps at the fourth or fifth delivery, if there is nothing in the doctrine to interfere with income, the world may consent to listen. Even then the Sage must go on repeating his message, else the whole will be speedily forgotten. At this House there were so few words spoken that everyone had a chance of being heard. 'Let your soul lie open to the light,' Cicely said. 'Lie open to the light!' And his presence in the House was due to such a purpose! If she only knew! The incongruity between purpose and pretence—if he had made pretence—was ridiculous. In the silence of the garden the words rang in his brain— 'lie open to the light.' What things had to be done before that opening of the soul to the light!

But he had resolved to defer this purpose while he observed the ways of the Community—a relief, for a time, to forget this terrible purpose. And he fell once more to considering the place where he had found his enemy. A strange, mysterious place! The retreat of rustics, apparently—yet, of rustics who fell into trances, had raptures and saw visions. Well, if it is given to any people to see visions, it must surely be to the country folk, who work alone in the field and forest, that such privilege is given. A place dominated by a man of strong magnetic force, who certainly believed what he said, and might, had he chosen to remain among men, have drawn multitudes to follow him, such was the power of his voice and of his words. A place with something of the desert about it, situated, like an abode of Eremites, in a lonely place under the everlasting hills, with a rushing stream to sit beside (nothing assists Meditation more than a running stream); a place outside the world; a place whither came no letters or news or papers; dedicated, like a Buddhist monastery, to that sublime selfishness in which no one cares for his brother, but is entirely occupied with his own advancement; a religious house in which there was neither chapel nor service—where the mind, stripped of dogma and creed, of teaching and of teacher, looked inwards for nourishment and for inspiration.

Thinking these things, he waited till Cicely, in her round, again drew near to him. Then once more he spoke to her. 'Those heights, Cicely—those levels of which you speak. What are they like when you reach them? What are the dreams and visions which come to you in your trance?'

'The levels are spiritual levels. The place is always the world. How can I explain? This world will always remain. There are as many worlds as there are men, yet only one real world. It is the perfect world which we are trying to see and to understand. To all of us there are worlds of different levels, invisible to each other. Outside our own world, above us and below us, are infinite worlds, always the same. When we are ready to go up to the world above us, we are taken up. Yet there is only one world, and that world you are not able to see or understand. What you see with your short sight is only a fragment.'

As she spoke she became like the Master—transformed. She became glorified. Her eyes were filled with light—she became a goddess.

'Then you will soon be taken up, and we shall lose you, Cicely.'

She shook her head. Compliments she did not understand. 'We live out our lives. We are called away only when at this stage we can learn no more.'

'Well—but always the same world? Always pie and pork and beans?'

'Don't look like that, Gilbert. I cannot tell you anything if you look like that. It makes me feel ill; it makes your soul black when you mock. You must not think of things gross and material when your soul should lie open to the light.'

'I will not. But there will be always this House?'

'There will be always, I suppose, some company of men and women trying to rise higher and higher to the greater happiness.'

'The greater happiness,' he repeated. 'That is what I cannot understand. What constitutes the greater happiness? What will you do with it when you have got it?'

'You cannot understand. Why talk any more? First, you must clear your mind of the Past, and then you must learn how to rest before you are able to take a single step.'

She turned away and continued her work. Gilbert looked after her, moved by her sincerity and her earnestness.

There are moments for some men — not for all, because most men are unable to feel these things, and for the few only in youth and early manhood—when it seems really possible to stand outside the environment of time and matter; when the raptures of saints, the visions of nuns, the ejaculations of anchorites, the stories of spiritualists, seem not idle dreams and fond imaginings, but true liftings of the Veil which hides the only things that are real and everlasting. At such moments a cloud rolls over the eyes; the walls of the room vanish; everything vanishes, and one is alone in space. It passes quickly for the most part; the strange feeling, which was always in the mind of the Master, has come and is gone in a moment, before one has had time to consider what it means, or to ask any questions, or to learn if any questions may be asked. While the Master spoke to him, Gilbert experienced this feeling. When Cicely spoke to him in the garden, he experienced it once more. It was not the first time. When he was a boy of seventeen, certain poetry drew him out of himself. When he heard music of a certain kind, he was fain to sit down and surrender himself. So, when he travelled abroad, and made the acquaintance of dervishes, fakeers, Moravian missionaries, and sometimes Catholic priests, worn and devoted, the same emotion seized him. Some books of biographies filled him with this sense; some flowers inspired him with this yearning after the power of living outside life—the power, in short, claimed by the people of this House. Now his brain was filled with a kind of glory, left there by the words and the voice and the eyes of this girl. At such a moment, if self-surrender were possible, everything would be possible: trance—visions—voices of the dead —and the lifting of the Veil.

His heart glowed within him. He could not choose but believe the girl. Her eyes were as sincere as her heart was pure, as her maiden soul was innocent. When he should be able to rest . . . but the Purpose stood between.

'You want rest?' It was the voice, cold, hard, and

metallic, of the man he was hunting. He stood with his hoe over his shoulder on the other side of the bushes. 'I have overheard your conversation with the girl. Rest is what we all want, isn't it?—rest and Meditation and Elevation. Yes—oh yes—Elevation!'

The glow and the joy of his dreams fled shrieking, driven away by this evil presence.

'You had better go on with your work,' said Gilbert shortly.

'Presently — presently. All in good time. You needn't break your back in this place. As for work, I suppose you don't really like blistering your hands and cramping your legs over a beastly hoe any more than I do. I chose gardening because no one knows whether you do anything or not.' He sat down on a barrow. 'I'm going to take a spell of rest. Let us talk. I was astonished, last night, to see you come in, because you have the appearance and the manners of an English gentleman, and you don't look like a Crank. As for me, I come here because I want complete rest, which a man can't get anywhere else. It was over-work—intellectual kind—writing. My doctor told me of this place. Light physical exercise, simple food, absolute silence, no telegrams, no letters, no newspapers—that is what I get here. I do not pretend to meditate, as they call it. I am never carried away in a trance; but I am quiet. That's my little simple story, Mr. Maryon. What is yours?'

'Mine? Oh! mine is still simpler.'

'You are not a religious Crank, like the rest of them. And you don't look as if you were nervous. I heard you talking to that girl just now. Well, she's the only pretty thing in the place. You look that kind of man —I shan't interfere. Besides, I shall be going in a week or two. Don't mind me.'

His cold face showed neither leer nor grin: there was nothing of the Satyr in the man; but it expressed evil of the most evil.

Gilbert felt an intense desire to kill the creature, but refrained.

'How long did you say you were going to stay?'

'Probably a week or two longer. The people are rustics; the food is coarse; there is nothing to drink; there is nothing to do; there is nothing to talk about; but one can be quiet. As for you, I suppose that little girl—well, they are all blind and deaf and dumb: you can do just what you like—I shan't interfere.'

Gilbert stepped across the beds and stood over him. He was a big strong man, and the other, though as tall, was slight and spare.

'Look here—you—Charles Lee, as you call yourself. I dare say I shall have some little accounts to make up with you presently. Meantime, be very careful never to mention that young lady's name again in my presence. If you do I will horsewhip you.'

The man looked ugly, but he made no reply.

'As for your coming here, we know all about that. It is a convenient spot for a man who wants to be out of the way; a place not likely to be suspected——'

'Out of the way?' The man changed colour. 'What do you mean?'

'Such a man, I say, might very well think that no one would look for him in such a place.'

'What the DEVIL do you mean, sir?' The man spoke with a poor show of surprise.

'I mean just what I say. Mr. Charles Lee thinks that he is safe so long as he remains in this House—so long as no one suspects this House—so long as no one comes to look for him. Very well, Mr. Charles Lee is quite right. The police are not suspicious about this place; they are looking for him in all the dives from Chicago to New Orleans. But they will not come here to look for him *unless they are sent for.*'

Mr. Charles Lee sat down again upon the barrow. 'The police?' he repeated. 'The police? What have the police to do with me?' He watched Gilbert with unmistakable terror in his eyes. He looked furtively about him as if meditating flight.

'That is your business, not mine.' He had gone so far, he thought, that he might just as well go on and complete the job on the spot—say, after breakfast.

'Who are you? What do you want with me? Who told you?' Then he suddenly threw up his arms. 'Oh! I remember now. You are Gilbert Maryon. You are the son of General Sir Harry Maryon, K.C.B. Oh yes! What the DEVIL are you doing here? I never met you at home, but I have heard about you. Yes: you were in the Foreign Office; you became an unpaid *attaché*— I remember.'

'I would not remember too much if I were you.'

'Why not?'

'Because you might happen to remember what your own name used to be and why you left England. I don't ask you to tell me, understand. It would be a pity to give yourself away, wouldn't it?'

In spite of his proud bearing, the man shivered from head to foot. There was one thing, then, that touched him still: his own disgrace; the memory of what he had been.

'What have you done?' he asked. 'Why are you here? How do you know—what you do know?'

'It is full early for personal and private conundrums, isn't it? Wait a bit. I do not desire your society, but I shall have to speak seriously to you very soon. Of that I warn you. We may, some time or other, perhaps this day, exchange confidences and confessions.'

'What confidences?'

'As to why and how you left your native country. Already I have learned that it must have been a very short time ago, because you knew that I was in the Foreign Office; and that you must have been a man of the Piccadilly End, otherwise you would not have known that little fact. Besides, you have the survival of manner, although your face must have changed since you were received in London houses. Your story, in fact, should be interesting. Mine, I confess, would be commonplace in comparison.'

'Then tell me,' he insisted, still with that terror in his face, 'why you have come here; how you learned—what you know.'

'Not yet. It is the story of a villain and his punishment. I will tell you presently—after breakfast, perhaps. There goes the bell. Go now, and feed.'

He left the man on the barrow, his face full of fear and suspicion and uncertainty, and turned his steps towards the hall and breakfast.

He was joined by Cicely, who laid her hand upon his arm.

'Brother Gilbert,' she said. 'Not to-day. Promise me, not to-day.'

'What?' he asked. 'What am I not to do this day?'

'Not to-day,' she repeated, as if she divined his purpose and knew his secret. 'Promise me, not to-day.'

'What is it, Cicely? Put the promise into words: what is it that I must not do this day?'

'I do not know what they mean'—she did not explain who 'they' were. 'They told me to make you promise, not to-day. You must promise, Gilbert. It is my mother's order. Not to-day.'

'Your mother's order? Your dead mother's order?' He hesitated. One look at her serious face determined him. He obeyed. 'Well, little witch, I promise. Not to-day.'

CHAPTER VI.

'NOT TO-DAY.'

THE House breakfast proved to be very nearly the same as the supper. What can one ask that is better than steak, bacon, ham, pork and beans, with hot cake and all kinds of cakes and jam? The body, as the Master said, must be kept in good case and painless, in order for the soul to be free. When hunger gnaws, or when rheumatics bite, the soul becomes nothing better than a groaning prisoner—which shows how mistaken the ascetics and eremites have all been in mortifying the flesh. Twice and three times as spiritually disposed is that soul which reposes in a body well fed and nourished and comfortable.

The one o'clock dinner was also very nearly the same as the breakfast and the supper. The Fraternity, in fact, had but one meal—a square meal, quadrilateral and rectangular—taken three times daily. As they knew what to expect, they were saved from vain lookings forward and from speculations as to possible or unattainable good things which trouble some folk. Iced water, tea and coffee were served at every meal, and of course if the food was coarse and indifferently cooked it was exactly what most of the members had been accustomed to receive all their lives.

In every kind of hunt, the sympathy of the onlookers is always with the hunter, seldom with the hunted. Especially is this the case with the hunt of man. He has to be run down, he has to be caught: how will it be done? That is what everybody asks; in certain circles, however, the question is—how will he escape? Great as is the ingenuity of the man hunted, still greater is the ingenuity of the detective. The hunted man flies, he runs out of sight, he disguises himself, he hides, he assumes a beard, he cuts off a beard, he puts on eyeglasses, he takes them off, he puts on a wig, he changes his name, his dress, his carriage, he has a thousand tricks and turns; yet in the end he is caught, generally by some accident which Mr. Sherlock Holmes, the detective, turns to his own account. Can we not admire the cleverness of the man who is hunted? Never mind why he is hunted, probably in order that he may no longer eat up other men; let us watch the cleverness of the quarry.

Here was a man whom all the police in the United

States were looking for; in every town they had his portrait and a description of him and information of his way of life. Every place closed to him, except this. He knocked at the door of this House and was admitted. Here he was quite safe; no police ever came to the place, it was unsuspected, it was a modern sanctuary. And here he had rested for three weeks and more, feeling himself for the first time in absolute security. There were certain drawbacks in the life here, but he was safe from pursuit. And then came this young Englishman. Why did he come to the place?

There is one branch of thought-reading which is common to all mankind, except the very stupid. This class, as we know, feel nothing, fear nothing, anticipate nothing, and desire nothing. They are incapable of imagination, love, hatred, or any other passion whatever. All but the very stupid, however, possess the power of divining whether another man is a friend or an enemy. This instinct is a survival of the days when man was a fighting animal, and a hunting animal, and a hunted animal. He could then hear and see his enemy miles off; he could scent his enemy when he was invisible; he acquired this power through the instinct of self-preservation: even now, when he hunts no longer, he can perceive at first sight if a man will prove a friend or an enemy. The man Charles Lee, who was at the moment a hunted animal, recognised, at the first sight of Gilbert, an enemy. This made him uneasy, particularly as he could not by any thinking arrive at a working theory as to why this young fellow should be an enemy, what he was doing in this House, and how he came to know anything about that ring—if he did know anything. He felt so uneasy that he would have gone away but for the absolute certainty that nowhere else could be found a place of such safety: the only place in the world where the residents showed no curiosity at all about a new-comer, and did not question him and did not talk about him. Such a place

was to a hunted man like a Fortress Impregnable, a
Château Gaillard. For three weeks he had lived unnoticed among them; nobody spoke to him except the
Master and this girl. And now came this young
Englishman, who knew at least that he was in hiding.
He was very uneasy indeed.

Other things made the fugitive uncomfortable: lesser
things; everything that must be expected when one has
to run away: part of the stage management, the 'business' of running away. The ring had been conducting
its operations, having acquired the power of spending
freely, in great cities, where there is variety of meals,
not the same meal; and variety of food, not the same
food; where there are hotels, and where there are,
sometimes, cooks; where, also, there are drinks like the
juice of the grape and the juice of the barley. How
dreadful, therefore, were the sufferings of this unfortunate
man, condemned to feed upon nothing but tough steak
and pork and beans, and to drink nothing, either with
his meals or between them, but tea and coffee and iced
water! There was no tobacco, there was not a cigar in
the place, and he had no money to buy any. That
there was no conversation under the circumstances
mattered little. And he had to do manual work. He
was expected to take a rake or a hoe or a spade, and to
work, actually to work, in the garden.

There was once a great criminal, almost as great a
criminal as this person. They tried to convert him
with prison, but he found himself among old friends
and was comparatively happy; at all events, he continued as far removed as ever from penitence. They
flogged him: he took his flogging as one of the disagreeable accidents of life—like toothache, but sooner
over—and went back to his old friends; they locked
him up quite alone—as soon as he was let out he went
back to his old friends; they gave him a kind chaplain
and a sympathetic visitor who prayed with him and
wept with him; he enjoyed the weeping very much,

and he then went back to his old friends. Finally they hit upon a plan which at least made him entirely miserable, because there was no hope left to him: he was never allowed to go back to his friends at all, and he had to spend the remainder of his life among people who neither drank nor gambled, nor thieved, nor planned iniquities, nor committed crimes, great or small, but lived with the most disgusting and intolerable purity, temperance and virtue. This seemed, for the moment, the only future possible for the man who called himself Charles Lee. He could not go back to his old friends, first because they were dispersed, and next because at every road which led to the former haunts of these interesting people stood the sheriff with an order for his arrest. And oh! how he hated the place he was in!

After breakfast they went back to work. Mr. Charles Lee, hoe in hand, contrived to keep within sight of Gilbert. Nothing at all happened. Gilbert went on quietly with his work; there was no conversation at all between him and the girl; nor did Gilbert address any remarks to him. What did he know? What did he mean by settling accounts? Nothing, either in London or in America, had ever passed between him and that young man. How did he learn what he evidently knew? The more he thought about it, the more uneasy he became.

At one o'clock they sat down to dinner, which was, as has been stated already, exactly the same as breakfast and supper. Gilbert observed that his left-hand neighbour, Brother Silas, devoured the same meal three times a day with the same voracity and despatch. He was a heavy-looking young man, square jawed, with high cheek-bones, big limbed. Like all the men in the place, he had a ruminating eye. The man who ruminates is not always the man who meditates. Brother Silas ruminated. He fed slowly, but steadily and thoroughly, like an ox, gazing into space the while.

Was it possible that this dull and clownish head contained a brain capable of seeing visions, and dreaming dreams, and taking flights into other worlds? Gilbert endeavoured, out of curiosity, to make the man talk: he put forth tentatives, he suggested questions, he gave openings; nothing could be got out of the man but a grunt. It might be imagination, but Gilbert thought that a gleam of light shot across those ruminating eyes once or twice, when the man turned his head slowly and his eyes fell upon Cicely, the one sweet and dainty figure in the whole company. Could he have so much grace as to admire this girl? Was Love admitted into the Community?

After dinner the people separated slowly and silently. A few turned them round in their places and, leaning back as if for Meditation, frankly dropped into slumber. There was no mistaking the difference between the Meditation of the evening and the sleep of the afternoon. The latter was honest, drowsy, afternoon doze; the former was trance. Others rolled slowly—the rolling gait comes to those who loaf as well as those who tread the yielding deck—out of the hall and took their seat on the benches in the verandah. Some walked up and down the wooden walk before the House, languidly, with hanging hands and vacant eyes. Some stood still and looked out into space, seeing nothing; some set off with briskness and then changed their minds and came back again: there was no sign of settled purpose, or of any brain activity at all. Upon all there lay the same dull and vacuous look. Not without wisdom did Benedict enjoin in his brethren the work of the body or the work of the mind when they were not chanting hymns in the abbey church.

Gilbert moved about among them and spoke to one or two. They were morose in their manner; the words seemed to irritate them: they answered in monosyllables. Their irritation was not altogether disinclination to answer, it was partly inability. If you remain absolutely silent for a long time—for many years—during which you read nothing, hear nothing, and speak nothing, you will become, like Alexander Selkirk, unable to speak except with great difficulty. At the very best our powers of speech are extremely limited : under such conditions they may vanish altogether, more especially with men no longer young, who have never received much education; who have lived solitary lives in the fields; and have never at any time enjoyed much converse with their fellow-men.

The women were brighter and more alert both in face and in movement. To begin with, it is impossible to keep in silence a company of women working together. Those who sit and sew, those who make and mend, those who cook and wash up, those who order dairy and laundry, have a great deal to say over their work. Here they called it necessary talk, not frivolous talk ; and this talk kept them alive, even though for the rest of the day they observed the wonted silence of the House.

One of these, a little slight woman, between forty and fifty years of age, her hair streaked with gray, with bright, beady eyes, and a sharp face, attracted Gilbert, because she looked so much more alive than the rest. He ventured to address her. She was sitting in a corner of the verandah, and she had some knitting in her hand ; she was the only woman who was occupied in this feminine manner, and she looked curiously natural and, therefore, out of place.

'Well, young man,' she said, 'if you want to talk about the House, you may. That's improvin' talk. We're set against idle talk, but you're a new-comer and perhaps you want to learn. Sit down, then, and ask.'

'Tell me,' said Gilbert, 'about your Meditation.'

'That's always the trouble, at first. You can't meditate, not worth a cent, can you? I couldn't when I began. I came here twenty years ago, soon after the Master started the House and just before Sister Cicely was born. I was in terrible trouble, I remember, about something or somebody; you wouldn't believe what a wrench it took to get all that trouble out of my head. But I persevered, thank the Lord! and forgot everybody and had my mind clear at last; and I've never thought about my own trouble ever since. And I meditate lovely every night.'

It seemed, to the new-comer, rather a selfish way of getting higher up; but he refrained from saying so.

'If it's any comfort to you, young man—you look as if your thoughts were elsewhere, perhaps with some girl or other—I may tell you that in a very few weeks I was able just to sit down, fold my hands, and go off—go off—up into the clouds.'

'Yes. And what do you see when you are up in the clouds?'

'It might be the New Jerusalem, for all I know,' she replied vaguely. 'It's jest grand and glorious; it fills me all over with a kind of warmth——'

'But what is it you see when you get there?' Gilbert persisted.

'Don't I tell you? It's grand and glorious. I come back all in a glow. Isn't that enough?'

'Then you see nothing?'

'When you come back from the other world,' the woman replied without hesitation, 'you can't never tell what you've seen; everything goes clean out of your head; you jest remember where you've been. Nothing is left but the glow.'

'I understand. Do you think the other people here enjoy the same glow, the same experience of the other world, as yourself?'

'We don't know much about each other. Sometimes there's whispering about this one or that one— and what we see, and what we hear, and what we remember. We women talk about it a little over our work. There's jealousies sometimes about who gets highest. Sister Cicely goes up ever so high. But the Master soars higher than anybody else.'

'Quite so. And what is your own work in the morning?'

'I work in the dairy. Young man, mind you choose the hardest, not the lightest work. Dig in the garden, if you can. Take a spade and dig. Do something to make the body tired, if you wish to meditate quickly and easily.'

'I will remember. And now tell me who they are, and where they come from, and why they come here.'

'I don't know who the brothers and sisters are, nor where they come from. It isn't any business of mine where they come from. When first they come they talk sometimes. Some of the women were driven here by cruel scorn. Oh, but it is for their own good, and after a bit they know it. Then they forget the Past—it drops clean from their souls like a garment that one takes off. Yes, young man, your Past will fall from you: perhaps you've been wicked—it doesn't matter; or unfortunate; or perhaps you've been disappointed in love—nothing matters. After a bit the world will be quite dead to you: nothing will be left but the care of keeping the body from pain and the mind from thought, so as to leave the blessed soul free to soar. You will get to understand by bits that you are all by yourself in space, and no concern with anybody else.'

'Isn't that rather a selfish way of looking at things?'

'It's the Lord's own doing, young man, and you can't undo it. Therefore, I say, forget your Past. It is gone by; you can't alter it. Bury it and forget it.'

'I have always thought that the Past never dies and can never be forgotten. What if one cannot forget the Past?'

'Then you will be criticised by the Committee. It is a dreadful thing to be criticised by the Committee.'

Cicely said the same thing to the brother with the hoe.

'Oh! What is the Committee?'

'Young man,' she took up her knitting, 'I've talked enough.'

'One moment.' Gilbert laid his hand upon the knitting, which is well known as a narcotic. 'One moment. Is the Past really forgotten? Have you really forgotten that old trouble? Do you never ask what became of him? Do you never wonder why he wronged you? Do you never ask why he married the other? Or if he repents his wickedness? Or if——'

'Oh!'—she dropped her knitting with a cry of pain, and answered as one who must,—' if I remember! Yes! yes! I think I forget; but I don't. Oh! I remember all day long, except in the evening, when I force myself to forget and so to rest for an hour.'

'Just so,' said Gilbert. 'The Past can never be forgotten. It is like your shadow; it can never be cut off.'

He left her, shaking and trembling, hands and head and shoulders. He had recalled something of that past trouble. He sighed in pity for the poor woman, who was trying her best to live in a fool's paradise, and turned away.

Gilbert retreated to the garden, where Cicely was still among her roses, walking about with clasped hands and thoughtful face. What were the thoughts of this girl who knew nothing?

'What do you do,' he asked, ' all the long afternoon?'

'Generally I am out here. Sometimes I sit indoors. The time seems long to you because you have forgotten how to rest.'

'I should like to read.'

'Oh no!' she said, 'you must not read. Nothing hinders rest more than reading. I used to read before I arrived at the age of Meditation—not since. Go and sit down somewhere by yourself in a corner; shut your eyes; try to forget the Past. You are in the world still; you are thinking of it all day long; and you are disturbed by something evil that has come to you out of the world. Forget the Past, Gilbert, and be happy with us. Oh, if you only knew it, this is the most beautiful House! There can be no place more delightful—if you only knew it.'

'I wish I did know it, then. But tell me, Cicely, what do you see when you meditate after your wonderful dance?'

'I see my father and my mother. Every night we are all three together on heights far above this. They tell me things.'

'What things do they tell you?'

'When I return to earth I have forgotten. That is to say, for the time. I shall remember everything when I am worthy to speak and this House is worthy to hear. The words come back to me when I go back to them, and my heart is so softened, so warm, and so happy. Oh, Gilbert! if you knew. Only to think of it makes me long for you to feel it too.'

'Child, what is the good of hearing things you can't remember? How can they affect your life?'

'My life? You mean my life here? Oh! but that doesn't count. I have nothing to do with my life here but to get through it.'

'Well. Then what do you see? What is your mother like? How is she dressed?'

'I don't know. When I come back to earth I have no recollection of such things. Yet, when I see her again, I know her again.'

'What is the good of seeing them if you cannot tell what they are like?'

'Gilbert, you know nothing. That *is* my true life— to be with them. It is my happiness and my joy. All the rest is show and a weariness—unless it is to see the flowers grow. Go away now, Gilbert. You disturb me too much.'

He obeyed. He wandered about the gardens, finding no rest or peace. The place was interesting, the girl was interesting; he was a young man open to impression and interested by this kind of profession or pretence; but everything was marred by the presence of the man Charles Lee, and the thought of what had to be done.

He found himself presently in the shrubbery where were the seats. He sat down, his mind agitated, as far from rest as is possible for any man, even outside the House of Meditation.

Presently the man himself who filled his thoughts came up to him and stood before him, dark and threatening.

'I want to know,' he said, 'what you meant this morning when you said that you had accounts to settle with me.'

'Did I say so? Well, then, in good time. Not to-day—I have promised. Not to-day. I shall settle those accounts with you another time.'

'You will explain now.' The man's face grew darker and more threatening.

'I shall choose my own time. Do you understand? My own time.'

'I have seen men shot for less.'

'You will not shoot me, Mr. Charles Lee. At least, not yet.'

'I have a right to demand an explanation. Come, Mr. Gilbert Maryon, you were once an English gentleman, whatever you are now. Suppose you had used those words to a man in any club of which you were a member?'

'I cannot suppose such a thing possible.'

'You charged me, in so many words, with hiding from the hands of Justice. Will you tell me, I ask once more, what you meant by that?'

'Well, I don't mind explaining so much. You have been, among other things, a leading member, perhaps the cleverest member, of a certain ring or long firm, or whatever it was called: a combination for purposes of plunder and robbery. You possess a certain distinction of appearance and manner, and generally played the part of the moneyed man, the aristocratic traveller, or any part requiring manners and appearance. At last you were everywhere blown upon, the police took up the case, the gang was broken up; you are now all separated and either arrested or in hiding. That is what I meant, Mr. Charles Lee.'

The man laughed, but without much merriment.

'I dare say,' he replied, 'that you are right about the gang. It does not concern me, because, you see, I am not the man in question. His name may be Charles Lee, or it may be something else. I don't know or care.'

'In that case you have only to march out of this place, which evidently does not suit you. But you will not leave it yet.'

'Why not?'

'Because in whatever American town you venture to show your face, you will find that they have got a photograph and an exact description of your personal appearance. Because, my friend, you are wanted very badly. Oh no, you will not leave this place.'

'I shall leave it,' he replied, with a very good assumption of dignity, 'when it suits me.'

'If I thought you were going to leave us before it suits *me*,' Gilbert replied, 'I would call in the sheriff of the nearest town.'

'By ——,' the man swore a great oath, 'I will kill, you, Mr. Gilbert Maryon.'

'No, you will not, unless you wish to see the sheriff, because in such a case he would be sent for immediately.'

'What do you want, then?'

'I want to settle accounts with you. Not to-day. Perhaps to-morrow.'

'How have I injured you?'

'That you will learn when the day of settlement arrives. Look here, Mr. Charles Lee, you are a prisoner in this House. Outside, all round you, you are waited for. You will continue to be a prisoner in this House until you are arrested, or until your death. Yes—until your death. It is all you have to look forward to. Now, Mr. Charles—shall I give you your right name? —go away and wait for the day of settlement—perhaps to-morrow.'

With white face, but with the affectation of carelessness, Charles Lee walked away. Heavens! and only two years before the man was a member of the English Government, a statesman, a gentleman of unblemished character!

CHAPTER VII.

A SECOND AND A THIRD MESSAGE.

GILBERT sought no more conversation that afternoon. He wandered about by himself in the grounds and garden and fields belonging to the House. The first curiosity once over, he felt himself out of harmony with the place, for everything jarred upon him: the sight and speech of the man whom he purposed to kill; the presence of that purpose; the postponement of the thing —on account of the vague request of a brain-sick girl, a visionary—lay upon his soul like lead. Why did he put off the thing? He had no right to stay an hour longer in the House; he should have sought out the man without going into the House—and so on. His spirit was disquieted within him as he strolled about the hedgeless fields. Presently he came upon a stream, a bright shallow stream which babbled with so sparkling a voice and laughed so merrily over the stones that it mocked him; the sunshine mocked him; the clear blue sky mocked him; the fresh breeze mocked him; everything mocked and scoffed at the man who bore about so grievous a burden.

The thing should have been done in a gambling den —in a saloon of desperadoes in the Wild West, if there is any Wild West left; even there it would have been a task heavy enough; but it had to be done in a house of religion. To this quiet peaceful retreat he had come to force a man, perhaps against his will, to mortal combat.

And no other way out of it—none. Even if the man were arrested, tried, and sentenced to a lifelong imprisonment for complicity in murder and companionship in robbery, his wife would not be free. Nothing, except his death, could set her free. He thought of her tears and of her shame; of the boy, whose name could only be preserved by the death of his father; of his own promise; and so he strengthened himself. Yet his heart was as heavy as lead.

Suddenly while he meditated—not in the Master's sense—a hand was laid upon his shoulder. It was the Master himself. Gilbert turned promptly.

'You, Master? I did not hear your footstep.'

'Worldling!' said the Master, using a word common on the lips of the converted and convinced and the saints in evangelical circles fifty years ago, 'your thoughts were far away from this House. You were back again Outside, as absorbed and entranced as we when we leave the House.'

'I was thinking——'

'Brother Gilbert,' the Master interrupted, 'I have been disturbed in Meditation on your account. I have been moved to rise and seek you out and to speak to you. It is laid upon me to speak to you. First of yourself. Something—I know not what, and I will not ask—troubles you. Something stands between you and the repose which you need. Am I right?'

'You are indeed right. I am deeply troubled.'

'You have not left Outside though you have come here. You come not with crimes upon your soul, like that other Englishman, but with a purpose not yet accomplished. Again, am I right?'

'How did you learn that?'

'Anyone can read trouble and doubt in your eyes.

But I have a more certain source of knowledge. When that which you think must be done shall have been done, you will be easier in your mind.'

'I think so. It will be finished.'

'Then, Gilbert, I have a message for you. One for your private ear.'

'A message?'

'From a person whom you know not—yet. Perhaps you will know her—some time or other. A message from her.' His low, soft voice was like music. 'For some reason which as yet I know not she takes an interest in you. She is Cicely's mother, and my very dear friend with whom I hold sweet converse every day.' His voice faltered; his eyes became once more filled with that strange, soft light—of what? Enthusiasm? Credulity? Imposture? Not the last: not imposture. 'She is my oldest friend, my dearest friend, for whose sake her child Cicely is dear to me beyond all earthly things. I say, for her sake; you would say, for her memory. To me it is not memory, because she lives with me still and daily speaks to me.'

'And the message?'

'Yes—the message. "Tell Gilbert Maryon," said Cicely's mother, " that what has to be done may be done without him. Tell him to wait; tell him to believe that what has to be done shall be done without him." That is the message. As I understand it, the time will come soon when the arm of the Lord will be stretched out—when some who now cumber and trouble the earth will cease their troubling. How do you understand it?'

'Why! how should she know? How should anyone —you—Cicely—anyone know anything? She cannot. What does she mean, then?'

'I know nothing, young man. Yet I can read the signs. I do not ask your purpose—I do not ask your Past. There is, however, a plain promise with a plain command, from one who cannot deceive and can foretell. On her heights the future is spread out before her like a map. This thing, whatever it is, will be done without your aid. Very well, then. You are troubled about the event and your own action in it. Let it trouble you no more. Suffer your mind to be at ease. Believe the promise, obey the command. So all will be well with you.'

The Master turned away and left Gilbert staring after him stupidly.

Now, observe. If one of our friends were to tell us that a telegram had just arrived from a dead man and that it was lying on the study table, we should treat that communication with contempt, and that friend as a person of strong imagination or of unsound mind. Such a thing would not be received seriously in London; I mean, outside one of the Houses of Pretence. Yet when such a message was brought to Gilbert in this House, whose atmosphere was charged with mysterious trances and wonderful ways, he received it with meekness. The man who gave him the message was a stranger, an acquaintance of twenty-four hours' standing, the friend of a day; he brought no credentials of veracity, he gave no proof of credibility; he simply said, 'Behold a miracle: I bring to you a message from the dead. Why they send you the message I do not know.'

Yet Gilbert received the message with meekness— with that rarest of modern virtues. Why? I suppose it was partly because the atmosphere of the place was so strange and weird; partly, perhaps, on account of the man who brought the message: a strange, remarkable man, picturesque, persuasive; a man with a soft voice, with eyes deep set, searching, luminous; with a high, square forehead; with white flowing hair. We probably ask ourselves how certain persons—impostors —could ever, under any circumstances, be believed. The things they pretended were incredible and absurd, yet they deceived multitudes, and will still deceive multitudes so long as they have the persuasive voice, the deep-set eyes, the face of candour, the manner of authority. Cagliostro is a case in point, and, I believe, Mohammed, and the late Mahdi.

With meekness Gilbert received that message. Why, he had already received and obeyed a warning from a girl—to be sure she looked like an angel or a spirit. He was also ready to obey a message given him by a man who looked like a Prophet. He received the message with meekness, and he allowed it to bring him consolation and relief.

'What had to be done would be done without him.' If that were so, really: if that should prove to be so—if he could only believe this—why, the rippling of the stream and the whisper of the breeze would be an echo to the joy of his heart; his soul would lie open once more—not to trance, but to life and light and action. Anything seemed possible in such a House as this—even a message from the dead: even the postponement at their command of a killing which he persuaded himself would be no murder, but the ordeal by battle.

One must own that, in any case, it was really a remarkable thing for two such messages to be delivered by two persons independently. Certainly the Master could have no suspicion of his intention, nor could the girl.

But another and even a more remarkable thing was to happen in the evening, as you shall hear.

At supper in the evening he sat, as before, opposite his enemy. Mr. Charles Lee retained so much of his English manners that he could and did sit at the table as if at a *table d'hôte*, without the least consciousness of the presence of anybody else: with icy separation he gazed across the table through the body of the man who was going to settle accounts with him. He sat in silence; he took such food as he desired, and in silence he presently rose and walked out of the hall. But Gilbert was no longer concerned about him. 'What was to be done would be done without him.' There was once a gallant knight who set forth to kill a loathly worm for the sake of a lady. On the way he met a fairy who bade him ride on and see the worm killed, but not by himself. So he marvelled greatly, but rode on with uplifted heart. For though he desired very much the death of the worm, without which the lady could never be happy, he could not choose but bethink him that it was a powerful creature, and one that had already killed many, and that the killing of loathly worms was a kind of poaching, because these creatures were strictly preserved for the hunting of the seigneur. Yet a gallant knight. Gilbert was like his valiancy, with differences: for the mediæval worm was sure to fight on provocation, and this, his modern successor, might refuse absolutely to fight. In that case, what to do?

After supper, the brothers and sisters, as on the preceding night, changed their positions, but not their seats; leaning back against the table with outstretched feet and folded hands, and heads slightly inclined backwards. Then, as on the evening before, the man at the piano played a stately march, with repetitions and deep-voiced chords; and life and thought went out of the rows of vacuous faces: all but a few were lost to sense and feeling, or understanding. They fell into trance. The restless few—among them was the little woman, now restless, with whom Gilbert had talked in the afternoon—got up and shuffled through their clumsy, ungainly dance on the platform. When they left off and descended, the veil of nothingness fell upon their faces too: they, like the rest, sat without their souls— a strange, uncanny sight.

Then Cicely sprang upon the stage, and with untutored feet performed again her wild fantastic dance. It was not the same dance as that of last night, but it was no less graceful, natural, spontaneous, fantastic. Gilbert watched it with increased interest; for now he understood something of what it meant: it was like listening to a sonata of which one understands a little,

and listens to learn more. Last night it was a mere
unmeaning dance that he saw. This evening he understood that she was seeking to bring body and mind
together into the condition necessary for perfect rest.
The rhythmic action of the body signified and accompanied the movement of the mind: first the limbs
fell into cadence; then the mind fell into repose as the
music grew fainter; lastly, with the whirl swift and
simple, the brain dropped into rest absolute. She sank
unconscious upon a seat on the platform, her eyes open,
her hands folded, her sweet face vacuous, with none of
its ethereal beauty left in it, save of shape and line.

The musician stopped and leaned back against the
wall, also in trance. And now the hall was perfectly
silent: not a breath, nor a cough, nor the movement
of a foot, disturbed the ghostly stillness.

Suddenly, Cicely rose; and, still with folded hands
and open eyes that saw nothing, she walked as a
somnambulist walks straight through the double file
of that enchanted company to Gilbert, as he sat at the
end of the table in his place near the door.

'Brother Gilbert,' she said, 'I bring you a message.'

A third message? He gazed into her face: it was
lifeless; no gleam of life or sight in those open eyes;
her soft, sweet voice was changed: it was now metallic,
and though she spoke in low tones her words echoed
from wall to wall in the silence of the place.

'My mother sends you a message.'

'Good heavens! Your mother?'

'First, for a token, and to show that it is really my
mother who sends it, she bids me tell you that she was
in Lucknow, a child of four years, when the English
troops relieved the place: and that your father, who
was with them, a young lieutenant, took her in his arms
and kissed her. That is a token.'

'My father went through the Indian Mutiny, certainly.'

'This is the message. "Tell Gilbert Maryon that
what must be done shall be done: but not by him.

Bid him put the thing out of his mind. During five weeks longer the sinner shall have time to repent. At the end of that time, what must be done shall be done."'

So saying, Cicely glided back to her seat, still with the somnambulist's certain walk, and the strange fixed gaze of her open eyes.

Again, one remarks that it is, of course, perfectly impossible for a man of Gilbert's education and antecedents to believe such things. They are too absurd for human reason. That is the way we talk. But there are certain considerations which we overlook. For instance, the condition of mind in which such a message is received. Gilbert was in a highly sensitive, excitable condition. The man he had hunted for two years was in his grasp. He was going to fulfil his pledge; he was going to set his old friend free. This fact alone made him excited and excitable. Then, in our casual talk, we are apt to forget the influence of voice, eyes, touch, surroundings. This message came to Gilbert, for instance, out of the silence and the stillness of a whole company of men and women entranced, by means of one of that company, herself rapt in an undoubted trance. No message could well come more solemnly. And then, again, one message corroborated its predecessor: Cicely could not know anything of the Master's communication. Yet here was an exact repetition of it. For the moment, at all events, Gilbert believed both messages. All his trouble left him. His eyes saw red no more.

If you please to take the trouble, you may construct a very reasonable explanation of the whole phenomenon. The Master imagined that every day he conversed with his dead friends—that was his fixed craze. Now, he was greatly interested in this pleasant, comely young Englishman who had come thus unexpectedly into the House. He observed—anybody with any penetration could observe—by the usual outward symptoms, that this new-comer was in trouble, or doubt, or anxiety about something. What more probable than that he should imagine a vague message and communicate it himself, believing it to be true? Nothing more natural. As a good child of his generation, Gilbert put the thing, next morning, in that way; he wrote it down in his diary, because most men argue best with a pen in hand. And yet, in spite of this rational interpretation, he continued to believe in the message.

Exactly the same thing with Cicely's message. She imagined this message, because, like the Master, she conversed with her dead parents every evening; she, too, was interested in the new-comer; she, too, had observed the signs of trouble. She dreamed the message; half asleep she carried the dream to him.

A perfectly rational explanation, you see. Not a spark of the supernatural about it. Gilbert wrote a short account of the two similar phenomena with this explanation. Much is due to one's self-respect in this age; but, being a descendant of so many ages which have all believed in the uncanny, he continued to believe in the warning and the command; he received the former; he obeyed the latter; and he said to himself that he disbelieved the whole business.

When the trance was over, he looked for some repetition of the message, some confirmation from Cicely. She made no sign; with the rest of the sisters she filed off to the gynæceum and vanished for the night.

Gilbert, a long way from the repose of meditation, sought his own room. He had the curiosity to look into his neighbour's room: it was again empty. What did the man do all the evening in the dark gardens and the empty workshops of the House? In the middle of the night he was again awakened by belated footsteps in the corridor; they passed his room, they entered his neighbour's room. Mr. Charles Lee, then, came up to bed at the fashionable hour of two. What had he been doing from seven o'clock in the evening until two in the morning? Wickedness, somewhere. Mischief, somewhere. Never mind. In five weeks' time all would be cleared up. So, relying on those two messages, Gilbert went to sleep again.

In the morning he made a curious discovery. When he exchanged his clothes for the livery of the House, he had placed all his money with his watch and a ring or two in a drawer. There were about six hundred dollars in notes and a letter of credit. All the money was gone. 'So,' said Gilbert, 'there is a robber in the House of Meditation.'

It was impossible not to connect the deed with the man named Charles Lee. 'Poor devil!' said Gilbert; 'he has sunk low indeed. But he cannot get away from this House. That is impossible.'

He resolved upon saying nothing, for the moment, about this loss, and so he went downstairs to the morning work.

The man whom he suspected was already in the garden, rake or hoe in hand, pretending to a zealous performance of his duties. When Cicely walked over from her place to speak with Gilbert, the man gazed suspiciously, his face pale with anxiety. They were talking about him. This he saw quite clearly. Everybody knows when other people are talking about them; some men pretend that they can hear what is said— which we need not believe. He was quite right. The conversation did, in fact, concern this sinful brother.

'My heart has been troubled about you all night, Gilbert,' said the girl seriously.

'It is very good of you to think about me at all. I do not forget what you said last night.'

'What did I say last night? I wish I could say or do anything to remove the trouble.'

'I am not so troubled, I say, Cicely, since I received your message of last night.'

She seemed not to hear. 'The bad influence,' she said, 'is connected with the other Englishman over yonder—the man with a soul as black as night. He has no business here; he belongs to lower levels: in his next world he will be a pig, I think, or a rattlesnake. You know that after death we all go to our own levels. This man fears you, Gilbert, for some reason. I see very plainly that he would do you some harm, if he dared. You are very hostile to him, and he knows it. But he cannot get away. I know not why. He would like to fly, but he is afraid.'

'How do you know this, Cicely? Are you a witch?'

'What is a witch? I know because I can read what is written on your face and in your eyes as plainly as any print: and on his face, too. Gilbert, put that purpose of yours out of your mind. Let me try to work upon that evil spirit of his and to calm him into forgetfulness. Oh! how restless he is! What a terrible punishment it is for wickedness, that one cannot forget! To be tied and chained in the lower levels—oh! it is dreadful!'

'You will never calm that restless spirit, Cicely. But try, by all means—after your mother's message.'

'My mother's message? What message? You keep talking about a message.'

'You gave it to me yourself, Cicely, last night, while you were in trance. Have you forgotten?'

She became greatly agitated. 'Oh, Gilbert! what? I remember nothing of what happens to me in trance. Tell me, Gilbert, exactly what it was. Ah! my mother! She sent herself—my mother—a message to you? Oh! what does it mean that she should think of you?' The tears came into her eyes. 'Yet, she is so good. She thinks of everybody.'

'She says that she knew my father long ago, in India, when she was a child.'

'Oh! Yes, yes—she was born in India: she was in Lucknow when the rebels. . . . Oh! it is wonderful. But the message. Tell me exactly what she said.'

'She said, "That what has to be done will be done,

but not by him." That is, by me. "And now he is to put the thing out of his mind. For five weeks longer the man shall have leisure to repent." The man is Brother Charles. "At the end of that time what has to be done will be done." That is the message, Cicely. The Master brought me another to the same effect from your mother.'

'Oh! Through the Master, too! Gilbert, there is some reason—I know not what—why she should give you her protection. Oh! but you must believe what she says: she cannot deceive you; she is so high that future and past and present are all visible to her. Oh! that my mother should send a message, and to you! Oh! she will look after you now! Oh, Gilbert! oh, how glad I am that you came!'

'But about this message?'

'You must obey—you have no choice. Tell me, Gilbert, you believe it?'

'Belief, my child, in such a thing as this is contrary to reason. The thing is preposterous. It is likewise ridiculous. I have said this to myself a dozen times. Yet, Cicely, I do believe it.'

He took her hand. The other man looked on with a scowl; he could see, but he could not hear—he could see her sweet, earnest face looking up in prayer—and he could see the man's face softening.

'I believe it, dear child. I will obey. I will wait for five long weeks. And meantime you will talk and tell me things out of your innocence and your faith. These things are too high for me. Let me lean awhile, Cicely, on your more stalwart arm.'

BOOK II.

AFTER FIVE WEEKS

CHAPTER I.

STRAWBERRIES! FINE STRAWBERRIES!

ONE afternoon, about four weeks after these beginnings, a certain English traveller, whose gray hair and gray moustache proclaimed his more than fifty summers, was standing in the portico of the first hotel of Aldermanbury City, New York State. Aldermanbury is not a very important place, but a good many thousand people worry through life there; it possesses at least one fine street; it has its public buildings—which are new and ambitious; it has a beautiful park; it has a noble river, which flows past its quays and wharves; it holds a daily exhibition of activity and industry; it boasts an electric tram as well as a horse tram; it has two, or perhaps ten, daily papers; there is a lecture-hall; there is a college for men and women: and it is old enough to have a few houses of the eighteenth century, with a church, wooden pillars and all, actually of the seventeenth century. In all America you cannot very well expect to find a church much older than that.

It was a sizzling hot day in June; the outlines of things quivered in the heat; the electric cars ran clicking noisily up and down, looking like red-hot furnaces for the accommodation of the wicked; if any man chose to walk on the sunny side it was equivalent to committing suicide—the coroner's inquest would certainly bring in that verdict; the broad shady hall of the hotel was filled with citizens sitting about and transacting business; they all drank iced water; the young men tried to preserve the stiffness of their collars scientifically by sticking a handkerchief between collar and neck. The heat, which overcomes the body and brings limpness and languor to the limbs, has in America, apparently, no such effect on the mind; the flow of business was not arrested; in the shops the electric fans went whizzing round and round, and then went whizzing back again; they fanned the cheek with the burning air, but they could not cool it.

The Englishman looked up and down the street lazily. It was his second day in the place : he had seen everything there was to see; he felt like going on to the next place. Why should he not go on? On the other hand, why should he go on? He had been going on for the best part of a twelvemonth. To one who goes about the world for so long there cometh in the end satiety of newness—enough of new places and new sights. This American city interested him not : on the other hand, if he went on to Boston or New York it would be hotter and noisier, and not much more interesting. Perhaps he might as well stay there—continuance of heat when there is not noise therewith is not unpleasant, and in the evening one can drive.

The Park of Aldermanbury is a mighty pretty place —much prettier than Hyde Park or Green Park, or even St. James's Park—with its ornamental water, its bridges, its islands and its hanging woods, and, after sunset, its countless points of fire in its millions of fireflies. The soft, cool air of this park, and stillness therewith, would be far better, he reflected, than the noise of New York, even with a drive in Central Park. Perhaps he would stay. In this irresolute condition of mind, he looked up the street and down the street, expecting nothing. He looked into the twilight of the hall, and he considered with pity the energy of drummers and those who hunt the nimble dollar all day long ; and he admired the hotel clerk, who, alone of mankind, remains unaffected by heat or cold ; who stands while others sit ; who is never idle and seldom silent ; who works right through all the hours there are, and never has a rest or a 'let up' or a holiday ; who is never hurried, never out of temper, and always knows everything connected with the service of life, the freight of human bodies, and the times of all the trains to everywhere. At this moment, just as if time was of no consequence whatever, the hotel clerk was carefully explaining to an extremely dull lady how to get from Aldermanbury to San Francisco.

The Englishman turned lazily to the street again, thinking that perhaps a cigar would help him through the time. And he then became aware of a man slowly getting along the street on the shady side. The man was too far off for his face to be visible ; but something indefinable in his manner of walking suggested, even at a distance, a certain street called Piccadilly.

The man drew nearer : the traveller could not choose but watch him. Why? Perhaps because there was no one else to watch : perhaps on account of that suggestion of Piccadilly.

The man carried a large basket ; he went into the shops with his basket, evidently offering his wares for sale ; he also offered them to the passengers on the wood pavement. There were two or three remarkable points about his manner of offering the strawberries which leaped to the eyes at once. First, he did not bawl or cry his wares, like the British costermonger. Secondly, in presenting his basket to ladies he politely took off his hat with a bow. The action once more suggested Piccadilly—not that hats are not removed in the presence of ladies at the city of Aldermanbury, but that there is a Piccadilly fashion which varies from year to year—or is it from month to month ?—and this was the fashion of two years ago. Thirdly, that the man stepped like a guardsman, being as tall as any in the Household Brigade and as upright; that he carried his head as if he was a belted earl; and that he handled his basket with the left hand much as if he had been handling a sword: further, that he proffered his basket as if it was a princely gift. And then, suddenly, the traveller's thoughts flew hither and thither in the most tumble-down, topsy-turvy, absurd manner possible: they became a kind of waking nightmare: he saw this itinerant merchant standing in a drawing-room filled with people, dressed just as he was in Aldermanbury, offering his strawberries—they were strawberries in a basket—for sale to the ladies who were too well-bred to show any astonishment, and only bowed, and said 'Thank you,' and bought the fruit. Then he pulled himself out of this ridiculous dream, and suddenly recognised the merchant and ran out into the street and slapped that merchant on the shoulder, crying, 'Gilbert Maryon! By the Lord! What the devil are you up to now?'

Gilbert Maryon—who was the strawberry vendor—turned his head, put down his basket, and without the least show of surprise, or shame, or confusion—yet most young men of London would be abashed at being caught in such an occupation—held out his hand with a frank smile of welcome.

'You, Annandale! Why, what are you doing in Aldermanbury?'

'I am going home, gradually. I have come here by degrees from San Francisco, and Chicago, and Buffalo—I have also come from Japan. I am a globe-trotter—by your leave.'

'Certainly—with my leave.'

'And you? What are you doing?'

'You see—I am selling strawberries.'

'That is what I do see—Gilbert Maryon is selling strawberries in the street! Why is Gilbert Maryon selling strawberries in the street?'

'Strawberries, you must admit, are grown to be sold.

Therefore, the end of their existence must be achieved. Someone must sell strawberries. Why not I? It is not, I believe, in any way disgraceful to sell strawberries in the street.'

'Well, if you ask my opinion, I think it is—as one may say—mildly disgraceful. Not like some things. But still not what a gentleman should do.'

'I have ceased to recognise the distinction.'

'Yet it exists. Why have you abolished the distinction?'

'They are very good strawberries,' he went on, without answering the question. 'Have some. They are cheaper than any you can buy in the shops; they are also fresher—I helped to pick them at six o'clock; and they are finer. We pride ourselves particularly on our strawberries, our peaches and our pears; no finer fruit of the kind is grown in the States. Our potatoes also are acknowledged to be the best in the market, and I believe that in peas and asparagus we are well to the front.' Gilbert shovelled up a few strawberries in his scoop, and offered them to his friend. 'Try them. I assure you that they are very fine strawberries.'

'No, thank you. Tell me what it means.'

'These are the strawberries of our Community.'

'Your Community?'

'My Community. I am at present a brother of the Community. We are monks and nuns. This is my monastic garb.'

His friend looked at it with disdain. It was a gray suit, quite simple, a jacket with side pockets, not quite in West-End style, and a round hat.

'It hath a reach-me-down appearance. Does the whole Community dress like this?'

'All the men do. I wish to goodness the women did as well.'

'What Community is it?'

'One in which we live the life in common, like the early Christians. We live by the labour of our hands;

we leave our wealth behind us when we enter. For my own part, I work in the garden. Sometimes I am sent here to sell fruit. Do have some.'

The traveller observed that, though the voice and manner were those of Gilbert of the London clubs and of London society, his face was somehow changed.

'Old man,' he laid a hand upon Gilbert's shoulder, 'what did you do it for? There is something behind this: you've either got a bee in your bonnet or you've got something up your sleeve.'

'I can only repeat that I am, for the present at least, a member of this Community——'

'Nevertheless——'

'The Community is not, like some, composed of people who have found the world hollow or discovered that society is tinkling cymbals. Not at all. Don't think that.'

'I won't. You find the society of the Community superior to that of London: is that the reason of your retreat?'

'Nine-tenths of us are half-taught rustics; one or two are German enthusiasts; there is a repentant burglar or two; there is a late leader in a notorious long firm: there are one or two ladies with a tempestuous Past. These constitute our Society.'

'What are you doing in it? Gilbert, there is something behind.'

'It's a very interesting Community. We do not talk; we do not read; we do not sing hymns; we have no chapel and no services; we do not fast or macerate ourselves—we have, on the contrary, three square meals a day, and they are always the same: the delicious steak of the American up-country hotel, with the refined yet tasty dish called "pork and beans," form the principal part of each meal.'

'Gilbert, once again, in the name of wonder, what are you doing in this awful place? If you cannot tell me, say so.'

He began, as men will, to think there must be a girl

of some kind at the bottom of the mystery. Yet Gilbert was not a *coureur des femmes*.

'We meditate; sometimes we dance; we fall into trance——'

'You don't mean to say that you've struck the Buddhist rubbish?'

Gilbert shook his head. 'The Buddhists are not in it, my dear friend, compared with us.'

'Well, come to the hotel, and let us sit down and have a drink.'

'Certainly,' said Gilbert. 'Carry the basket for a bit, will you?'

Mr. Annandale looked to the right and to the left of him, also before him and behind him, for he was blushing like a schoolgirl, while he obeyed, and carried the basket of strawberries into the porch of the hotel.

There they sat down. Mr. Annandale produced his cigar-case.

'Thank you,' said Gilbert; 'for the time I have renounced tobacco.'

'Have a drink, then—a whisky-and-soda.'

'Thank you,' said Gilbert; 'for the time I have renounced whisky.'

There was a cheerful light in his eye; there was a smile upon his lips—which showed that, in spite of these privations, Gilbert was not treating the Community very seriously. This made the other man still more curious to understand what it meant.

'Let me see,' said Annandale: 'it must be two years since you disappeared without giving notice. Two years; it was either just before or just after the breakdown of Sir Charles Osterley.'

'Just after that event. Lady Osterley, I remember, told me about it.'

'Yes—the divine Dorabyn. I remember you were an old ally of hers; as for me, I am only an old lover, you know. Yes—after that event. Have you heard, by any accident, where the man is and how he is?'

'He had to go abroad, I believe,' Gilbert replied evasively.

'So they said—so they said. Under certain circumstances people will say anything. His own people are in the same tale. Gone abroad—gone abroad. My dear Gilbert, when a man disappears suddenly and is no more seen, when nobody hears anything about him, when he is never met abroad, when his own people never mention him, when his wife will not talk about him with her oldest friends—meaning me—what is the conclusion?' Mr. Annandale touched his forehead. 'That's the conclusion—that, and no other; and poor Dorabyn is a widow, yet not a widow.'

'A good many people have come to that conclusion,' said Gilbert.

'There can be no other conclusion. And I'm awfully sorry for poor Dorabyn—the matchless Dorabyn. He was a cold-blooded beast; he always looked as if he was devising something dark and treacherous, but statesmanlike, such as the murder of Mr. Gladstone and the burial of the body under the stairs in the Tower. Dorabyn would have him; threw over all her old admirers—even me, sir, me, who was old enough to be her father—in order to marry a man going to be Prime Minister. And this is the end of her ambition. Whereas——'

'If she had married you, she would now——'

'Well, it's the month of May, isn't it? She would now be the Queen of her own world—and a mighty fine world it is. But she would have made it finer. Poor Dorabyn! She is travelling about the world with her little boy.'

'So I understood when last she wrote to me.'

'And you too have disappeared. Why?'

'There seems no reason—does there?—why I should communicate to the papers what I am doing and where I am staying. The world cares nothing about my occupations.'

'A small part of the world does care a great deal, Gilbert.'

'Thank you. Well, I came abroad—I have been travelling about for two years. That is really all there is to tell you.'

'Oh! and this precious Community?'

'I have not been there very long: a few weeks; the thing interests me: I don't know how much longer I am going to stay—probably not very long.'

His friend nodded at the basket at their feet. 'Do they make you do that every day?'

'No; strawberries are only in season for a few weeks. I do other kinds of work. Mostly, however, I work in the garden. One of our principles is that one should not work too exclusively at one thing, or the work itself may become a hindrance by occupying our thoughts. So I sometimes make wooden traps, or turn chair legs—we are great in chair legs—in the carpenter's shop. Sometimes I am sent into this city to sell our fruit and vegetables.'

'Are there any gentlefolks at all where you are living?'

'The distinction is invidious.'

'Have they good manners?'

'No.'

'Is the cooking good?'

'It is detestable.'

'How is the wine?'

'There is none.'

'You are taking notes and making up a novel. Well, everybody does that nowadays.'

'I no longer read or write anything. There are no books in the House. For the attainment of the Perfect Life, which is the *raison d'être* of the House, books are found to be a hindrance.'

'Do you propose to stay there much longer?'

A curious change fell upon Gilbert's face, a black cloud. His eyes darkened. 'Perhaps I may come out of it in a few days. Perhaps I may stay there longer.'

'Are there any girls to talk with—*pour conter des fleurettes*, after the fashion of the world—your favourite amusement?'

''There are sisters——'

'In so large a family some of the sisters must be young.'

''To whom we are brothers.'

'It is a kindly tie, Gilbert. Tell me truly: do you like this abominable life? Do you really endure it with patience?'

'Work is not degrading. There might be things much harder to endure than work. In order to carry out certain purposes one would willingly suffer much worse things than work.'

'Well, but the change, the companionship. Remember your companions at home. Remember Dorabyn.'

Gilbert flushed suddenly. He could not tell this man that he was in the place solely for the sake of Dorabyn.

Mr. Annandale changed the subject: there was something behind; if Gilbert were really drawn by the strange doctrines of this Crankery he could not speak of the House in this light and careless tone; if there was nothing, why was he confused at the mention of his old friend's name? A girl must be at the bottom of it —*Cherchez la femme; cherchez la femme.* Perfect Life, work necessary for the Perfect Life—heard one ever such stuff and nonsense?

They talked all the afternoon; they went back to club-land; they talked about people; they talked scandal; the last scandal but two; the sun went down; they dined together at the hotel—a table decently ordered and served; they had a bottle of fair claret with the old talk. These things refresh the soul after a course of House dinner and silence withal.

It was eleven o'clock when Gilbert left the hotel.

In the morning the darky sweeping the floor found the strawberry basket which Gilbert had forgotten; this shows that when he went away he was not thinking of his mission: to sell those strawberries for the good of the House.

Eleven o'clock when Gilbert turned into the street; a clear moonlight night; the air as warm as in the day. He looked about him: the street was almost deserted; he felt like one who has escaped from prison; it was delightful only to be in the street among men and not in a cell among Cranks. He threw up his arms and could have shouted in the joy of momentary freedom. He strolled down the side walk. Presently he came to a cross street, at the end of it: on the right rose the public buildings of the city; in the moonlight they looked imposing—the moon is very kind to inferior architecture as well as to ruins: on the left the street sloped to the river; the moonlight lay upon the broad bosom of the noble river; half-way across there floated rather than sailed, for there was no wind, a small boat with her white sail spread—who was in that boat? Why did she sail at midnight? Gilbert turned down this street and stood upon the quay. Lower down were moored two big river steamers; behind the quay rose two or three saloons, their electric lamps burning brightly, and a confusion of voices showing that men were still awake.

'I have not seen real humans for a month,' said Gilbert. He walked over to the entrance of one place: it was a dive; he looked in; there was a bar with half a dozen men lounging around; along one side of the room was a bench where two or three men were sitting; they seemed to be seafaring men—probably connected with the river steamers. In one corner was a table with four men playing cards. Gilbert drew back suddenly. For one of the gamblers was the man who was going to —what? He knew not what would happen to that man. But something.

There he was, playing with passion and intensity, his face drawn with excitement. The other men took their gains calmly; this man, Charles Lee, was absorbed and carried away with it.

There was no danger of being seen by him. Gilbert stood in the shade of the entrance. He watched for a few minutes. Then he turned away. 'There goes my money,' he said, 'the money that he has stolen. And this is what our friend does all the evening! Is he not afraid? Is he going mad to venture where the police are looking for him? Will it end in his being arrested? In that case where is Dorabyn's freedom? And where is my promise? And what about that message from the skies?'

CHAPTER II.

VOICES IN THE NIGHT.

This unexpected meeting with his old friend—Colonel Annandale, the old friend of his father, the old friend of Dorabyn, the former friend of Charles Osterley— rudely recalled to Gilbert's mind the purpose for which he had come to this place. Further, the sight of the man for whom he came to the place, gambling with common stokers and firemen of the river steamers, also recalled to him the purpose for which he had come to this place.

If you remember, he had come to kill this man. That is to say, he would make him fight, somehow, and either kill him or be killed himself.

A very serious purpose. It would be difficult to find a more serious purpose.

'I go out to kill a man, or to be killed.' It was like the Ordeal by Battle, except that in the old Ordeal the guilty man had to swear by the Living God and by the dead saints that he was innocent: a perjury which generally afflicted his heart with terror, and took the strength out of his hand and the keenness out of his sight. In this Ordeal the guilty man would not have to make any pretence or commit any perjury; he would simply fight, his guilt being known, in order to save his life, if he could.

A very serious purpose, indeed. Yet Gilbert had managed to forget it; or, at least, to put it out of his mind for five weeks.

It seems a good deal to forget. Yet we are all of us constantly forgetting and putting out of sight a vast number of things, to remember which would poison the present. One could not live if one had to be always gazing back into the past, or always anticipating the future. Which of us loves to dwell, except at rare intervals, on the early days of struggle? Yet it was a healthy and invigorating time. Which of us dares to anticipate and realize the pains of eighty; the chamber of torture; the slow dragging of life out of the body by long agony? No one. We can bring ourselves to forget everything. Yet, it must be admitted, to forget such a purpose as this required considerable power of forgetting.

He had come to kill a man. The man was there, waiting to be killed: yet he had done nothing. Why? Because a girl brought him a message which she said came from the dead.

Five weeks the Message asked for—five weeks' respite. Four weeks had gone; but one remained—only one week: the respite had been asked for on the ground of possible softening and repentance.

Every day, three times a day, the two men sat opposite each other at the table in the Hall. The man who called himself Charles Lee appeared with regularity at the common meals of the House: he took his seat with calm insolence; he looked through his opposite neighbour as if he were not there—it was in the highest style of the best and most popular British manner: it

was just as if he was taking his place at **a Continental
table d'hôte**; he sat in silence, pale, self-contained, and
with the well-bred manner of superiority which still
remained to him. Gilbert talked with Cicely; neither
of the two addressed a word to this man. The meal
despatched, he rose and departed, silently. In the
morning he pretended to work in the garden, but did
nothing; in the afternoon he strolled about under the
shade trees and slept on the benches. This silence and
deliberate separation helped to make it possible for
Gilbert to set his purpose on one side and to forget it.
Had the man talked or blustered or pretended, the end
would have been forced upon Gilbert.

It was nearly midnight when he reached the House.
Lights were out: the Community were long since
sleeping peacefully.

He mounted to his room, undressed quickly, and lay
down.

Sleep came, and with sleep came Visions. They were
terrible Visions, born of the purpose in his mind, thus
awakened and returned to him. The Visions showed
him the flower gardens of the House; among the
flowers moved the girl, pure and white, neither fearing
evil, nor thinking evil, nor knowing evil; and beside
her stood an Evil Presence—whose soul was black
through and through; but it could do no harm to the
girl. And then he saw in his Visions a Figure, marching solemnly and slowly, though still at some days'
distance. It was the Figure of Death himself; not a
grinning skeleton, but a strong man armed, with purpose in his face—and lo! the countenance of Death
was not his own, but some other's whose face was
hidden; but the shape and the height and the carriage
of the shape were like unto the shape and the height
and the carriage of Sir Charles himself. The Vision
was so vivid and clear that he must have been asleep,
though he thought he was awake: it is only in sleep

that we are enabled to receive such Visions. He sat up, trying to bring it back, especially the Vision of that Death, the Avenger who was not himself, but another. What other? Oh! a dream—a dream.

Sleep would come no more. It was a hot night; he got up and leaned out of his open window, trying to think coherently. This was difficult, because he was tired, and in that condition of half sleep in which the mind will not work. Only a week remained. He must resolve on something; he must be ready for action. What?

Dorabyn was in America. The thing must be done without further delay. How should it be done? How should it be begun?

First, he discovered sleepily that he could not answer that question. Then he woke up a little more and tried again. Still he could not find out any answer. Then he became quite broad awake, and yet he could not find an answer. He tried other things; his mind was quite clear and able to work upon these; but in this line he could not think at all—it was just as if a high brick wall stood up before him if he moved in this direction.

He looked out into the night—a dark, black, moonless night; as breathless as, in the early summer, the State of New York often sees the night. It was as hot as one may experience in the Red Sea at the same season; away over the hills there flashed incessantly gleams of lightning with low growls and rumblings of thunder.

He stood leaning out of the window, watching the flashes which lit up for the moment the farm buildings and the gardens of the House; and he wondered when this brick wall would vanish, and when he should find an answer to that question. Because, you see, it was now really necessary that an answer of some kind should be found.

His thoughts kept coming back to this question. He tried to think of other things: of the House; of the girl Cicely, thoughtful, serious, sweet of face and firm of eye and innocent of brow; of the men and women in trance; of the grim and mournful listlessness which they called Recreation; of the dulness; of the sadness; of the strange unreal futility of a place whose people were nourished and kept alive by illusions and self-deceptions, like those islanders of Rabelais who fed upon wind: all these things he could think about clearly. He could even picture to himself the degradation of the man gambling in the lowest den of an American town; and the despair of the man hiding in the last place of concealment possible: the man hunted; the man disgraced. He could remember his promise to Dorabyn in her agony that he would set her free. And then? Then he could go no further. If he asked that simple question, 'How?' the high brick wall rose up before him over which he could not climb; over which he could not even look.

'What must be done shall be done, but not by you.'

It was a promise. Whose promise? Cicely said that it was the promise of a dead woman. What matter, so long as the charm acts, whether it is illogical, absurd, contrary to reason? Charms have healed people ever since the world began. The words, like a charm, fell on Gilbert's disquiet soul. They were as the cold blade upon the burning wound of the soldier. His restlessness suddenly left him; there returned to his soul once more the sense of reliance with which Cicely had bewitched him when she first brought that message; with which the girl had held him patient and contented for four weeks.

'What must be done shall be done, but not by you.'

Had this thing been known to the world concerning Gilbert, who was not a visionary, nor a crank, nor a dreamer, nor a ghost-monger, but a sane and simple man, who troubled his head about no such matters—had it been spread abroad in his club that Gilbert Maryon, of all men, had yielded to such an influence, there would have been derision. But no one in any club will ever be able to connect the name of Gilbert Maryon with this sad softening of the brain, because Gilbert Maryon keeps the story to himself.

He felt no further desire for sleep; he continued to lean out of the window, watching the play of lightning and listening to the rumblings among the hills. The air was in that condition which unscientific people who wish to be thought scientific love to describe as 'charged with electricity.' The exact scientific description of that condition I do not know; in common parlance, however, men speak of it as 'jumpy.' Perhaps the lightning made the night jumpy. Now, when the air is jumpy, you may experience all kinds of strange, impossible and incredible things. A man speaks afar off; his voice is close at your ear. You reply, your voice is far off; the closing of a window is like the firing of a cannon. One man—a visionary, he—walking once in the poetical neighbourhood of Bloomsbury (London, West Central), the day being Sunday, the season early summer, the time evening, the air very jumpy—it was, in fact, only five minutes before the breaking of the great thunderstorm that o'er pale Britannia passed exactly twenty-five years ago—this man, I say, heard people talking in their houses behind the closed windows —yea, heard what they said; as a proof, he reported that the language and the ideas were for the most part creeping and common. I tell this anecdote, not because I hope to be believed, though it is quite true. This Visionary has never been believed. Whenever he relates the incident allusions are made to his calling, which is that of *Raconteur* or Story-teller. Yet for once he stumbled into plain, naked truth. I tell it here because it illustrates, as pat as possible, the adventure which came to Gilbert on this night of wakefulness and visions, and hot, still air, and general jumpiness.

It was about two o'clock in the morning—the time

between the two days, when the memory of the dead day has wholly gone out of the sky and the anticipation of the new birth has not yet begun: not a time for ghosts, who come earlier or later; when the whole world is asleep, even the watch-dog. Now please to remember, before you read what may appear incredible, the exact position of Gilbert's room in the House. The latter faced full south: in its western wing were the cells or sleeping rooms of the men; on the west side of this wing, and on the third floor, was Gilbert's room. The eastern wing was given to the Sisters; beyond that wing ran, open, hedgeless, straight, the road to Aldermanbury. In other words, Gilbert was as far as the position of the House would allow from any persons walking on that road.

In such a place, at such a time, in such a position, the following remarkable experience arrived to the man leaning with his head out of window.

First he heard footsteps on the road at some distance from the House: that would not, perhaps, be so very strange a thing on a metalled road, because, on such a road, a man's footsteps might be heard a long way off, in the intervals of growling thunder: but the road was not metalled; it was a plain dusty cross-country road, used for no other purpose, at this end, than for communication with the House.

There were two distinct footsteps; he heard them and distinguished them quite plainly: one step belonged to a man, the other to a woman. What man—what woman—could be walking along this road at such an hour? Tramps, perhaps: but tramps never came to this House; first, because it stood well away from the main road; and, next, because those tramps who had tried it reported of the place that a real bit of work had to be put in, and at least a third of a day's work before any grub was exhibited. Now, work to a tramp is like the other end of a magnet to the needle: it makes him turn and run away. The footsteps were not those of tramps. Further, it became apparent to Gilbert that the feet were moving in different directions.

Gilbert listened curiously; his senses were strangely quickened, yet he neither marvelled nor asked how he came to hear and to understand things so far off. As for the footstep of the man, though it was still a long way off, on the other side of the House, still on the road which led to the city of Aldermanbury, he recognised it as that of the man who called himself Charles Lee.

'He is coming home after his gambling bout. He has lost all my money,' said Gilbert.

The other footstep, that of the woman, was in that road also, going to meet this man.

'What woman is it? What can she want with this man in the dead of night?' He listened again with curiosity. Surely, surely—the footstep of the girl Cicely. Of Cicely! Then he leaned out of window and listened with all his ears. What was Cicely, the child Cicely, doing with this fallen gentleman in the middle of the night? The flashes of lightning lit up the farm buildings and the gardens; but they could not show him this couple meeting in that road on the other side of the House.

But he could hear. He heard not only footsteps but also words.

Outside, the man Charles Lee was walking home to his retreat. Night after night he ventured forth in the darkness to a den frequented by certain persons of the baser sort, where, if he could show a single dollar, he could gamble as long as the money held out. This evening he was returning home stone broke. It has been indicated how he was able to find money for the last gamble: that plunder was now, after four weeks' changes and chances, mutabilities and variations, entirely vanished, and he knew not where to turn for more. He walked slowly; he hated walking along the rough and dark road—it was four long miles from Aldermanbury to the House which he loathed but could not leave.

All day long he devised plans for disguise and escape; yet what disguise would hide him? And where could he find any disguise? Spectacles, a red wig, a beard, a patch over one eye; but how to get these things? And when he had them, where to go without money? And every day and all day long his heart failed him for fear and rage, because he saw no way of escape and no choice but to stay where he was.

Presently, when the House was almost in sight, Brother Charles heard footsteps approaching. And he stopped with a great curse upon his lips.

'That girl again!' he swore. She drew nearer. 'She is mad. She is put up by that damned Maryon fellow! She tries to frighten me.' He had made up his mind by this time that Gilbert, too, was a refugee, and that he would not bring the police to the House for his own sake. 'Frighten me,' he repeated. 'To frighten me away!' He straightened himself and walked on with resolution. The man was truly a most deplorable and a most disgraceful creature, but he was not to be alarmed by bogies.

Then the girl met him, clad in a white dressing gown, with no hat. She stood before him and threw out her arms to bar the way.

'Well? You are here again? Do you think I shall take you for a ghost?' asked Charles Lee. 'What is the meaning of this play-acting? Are you not afraid to come out by yourself in the middle of the night? Are you going to give me some more messages from dead people? Pray do not trouble. The dead, my girl, sleep very still. They know nothing that is done. They neither hear nor speak, nor understand anything.'

'I am sent, Brother Charles.'

'Sent!' he repeated. 'Once for all, I am not the man to be moved by rubbish of that kind. Confess that young Maryon sent you. He wants to get me out of the place. Why does he want me to go? You girl

—Cicely—go and tell him that I won't interfere with him if he lets me alone. If he won't——'

'I am sent,' she repeated. 'You have hitherto paid no heed. I am sent to tell you that the allotted time is well-nigh over; there remain but six days; and then——'

'What then?'

'When a man has done all the evil that he is permitted to do, when there is no more hope that he will forget the Past, he is called away.'

'You mean that I am going to die in a week? Perhaps. But how am I to die? I am perfectly well; as well as this infernal place will let me be.'

'You are such a man,' said Cicely, without answering his words. 'You will not be permitted to do any more evil.'

'If you were a man!' he replied weakly.

Then she raised her hand and became like the Master, a Prophet. 'You will not forget the Past: you are tied with a chain of shame and wickedness: you feel the shame, you cannot feel the wickedness; that is your punishment already: it will be a part of your next existence that you will feel the misery yet not be able to give up the cause. Oh! you must sink far, far below this present life: you have I know not how much trouble and suffering to undergo before you can rise again to what you were in the days of your youth. Only a week left; and then—Charles Osterley——'

'What?' he cried. 'Who told you my name?'

'You will suffer what men call death.'

'Who told you my name? Was it Maryon? What do you know about me?'

'That you will die, Charles Osterley. There are still before you six days. There is yet time to cut the chain and to forget the Past.'

She turned and left him, speeding swiftly home. The man stood still, pale and trembling. The sound of his own name, which he had not heard since he went out of the presence of the man whose name he had forged, made him tremble. The after story was nothing—only followed as a corollary on the first: that he had become rogue and sharper and conspirator was nothing, compared with the memory of that forgery.

Gilbert, from his window, listened. The girl's voice ceased; he heard her light footstep as she returned to the House. The man for some time remained still. Was he terrified? Was he moved? Was there any hope at all that he could, if he would, forget the past?

Presently his footstep was heard again; but it was slow and heavy, as of one oppressed with weariness or heaviness of mind. It reached the House; it passed along the gravel walk before the House; it reached the entrance to the wing, which stood open day and night; it came slowly up the stairs; it passed along the corridor. Gilbert left the window and turned to the door. That night—that very night—he would tell him all, and why he came: he would warn him and bid him prepare. But his hands in the dark fell upon the bare wall of the room; he groped about, feeling for his door: he could not find it. The wall of the room was exactly like the wall which stood between him and the answer to that question. It would not suffer him to pass through in order to get at the man. Gilbert desisted: you cannot fight a brick wall; he lay down and fell fast asleep.

In the morning the thing was like a dream of the night. Cicely greeted him in the garden with her serious smile.

'You should look tired this morning, Cicely,' said Gilbert. 'You had a broken night. Yet you look as fresh and as sweet as one of your own rosebuds.'

'I had a very good night, Gilbert. I always sleep well.'

'Oh!' It was, then, as he knew beforehand, a trance or a sleep-walking. 'Did dreams visit you?'

'Dreams? Yes, I dreamed about Brother Charles.' She shuddered and looked round. 'To think about him gives me a kind of sore throat: it pains me only to look at him. Oh! Gilbert, his soul is black through and through. What does he stay here for? Something will happen to him—I am sure that something will happen to him.'

'I think it very probable—more than probable.'

'His heart is full of hatred and of fear: I feel it when he sits beside me in the Hall. Perhaps he will be criticised.'

'You are a witch, Cicely. Will criticism—which I take to be a fearless expounding of one's faults—quite meet the case?'

Cicely shook her head. 'It must be a dreadful thing,' she said, 'to be criticised.'

Gilbert laughed. 'I do not think the criticism of the Fraternity would be very formidable. However, you do not always dream about this nigger heart. Have you no more pleasant dreams?'

'Oh yes. I dream of you sometimes. And my mother always talks to me every morning. When you have quite forgotten the Past, Gilbert, and can meditate like us, you will be able to talk to your own mother, perhaps.'

'Perhaps. And to dream of you, Cicely, which would be very delightful.' He looked round the garden. The man Charles Lee was not there. 'Where is our cheerful neighbour, the Black heart? He came home so late last night that doubtless he sleepeth: much the same sort of sleep, no doubt, as is granted to the White heart. Don't you think it *was* very late?'

No; she remembered nothing. 'I don't know,' she said. 'I suppose you went to bed at the usual time?'

Gilbert changed the subject. 'Cicely, do you remember bringing me a message? I was invited to postpone a certain purpose for five weeks. Do you remember?'

'Yes, I remember something about it.'

'Do you know what the purpose was?'

'No.'

'Did you connect that message with the man—of whom you dreamed, last night?'

'No.'

Then the breakfast bell clanged and clashed.

'We will talk about this, later on, in Recreation,' he said.

Brother Charles was late in Hall. Something seemed to have happened to him. He was always pale; this morning he looked white; his eyes were underlined: not that he had lost anything of the Grand Manner— that is, consistent with trembling hands, with meaning or suspicious glances: even the greatest man, Charlemagne himself, could be suspicious at times. Yet there was something in his manner, to one who knew the truth, as of the hunted creature, nearing the spot where he will stand at bay.

In the garden, after breakfast, he wandered about aimlessly, carrying a hoe and doing no manner of work. Presently, with an evident effort, he accosted Cicely, who was among her flowers.

'Tell me,' he said—'I have, I suppose, the right to ask—how you have managed to learn my name? What I want to know is—who told you? and what has he told you besides?'

'I do not understand,' she answered, wondering.

'Your name? It is Charles Lee. What more is there to know?'

Either the most consummate actress in the world, or perfectly ignorant and innocent. Was she sleep-walking? Yet could there be such sleep-walking as would reveal a hidden name?

'Come,' he said. 'It is your humour not to understand. Suppose we put it in another way. Why have you been meeting me every night for the last week and more in the dead of night, bringing your pretended warnings and prophecies?'

'Brother Charles!' Cicely answered in amazement,

'you are wandering in your wits. Indeed, you look ill. Had you not better lie down, and, if you can, seek forgetfulness in Meditation?'

'No—no. But you met me last night—again—in the middle of the night.'

'How could I meet you in the middle of the night? You are dreaming. In the middle of the night you are in your room and I am in mine. Your words are foolish. Go away and lie down. Perhaps the sun has touched your head.'

'I believe it is a House of Ghosts,' said Mr. Charles Lee. He shouldered his hoe. 'You are all ghosts together.' He turned away, but came back again. 'Do not imagine,' he said, 'that I am afraid of ghosts, or of madness, or of mad women, or of sham messages. But about that name—how did you learn my name?'

'Go away, and lie down,' said Cicely, 'till the fit has left you. All this, Brother Charles, is part of the Past which you will never even try to forget. One of these days they will criticise you. I am sure they will; and then—oh! I don't know what will happen then.'

He looked into her serious eyes—*was* the girl a consummate actress? How else could she pretend not to know about these nightly meetings? He looked across the garden and saw Gilbert working among the strawberries. Of course they were in collusion.

'You refuse to answer me,' he said. 'As you please, then; I have no more to say. Do not, however, bring me any more sham messages.'

CHAPTER III.

ON THE VERANDAH.

GILBERT deferred further explanation till after Recreation.

It was Cicely's custom at this time to remain behind and to talk awhile with the Master. It was the time that in her father's life belonged to him. It is not good for a child to grow up altogether in silence; and when he died the Master carried on the custom. What did they talk about? Indeed, one knows not. The flowers, the birds, the sky, the other world chiefly, I think—the other world, which thus became to the girl as real as this. She saw it plainly: a world very much like her own; a garden closed, roses in profusion, lilies red and white and yellow, the distant hills yellow with the golden rod; and on the lawns and under the shade of the trees her father and her mother, whom they called, while still on their earthly pilgrimage, Brother Raymond and Sister Alice. They were in white—the old Baptist's early reading gave him a New Jerusalem, in which the saints were clothed in white; but he turned the city of the jasper gates into another House of Trance, and the place of a thousand joys into another pilgrimage to another New Jerusalem. But the child saw it all so plainly that when she joined the rest in Meditation she flew off without the least delay and embraced her mother and kissed her father and held high and saintly discourse, insomuch that when the time came to return it was with a glowing cheek, a beating heart, and a humid eye. All this she got, I believe, from this after-dinner talk. And as for the Master, though he very properly insisted on the loneliness of each individual—each standing in the Universe apart and alone—in the society of this young girl, the daughter of the House, he even forgot for the moment that loneliness of Elevation which he proclaimed and preached.

Again, every prophet must have his favourite; his feminine believer and disciple. It is impossible to be complete as a prophet without a favourite. Mohammed had Kadijah; St. Francis of Assisi had Lady Clare; every vicar has his pew-opener; the Master of the House of Trance had one woman whom he specially loved and who entirely believed in him. To this good

and faithful disciple the Prophet confided everything;
he clothed, for her eyes first, his visions in words; in
her simple and unquestioning faith he found a reflection of his own; and because it was so unquestioning
and so simple, his own faith was strengthened and his
own confidence in his own Mission was proved to be
founded on the solid rock. But for this afternoon talk
the girl, before Gilbert arrived, had no opportunity of
speech at all. But for this she might have lost altogether the power of speech, as some of the men had
done, simply for want of practice. One may very well
forget how to talk if one remains silent long enough.
There is the leading case of Alexander Selkirk. People
who live much alone become unready with words; the
mind works, but no record is made by word of mouth
concerning its operations. It is interesting to reflect
that thus the greatest discoveries may have been made
and lost, simply because the discoverer could not speak,
or read, or write. Cicely, in this way, preserved the
(possibly) useful faculty of speech; yet she spoke little
and always slowly and with thought, as if words were
precious, and not to be wasted and lightly thrown about.

This day the Master remained as usual sitting in his
armchair. Cicely sat at the end of the bench, her head
on her hand and her left arm on the table.

'You look troubled, dear Master,' she said. 'Your
eyes are full of trouble.'

'There is something in the House, child, that pains
me. I know not what it is. It jars and frets; something that concerns our peace and tranquillity.'

'Indeed, Master, I know of nothing. Everything is
quiet. For the moment, I suppose, they are nearly all
asleep.'

It has been explained that most of the Community
thus interpreted the uses of Recreation.

'No,' he went on fretfully. 'There is something that
threatens. I feel it, though I cannot tell you what it
is. I have asked your mother about it.'

'What does she say?'

'I cannot remember all she says. We are imperfect —the best of us. I cannot remember, much as I desire to remember. She told me what to expect. But I have forgotten. Yet I remember her assurance that it should not be allowed to drag me down. That is everything; I ought to ask no more.'

'Then, Master, why should you vex yourself about it? Nothing can hurt you that does not drag you down.'

'It may drag others down. I look round the Hall, dear child, and I like to think of their souls as I knew them when they first came; so simple they were then, and so common and uncultivated, most of them. And I like to think of them rising by means of Meditation to heights unknown Outside, where they must needs, in order to rise at all, call in the aid of services and sermons. Well, it is to pass without harm to me—and without harm to you. I remember so much, Cicely. I remember, too, that your mother is concerned very strangely with Brother Gilbert. She talks to me about him. It is a good thing for him that he came here. Something troubles him, but it will pass: he is to possess his soul in patience. Why she is interested in Gilbert, I cannot tell you. Hush!'—he sat up and listened, his eyes suddenly gazing into space. 'Go, dear child, go—she calls me. I hear her voice. Alice, I come—I come.'

His head fell gently back; his eyes became fixed: he was in Trance again.

Gilbert waited for Cicely on the verandah with the greater part of the Community. It was no afternoon for croquet on the lawn, even if anybody had been willing to play; the sun was too fierce and the air too hot. Many of the members were sitting on the long, low bench that ran round the deep verandah: they were mostly fast asleep. Beyond the lawn, under the trees, sat others, also fast asleep. One or two paced the floor of the verandah, restlessly, not together, not talking, but separate and apart; there was no murmur of voices, no sound of talk, no rustling of whispers; every soul was consciously alone, selfishly absorbed; to each, amidst the crowd, the others did not exist at all. And their faces were so heavy, so vacuous, that Gilbert's heart was filled with pity for them and for the experiment and the doctrine.

Among those who walked up and down the verandah was a woman—still young—apparently under thirty. She was a big-boned woman, tall and angular, with no figure to speak of. The dress of the sisters seemed to suit her, hideous as it was; her hair was cut quite short; she had no ornament at her throat; and she walked with something of the firm and plodding step of the farmer. Her features were shaped with a rougher, even ruder, handling than is generally considered suitable for a young woman; it was essentially a hard face, such as belongs to one of a hard and narrow creed, belonging to a family of that old Puritan stock which for generations has known no life without struggle and endurance; which has forgotten whatever desire for or knowledge of beauty it ever possessed—whether beauty of form or thought or expression; of music, poetry, or art. The face of the woman was resolute, hard, and keen; yet the eyes, as becomes a member of the Community, could soften and become the eyes of a dreamer: all the members of the Community had this dreamy eye at times; it was their common possession; they could be classed and recognised by their eyes; without the possibility of the dreamy eye the crank became impossible. With some the dreamy habit betrayed itself in a soft and limpid eye, like Cicely's; with this woman, even at her dreamiest, which was just at the commencement of Meditation, her eye retained something of its hardness. It was as if at that hallowed moment there was something to be endured —something of the struggle of New England life.

The name of this saint was Phœbe—Sister Phœbe:

she sat in Hall on the right hand of Mr. Charles Lee; therefore nearly opposite to Gilbert. She never spoke at meals; seldom at any other time. Her work lay in the farm, among the poultry and in the dairy. No one could equal her in the rearing of these interesting creatures or in the management of the eggs. No one could approach her for butter, cheese, or cream; and she was not unacquainted with the common pig. She worked every day with honest zeal and energy; she loved the work; she believed in the House; there was not any member of the whole Community who better understood the Rule and the day's routine, and what it meant, from Fatigue, which began it, its every Restoration, Recreation, Elevation, and Meditation, down to Retirement, which ended it. She loved the Rule; she loved the House; she wanted no change—until there came to the House a disturbing element, in the shape of a young man of strange and unusual make.

This afternoon she walked backwards and forwards restlessly, her mind evidently agitated by some troubling of the peaceful waters. From time to time she glanced at Gilbert; then she turned away; then she glanced again; her eyes were full of hesitation and of doubt. She looked, and turned her head, and looked again. These little indications might have been legible to any who understand the simple voice of Nature. And she drew nearer, gradually, to the strange young man of unusual appearance and speech; it was as if she could not choose but draw nearer. She gradually approached him, still with hesitation in her manner and in her look, and still with rebellious turnings of the head and eyes.

'Brother Gilbert,' she began at last, abruptly; and as she spoke her cheek became aflame and she stopped short.

'What is it, Sister Phœbe?' True to the principles of the House, Gilbert, entirely occupied in his own reflections, which concerned Cicely, had paid no attention to these symptoms.

'It has been in my mind to warn you, for a long time——' and she stopped again.

'To warn me—for a long time,' he repeated.

'That we do not encourage frivolous conversation. I overhear you every day at Restoration engaging in frivolous talk with Sister Cicely—about Outside. It is not good for us to talk, or think, about Outside. It agitates the mind.'

'Serious conversation is, I believe, held to be permissible.'

'It may be improving if it leads to Elevation. Let me talk seriously with you.'

The ice once broken, the fires of modesty left her cheek. She became once more cold and hard.

'Shall we sit down?' asked Gilbert. 'Sitting down may be frivolous. On the other hand, when accompanied by such serious talk as yours——' He sighed, and took a seat on the bench.

She sat down and folded her hands and straightened herself. She looked very, very straight.

'We do not encourage Single Attachments,' she began. 'They are accounted in this House to be injurious.'

'Indeed! I think I have heard of that superstition.'

'We come here,' she added, 'for Elevation, not for Single Attachments.'

'That is, I suppose, your reason for coming here.'

'They do say, in the Laundry, where you can't prevent talk, that you and Brother Charles are two English noblemen, obliged to quit your country on account of your dreadful profligacy.'

'Really! That is what they say in the Laundry? They have an excellent motto in the Marischal College of Aberdeen—I recommend it for Laundry use, with Cleaver's soap, unless you prefer Pears', to rub it in. 'It is this: "They say—what do they say? Let them say."'

'Not that we mind what you have been. There's a

heap of wickedness behind us in this House. But it is all forgotten. Even a British nobleman is welcome here if he forgets the Past. I hope you have forgotten the Past, Brother Gilbert?'

'One cannot always forget the Past. Besides, that of a British nobleman is too awful for anything. Let us try to forget as much as possible—all the uninteresting bits, at least. You, Sister Phœbe, without doubt had nothing to forget.'

She considered a little.

'No,' she replied, perhaps with some regret. 'I've nothing much to forget. I was never one of the scoffers. I came here because I wanted quiet.'

'You wanted quiet? Strange! I thought that you all wanted as much noise as ever you can possibly get: doors that bang in railway carriages; bells that ring and ding and cling and clang along the street; electric cars that click. But you, actually alone of your country's women, wanted quiet!'

'I wanted to be alone sometimes. There was no loneliness at home. We had crowds in chapel; crowds in Sunday-school; crowds to prayer-meeting; crowds in the workrooms; even at night I couldn't be alone in a bedroom to myself. So I came here to be quiet, all alone with my own soul. And the Master took me in.'

'Your soul and you. The pair of you.'

'I wanted to be quiet. So I came here. I never knew what happiness meant till I came here.'

'Here you are quite lonely in a crowd. I should have thought—but it doesn't matter. I suppose if you were to marry it would be in order to become more lonely. But of course the sisters do not marry?'

'Some do. Oh, yes! And some say it helps Elevation. I might marry'—she looked at him strangely—'I might marry, I say, if I found a man who would help in Elevation.'

'Who would make himself a ladder. You would climb up your husband?'

'There's ways. Outside, it's good to have a husband to work for the house. Here it may be good—I don't know—to have a husband just as a kind of support. Sometimes one feels lonesome. Sometimes it's good to talk about your experiences, and there's no one here who cares to listen. A husband would have to. That's his duty.'

'Yes. And what would the husband get by it?'

'Brother Gilbert—he'd get ME! What more would the man have?'

'Ah! That, indeed!' said Gilbert, in his softest, most sympathetic voice. 'That, indeed!'

'Brother Gilbert'—she laid her hand, a rough and osseous hand, upon his, and a strange and terrifying softening came into her eyes—'we must talk again. I think you want some one to be pulling you up all the time. By yourself you'll never get up, you're that light in your talk. Sister Cicely is a good girl, but she hasn't begun real Elevation, not yet. She wouldn't be any use to you at all. Besides, we don't allow of Single Attachments. If you got to be thinking all day about Cicely, you would never rise; you'd just sink down, ever so much down.'

'Well, but when a man is married Attachments begin. That's the proverb.'

'There's no Single Attachments in this House,' she repeated, 'married or not. Remember that. There is Selection, not Attachment. If I were to think of marriage, Brother Gilbert'—again that incongruous softening of the face fell upon her: Gilbert shuddered and sprang to his feet—'I should want one quite different from my own people, so as I could never fall back into the old grooves. He should talk different; he should think different; he should talk gentle and soft, like you—and he should have parlour manners all the time.'

'You like parlour manners? So do I, Sister Phœbe. I think you ought to be married, if the laws of the

Community allow it. You should marry a man, say, like Brother Silas. He isn't a bit like the people you remember, I am sure: they were spry, he is dull; he has always lived in loneliness, not in crowds; and he knows the people you remember, I dare say, if you come to examine him. He would every day illustrate for you the difference between kitchen manners and town manners.'

'I wasn't—just—exactly—thinking of Brother Silas,' said the maiden, with the strangest possible touch of maidenly modesty.

But Gilbert turned on his heel and walked away.

At the other end of the verandah he found the little lady whose peace of mind he had disturbed on the very first day.

She looked up from her knitting; laughed cheerfully, and motioned him to sit down beside her on the bench.

'Come and talk,' she said, smiling graciously. 'It does me good to have a talk with you. Why, since you came here it hasn't been the same place. You shall stay always, and always, and always.'

'No, my dear.' Gilbert's charm with the other sex partly lay in his consideration for all alike, young and old, pretty and plain, one with another—he called this little lady 'my dear,' and she liked it. 'I do not think I shall stay here always, or much longer.'

'Are you really, Gilbert, as they say, a British nobleman in disguise, run away from the people you have ruined by your horrible profligacy?'

'Do I look like a profligate peer?'

'No, you don't. So I told them. Though how they got to think so, I don't know. I should like to see, just for once, a British nobleman—a real, downright wicked one.'

'I'm afraid he won't come this way. Now, tell me you have quite left off forgetting?'

'Oh, yes! Quite. That's all gone. At first I thought it would be terrible to be remembering again what I had such trouble in putting away. I thought it would just spoil Meditation.'

'Well?'

'It hasn't, not worth talking about. Brother Gilbert, if you'd been the Master himself you couldn't have helped me more. Why, every afternoon I live in the Past again, and at night I meditate better than ever.'

'That's brave. Is it a very miserable Past?'

'You've got such a way with you that one can talk. I can't talk to those stocks and stones.' She pointed to the vacuous ones who wandered about or slept on the bench. 'Well, I said to myself, "What is past is past. He can't come back to me, because he's married the other one"—Mamie she was. So I set to work to remember again—and as I don't know what they did nor how they fared, after they married, I've been making up ever since. And now I seem to know all just exactly what happened. It's twenty years ago: Mamie's got half a dozen children, and Jacob's partly bald and partly gray. As for flesh, he was always inclined to put it on. And it actually makes me happy just to feel that they're happy.'

'How can you feel it?'

'Young man, if you ever loved anybody—same as I loved Jacob—you'd understand how. So you see, I do forget the Past. I've buried the Past. But I go along with my dear friend in the Present. And oh! my dear boy, I don't feel bitter nor angry, nor revengeful, any more.'

Then she showed how radical had been the change in her, for she became what every woman Outside is—a matchmaker.

'I've got my eyes back again,' she said, 'as well as my memory. Oh, yes—I see things, I see things every day.' She nodded her head and laughed, and looked whole comedies.

'What things do you see? You are a very crafty, cunning, and dangerous creature. I must take care. What things do you see?'

'I see things,' she repeated. 'In the garden, under the shade trees, at meals in Hall, at Recreation and at Restoration. Oh! I like to see things; only, Gilbert, my dear boy, be careful. Don't be too open. There's dangers. It's a very rigid rule with the Master—he's hard as rock about it—there must be no Single Attachments. The only way for you to get her is to pretend that you'd rather not. I shall warn her, too. She shows her feelings by her eyes. Oh! she follows you about, Brother Gilbert; if you tamper with that poor girl—I'll—I'll stick a knitting-needle into you. I will indeed! But you're not that sort, you dear boy, are you?'

'No. I'm not that sort, where Cicely is concerned.'

'There's dangers abroad. Brother Silas, he wants her himself; he's just sick for the girl. You think he's a fool: he isn't; only he won't speak; he's just finding out by degrees that he's a man, and he's as obstinate as a Western mule. Speak to the Master, quick, Gilbert, or it may be too late. Then there's Sister Phœbe—I saw her just now talking to you. Take care—take care! She's falling in love with you fast. And she's quite ready to pretend that it is no Single Attachment: she's that cunning, and mean, and artful. Worse than Silas, because it's the nature of a man to yearn after a pretty girl. Take care, Gilbert, and speak to the Master quickly. She's a strong woman, and she'll do her best to get what she wants. That's you, my dear boy—you—nothing short of you.'

He laughed and patted her hand again. And at that moment Cicely came out of the Hall.

CHAPTER IV.

SINGLE ATTACHMENTS!

CICELY came out of the Hall and looked around, shading her eyes with her hand, for the sunlight outside was dazzling. Then she saw Gilbert, and with a nod and a smile she put on her straw hat and came across the lawn to the shade trees beyond. Her nod and her smile were a direct invitation to follow. In fact, she meant that invitation which in the innocence of her heart was not coquetry or part of a flirtation, but an acknowledgment before all the world that she desired Gilbert's society and found it delightful.

Brother Silas saw this invitation, and he became red in the cheeks and dangerous in the eyes.

Sister Phœbe saw it, and her mouth closed with firmness.

Sister Euphemia saw it, and she smiled; then she looked at Sister Phœbe and she smiled again, but, as heralds say, with a difference.

Gilbert would have followed, but was met by Brother Silas, who without a word held out his arms and barred the way. He would have spoken; he was most desirous of expressing his feelings and views on the subject; he wrestled with his memory, but in vain; he had not spoken at all for many months, and the words refused to come; he could not remember the right words—the words which should have been used to explain his unexpected action. Neither tongue nor brain would work. His face was red and his aspect was threatening. It looked for the moment like a fight.

'Friend Silas,' said Gilbert, 'what the devil do you mean by sticking your arms out like a windmill?'

'Single Attachments,' Silas followed it up at last with an immense effort. 'Single Attachments,' he repeated.

'Single Attachments,' he said a third time—because no other words suggested themselves. Remember that he had not spoken for months.

'Dear me!' Gilbert replied sweetly. 'Are you contemplating a Single Attachment?'

'I hate a Britisher.' It was a very, very weak thing to say—it had nothing to do with the business in hand; but it was the first sentence that offered: he had been taught and encouraged from childhood to entertain this tender feeling towards his trans-Atlantic cousins; he had it rubbed into him as a schoolboy in the State of Maine, to which he belonged. And they were the readiest words that occurred to him.

'Do you?' Gilbert replied. 'Well; but that is such a very common feeling with your class that it hardly deserves remark, does it? The symptom presents, I assure you, nothing unusual. Will you lower your arms and stand out of my way?'

'No,' said Silas. 'You shan't follow her. I've seen you'—he partially recovered the gift of speech—'I've watched you. No—you shan't follow her.'

'Silas—you are a big man and a strong man. When I hit out you will probably hit back, and there will be a free fight such as this House has never before witnessed. It will be a fight fit to wake up these sleepers. Now I put it to you with fraternal affection: if you want to fight, just stay where you are. If you don't want to fight, get out of my way. Fighting, I am told, is, on the whole, a hindrance to Meditation, also Elevation. It is said to be even worse than a Single Attachment.'

The man growled, but lowered his arms and stood aside. His face, which commonly resembled that of the labouring and patient ox, became that of the bull, and in his dull eyes there shone an unusual light which meant jealousy, rage, revenge, with a little hatred, envy, wounded pride, and a few other passions, all incongruous as regards Elevation. Still, he stood aside and growled, inarticulate.

SINGLE ATTACHMENTS!

Do you suppose the bull who growls on the other side of the hedge would not much rather speak if he could? Of course he would.

'The man is jealous,' Gilbert thought. 'He desires that pearl to be thrown unto him—unto him! And Phœbe—poor thing! She's jealous, too! Phœbe! Sister Phœbe—the love-smitten virgin! Phœbe! After all, there are two human creatures at least in the House quite ready to create a new Past with the greatest rapidity possible.'

'Come away from this place, Cicely,' he said. 'There are too many of our people about. I want to talk to you seriously. Come with me beyond the farm. I know a place where there is a shelter from the sun beside the stream. Nobody ever goes out there except myself. There we will sit and talk.'

You have already heard of the stream which ran past the House. It came down from the wooded hills a mile or two on the north of the estate; its waters, cold as ice and clear as crystal, ran swiftly over a shallow bed of gravel, winding in and out here and there; on one side were the woods; on the other bank rose a low cliff, sometimes advancing to the water's edge, sometimes receding and leaving between rock and river tiny plains grass-covered. Over the cliff behind hung wild vines and brambles.

To one such spot Gilbert led Cicely; in the middle of the little meadow stood a boulder for a seat; at the back the rock jutted out and formed a natural table or shelf which, for reasons which you will presently learn, Gilbert will remember for the rest of his natural life. The cliff at this place faced north-east, and cast a deep shade over the grass; the hanging vines and the woods on the other side of the stream made a grateful and refreshing greenery; the cliff and the trees on either side closed in; the stream flowed chattering and babbling over its bed; the fish darted about, backwards and forwards; there was no sound of birds this hot afternoon from the woods; the ground was broken and stony, so that no one ever came to clear away the trees; there was no road to the place. The two were quite alone.

Cicely sat down on the boulder and took off her hat. Gilbert stood over her silent. They remained in silence while one might count a hundred.

'I know this place, Gilbert,' she said. 'I used to come here when I was a child. I used to come here all by myself to find out what Outside was like. I thought the whole world was desert and solitary except our House.'

'Why do you not come here again, sometimes?'

'I don't know. I suppose that I am no longer curious about Outside. Yet I like you to tell me things. It does not disturb me in the least when you tell me about Outside.'

'Surely, dear child, you want sometimes to get away from the ugly House and the ugly people in it.'

She turned her large, serious eyes upon him with reproach and wonder.

'Ugly, Gilbert? Why do you call them ugly? There are a hundred of them and more; and they are all mounting upwards.'

'Are they mounting upwards? It is good for you to believe it, at any rate. But the House is ugly. You will admit so much.'

'I don't know what you would have, Gilbert.'

'No, you don't, that is the curious thing. There is no beauty in the place except your own; and you know of none except the beauty of your own soul. Strange! To grow up without any knowledge of beauty—no art, no music, no poetry, and to become—what you have become.'

'My mother teaches me, Gilbert.'

'Yes. And not to know even what a lovely face means.'

'Well, but you can tell me, Gilbert.'

'Do you think, for instance, that Phœbe has a lovely face?'

SINGLE ATTACHMENTS! 141

'I don't know. Oh, Gilbert, what does it matter about faces? The Master's face is lovely to me. So is yours. What is the good of thinking whether a face is beautiful or not?'

'Outside, my child, a lovely face is considered by the woman who possesses it as a very great treasure indeed; far above rubies and more to be desired than much fine gold. Don't you *like* to get away from them all?' Gilbert insisted with a kind of jealousy.

'No. Why should I? They belong to me, and I to them, as much as one person can belong to another. Of course, with the Master it is different. He takes me with him to talk with my mother.'

'But what is the good, when you forget what is said?'

'Sometimes I remember a little. I gave you my mother's message, some time ago. You see I remembered that.'

'What message did you give to Brother Charles last night—yesterday?'

'None. Why do you ask? He came to me this morning and asked the same question.'

'You do not remember receiving or giving any message?'

'No.'

It was impossible to doubt this assurance. Such a girl could not possibly deceive others.

'Gilbert, you are still hostile to this man—I don't know why, except because he is a bad man who won't forget his Past; but you are not so troubled about him as you were. Your mind is more tranquil than it was.'

'He does not trouble me much. Only occasionally. Your message, if you remember, bade me wait for five weeks. Four have passed. There remain only six days—after to-day, five days. Sometimes I doubt, Cicely. Sometimes I ask whether that message was really from your mother.'

'Oh! but since she sent that message, how can you

doubt? Of course it came from her. Oh, Gilbert! you cannot doubt my mother. Have faith. Whatever was promised will be done. Have patience.'

'I come to this House.' Gilbert addressed the running brook, which carried his words to the Atlantic, where they were sucked up by the sky and carried across the ocean and there fell in rain upon the thirsty earth, whence, no doubt, they got into the papers. 'I come here with a certain very important purpose. On the very first day I receive a message from a damsel —a very charming damsel—to——'

'Do you mean me, Gilbert? Why do you call me charming?'

'Because you have charmed away my senses, so that for your sake, Cicely, I would throw away the world. You command—and I obey.'

She looked at him in wonder unspeakable. What could he mean?

'You tell me to wait, although it is a most serious and important business—and I do wait. You tell me that it is a message from the dead, and I believe it. I actually believe it. A message from the dead to me! And I believe it! Why? Because it comes through you. Cicely, if you bade me drown myself in the stream in your mother's name, I should do it. Because I cannot doubt you. It is impossible.'

'If the message had to do with Brother Charles, believe it all the more. For your mind grows black whenever you think of him.'

'A mind is white, Cicely, according to you, or it is black. That is elementary. Some day—soon—I will teach you that the mind of a man is very seldom black, and never white. Some minds are variegated; some minds vary; some are quite pretty in their colours— azure blue, emerald green, rosy red, violet, green, golden yellow; some sparkle like diamonds; some are as dull as a muddy ditch. But the mind of the man you name, child, will always be black through and through.'

'Not if he could forget the Past.'

'No one can forget the Past. Least of all such a man as this. I will show you some day, in a more convenient place than this, that the Past can never be forgotten, or put aside. Your people here think they have forgotten it, when they have only dulled their senses to it. The Master thinks that he forgets the Past; yet every night he goes away in imagination to talk with his friends of the Past. You yourself do the same thing.'

'Gilbert'—she avoided the point: she could not argue; but she could feel—'you are always telling me that you will show me this or that. But all these things are Outside.' She looked round her with a shudder: were they not already in the dreaded Outside —which lay all round that end of the Universe, the House of Meditation?

'You are going Outside, Cicely,' Gilbert told her firmly. 'You are going with me—soon—some day— when your mother's promise has been fulfilled.'

'But I can never leave the House and the Master.'

'There is an old Book on which, as on a foundation, this House is built. You have never read in this Book, Cicely, which is a great pity, because it is full of humanity. Well, it is said in that Book, as a common and well-known law of nature, that a man shall forsake his father and his mother and shall cleave to his wife. The same law rules the woman, who every day forsakes father and mother and clings to her husband. We shall together obey that universal law, Cicely, and cleave unto each other.'

'There are laws—Outside—which do not belong to us. The laws of the land do not touch our Community.'

'This is not the law of the land, Cicely. It is a law of nature—which makes me love you, dear child.'

'Oh! Gilbert,' her face flushed with pleasure. 'It makes me so happy. And I love you, too, as much as I love the Master—far more than any of the others.'

'Haven't they taught you to avoid Single Attachments?'

'We are not to think too much of one person. That is the Rule.'

'What is "too much"? I think of you, Cicely, all day and all night. Is that too much? Do you think of me?'

'Oh yes. But I think of the Master as well.'

'In that case you are quite safe. Certainly, I cannot think too much of you. In this dreary House, full of dreary people who delude themselves with a belief worthy only of the highest visionary like the Master, which is perfectly unfit for the boor, which can only be true with a soul as pure and innocent as your own—what is there to think about but you? Cicely, you are the one pleasant spot, the solitary flower, in this mass of stupid selfishness.'

'No—no—Gilbert. You don't know us. Oh! ask the Master to tell you what we are.'

'The Master? He will tell me honestly what he believes the House to be. Never mind that, Cicely dear.' He took her hand. 'Something I have to tell you, dear child.' He raised the hand and kissed it. She sat quite still, bathed in the glow and warmth of this young sun-god—her Apollo—who said that he obeyed her, but who commanded her in everything. 'In a few days—six or seven at the outside—something will happen in this House—something decisive, something that will change all my future; I know not, yet, what it will be; yet, if the message is true and the promise be fulfilled, it will bring no harm to me. Sibyl, Delphian, Priestess of the Sacred Grove—what do you think of the coming event?'

She dropped her hands; her face turned white; she fell back and would have fallen, but Gilbert supported her. Her eyes closed; she was in trance again.

The soul remained outside the body for two or three minutes only. She opened her eyes; she blushed to find herself lying on Gilbert's arm; she sat up. 'Gilbert!' she said, 'I have seen my mother and I have asked her what this means. "Tell him," she says, "that nothing will happen to his harm."'

'How do you know, Cicely, that it was your mother?'

'Oh! Gilbert! As if one could be deceived in such a thing as that! Not to know my own mother?'

'Well, Cicely, I accept your assurance. I am very glad to accept it, because otherwise the next few days would be an anxious time. After they are over and done with, and we have found out what the message really means, that question will arise between us.'

'What question, Gilbert?'

'The question of the universal law. Whether a girl shall leave her father and her mother and shall cleave to the man who loves her.'

'Oh, Gilbert! Go away? Leave the Master? Go into Outside, where there is nothing that we love—not even Meditation?'

'You shall have Meditation, if you desire it.'

'Oh! Gilbert; you must not go. Oh! you have made me so happy here!' The tears welled up into her eyes. 'What should I do without you? Oh, yes —I understand now. Before you came the place was dull and stupid. Every night I look forward to the morning when I shall talk to you again; and every morning I look forward to the long day when I shall talk to you again and listen to you. Oh! Gilbert— Gilbert—you must not go away and leave me.'

They were the words of love, in the voice of love, with the passion of love, and yet Cicely knew not the meaning of love; nor did she know that she loved the Master in one way and this man in another; nor did she know that a man could be to her more than a brother.

Gilbert took her hand again. He sat down beside her on the boulder; he laid his arm round her waist just as if he had been a young man courting his girl on Hampstead Heath on a Sunday evening in July—but Love is a mighty leveller. He drew her closer; he kissed her shapely head. 'My dear—my dear,' he said, 'I must indeed leave the House; and yet I shall never—never leave you. For you will leave the spirits of your father and your mother and cleave to me; and we twain shall be but one soul—not two standing lonely in the universal space, but one.' He kissed her again and again.

She offered no resistance. Perhaps it was gradually dawning upon her that here was a different kind of man—not a Brother at all.

So much were these two people occupied and carried away that they did not hear a footstep which approached; so much were they wrapped up in each other —which can only be understood by thinking of the common roll jam pudding—that they did not look round. This was perhaps fortunate; for they would have seen a red and angry face looking on from the angle where the cliff ran down to the stream and turned again—a very angry face; with burning cheeks, with flaming eyes, with trembling lips, and a figure trembling all over with the madness of rage and jealousy.

It was Sister Phœbe. She had followed, to watch and spy upon the guilty doings of the wicked pair.

She stepped forward, her foot unheard upon the grass; she laid her hand—a firm bony hand with a good muscular grip in it—upon Gilbert's shoulder.

He turned guiltily. He started to his feet.

'Single Attachments!' she said, with a hiss—there was a sibilant at the beginning and a sibilant at the end—and a menace in her voice.

Only one of the guilty pair blushed. It was the man. Cicely looked up without the least confusion, yet with a little terror, for the woman looked so fierce and so threatening. Besides, the Master did not approve of Single Attachments. But she was going to leave the Community; she was going to leave father and mother and all and to cleave unto her lover. It mattered nothing, she understood now, having learned this wisdom in the last five minutes, whether Sister Phœbe approved or disapproved.

'Single Attachments!' Sister Phœbe repeated.

She brandished a long and bony forefinger in their faces—one so young ought not to have had a finger so bony—and she turned and disappeared. She would have spoken, but, as with Silas, the words proper for the occasion refused to come. Therefore she walked away.

'She followed and listened and watched,' said Gilbert. 'Very good. It is what I should have expected of her. Never mind, Cicely: in a few days we shall depart to a place where Sister Phœbe can neither follow nor listen. Don't be afraid, my dear—my dear—my dear!'

'I am not afraid with you, Gilbert. But why did she look so angry?'

'It is the jealousy of the slighted woman. Think no more about her. We will make ours a Double instead of a Single Attachment. That is not against the Master's rule, is it?'

CHAPTER V.

AN EXPLANATION.

LOVE-MAKING on the edge of a precipice would be incongruous—but suppose one is perfectly certain that there is to be no falling over that precipice? Once assured, even on such imperfect evidence as satisfied Gilbert, upon this point, why should we not make love? It is a healthy and a natural occupation. It had interested Gilbert first of all; then it began to interest him more; then it absorbed him, insomuch that he forgot for the time his purpose and the precipice: the end of his stay and—very possibly—the end of himself.

It is always so, to forget everything in the contemplation of another soul; and now, for one week at least, courtings and contemplation, love-making and dreams and tenderness all had to be put aside for the time. This chance meeting with Annandale brought back Gilbert from the land of dreams to reality—with the man in the foreground whom he had almost managed to forget. Only a week; only six days; only five. And something on each one of the days to keep him well in the front.

Only five days. It was the morning after the disgraceful experience of the Single Attachment beside the stream. The day began with the arrival of two letters for Gilbert. Never before had any member of the Community received a single letter. The Master received them, and hesitated before he passed them on.

'Brother Gilbert,' he said reproachfully, 'when do you intend to sever yourself from Outside?'

They were, both of them, letters of the greatest importance. The first was from Mr. Arthur Annandale, still staying at the hotel of Aldermanbury.

'I told you,' he wrote, 'that Lady Osterley had arrived in New York. Naturally I have informed her about yourself—she always took an absurd interest in you—and I told her of your present religious or social convictions, and of your soul-elevating occupation. She telegraphs that she is coming here from New York tomorrow and that you must meet her. So you must come. If you are prevented by the exigencies of your new profession—such as bawling potatoes in the street with a pal and a donkey cart—and so cannot come, we will drive over and visit the place and see the monks and their monkery with the nuns and their nunnery. Do you know that you forgot the strawberry basket—left it in the porch of the hotel? It wasn't wasted. Six little nigger boys found it, and attempted to commit suicide with the contents. I saw them. By the way, you may perhaps be able to leave your cart and your pal outside the hotel.'

AN EXPLANATION

Dorabyn in Aldermanbury, within four miles of her husband! And within five days of that appointed by fate! Strange that she should be brought to this place at such a time!

He opened the second letter. This was more important still. It was from his private detective in New York, who had been employed in following up the man Charles Lee.

'I assume,' he wrote, 'that you desire to keep this man out of danger. Therefore I must warn you that there has happened a very serious development of his case. The whole business of the death of the young Mexican, about which I have already given you a hint, has now, I am informed, been unravelled by the police. The body of the man was found under some shrubs in the street; his pockets were empty; he had been killed by a knife-thrust in the back. It was learned that he had been staying at a hotel; he left this hotel with another visitor, who came home at midnight without him. In the morning the other visitor went away. There was no suspicion of anything against him: he was allowed to go away. Then the body of the man was found, and it was buried after examination. This other visitor was Mr. Charles Lee; the place where he took the young Mexican was a gambling den. Now, two of the gang have been arrested in different towns, and without communication with each other have confessed the truth. I have not seen their confessions; but they agree in the main point: the pigeon was brought to the plucking by Mr. Charles Lee, and it was his knife in the end which killed the man as he was trying to get away with money he had won. If, therefore, Lee is arrested on a charge of fraud, he will be immediately afterwards accused of wilful murder. Lee should therefore remain perfectly quiet where he is. A description of his appearance, station, etc., has by this time been sent out broadcast all over the country. If one of these papers falls into the hands of any one in your Community, the man will probably be denounced. If not, there is no other place of safety for him in the American continent. They have no photograph of him, which is one point in favour of his present safety and future escape. But the description of him is clear.'

The description was very clear; a handbill was inclosed:—

'REWARD.—Five hundred dollars for the capture of Charles Lee, charged with conspiracy and fraud. The said Charles Lee, who has been known as Charles Hamilton, Charles Gordon, Charles Courtenay, and other *aliases*, is believed to be an Englishman. He is six feet one inch in height; he is about thirty-four years of age; he has black hair and black eyes; he wears no beard nor moustache; his features are straight and regular; his face is extremely pale; he is grave and austere; his manners are polite and cold. They are those of a refined gentleman.'

For the moment—what next? He must certainly keep the man at home. Therefore there must be some explanation.

Generally, after dinner, Lee retreated to the shade of the trees beyond the lawn, where, with feet outstretched, he seemed to sleep away the afternoon. To-day, however, he was not in his usual place. Gilbert looked about for him: in the Hall; in his bedroom; in the verandah; but found him at length alone in one of the empty workshops, where none of the members were ever found in the afternoon.

He was seated on a humble three-legged stool before a carpenter's bench; it might have been an armchair before a table in Downing Street. He had a pack of cards in his hand, and he was intent upon some kind of game—was it some problem in High Diplomacy?— he was as much interested as if it was that; or, was it some innocuous form of Patience? or was it some one

AN EXPLANATION

of the many thousand varieties by which unhappy cards are forced to deceive the credulous?

One knows not. It is only certain that he had retired to this place in order to be quite alone.

He looked up when he heard the footsteps on the floor. His face showed neither annoyance, nor astonishment, nor embarrassment at the interruption; he preserved the same perfect calm and tranquillity; nothing was more astonishing to Gilbert than the contrast between this face, which was as a mask never to be lifted, and the face which this man's past ought to have worn. Every mean and miserable and violent crime ought to have been stamped upon that face; yet behold! it was the face of a plenipotentiary—calm, judicial, quiet, fearless, immovable: the face say, rather, of an Oriental king who must be just and stern and pitiless to punish, and must also be generous and sorrowful and quick to reward. Such was the face of this man; so strong, so set, so encouraging to lovers of virtue.

He looked up, then, and stared with icy insolence, as one who is too proud to be disturbed by people of the baser sort, yet wants explanation.

'I have come——' Gilbert hesitated. The man's calmness was a kind of insult, considering everything. Has a man who has dropped down, down, down into such depths of infamy, the right to assume any dignity at all? 'I have come,' he went on, 'for a few words of explanation.'

'Go on, sir.' He swept the cards together and held them in his left hand. They might have been a bundle of despatches.

He half turned round, leaning against the wall, with his long legs crossed. He was exactly like a State Minister about to give audience.

'I must begin by telling you that I know pretty well the history of your two years' residence in this country. Shall I remind you?'

'As you please.'

'You arrived in New York just two years ago. You came over under the name of Charles Lee. You travelled as a second-class passenger, and you remained in your cabin most of the time in order not to be recognised by any of the first-class passengers. You very soon found your way to some gambling hell, and there you lost the five hundred pounds which was all you had.'

The Court inclined its head, gravely.

'As you had no more money, you were turned into the street. You were presently picked up by one of the company who had cheated you. He gave you assistance and made a proposition to you.'

'A proposition,' murmured the Court.

'Very well: I have traced you from town to town. I know everything that you did, including the last business which caused the dispersal and flight of the gang.'

Another gentle condescension of the proud head.

'Some of your friends are already in gaol. The police are naturally anxious to include you in the number. So far, they have failed to find you. They have no suspicion of this place. You are perfectly safe here. They are looking for you in the places where such persons as yourself are generally found.'

'You are going to put them on the right scent?' There was a concentration of contempt in the question which made the innocent man writhe.

'You will be arrested, if at all, not on a charge of felony, or fraud, but for the wilful murder of a certain young Mexican.'

The man dropped the cards out of his hand. They fell upon the table. He turned quickly and picked them up again. 'Go on, sir.'

'If I wished you to be arrested and tried, I should arrest you myself.'

'What do you wish, then?'

'I wish to see you dead, Sir Charles Osterley,' he answered bluntly.

Sir Charles bowed gravely. 'Yes, I have thought so for some time. Well, in my turn I will tell you something. I have myself been very strongly tempted, sir, ever since you came here, to put you out of the way. I knew, from the first, that you came here in search of me. I wish I had killed you. A dead enemy is better than a living one. Once or twice I have been very near it. It would have been quite easy to do it. I have gone so far as to get up in the night and to take my knife—but, somehow, there's always something to interfere in this cursed place. Sometimes I think it is haunted: I couldn't find the door of my room; I felt round and round the room, but I couldn't find it. Then there was another time: I walked up the stream in the shade of the woods, and I came upon you lying under a rock fast asleep. Then I could have done it. I should have done it, too, but that little devil of a girl, whom you are always sending to me with messages, trying to frighten me, ran out of somewhere and stood between. I couldn't very well kill her as well. So you escaped for that time.'

'Thank you,' said Gilbert. Cicely, then, had saved his life. It was something to remember.

'And when shall we proceed to the next—or final step?'

'I believe—on Saturday.'

'On Saturday,' he repeated. 'Something will happen. Will that something—may I ask?—take the form of a—a personal encounter?'

'Perhaps. Most probably. If you please.'

'It will please me well. Nothing will please me better. When you are once out of the way I shall feel more tranquil. Mr. Maryon, I was once assisting at the adjustment of a quarrel such as ours. It was a pretty sight. They played a game—a single game—for a revolver—do you understand? Only one revolver. The revolver lay between them. It was a game worth playing. At the end of it, the winner——'

'I understand. On Saturday you will bring a new pack of cards unopened. For my part, I will bring a revolver loaded. We may as well settle the quarrel that way as any other. But meanwhile you will engage not to precipitate matters, or to spoil the game, by going into town and getting arrested and hanged?'

'And your friend the detective will not bring the sheriff here? Very good. Till Saturday, then——' He inclined his head slightly: he was the Minister dismissing a deputation of one. 'Good morning, Mr. Maryon; I am pleased to have had the opportunity of hearing your views.'

CHAPTER VI.

LADY OSTERLEY'S ARRIVAL.

THUS dismissed, Gilbert retired with some feeling of humiliation. He had advanced as one about to dictate terms; he withdrew as one who had accepted terms.

However, there was something gained. The man would not appear in Aldermanbury, and it would be easy to keep Dorabyn from visiting the House.

Lady Osterley occupied a suite on the first floor. There is an admirable arrangement in the American hotels by which a travelling party can take a suite of rooms like a flat—bedrooms, sitting-rooms, bathrooms, all complete, in a ring form, separated from the rest of the house. This is a much more convenient arrangement than the private room in the English hotel. At the same time the rooms—living and sleeping rooms—are far better furnished than in our best hotels. There are electric lights, electric fans, electric bells; there are most comfortable chairs and most useful tables; a lady may use her bedroom for other purposes besides sleep: she may write in it, read in it, receive her friends—at least her lady friends—in it. Lady

Osterley had taken a suite with two sitting-rooms; in the first Gilbert found her nurse and her maid, with the boy, now nearly four years old, a bonny boy, playing about the floor; in the inner room Dorabyn herself sat at the open window, looking down upon the clicking electric cars and the shops with their revolving fans, and the stream of men with the eager, nervous faces—compared with them our City face is vacuous and bovine—yet we do a good stroke of business year in year out; and the women so extravagantly well dressed slowly going into the shops or coming out of them. She had already communicated a sense of herself to the room. The table and the chairs were littered with her things: her books, her sketching-blocks, her paint-box, her desk, her work. At the sight of these familiar objects, and of Dorabyn herself, there came back to Gilbert the memory of a certain dressing-room; a confession of suffering and shame; that solemn pledge, to redeem which he was now a member of the Community of Cranks.

Dorabyn sprang to her feet and welcomed him. 'My dear Gilbert!' she cried. 'To find you here! How long is it since I heard from you?'

She did not ask him how he had fared, and why he did not fulfil his promise. 'I heard you were here,' she went on with a smile—an unwonted smile—upon her sad face. 'Therefore of course I came on at once. To be sure, it matters very little where I am so long as I am not at home.'

'You are looking well, Dorabyn. A little pale, but as stately as ever. When were you not stately, I wonder?'

She had preserved that quality, whatever else she had lost. She still moved and stood and spoke like a queen.

'I am tired of wandering, Gilbert. That is all I have to tell you. And I see no end to it. Things are exactly as they were, and I have no hope of any change.'

'Yet there may be change—at any moment.' Had

she forgotten his promise? It seemed so. She made no allusion to it, neither then nor afterwards.

She shook her head.

'There can be no change but by death. I must not dare to hope for any man's death. Yet, surely in this case, it could not be more awful or more terrible than his life. I pray for nothing now. I hope for nothing.'

'Yet there may be change at any moment. My poor Dorabyn, now I look closer, you have a harassed look.'

'Harassed? I am hunted. No deer in the forest could be more hunted than I am. They hunt me everywhere. They find me out wherever I go. They find me out and write to me. "Where is Charles? For Heaven's sake"—it is his mother or his sister—"where is Charles?" Then I run away again. As yet they do not know that I have crossed the ocean, but they will soon find out, and then the hunt will begin again. Find me, if you can, Gilbert, an uninhabited island.'

'Can you not invent something?'

'Oh, Gilbert: everything is so much more difficult than I thought it would be when I told you—have you forgotten? No: how could any one forget?—about—about that—that shameful business. I knew there would be that kind of trouble. No one, Gilbert, if I can help it, shall ever learn the truth. You, my cousin, and myself, we three know, and nobody else. Even the respectable old solicitor does not know all. My son's fair name shall not be tarnished. The man has relations, you know: everybody has; but this man has got relations by multitudes; never was a man with so many cousins. He has a mother—poor soul! and a sister or two—his elder sister Alice died over here somewhere, I believe. Poor mother! Poor sisters! They shall never know if I can help it. They send letters to me—letters by the dozen, the score, the peck, the bushel. Oh! Gilbert, Gilbert, if you could only read those letters. They are angry, tearful, expostulatory, threatening, everything. "Where is he?" they ask: "what is he? How is he? What is the matter with him? Who is his doctor? What are the prospects of recovery? Why—why—why will I not answer, or tell them even where he is?"'

'Yes. It is only in novels that a man can act without a crowd of cousins knowing all that he does.'

'You see, the man, to them, is still the splendidly successful young man; the young man of principle; the young man quite safe to become Prime Minister. They were so proud of him, poor things! His breakdown was the bitterest blow and disappointment to them. Oh! Gilbert, men don't understand how their belongings glory in their ambitions, and how the cousins become distinguished through their distinction! I never understood this fully until the man broke down. Oh! the bitter blow—to his people; the cruel disappointment—to his cousins! Why, he was going to elevate the family, which had just a baronetcy in it, with never a man of any distinction, into an illustrious house headed by a great statesman! Think of it! Think of becoming first cousin to a Palmerston or a Pitt! There is true distinction for you! And they missed it.'

'And do you never answer any letters?'

'None at all. It is the only safe rule. Nor will I ever see any of them if I can help it. Sometimes they have tried to get at me. I ward them off, put them off and run away.'

'Why not tell them something? That he was a gambler, ruined himself—had to go away?'

'No. There is disgrace in having to run away; and a kind of disgrace in being a gambler. At least, I suppose so. My boy shall never know his father's madness, nor his father's iniquity. No one shall ever, if I can help it, get a clue to the secret. He, above all, shall never entertain the least suspicion.'

'You must tell him something about his father.'

'Yes. I have thought it out. I shall tell him what the world knows; what his father's family will tell him: that a breakdown of health sent him abroad; that he died alone somewhere, in some place in Italy, or Spain, where there is no Protestant cemetery, so that he was buried without a tombstone in a garden or a field. That is what I mean to tell him, Gilbert.'

'I see.'

Gilbert looked at her curiously. If she only knew that but two or three miles away the man himself was in hiding. But she should not know. And he looked for some sign in her manner, in her voice, in her face, that she remembered that promise of his. Dorabyn gave no sign. If she remembered his words at all, it was only to remember as well that no one could help except Death the Deliverer.

'I am so tired, so tired of wandering,' she went on. 'And for the boy's sake I must some day soon settle down in some obscure place—some such place as this, where English people are not often seen. I will not, if I can help it, live under an assumed name. The boy will have to be educated. Oh, Gilbert! the situation is full of trouble and danger. As for the man, I have made inquiries. The respectable old gentleman, his solicitor, has heard nothing about him. He says so, and I believe him. He has quite disappeared. He may be dead. Sometimes I think that he must be dead, because—what could he do for a living? If he is not dead he must be passing under another name. How can I learn whether he is alive or dead? Why, he might even appear before me at any minute! Fortune brings about strange coincidences. I dreamed about him last night. I dreamed that he stood before me, cold and proud and austere as ever; giving no outward sign, though all his crimes were flaming and burning in his heart. Nothing—no shame, no exposure even, could take the pride out of that man's face or make him betray the least emotion or bitterness or self-reproach.'

'Such coincidences do sometimes occur,' said Gilbert. 'But one need not think about them nor anticipate them.'

'Well, that is enough about myself. Now about you, Gilbert. What is it I hear about selling strawberries in the street? And what is this Community?'

Gilbert made up quite a pretty little story of this House of Industry and Trance. He said nothing about the rusticity of Brother Silas or the hardness of Sister Phœbe, nor did he discuss the attractions of Sister Cicely.

Lady Osterley listened with interest, but without enthusiasm. One sometimes reads about these communities, of which there have been so many in America, but to converse with a member is a privilege seldom accorded to anyone. However, she was not carried away, although Gilbert spoke with animation of this beautiful House.

'I gather,' she said, 'that your people are not gentlefolk, to begin with.'

'They are not. I concede the point. There is no distinction of class among them.'

'Nor is there among us. My dear Gilbert, real gentlefolk know no distinctions among themselves. If you want the society of persons who are not real gentlefolk, any part of London will provide it for you in plenty. They are the people who cultivate distinctions, not we. No need to cross the Atlantic. Then you talk about the perfect life. My dear boy, is there, in all the world, any imaginable life more perfect than that of the best society in England? There cannot be, I assure you. Which makes me regret all the more my enforced exile.'

'It is not quite the same thing. You do not understand.'

'It is only one of the ways of thinking about going to heaven. My dear Gilbert, it was never your weakness to change this life into a dream of going to heaven. It never was your custom to take up with fads and fancies. Why do you not go home, if you want a monastery, and build one there for gentlefolk, and lead the most perfect life you can? Perhaps I would come and live there too, if those people could be kept from worrying me with letters. Your present House, I am convinced, is full of dull men and women with no manners.'

'About the women,' said Gilbert. 'Most of them, it is true, have, we will say, few manners, poor dears; yet they are for the most part dreamy and gentle; they are not obtrusive in their mannerlessness; they neither disgust nor repel one. I am on very friendly terms with several. I could, if you would allow me, Dorabyn, bring you one whom even you, I am sure——'

Dorabyn clapped her hands and laughed gently.

'Oh! I knew it! I was sure of it! You to go hawking strawberries about the street! You to become a gardener and a costermonger! You to sit down every evening and to look on at a company of cranks going off into trance! Ridiculous!'

'In fact,' said Gilbert truthfully, 'the company of cranks is not the sole object of my stay at the House.'

'It is, on the other hand, ... what is her name?'

'They call her Cicely.'

'Cicely what?'

'I don't know. I don't want to know her by any other name. I am very seriously in love, Dorabyn. For a good many years your letters prevented me from falling in love. I wanted no meaner creature, you know.'

'Gilbert!'

'And now I have found—no meaner creature.'

'What are her belongings—her people?'

'I don't know. She must be a gentlewoman by birth as she is by education. Her father, who died the other day, educated her. Of her mother's part I do not at present speak, because she died in giving birth to Cicely. There are many strange things at the House, but Cicely's case is the strangest. I do not know even her father's name. But you shall see her. Prepare yourself for a hideous dress—it is the dress of the Sisters; prepare yourself for the sweetest face in the whole world; her cheek is too pale, her eyes are too serious, her lips seldom smile; it is because she lives too much in the other world. I shall teach her to live below. But I cannot talk about her, Dorabyn. I must bring her.'

'Is it settled, Gilbert? Are you formally engaged?'

'She understands nothing. She is a child in innocence and ignorance. She knows that she thinks about me all day long; and she likes to be with me and is never tired of talking to me. All that she confesses. As for the rest—she knows nothing.'

'Bring her to me, Gilbert. And — afterwards? When you are married there will be no more nonsense about the House of Trance, will there?'

'I have ideas. I do not know, yet, what is best to be done. There are difficulties. But I think they may be overcome. I do not desire to stay longer than is necessary'—his face fell suddenly—'I must wait to see what will happen.'

Dorabyn looked at him with wonder. Why did he become black all at once, like the sky before a sudden storm?

'Why do you look so gloomy, Gilbert? Is there anything disagreeable behind?'

'Do I look gloomy?'

'You turned suddenly into gloom. Gilbert, what is it? I told you my trouble. Tell me yours.'

'It is not trouble exactly. I will tell you—say—on Saturday. Something is going to happen on Saturday. I know not what. I am anxious.'

'Does it concern yourself, or your mistress?'

'It concerns both. It concerns everybody. That is enough, Dorabyn. Now for yourself again. Let us have dinner early. They call their seven-o'clock meal supper here. And then we will drive in the park in the cool of the evening, and see the fireflies in the shrubs

11

and the stars in the sky. The American stars are splendid. And the quiet of the place will calm your nerves—and mine as well.'

They dined together—these two and Annandale. The talk was the old familiar talk which one only gets with the old familiar people. The House was forgotten, and all three were back in London.

After dinner they drove out to the park, which is a very lovely park, with ornamental water and valleys and cascades and hanging woods; there was a little moon, but not much, and the skies were brilliant, and the fireflies illuminated the shrubs with myriads of tiny electric sparks. But they noticed nothing, for two had been out of London for two years and one for eighteen months, and they all three thirsted for the old talk.

'Gilbert,' said Dorabyn, when they alighted at the hotel, 'you have been talking quite in the old way. You forget the Community very easily. If you were never to go back there any more——'

'I forget everything with you, Dorabyn—except one thing, and that is always with me, day and night, wherever I go.'

He meant Cicely, not the unspeakable Man.

In the evening, when he climbed the stairs at about eleven, he heard the Man moving about the room. What was he doing? At least he was keeping his promise not to venture into Aldermanbury even at night.

CHAPTER VII.

PROPOS D'AMOUR.

'CICELY'—it was in the early morning before breakfast, the morning after the talk with Dorabyn, and they stood among the flowers—'I want to talk very seriously to you.'

'I like you best when you talk seriously, Gilbert,

though it is very pleasant to listen while you talk about men and women as if you meant something else.'

'You must talk seriously too, my dear Cicely—very seriously.' He took her hand and held it lightly. To take a girl's hand and to press it softly but firmly is accepted all the world over as an assurance of love. Everybody knows so much of the language of love. But when you keep hold of her fingers lightly without pressure, it is a token, or a reminder, of ownership: of chains and bonds. I believe every girl understands this symbol; and most girls prefer it to the former.

'I want to talk seriously, then, about ourselves, my dear. First of all, you know that I love you, Cicely.'

'Oh! yes.' Three weeks before she would have replied with a childish look of innocence in her eyes. Of course she loved him. Now, she had advanced so far under his tuition that she blushed when she made this confession.

'Then, dear, we must understand what love demands, in our own case. You know that when two people like ourselves love each other—I mean two people like you and me, not two people like the Master and you, who also love each other—they want to marry: that is to say, to be together constantly as your father and mother are together—perhaps, like those to whom is granted the perfect love, to be together and never tire of each other, not only in this world, but also in worlds to come. I speak, my dear, as you believe.'

'Those who love each other, Gilbert, never cease to love—oh! never—never—never.'

'Wisest and sweetest! never—never—never.' He kissed her white forehead. 'Now, my dear, what I want to say, very seriously indeed, is this. If that message of your mother's proves true——'

'It must prove true. My mother could not—oh! she could not—at her levels it would be impossible—she could not send a message if it was not true. You may depend perfectly—perfectly—Gilbert, on what she said.'

'Then, my sweet mistress, on and after Saturday next I shall be free to leave the House.'

'Leave the House? Oh! Gilbert!'

'Yes. Leave the House, my dear. But don't look dismayed. Don't think I shall leave it without you. I am going to take you away with me. I am going to take you with me right away into that mysterious abyss which you call Outside.'

She shuddered. 'Will my mother let me go?'

Gilbert received the question quite gravely, and answered as if her mother were still living. 'Cicely dear, your mother has had every opportunity, for a month past, of observing that I have been diligently endeavouring to steal away her daughter's heart. If she had objected, she would have interfered and stopped it, somehow, long before this. But she has not. On the contrary, she has sent me messages, through you, and through the Master as well. She has shown an interest in me from the beginning. I think, my dear, that since she has herself been perfectly happy in her love, she desires you, too, to possess and to impart that blessing. Sure I am that there can be no greater happiness for me, my dear, than your love.'

'I think she loves you, too, Gilbert. But to leave the House—and the Master—and the brothers and sisters?'

'You will leave it with me, not alone, my dear. I know Outside pretty well. I can promise that you will very soon find life there infinitely more attractive than life here. There is so much to do and to observe. At first you will find everything new and strange. And you will also find, among the people you will know, most things with the prettiest possible covering, lid, casing, dress, or external wrapper, so that at first you will be quite delighted with all that you see. Afterwards you will naturally cease to be quite so much pleased with things. You will find, here and there, I am afraid, pretence and assurance.'

'But in Outside they cannot meditate. The Master says that there is no Meditation anywhere in the world except in this place.'

'You shall go to your mother for direction. As for your Meditation, I confess I doubt its value even in the life that the Master desires. However, I should think that to go into your own room and to lock the door would be quite easy anywhere in the world. It is, true, however, that people Outside do not as a rule meditate—as Sister Euphemia says—worth a cent.'

'Without Meditation how can one rise?'

'You ask more than I can tell you. Cicely, my child, I am one of the world: I have always lived in the world. I have hitherto cared no more about what you call Elevation than the rest of the world. But I should say from observation, that methods of Elevation, that is, of attaining to a higher level of the mind and the soul, should be as easily learned in the world as here.'

'How should I learn them?'

He shifted the responsibility once more.

'Again, if you still, after some experience of the world, desire them, ask your mother.'

She was silent. To leave the House! It frightened her. To go into the raging, roaring, noisy Outside, of which they spoke with a kind of terror! The thought made her shiver. But that Gilbert should go away without her! That would be worse.

'I shall take you with me, my dear,' he went on, reading her thoughts, 'this very day to a friend, an old friend of mine, who is staying at a hotel at Aldermanbury. She will tell you that it is not so very dreadful a thing to live in the world. I do not think she ever meditates, but it would be difficult to find a woman of a nobler nature than this friend of mine. She has promised to interest herself in you. We will go over in the afternoon—to-day—we can easily go there and get back in time for your Meditation.'

Man proposes—but the event is not always exactly what he designs. You shall see what happened as regards this proposed visit to Dorabyn.

'And now let us sit down, my dear, and talk about the world.'

They sat down on the bench occupied by Brother Charles in the hours of Recreation ; it was close to the flower-bed which marked the grave of Sister Alice. Gilbert laid his hand on the girl's waist and began to talk.

'I mean to take you away with me when this business of mine is over,' Gilbert went on. 'I have arranged it all in my own mind. Dorabyn—my old friend—will receive you, I am sure. I shall take you to England, where I have a house. It is not a large house, my child, because I am not what they call a very rich man : but it is a pretty house and an old house. Part of it was built in the reign of Henry the Eighth : there are ghosts in it and secret chambers : there are gardens round it, and a Park and the ruins of an old Abbey : outside the Park there is a village church and a churchyard full of solemn trees. Swallows fly about the churchyard ; rooks caw in the branches : it is one of the oldest and most venerable churches in the country : there are cottages with thatched roofs and green palings : there are cottage folk, soft-mannered, respectful—you will love them, Cicely : not far off there are other houses, where you will find certain gentlewomen who will welcome you for my sake first, and your own next ; they are soft of voice and of manners : they are kind and gracious : you will love them and they will love you. My dear, I promise that you shall find the place full of love—far, far more full of love, believe me, than you will ever find here. Such love as you desire—which is your very breath— you can only find among gentlefolk.'

'Gilbert, why do you think so much of gentlefolk? Here we have no such thing.'

'Apart from the Master, who has been made a gentleman by your mother, and you, dear child, we have not, indeed.'

'But how will these kind ladies receive one who is not one of themselves—a gentlewoman, as you call it?'

'You are one of themselves, my dear. They will never entertain the slightest doubt upon that subject. Your face, your manner, your voice—everything proclaims that fact aloud.'

She sighed. 'I am afraid,' she said. 'I am sure that I do not know their manners or their speech. Gilbert, it terrifies me more than I can tell you to think of going among all these strangers.'

'You will learn all there is to learn very soon. And you need not be frightened in the least. In this village, among these quiet, kindly folk, you will learn certain little differences in a very short time. My dear, our farms and gardens are far more beautiful than these. You will find among these people a far more beautiful life than this of the Community. Here you have no village church and no churchyard: no beautiful service of rich and poor, old and young, all together: no refined and gracious ladies. You will grow, my dear: you will put on new ideas, just as you will put on dresses far more beautiful than this.'

'Oh, Gilbert! you make my heart beat. But I am afraid.'

'You will change through and through: you will learn that you belong to the past in a way you have never before understood; that you do not stand alone in the universe, that you are one of an infinite multitude——' He stopped, for she was no longer listening. Her eyes were again far away. Her face was white, her breathing was suspended. He was not in the least alarmed or anxious. She was again in a trance or catalepsy. He laid his arm about her waist to keep her from falling, and sat patiently waiting her return.

He waited ten minutes: then her lips parted: her colour returned: she opened her eyes. 'Gilbert,' she said, 'you were talking about things which I could not understand—about villages and churchyards. Do not tell me too much. Let me learn everything gradually. I get frightened when you talk about what is coming. And then my mother called me. She is always watching over me, you know.'

'Yes, I know. That is—but what did she say?'

'She kissed me, and told me to follow my heart, and be happy.'

'And that, dear Cicely?'

She moved towards him, and lo! it was heart to heart and lip to lip.

CHAPTER VIII.

CRITICISM.

THE Committee of the Community sat in deliberation in the Common Hall, which was at once refectory, chapter-house, calefactory, chapel, and place of Meditation.

The Committee did not meet to consider the affairs of the Community. These were all in the Master's hands; he kept complete control of the business side of the Society; nobody knew, nobody asked, what was its income and what were its resources; sufficient for the members to know that the three square meals suffered no diminution in quantity. Who would confuse the finer parts of the brain, those which go to Meditation, in order to study finance? Fortunately, as is generally the case with a successful founder, the Master was as good in administration as in Meditation.

Nor did the Committee meet for the passing of new laws or the alteration of old ones. There were no laws except the simple routine of Fatigue and Repose, Restoration and Meditation; every day was like its predecessor, save for the change of season; summer followed spring, autumn followed summer, winter followed autumn. There was no first day or Sunday, no seventh day or

Sabbath, no saint's day, holy day, commemoration day,
or anything but the same day with the same routine.
Nothing, in fact, to disturb the mind or to hinder
Meditation.

The Committee, whenever it was called together,
which was a very rare event, met to deliberate on the
conduct of a member, and especially on that part of his
conduct which might affect the others. The delibera-
tions were carried on in the presence of the member
concerned, who was thus 'criticised' to his face. He
was invited to attend and to stand at the end of a long
table, while a frank and completely outspoken criticism
of his behaviour, his discourse, and the general conduct
of his own life was carried on before him. This criticism
of a member was an ideal arrangement made by the
Master at the outset. You shall see, immediately, how
well it worked. The leading thought in the establish-
ment of the institution was that, in a spirit of love and
faithfulness, a brother might be openly admonished of
his faults, and so gently and lovingly led back to the
better way. Like other ideal institutions, it was not
always carried out quite in the spirit intended. Indeed,
for some reason or other, the one thing which the
members most feared was criticism. It is strange, for,
if you think of it, how beautifully we should all behave
if we were faithfully admonished of our faults! The
members, indeed, lived in daily terror of being criticised.
Perhaps the critics were too faithful. In other depart-
ments of human activity the too faithful critic is not
popular. Again, if you think of it, the man who aims
at such a tremendous achievement as the Higher Life—
the life of the next world, or even the next after that—
ought surely to welcome a frank, outspoken, plain, un-
varnished account of how his conduct appears to his
brother members. Nothing should be more helpful.
Yet, for some reason, nothing was more dreaded by
the members. The sisters went to be criticised with
trembling limbs, and returned with cheeks aflame.

The brothers obeyed the summons with temper, and sometimes came away in a rage so blind that they had actually been known to leave the Community. Yet, surely, the Master was right. One cannot imagine a more effective weapon in the cause of righteousness than the candid criticism of one's own loving brothers and gentle sisters. Perhaps, if the subject of discussion were allowed to take chloroform or ether or some other anæsthetic, the institution would be more popular.

The Committee of the Community was a body of twelve, the Founder being President. They filled up death vacancies by themselves; the Community had no vote in the election. Since the only function of the Committee was to criticise, it will be understood that they were great sticklers for the Rule. Fortunately it was a simple Rule, because the Committee were like the Pharisees for dividing the word. The body consisted of women as well as of men; they all belonged to the same class, that of the imperfectly educated; and they all entertained the same narrow religion, tempered by the revelations expected by him who Meditates.

'I suppose,' said the Master, with a sigh, 'that, as we have criticism to pronounce upon Brother Gilbert and Sister Cicely, we must have them both before us.'

'Both,' replied the Committee unanimously.

'But separately; not together,' said Sister Phœbe, who was on the Committee.

'I confess,' said the Master, 'that in the case of our young Sister Cicely, I would rather that she were placed in the hands of an elder member—say myself —for private criticism. She is young, she is inexperienced——'

'She must be made to understand,' interrupted Sister Phœbe quickly. 'She cannot understand too early.'

The Master sighed again. He would have saved the child if he could. 'Call Sister Cicely, then,' he ordered. 'Let us criticise the child in all tenderness. Remember, she is young; she is used to nothing but kindness; she is a daughter of the House; and her father was my first follower.'

'In tenderness,' said Sister Phœbe firmly. 'But in truth, always in truth, which is in love. Cicely's soul must be our consideration, until she makes it her own.'

The Committee murmured assent. Zeal for other people's souls was always a marked feature in the Committee. The Master looked round the table. He sighed; the words were his own words; he would have saved the child; but he said no more.

Of course one associates the criticising of Gilbert and Cicely with that evidence of the Single Attachment discovered by Sister Phœbe. It was only the last drop that caused the cup of toleration to overflow. For a whole month it was evident to the Community that these two openly and shamelessly sought each other, walked together, and talked together. What did they talk about? Subjects connected with Meditation and the Things Unutterable which nobody could remember? The Community feared not.

In fact, the daily conversation had drifted more and more away from the Community and into the wicked world, of which Cicely had now learned far more than she had ever imagined, insomuch that, like Eve, she was growing curious and wanted to learn a great deal more. So they talked while they worked in the garden, and they talked at meals, despite the presence of the Man of Marble, and they talked at Recreation, and the Community looked on and marvelled; and some were indignant, and some were jealous.

Cicely was in the garden tying up and weeding, as usual. She was quite happy; she was singing over her work—a song without words, a blithe song like the song of the lark, which she had never heard; yet not a loud song, lest some of the brethren might be disturbed; and while she sang she kept thinking about Gilbert—she thought about him all day long—and about what she could do for him to assist his spiritual advance, which was deplorably slow. Not once had he succeeded in getting into Meditation. And she had before her that vision of Outside.

Then there came to her one of the brothers.

'Sister,' he said, 'the Committee are in meeting. They have to speak to you. Come with me.'

She turned pale and her heart became as heavy as lead. She knew—who did not?—the trials of a Criticism: not that she had yet passed through the ordeal, but others had, and talked. Members had been known to run away rather than face a Criticism. Besides, what were they going to talk about? The Single Attachment? She blushed a rosy red, and again she turned pale. 'Come,' said the brother. Her colour came and went. She stood still, staring. 'Come,' said the brother.

She entered the Hall, bare-headed, carrying her hat. She stood at the end of the long table at which the Committee were assembled. She knew too well—this guilty criminal—that the criticism would turn upon Single Attachments. So that her cheek flamed and her lips quivered. The ceremony was exactly as if a penitent should kneel in silence before a company of priests, who should turn and turn about, recite and confess openly all that sinner's sinful deeds and all her sinful thoughts. It was as if the Father Confessor should confess in the name of the penitent.

'Sister Cicely,' the Master began, and paused.

Cicely lifted her head and looked round the table. There were but two faces which showed any sign of kindness or of sympathy. One was the face of the venerable Master. His patriarchal appearance conveyed an assurance of kindness; his long white hair, his benevolent face, his soft and gentle voice, soothed the fears of the girl. The other face was that of the little lady whose past Gilbert had restored to her. The rest might have been members of the Grand

Inquisition, so hard and pitiless and determined were they.

'Sister Cicely,' the President repeated; 'from time to time it is the godly custom of this House for the Committee, which is the body of Presbyters, I myself being the Overseer, President, Bishop, or Master, to call before them any of the brothers who may be exposed to special temptation, who may be falling into danger, who may be neglecting the one important object of human life; and, in a spirit of love, to point out their faults or dangers, and to lead that brother or sister back into the way of the Sinless Life. You are, very specially, Sister Cicely, a daughter of the House you were born among us, you have never been outside the House; so far as it is permitted to love one more than another you are very dear to me; your father was my earliest friend, he and I were the first members of this Community, which has since been abundantly blessed—yea, blessings fall thickly on our heads. Therefore, sister, we are, if one may say so, more than commonly concerned for the state of your soul. You have never known any of the temptations of the outer world; you should indeed be already well advanced, considering your advantages, in the Way of Perfection. Yet I hear, sorrowfully, of dangers. Remember, child, that he who does not advance, recedes. We must still press onward. Receive, therefore, dear sister, the admonition of your brethren and your sisters in the spirit of submissive love and Christian meekness.'

'I have observed for some time,' said an old man, with a harsh and grating voice, 'too much attention to the decoration of her person in our sister. She must be continually washing her hands and brushing her hair and keeping her dress clean. What matters a little dirt if the soul is right?'

'I have observed,' said another grimly, after a pause, 'that Sister Cicely is too fond of singing. She constantly sings at her work when she ought to be meditating.'

'I have observed,' said a third, after another pause, 'that of late she frequently laughs in her conversation. There should be nothing in the Community to laugh at.'

Cicely, her hands folded, made no reply whatever.

'She seems,' said an old woman critically, 'not to care any longer for the things of the Community—our blessings of the Common Life. She is languid in her intercourse with the members.'

'She chooses and selects her companions,' said another woman, 'as if one were better or more desirable than another in the Community.'

'You hear, Sister Cicely,' said the President, looking nervously at Sister Phœbe. 'Perhaps we have said enough. Remember that there must be no selection or comparison among us. We are all brothers and sisters, with the same hopes and the same dangers. No selections, sister.'

'There is more than selection,' said Sister Phœbe, who had hitherto only nodded her head. 'I have myself observed, for some time, the growth of a Single Attachment — an attachment towards the English brother, Gilbert. I have watched you, Sister Cicely, with this brother, who is less to be blamed than you, because he has not yet acquired the spirit of our Rule —a spirit which forbids earthly love even in those who marry by command and permission of the House. You know this prohibition; it is our most distinctive teaching that we are not to imperil our souls by the selfish passion of love.'

'You know this teaching, Cicely,' said the Master.

Cicely made no reply.

Sister Phœbe went on, acquiring fresh vigour as she proceeded. 'You have singled out this brother. You walk with him, you meet him every afternoon in the garden, you sit beside him and talk. I have listened to your talk: it is about books—worldly books; poetry— what has worldly poetry to do for the soul except to drag it down? And about Outside you listen with guilty pleasure; nay, I know not what he has told you, this brother who was once a rich young Englishman—that is, a profligate, whose life cannot be described by virtuous lips.'

She paused. Cicely made no reply, but the flush on her face continued.

Sister Phœbe went on.

'You whisper together; you take no pleasure in the society of the others; you no longer converse with the sisters; you stop in your work to think about him.'

Still Cicely made no answer.

'There is worse to follow.' Sister Phœbe looked round the room so as to collect and concentrate all thoughts on this one fact. 'Much worse. I have seen him kiss her! I have seen him kiss—her—head!'

The Committee murmured and shook their assembled heads, all but the little lady, who blushed and smiled.

'For my own part, I have not witnessed any kissing,' said the ancient brother with the harsh voice, 'but I have observed other signs of this Single Attachment. When such an attachment is formed there can be no longer any Meditation. This couple would separate themselves from us: they would like to live apart. Our ways and manners have ceased to be good enough for them.'

'She follows him about with her eyes,' Sister Phœbe continued. 'She draws him on. She is much worse than the other.'

'And he leans over her as if he wanted to put his arms round her,' added another member.

'It is her artfulness,' said Sister Phœbe. 'If she did not encourage him——'

'Enough,' interrupted the Master. 'Have you anything to say, Sister Cicely?'

'It is quite true'—Cicely drew herself up and faced her critics boldly—'that I take great pleasure in the conversation of Brother Gilbert.'

'Why!' cried Sister Phœbe, who was by far the most venomous of them all: 'she confesses it! She actually glories in her guilt!'

'There is no guilt,' Cicely replied quickly, 'in listening to the words of a well instructed man who fills one with new ideas. He has taught me things that I could never learn anywhere else. Ignorance is not spiritual elevation. I know so much.'

'Knowledge of evil,' said the Master, 'is always dangerous. You have been brought up in ignorance of evil, sister. I hoped that you would always continue in ignorance. Knowledge of the world is knowledge of evil, and evil easily assumes the guise of good. Talk to him no more, my child, of Outside, or of anything beyond the daily life of the Community. But you are accused not so much of conversation with him —he shall be admonished on that point—as of forming a Single Attachment to him. Tell me if that is true.'

The girl hesitated. But the truth had to be told.

'It is true,' she said.

The Committee groaned. It was a hollow, melancholy groan.

'Such an Attachment, dear sister,' the Master continued, but very gently, 'is dangerous in the extreme both to the Community and to yourself. It must be broken down, trodden under foot, resolutely put away out of your mind as an unclean thing. It is both selfish and sinful—though a selfish soul can never be free from sin. It is selfish because it draws away your thoughts from others and concentrates them upon yourself and upon him; so that, after the way of the world, there is nothing to be thought of in the whole world, by you and by him, but yourselves. Where are your sacred thoughts and holy meditations? Dispelled; driven away by this blind and unholy passion. Where is the way of perfection? It is lost. And it is a sinful passion because it causes you to neglect your duties towards the Community. Why do we live together?

In order that we may work each for the other. Why do we work each for the other? Because we would cause every one to walk in the way without cares and anxieties of this world: because we will not allow any thoughts or hope of personal gain or profit to interfere with our meditations. You break in upon this rule; you substitute thought and work for one—in place of thought and work for the Community.'

Then Cicely spoke—and she spoke with passion, and rebelliously.

'Since I have conversed with Brother Gilbert my thoughts have been on a higher level than they ever reached before. I have cast away my old selfishness. I have prayed for him, instead of myself, night and day. I am far holier of heart since I ceased to think about my own soul and have begun to think of his. It is better to think for another than for yourself. I shall continue to think for him.'

Sister Phœbe shrieked. 'This is rebellion,' she said. 'Shall we suffer a rebel to remain with us?'

The Master held up his hand. 'Listen, child,' he said. 'We cannot suffer you, our dear one, the daughter of my friend, to become a castaway. We might expel you from the Community, but that would be your destruction and our great pain and grief. We will save you, dear child, from yourself—even against your own will we will save you, by the wholesome order and discipline of the House. We shall break up this Attachment for you; we shall substitute another of a less destructive kind. Unhappy girl! Your meditations are no longer for yourself, but for another. What will it profit you if his soul be saved while yours is lost? For we are alone—each of us is alone in the world. We may support each other a little, and help each other a little. But each of us is alone. You must renounce, dear child, this Single Attachment.'

Cicely shook her head.

'There is but one certain way to break it up. For

the sake of your highest interests, we have resolved on adopting that way. We shall give you to another man in marriage.'

To another man! Cicely caught hold of the table. Things became dim: she was like one who has received a violent blow. She staggered and reeled.

'Give her a minute,' cried the little old lady whose past was so hard to forget. She jumped up and ran to hold her. 'Don't frighten the child. Goodness! This comes of a committee with no knowledge. What do you know'—she addressed the Master—'about a young girl's heart? Courage, my pretty! perhaps it won't be so bad, after all. Not one among you all, except me, who knows what is meant by love. Another man! Oh! dear Lord! another man!'

Cicely recovered. She stood upright again, though the sympathetic sister held her by the waist.

'We are too sudden for you, dear child,' said the Master kindly. 'Believe me, it is for your good—your highest good. We shall give you in marriage to Brother Silas here, who is willing, for his own Elevation, to take a wife.'

Brother Silas, to show his willingness in the matter of self-sacrifice, grinned from ear to ear. Cicely looked at him stupidly: she did not understand—except that she was to be separated from Gilbert.

'And now, dear sister,' said the Master, 'you have heard as much as is good for you. We want no more criticism, which may become a mischievous carping, unless restrained.' He looked at Sister Phœbe. 'Go now, and reflect on the selfishness and the dangers of the Single Attachment.'

'Not back to the garden,' cried Sister Phœbe. 'She will only meet the man there and make things worse.'

'I think, dear child,' the Master added, 'that we can excuse you from work for a day or two while——'

'In her own room,' cried Sister Phœbe.

'In the seclusion of your own chamber while you

consider alone the things that have been said to you this day.'

Cicely obeyed. She walked with hanging head and flaming cheeks and flashing eyes to the door of the women's wing, and disappeared.

They were very wrong. They should have married her there and then, before she knew what resistance meant. They let her go. At least those flaming cheeks and flashing eyes betokened a stormy honeymoon for Brother Silas. They let her go. The consequences to the bridegroom elect, as you will hear immediately, were disastrous indeed.

CHAPTER IX.

REVOLT.

'CALL Brother Gilbert,' said the Master.

'And what may the Committee want with me?' asked Gilbert.

'You've got to come,' replied the Summoner.

'They're going to criticise you,' said one of his fellow-gardeners, with the ready smile of pleasing anticipation with which one greets a person about to suffer. All those who have been publicly flogged, tortured, beheaded, or hanged will remember the universal smile which greeted the patient on his appearance. 'They will criticise you,' he said, 'for the good of your Elevation.'

'They will tell you your faults,' said another.

'Things you never suspected,' said a third. 'Ah!' with a long-drawn breath: only to think of the rage which would presently fill the soul of the sufferer !

Gilbert rolled down his sleeves—ask not what was his occupation—put on his coat and obeyed the summons.

The other men looked after him.

'Not before 'twas time,' said the first gardener. 'Light

conversation,' said the second. 'He laughs,' said the third. 'He talks,' said the first—there were three only. 'With Sister Cicely,' said the second. 'They should both be watched,' said the third. And so on, because criticism is the universal solvent; it loosens all tongues and stimulates the dullest imagination; even criticism of this kind, which is perilously nigh to scandal.

The Master opened the proceedings with much the same kind of general introduction as he had used for the offending sister. Gilbert stood at the end of the table listening with outward respect.

'Therefore,' the Master concluded, 'you will learn from what is said the judgment that is passed upon you by your brethren of this household and their opinion of your conduct. Remember that even if the judgment seems harsh it has been formed and will be uttered in the spirit of love.'

Gilbert bowed. 'In the spirit of love,' he repeated. Then he looked about him, found a chair, and sat down in easy attitude to receive what would be offered. There was no heightened colour or any appearance of terror or uneasiness whatever.

'It is customary,' said one of them timidly, 'to stand in the presence of the Committee.'

'I prefer to sit,' said Gilbert. 'The spirit of the Community is equality. Therefore, in a spirit of love, I take a chair.'

They looked at the Master, who passed over the incident.

'I have observed,' said the elderly brother with the rasping voice, opening the ball, 'that Brother Gilbert gives himself airs. He looks as if he were superior to us.'

Gilbert bowed. 'Thank you,' he said. 'Next!'

'I have observed,' said another, 'that he is dainty about his food; he has also been heard to find fault with the way in which some members take their food, as if the Higher Life could be troubled about holding the knife and fork. And he has frequently complained that the steaks were tough.'

'Excuse me for interrupting,' said Gilbert. 'Do I understand that the Higher Life requires toughness in the steak ?'

The critic grew red and rather angry.

'The question is flippant,' he said. 'The point of my observation is the daintiness of Brother Gilbert.'

Gilbert bowed again. 'Thank you,' he said.

'I have observed,' said a third, 'that Brother Gilbert has refused the coffee on the ground that it was mud.'

'Black mud,' Gilbert corrected him. 'It is quite true. Coffee ought not to be black mud.'

'And I,' said a fourth, 'have seen him turn up his nose because the sausages were fat.'

'These observations,' said Gilbert, 'are, I submit to this collective wisdom, wide of the mark. None of these things affect the spiritual condition as to which you are so tender. A man who is accustomed to food properly dressed is hindered by being invited to eat such things as are too often placed upon your table. If you have nothing of any greater importance than this I shall retire, and continue to state the fact when the coffee is black mud.'

He rose and looked round the table. Seeing another member about to speak, he sat down again.

'I have also observed,' said that other member, 'that our brother is a respecter of persons.'

'Which means, I suppose,' Gilbert replied, 'that I do not like the society of certain somewhat coarse members of the Community. Do you wish that they should drag all down to their own level ?'

'I have observed,' said another, 'hardness of heart. He does not keep himself open to the influences which we offer him. He has never been observed to meditate.'

'I have remarked,' said another, 'that in his discourse he is proud and particular, and that he uses words and sayings which some of us do not understand. This confuses us. And sometimes he speaks as a mocker, meaning the opposite to what he says.'

Then there was silence for a space. Gilbert looked round coldly. 'Anything more?' he asked.

Sister Phœbe here broke in. 'Oh! there is a great deal more—a great deal more: these things are but a beginning; there is a great deal more. I have observed that Brother Gilbert has for some time fallen into a Single Attachment.'

Gilbert smiled. 'Oh!' he said, 'you have observed that, have you? I thought we should come to it, after these preliminaries. Very well. I understand, Master, that I have given offence to some by making remarks when the food was coarse and unfit to be placed upon the table. Will you inform me if there is anything contrary to the spirit of the Community in this kind of complaint? If so, I will in future refrain.'

'All depends upon the spirit and the manner. If in your remarks you did not intend any reflection upon the members——'

'Of course not. Why should I reflect upon them? If they like black mud they may. Then it appears that I do not talk quite in the way customary to the members. The manner of talk will change insensibly, no doubt. And some members think that I give myself airs. Now, I would advise any such member to remember your own teaching and to confine his thoughts to his own solitary, individual soul. Then he will cease to notice my airs. So much for the preliminaries. Now, if you please, Master, we will take the next point of this meeting.' He addressed the Master, but he looked at Phœbe, who took the cudgels vigorously.

'He occupies himself all day long with Sister Cicely. He sits next her at meals; he works with her in the garden; he talks with her all Recreation; he laughs with her and makes her laugh even at Restoration; and I saw him, yesterday, as I have told you already, kiss her head.'

* * * * *

The stars indicate the Master's harangue which followed. With a few alterations, *mutatis mutandis*, it was exactly the same as that which had been delivered for the benefit of the other sinner.

'Therefore,' the Master concluded, 'for the sake of our highest interests we must exclude from the Community all these Single Attachments, with the uncontrolled passions, wild wraths, and fierce jealousies which disturb and drag down the souls of Outside. We have taken such measures as will effectually remove the object of your misplaced affection and place it altogether beyond your reach.'

'What have you done with that child?' Gilbert sprang to his feet and glared about the room.

'We are going to marry her.'

'To marry her? Marry her? Think what you are doing. There is not one in this Community who is fit to marry her—no one who can stand beside her even in the gifts you desire. If you give her to one of your rustics and boors, you will destroy her.'

'We have considered,' said the Master coldly, ' what will be best for her welfare. And we shall marry her. In the Community we allow marriages, provided they are not accompanied and made hurtful by the presence of Love. A calm, meditative union, which, although each stands consciously apart from the other, and alone in the universe, may be helpful. Therefore we are going to marry Sister Cicely to Brother Silas here.'

'Silas?' Gilbert looked down upon the bridegroom elect with withering disgust. ' You would marry that girl—Cicely—to this clumsy boor?' Silas stood up and opened his mouth to speak, but could find no words, and sat down again, confused and angry. 'Do you know—can you imagine—what that means? Good God! Are you human creatures?'

'I said he was a respecter of persons,' observed the member of the Committee who had made that original discovery.

'Master,' repeated Gilbert, 'you cannot possibly mean to give this delicate, high-strung creature, your own child —almost your own daughter—to that boor? It is degradation. It is more. You—you who love her—can you mean it?'

'We have considered the matter,' the Master replied, with a certain sadness. 'There is no passion of single love in the case. We are destroying that passion out of the love we all bear to her. You do not understand —you are still full of the prejudices of Outside.'

'It is you who do not understand. Marriage for such a girl as Cicely, without love, would be degradation certain and fatal.'

'Enough about Cicely,' said the Master. 'The whole spirit of the Community is concerned with this marriage. Now for yourself. You also, it is clear, are prone to Single Attachments. You also must be treated in the same way.'

'Why, you are not going to marry me?' He laughed aloud.

'We are. Sister Phœbe consents to take you.'

'Oh! Lord!' There was a world of meaning in the interjection. And he laughed again. The Committee looked on in wonder. The young man was capable of laughing at anything.

'Sister Phœbe is a maiden of great spiritual riches: one who will not expect any wasting of the soul in foolish fondness. Yours will be eminently a spiritual marriage, with no love either in the past or in the present. In your wife you will have a friend who will watch over you with the care of one farther advanced than yourself.'

'And this paragon is Sister Phœbe—this Sister Phœbe—this identical Phœbe?'

They were mocking words; everybody understood so much.

'Your wife,' the Master repeated, 'will be Sister Phœbe, who consents to take you as her husband.'

'Oh!' Gilbert faced the bride elect. 'It is as well to understand quite clearly what you mean, Master. You have never yet been married, I believe. It is a thousand pities. Your character wants just that one touch of human sympathy which comes of experience in love. There was a cardinal of the Romish Church; he had once been married: he was unlike any other priest ever known; he was the most human of creatures because, like yourself, he lived consistently with his creed, and, unlike yourself, he knew the meaning of love. Tell me again, Master, do you seriously order Cicely to marry this man, and me to marry this woman?'

'Since it is the only way to break down this Single Attachment, I do.'

Gilbert turned again to Phœbe. She was always hard-featured; this morning she was harder than ever; her mouth was set and her eyes were resolute. Heavens! what a bride! What an uncompromising bride! She looked straight before her; she pretended not to know that Gilbert was looking at her; she said nothing.

'Sister Phœbe,' said Gilbert: 'will you tell me before this Committee whether it is your desire to marry me?'

'It is,' she replied.

'And yours, Brother Silas, to marry this poor girl?'

'It is.'

'Then, Master, I accuse these two persons of Single Attachments.'

'This is trifling,' said the Master.

'It is nothing of the kind. I accuse them both of Single Attachments. The man has been unable to conceal his jealousy; in his way he loves the girl; the woman has almost in so many words offered to marry me. A Single Attachment which is not returned is, I submit, even a more fatal disturber of Meditation than one which is returned. Do you accept my accusation, Master? If not, you must be prepared for what will follow.'

A dead silence fell upon the Committee. For there was rebellion in that face.

Then Phœbe turned and looked upon his face. There was so much bitterness and loathing in it that the woman, though not given to blushing, changed colour; she started to her feet; she opened her mouth to speak, but she could not. The rage of the woman despised filled her soul; she sat down again and bent her head. Did she console herself with the thought that to-morrow he would be hers—her very own? Alas! There are some things that we never know, and among these things is the kind of married life which Sister Phœbe contemplated in the society of a man who was capable of Single Attachments.

'Remember, Brother Gilbert,' said the Master, 'that this criticism has been conducted for your instruction, and in a spirit of truth and love. As for your marriage, that is ordered for you in the certainty that you will thus acquire the help and guidance you need. Sister Phœbe is rich in spiritual graces.'

Gilbert bowed. Then he looked round the Committee.

'If nobody has any further observation to make——'

Nobody had apparently.

'Before I go,' Gilbert went on, 'I should like to point out to you that you must have spent a great deal of time, all of you, in watching for, and picking out, these various faults and weaknesses. The note, the distinguishing feature of this Community is, as the Master has insisted upon this morning, the isolation of the individual. He desires that we should be concentrated and rapt in our own meditations, the presence of the others being chiefly helpful in providing for each other the necessaries of life, and in the prevention of the evils which attend the solitary. Now, instead of following out the Master's teaching, you have all been diligently spying out the doings and the ways of two of the members. I observe, therefore, for my own part, a low spiritual level in all of you which surprises and pains me. You are not what you pretend to be. As for the trifles you have brought forward, I have sufficiently replied to them. As to my conversations with this girl, it has been to me most instructive to study the most pure and innocent soul in this House. The only good I have received, as yet, from this Community has been through her. As for this proposed marriage——'

'Nothing can be permitted on this point,' the Master interrupted. 'The thing has been determined by the Committee.'

'Where is Cicely?' asked Gilbert. 'What have you done with her?'

'She has been sent to her own room,' the Master replied.

'Out of your way,' added Sister Phœbe.

To the amazement of the Committee, Gilbert strode straight up the Hall to the door of the women's wing. He dared to invade the privacy of the gynæceum. What does the profligacy of the British nobleman respect? They heard him marching down the corridors; they heard him cry 'Cicely! Cicely!' They heard him mounting the stairs . . . and they looked at each other aghast.

Gilbert found the girl in her own room at the top of the house; a little room like his own, furnished in exactly the same manner. And at sight of the child's cell, so plain and mean, there fell upon him— not for the first time—an overwhelming pity for one who had been brought up with nothing beautiful or graceful or artistic at all about her except the flowers in the garden, the blossoms on the trees, and the clouds and sunshine of the sky. That so sweet a flower should grow up in a cell no better than is given to a prisoner in a gaol! But it was not a time for these regrets.

Cicely was sitting on her bed with folded hands— bewildered—disconsolate—tearful.

'Oh, Gilbert, Gilbert!' She started to her feet when he appeared. 'Save me! save me! Oh, I cannot, I will not marry that man!'

'My love! You shall not,' he murmured, kissing her and laying his strong protecting arm about her. 'I am come to save you. Quick, child! They may offer resistance; but I do not think they will. Take anything you value—if there is anything—and come with me.'

In the corner lay a desk of rosewood. Cicely took it up. 'It was my mother's. It is all I have of hers.'

Gilbert took it out of her hands. 'I will carry it. Come, child, you must trust yourself to me. Come, put on your hat.'

She obeyed. He led her down the stair and back into the Hall, where the Committee sat with minds astonished.

'Master,' he said, 'Cicely will go with me. She will stay with friends of mine until, at least, you have returned to your senses.'

Cicely laid her hands upon the Master's shoulders.

'Oh, dear Master!' she said. 'Oh, kind Master! Oh, my friend and protector and the friend of my mother. Think of her. Think of my father. Would they let me marry Brother Silas? Oh! I must leave you, but only for a time—only till you tell me that I can come back.'

She kissed his forehead and took Gilbert's hand again.

The Master rose, opened his mouth, looked round sadly, and sat down again in silence.

And the unhappy victims of a Single Attachment passed out of the door and through the porch, and were heard crunching the gravel without while the Committee sat helpless within.

CHAPTER X.

FLIGHT.

THE door slammed after them: it was always made to slam—it slammed of its own accord for everyone who passed through. This time it slammed reproachfully. It said to Gilbert: 'I have slammed for the House nineteen years and more. I have done my duty by you since you have been here. I have taught you to despise noise. When you hear the heavy bell of the locomotive, the whistle of the steamer, the click of the electric car, the slamming of other doors, you will suffer nothing, thanks to me. And now I shall slam for you no more.' An odd thing to think of, but at supreme moments of life we very often turn to trifles. To Cicely the door conveyed no such message; she could think of nothing except that she was leaving the Community and the Master—the place where she discoursed with her dead mother and recalled the teachings of her dead father—the place which had been a convent, a seclusion, a school, a paradise to her.

She shrank back in the verandah.

'Oh, Gilbert!' she cried, trembling. 'Oh! what shall I do—Outside? How can I live there?'

'Trust yourself to me, dear child. Have no fear.' He held her by the hand and gently led her along.

'Oh! to leave the Master! And the sisters! And my flowers!'

''There are other—and better—sisters waiting for you Outside, Cicely. And other—perhaps better— flowers. Come. Remember that if you stay there is Silas for you and Phœbe for me. Because I could not go away and leave you here alone, Cicely, you will not condemn me to Phœbe?'

He looked so brave and strong, his grasp was so firm and warm, his eyes were so full of tenderness, that

Cicely yielded: the woman yielded to the man and trusted him, and went out with him into the wide world of which she knew so little. She went with him; and in another minute they were beyond the Community precinct and on the world's high road. She looked before her along the straight road with expectant eyes, as one who lands upon an unknown shore and fears to meet strange monsters and strange wild people —monoculous people, unipeds such as Mandeville saw —hairy satyrs: on an unknown shore never before discovered anything may be expected.

It was not difficult to read the thoughts of the young traveller.

'In the world,' said Gilbert, 'you will find a good many things strange to your experience, which has been narrow. You must be patient and observant. You must not cry out with wonder or surprise. Look on at first in silence.'

'I will try. It is not difficult to be silent.'

'Not for you; your soul dwells in a perpetual calm. But you will have to unlearn a great deal that you have been taught. For instance, the Master has told you, thinking always of Elevation, that every soul stands alone in space. I would rather hold that everyone stands in a crowd. You converse with your mother, who is dead, as with the Master—who is living. You are not alone, then. There is an endless chain of life running from parent to child; there is the tie of love which can never be dissolved. Those who are worthy, Cicely, are only bound more closely by this tie. Your parents are not separated. Therefore they are not alone. In this life we are bound to each other—brother, sister, lover, children, all; so that there is never any solitude save for some hapless creatures who have no such tie. My child, you have never been alone all your life.'

'Yet the Master says so.'

'It is the inheritance of his former narrow creed—of

which you know nothing. Have you ever felt alone, Cicely? But of course you have not.'

It is not usual for lovers to begin with theological discussion and metaphysical distinctions. But the circumstances of this case were not common. Few lovers chance upon a mistress educated in such opinions; few girls have to make their entrance into society with such a past as Cicely possessed. Further, Gilbert was going to place this girl in the charge of one who was hard to please in the matter of girl.

Gilbert changed the subject, but returned to it. The only way to teach a thing thoroughly is to repeat it over and over again, to rub it in, to keep on repeating it in different words.

'Then about the Single Attachment,' he went on lightly. 'Why, you were always taught its wickedness. Yet, see! And now we are both turned out of the Community on account of having fallen into this wickedness.' He stooped and kissed her hand, which he was still holding as if afraid she might turn and run back home. 'Why, Cicely, who could help falling into this snare—this pitfall—when one talked every day with you and sat beside you and looked into your sweet serious face? Your name should be Cecilia, not Cicely. Well, my dear, in this terrible Outside, Single Attachments are considered the most charming things possible, also the most laudable things; young men are encouraged to form them, girls try to attract them, everything in Outside is built upon the Single Attachment and on companionship. This, too, you shall learn.'

'Perhaps,' she replied. 'Must I forget everything?'

'Not everything, dear Cicely. You cannot forget your sweetness and your loveliness. But you may forget, as soon as you please, the rustics and boors of the House in which the Master is the only gentleman. I am sure that your father was an English gentleman, Cicely, because he has made the Master what he is, and you what you are. In speech, in manner and in mind, you are a gentlewoman. You are just returning with me to your own class, which is my class too. Perhaps we may even attach you, as the heralds say, to your own people. Perhaps you may turn out to be an heiress—who knows? A long-lost princess in your own right—who knows?'

'Indeed, Gilbert, I do not know. But I do not understand, in the least, what you mean by heralds and heiresses.'

'No, you are just exactly as ignorant as Eve herself when she, too, stepped into Outside and looked round about her. But you will soon learn.'

It was a hot walk in the noontide glare of the road; there was no shade, no pleasantness, as in our English country of hedge, of wayside turf and wayside flowers: an open road and a lonely road, not even frequented by tramps, from whom the House exacted hard work before it granted relief. Gilbert marched along, carrying the desk under his arm. Presently he found that he was walking too fast for his companion.

'I forgot,' he said. 'We have four miles in front of us. Are you tired already? Shall I walk on and bring you a carriage of some kind?'

'I am not tired, Gilbert. And oh! you must not leave me.'

'There is no vehicle to be got nearer than the town. Let us beguile the time with stories and confessions. Tell me what you remember of your father. Had he any profession?'

'He used to work in the garden. He knew all the flowers and the trees.'

'Yes. But had he any profession?'

'I don't know what you mean. We all have our work. And he was a gardener.'

'Do you know where he came from?'

'Oh yes. He came from England.'

'Did he ever tell you about his people—or your mother's people—who they were?'

'No. In the House we never talk about such things.'
'Was he—was he—like Brother Silas, for instance?'
'Like Brother Silas? Oh no! My father was a very quiet man, who lived retired and talked to no one but the Master and me. He could not talk like Silas and the rest. He talked like you. He was always patient, though the others tried him sometimes. He would never criticise any one except quite privately.'
'Did he never tell you anything about himself?'
'Sometimes he talked as if I was going back to Outside. He taught me to read in case I went Outside. He seemed afraid of something for me. Then he would meditate and talk with my mother and would come back soothed and comforted. He always wanted to die—which is just to pass into the next stage, you know. Now he is gone and is with my mother again, unless one of them goes higher still before the other. And I don't think that will happen.'
'Yet you were told that every soul is alone. So your father told you nothing about himself in the old home. Did he leave you nothing?'
'There is my mother's desk which you are carrying. There was nothing more.'
'Did he teach you to dance?'
'No, I learned that by myself. He used to play, and I used to dance in the Hall when I was a little child while he played. I have always danced for amusement and for soothing.'
'You learned to read, but you have no books; you no longer read—in fact, you never have read: you know only what your father taught you orally; you are a living example, my dear child, of what very little use reading is after all. You know, in fact, a great deal. You are an accomplished gardener: what a field is covered by that science alone! You can dance, and you can sing. You can hold intercourse with the world of the dead, which no one who can read ever succeeded in doing. You are a profound hypnotist,

though you do not know the meaning of the word You are as full of graces as any girl out of a fashionable school. You will make the men fall in love with you far more easily than any professional beauty——'

'Gilbert, I don't understand what you mean.'

'The road stretches out straight before us and the sun is strong, Cicely. That is enough for anybody to understand. Sunshine and a long road and our two selves on the road. Did you ever hear the story of the Fairy and the Princess? I will tell you, to beguile the way—the happy way. The Fairy was a kind-hearted creature; she took the Princess away when she was a baby, and she placed her in an island where no one ever came and the people lived quite by themselves. They were simple, rather silly people for the most part, and not too well bred; they held a very beautiful faith, much too good for them—namely, that by the simple process of getting outside their own bodies, they could rise to unheard-of heights. They forgot that the soul, like the body, must be constantly nourished and fed with thoughts and instruction. They did get outside the body, but they starved the soul, and so they never got any higher. But the Princess and the King of that island used to converse together, and in this way enriched and nourished their souls—so that they did really rise, and that Princess grew mentally taller, taller, taller, till she far outgrew all the rest. Then, because to stay longer among this lower and baser folk would have made this sweet Princess deteriorate, the Fairy sent a Prince to her, who said: "Come with me. I will take you back to the real world, which has great need of your Royal Highness." Then the Princess arose and took his hand, and they went out together.'

'And afterwards? Oh, Gilbert, nobody except you ever told me stories!'

'Afterwards, dear Cicely? Well, I think you shall finish the story by yourself. The road still stretches out far before us, and the sun is bright and warm. It warms one through and through. Love is the sun, and it can never be too bright and strong. Now tell me more.'

'I have told you enough about myself,' said Cicely. 'The more I tell you the more you turn it all to praise and flattery. You must not, Gilbert, unless you want to make me ashamed.'

'You have but to command,' he said. 'I will praise you no more, my dear; I will only look at you.'

They walked on in silence for a space. Presently Cicely spoke again.

'Where are you going, Gilbert?'

'We are going first to the town of Aldermanbury, which eats up all your fruit and vegetables. There, my child, as I told you, is staying at this moment, by a rare and blessed chance, my best and oldest friend. I had already promised to take you to see her. Now I shall ask her to receive you. She will be prepared to love you first because I love you—such a good and faithful friend she is. To-morrow, of course, she will have learned to love you for your own sweet sake.'

She pondered for a few moments over this announcement. Then she asked, timidly—'Have you a Single Attachment for her as you have for me, Gilbert?'

'No, Cicely. You do not understand, as yet, the full meaning of the Single Attachment. You will master that matter before long. There can only be one real Single Attachment for a man in his lifetime. However, this lady stands in the place of a sister to me. She is married, though her marriage was—well—not one of the happiest.'

'I have listened to some of the married members,' said Cicely. 'I have heard them criticising each other very plainly. I suppose they married in order to tell each other their faults. I shall never mind your criticising me, Gilbert, as much as you please.'

A thousand epigrams might be neatly turned in answer to this innocent speech. Gilbert refrained from even the most obvious. 'You shall criticise me, dear child

It shall be your duty. It shall be my privilege to listen. I want no end of criticising. We all do. It is the crying want of the age. In fact, before I met you, I was thinking of becoming a poet, in order to get plenty of this wholesome criticism.'

At this point he remembered suddenly, and very disagreeably, the duty that awaited him in a day or two. What right had he to make love, when he was bound to attempt the life of another man? His face fell; it became overcast; the light and sunshine went out of his eyes.

Cicely saw the change, and shuddered. 'Gilbert!' she cried, 'what has happened to you? Oh! you hurt me when you look like that. I thought it had gone— that look. Your soul has become black. Oh! Gilbert, have you forgotten—— What was it?' She stopped; she put up her hand; she lifted her face; for a moment —only a moment—life went out of it: she had gone to ask her mother for that message again. Then she came back to life. 'What must be done shall be done, but not by your hands,' she repeated solemnly. 'I know not what it is, Gilbert; but can you doubt my mother—my own mother?'

He inclined his head. 'I must try to assume that faith, Cicely, even though it sometimes fails me, otherwise I should be doubting you and the sender of that message. What manner of woman must she be, capable of giving such a daughter to the world?'

Apparently faith really did return for his support, for his face resumed its brightness.

'I *will* believe,' he said resolutely, 'though why I should, the Lord knows—but I *will* believe.'

They approached the city of Aldermanbury. The world grew larger. Here lived, collected together, but not united, thousands of human beings without the pale of the Community. The houses, scattered at first, and mean and squalid, grew closer together and cleaner of aspect, for the suburbs of Aldermanbury are not the best and worthiest part of the city. Then they came to the streets, with the shops and the electric cars and the trams and the people. And now Gilbert had to lead the girl by the arm ; for she was like one who has been blind and has suddenly recovered her sight, and sees men as trees walking, and knows not the things she sees, or their proportions, or their distances, or their dangers, or what they mean at all. He led her through the streets to the hotel, where the hall was filled with men sitting about and talking. He led her up the stairs to the first floor, and to a set of rooms furnished in a manner amazing to the child who had never seen any furniture worthy of the name ; and in a long, low chair, with a little boy in her lap, sat a lady whose appearance filled the girl with terror, by reason of her dress and her queenly look.

'Gilbert !' she cried. 'You have brought me Cicely ?' She rose and held out her hand. 'You are Cicely, my dear ?'

'I have brought her, Dorabyn. She has left the House with me. Will you receive her ?'

'Of course I will. You have left the House, Cicely ? Who are her guardians, Gilbert ?'

'She has no guardians, no property, no relations—nothing, except this desk.' He laid it on the table. 'That is her sole inheritance.'

'Oh ! And she is quite free to leave the place ? I suppose no one will dispute her right ?'

'Quite free. In fact, they have turned us out. Cicely was ordered to marry a rustic, a shepherd—a swain, love-sick for his Amaryllis—who devours pork and beans; and I was ordered to marry a milkmaid—not a "Hey Dolly! ho Dolly! Dolly shall be mine." Not that kind of Dolly at all—an inferior kind—a harder, more elderly, bonier kind. But—well—another time. That is the situation, Dorabyn. We've run away.'

'And you've brought her to me. Quite right, Gilbert. Will you stay with me, Cicely ?'

'If you please,' she replied, with a little hesitation. 'If—if—Gilbert does not go away.'

'He will stay too. This is my little boy—you will like to play with him. And——'

She suddenly realised the enormity of the dress, and cold shudders seized her. 'And, Gilbert,' she said, 'as there is a great deal to be done between this and the evening, you had better leave us by ourselves. Go away and return at half-past seven. In the meantime you might also get yourself apparelled in Christian guise. At present you look like a shabby gamekeeper.'

Gilbert retired.

Lady Osterley called her maid. 'Doughty,' she said, by way of explanation and apology, 'this is the peculiar dress of a religious House in which this young lady has been brought up. Now that she has left the House, she will leave the dress. We must take her in hand at once. Do the best you can. Let me have her decently dressed by the evening.'

The maid neither shivered nor shuddered nor uttered interjections. She reserved these for her next conversation with the nurse. She just lifted Cicely's hair, which ought to have fallen to her waist, and suggested dexterously a more becoming way of dressing it; then she surveyed curiously the figure or model before her. It presented, she observed, great possibilities. Then she put a pin between her lips. This is an emblematic ceremony among ladies' maids and dressmakers, and betokens strict attention to business.

CHAPTER XI.

MARRIAGE FOR ELEVATION.

THE Committee sat looking in each other's faces in silent confusion. Brother Silas, by the jerking of his arms and legs, showed that he was struggling for words; Sister Phœbe sat with rage equally unspeakable—the rage of the slighted woman—stamped upon her face. For the rest there was doubt as well as confusion. What was to be done? There was no Rule concerning mutiny and disobedience. Had Phœbe known of the alleged immuring of monk and nun, I think she would have proposed that the rebels should be brought back by force and immured, or, at least, put under the platform and there nailed up. Unfortunately, she knew neither ecclesiastical history nor ecclesiastical slanders.

Presently the Master spoke, but in a low voice, as if to himself. 'They will come back to us,' he said. 'My child cannot leave me thus. The matter concerns her soul. She will endure anything in that cause. So too will the young man, who is reasonable and intelligent.'

He lapsed into silence. They waited ten minutes. Yet the rebels returned not.

'I think,' said the Master again, 'that some one might go out and bid them return. Not you, Brother Silas, nor you, Sister Phœbe.'

'If they come back,' said Sister Phœbe, venomously, 'they must obey. They must be made to obey. Else there would be no use in having a Committee at all.'

'Go, Sister Euphemia,' said the Master. 'You will speak very kindly to them. Tell them that we will overlook their disobedience and reconsider the question of marriage.'

'Poor dears!' Sister Euphemia rose to obey. 'I shall find them crying together under the trees somewhere. They will come back, I dare say, if they are not to be forced into marriage horrible to them. Master, there's some things even you don't understand: one of them is that a woman would rather die than marry a man she doesn't like. I would myself; such were my feelings when I was young. You will have to do more than forgive them if they come back.'

'They shall be made to obey,' said Sister Phœbe again. 'First, they must obey. After that, I will take care of Brother Gilbert.' She looked, indeed, as if she would take the fondest, the most loving and tender care of him. 'As for the girl, she should be corrected first and handed over to a husband afterwards.'

The Master looked at her with much surprise. ''Tell them,' he said sternly, ' exactly what I have ordered you to tell them.'

Sister Euphemia vanished.

'There is, perhaps,' the Master continued slowly, ' something that I do not comprehend in the marriage tie, which may make it in some cases a help, rather than a hindrance. The Single Attachment, I understand, may hinder by demanding too much thought each for the other; perhaps, however, a marriage ordered by the Committee may hinder by reason of discontent, or resentment, or even'—he looked at rustical Silas and remembered the dainty delicateness of his child—' even of positive repulsion. My experience in such matters is slender.'

'Let them obey,' said Sister Phœbe, while Silas jerked himself into convulsions.

Five minutes later, Sister Euphemia returned. 'I looked for them,' she said, a little breathless, ' under the trees; they were not there: one of the gardeners saw them walking away along the road.' She resumed her place and began to cry. 'They have left us,' she said. 'Oh! they have left us. We have lost them. They have gone Outside. And that tender lamb who has never seen anything and knows nothing!' She wiped her eyes and turned venomously to Sister Phœbe. 'And now,' she snapped, 'I hope you are all satisfied with your morning's work!'

'Send some one after them,' said Phœbe, springing to her feet. 'Let three or four of the brothers run after them and bring them back. That girl has bewitched him. Oh! I have seen her. I have watched her tricks. If she'd lived all her life Outside, she couldn't have been more artful. Silas, if you've the spirit of a sheep left in you, get up and fight this man for your girl.

Coward! get up and take a stick and bring him back again. You—an American—afraid of an Englishman! Shame! Or bring the girl. He'll follow then. He'll follow wherever she goes. Get up, Silas. Coward! Log! Oh! you've got no spirit left at all. You want to marry this girl, and you let another man carry her off! Coward! Shall I go myself with a stick after them?'

'Gracious!' cried Sister Euphemia. 'I thought the Committee were to countenance no Single Attachments. And here is Sister Phœbe appealing to Silas's Single Attachment for that dear child. I've seen him, too. I've watched, too, for months to see it growing and growing. And I've watched another thing, too.' She nodded viciously at Sister Phœbe, who now sat down and panted. 'Oh yes, another thing, which I shall tell in good time.'

'Let no one stir,' said the Master. 'We welcome all who come and are willing to work with us and learn to meditate—we keep none against their will. Our dear young Sister Cicely has been with us all her life; she has never known any other kind of life; I fear she will be strange and unhappy. Outside has many dangers for innocent girls. I always hoped that she would never leave us. I thought that she was happy and desired nothing—I never suspected this Single Attachment.'

'What does every girl desire?' asked Sister Euphemia. 'Cicely wanted love without knowing what she wanted. The same want made me unhappy enough, Lord knows! She got what she wanted, and you tried to take it away. She wanted love, and you offered her—THAT!'

She did not say what, but she pointed to the bridegroom elect.

'If she chooses,' the Master continued, hanging his head sorrowfully, 'she must—leave us—leave us.'

The Committee respected the Master's grief, and were silent. But Phœbe, perhaps with excess of sympathy, perhaps still agitated by the jealousy of the despised woman, snorted and choked.

Presently the Master lifted his head again and spoke. 'Perhaps I was wrong,' he said, 'to think of marrying this child at all. She was happy in the love of the young man. Perhaps it would have been a help instead of a hindrance. They might have gone on loving each other as brother and sister. Her sainted mother found marriage a help. There are great possibilities in that young man——'

'Ruined by his infatuation,' said Sister Phœbe.

'Brother and sister!' Sister Euphemia, the experienced, scoffed. 'Much you know about it, Master!'

'I shall leave it to her mother. This night I shall converse with her as usual. I shall ask for her guidance —perhaps for her rebuke. Yes'—his face cleared; he became hopeful—'I shall leave it with her. She has been—I know not why, much occupied of late with the concerns of the House. I shall put the matter entirely in her hands—the safety and the well-being of her daughter. She will tell me what to do.'

'Cicely wants love,' Sister Euphemia repeated. 'It is not safe with some natures—gentle, delicate natures—to rob them of love. That was done to me—and I have been here twenty years in consequence. Your method, Master, of preventing Single Attachments by regulated marriages may be very good for coarse and common souls; but not for girls like Cicely and me.'

'If she comes back she must obey the Committee,' said Phœbe, still jealous for order. 'Are we to have no authority in such a matter as this, simply because the Master talks with this rebellious girl's mother? The Committee have ordered the girl to marry Brother Silas and the man to marry me. If she comes back the Committee must be obeyed.'

The Master looked up again in surprised disapproval. It was the first time in the history of the Community that any claim to power had been put forward by a member of Committee. Was he not the founder and the prophet and the dictator of the Community?'

'I shall wait,' he said, assuming authority. 'I shall decide after consultation with her mother what shall be done.'

He looked round him. No one replied. 'Let us now,' he continued, 'proceed to the business of the day. We have next to consider the case of the man Charles Lee. I do not ask you to criticise this brother, because criticism in his case would be idle. If a man desires to become a member of this House, the way is plain. He must first of all conform to our Rule. This man came to us six or seven weeks ago. He understood the plain Rule of the House. He desired, he said, above all things, Elevation; he professed readiness to forget the Past—in his case, I fear, a Past of wickedness; he said he was willing to work for the subjugation, the health, and the fatigue of the body; also for the maintenance of the Community; he promised to meditate daily, or, at least, to endeavour after Meditation. These,' continued the Master, 'were his promises. His manners were those of an English aristocrat I confess that I was pleased to find our simple Community attracting a man of that position willing to forget the Past. Mostly, like the Apostles, we have been a simple folk. He came, therefore, as you know. He has been among us about six or seven weeks. How has he carried out these promises? He chose the garden for his work, but he has never done a stroke of real work: he only pretends; he sits about in the shade; he has no intercourse with the Community; he despises our simple, yet plentiful, meals; he does not even make an attempt at Meditation; on the contrary, he gets up and goes out. Where does he go? I was informed when in Aldermanbury last week that one of our members is seen nightly at a certain saloon where they play cards for money and drink whisky. What are we to do with such a man?'

'Expel him,' said the Committee, with the unanimity of the stage. In fact, Brother Charles was cordially hated by everyone in the place.

'If there were any hope I would bear with him. But there seems none: his heart is hard; his spirit is black and gloomy; he belongs to the Devil, not to us.'

'Expel him,' cried the Committee again.

'It is a standing mockery of our Endeavours after the Higher Life. How can we, with our aims, entertain among us one who still wallows in Outside? Let us, then, without criticism, which would be lost upon such a man, call him before us and order him to leave the House—say on Saturday.'

All assented except Sister Phœbe, still mutinous. 'I should like,' she said, 'to let him know our individual opinions. What is the good of a Committee if we are to have no voice in anything?'

'Brother Silas'—the Master paid no attention to this interruption—'bring Charles Lee before us.'

The offending brother appeared and stood at the bottom of the table. Nothing more incongruous was ever seen in any court of justice than the trial or the judgment of this man—so calm, so lofty in appearance, so completely contemptuous of the court was the prisoner; so simple, so rustic, was the appearance of the judges. He slightly bowed and waited.

'Charles Lee,' said the Master, 'when you came to us, you told me that your simple desire in entering this Community was to endeavour after Elevation. I believed your statement; it was manifest from your appearance and your atmosphere that spiritually you were very low down indeed; you carried about with you, in fact, the atmosphere of a lower world; it is such an atmosphere as was anciently described, for lack of a better word, as sulphurous. I admitted you, subject to the simple Rules of the House. Let me remind you of them. They were three in number. First, that all must work; next, that the Past is to be entirely set aside and forgotten; thirdly, that all must aim at rising to a higher level by Meditation. You promised to obey these three Rules.'

Mr. Charles Lee inclined his head.

'You have now been with us for seven weeks. I am willing to make great allowance for difficulties at the outset, but I expect——'

'The Committee expects,' interrupted Phœbe, stung into self-assertion.

'I expect, I say, to find an honest attempt at carrying out the Rules. It is now quite certain that you have made no such attempt, and that you do not intend to make any such attempt. You have done no work since you came; you have not earned one farthing for the House; you have made no attempt to raise yourself. About you still clings—I perceive it plainly—the sulphurous atmosphere of your level. Your soul is black through and through. I can see no single gleam of light in it to show a better purpose. As for meditating, you have not even begun to understand what it means. You spend your evenings in the world, in places where they play cards and drink whisky—places called saloons and dives. I have to tell you, therefore, that we cannot allow you to remain in this House. It is now Thursday: you can stay here, if you have arrangements to make, until Saturday. On that day we shall lock up your room and you will no longer be allowed in the Hall. Do you understand?'

The man bowed his head slightly, without the least change of countenance. Then he looked round the Committee as if expecting a few remarks from them.

'I have observed in this brother,' said Sister Phœbe, 'a pride intolerable. They say that in his own country he is a British nobleman; this is not the place for the superior airs of that profligate class. Let him go back to his own people.'

'You can depart,' said the Master.

Mr. Charles Lee bowed again, but continued to wait.

'He finds fault with the food—as good food as ever was placed before people,' another member interposed—

the man with the rasping voice. 'He sits at table as if the rest of us were mud beneath his feet.'

'You can depart,' said the Master. But the man called Charles Lee inclined his head to the last speaker, and turned again to Sister Phœbe, who showed further intentions.

'He should never have been admitted,' she said, 'without inquiry. Why did he come here? What has he done? It isn't for Elevation that he comes here. What has he done? Is the Community to be the refuge of the broken-down British aristocracy? Let them go and dump their vices and their pride somewhere else.'

'Be so good, sir, as to withdraw immediately,' said the Master.

Mr. Charles Lee inclined his head and walked out. The blow was unexpected, and it was fatal. There was but one chance left—to remain quiet, unsuspected in this place unsuspecting. And now this chance was gone. Yet he showed no emotion whatever. With just such an air, with such a smile, with such contempt, did the Marquis de la Vieille Roche receive sentence of death by guillotine from the Revolutionary Tribunal: a sentence that would not be carried out because outside the mob waited for the prisoners, roaring and shouting and singing for more blood—more blood; the mob who were to murder him, out of hand. With just such an air, I say, so cold, so calm, so unmoved, this man walked down the Hall and out of the porch. For that raging mob substitute the whole police force of the United States, all provided with an accurate description and a portrait of him; and his appearance was unmistakable—he had never endeavoured to disguise himself at all. For the roars and shouting of the maddened mob of Paris substitute the calm, cold voice of many-handed Justice, saying, 'Come, thou man of blood and destruction, I will have life for life.'

'The atmosphere is more fragrant,' said the Master,

sniffing. 'The presence of that man was like the breathing of the air in the worlds below. How low, I know not. He is not one of those who simply fails to rise: he has fallen, his former pride remains; there are those—above—who would help him if they could. I think they knew him formerly. What say they? That he was a British nobleman? I know not. When I lived at home I knew nothing of noblemen. Well—he is gone. I think he will remain in this world very little longer. They are mostly taken away when they prove to be hardened against everything.'

He paused and looked round the table.

'One duty remains,' he said, with something of a smile in the corners of his eyes, but that might be the observer's fancy. 'One duty. Not in itself a painful duty, but a necessary duty. I have to bring back to a sense of their position two of our own body—to rescue them from a grievous temptation. Brothers and sisters, we must proceed to criticise Sister Phœbe.'

Sister Phœbe jumped in her place; she opened her mouth; she shut it again; she folded her hands; she sat bolt upright.

'I have observed,' the Master continued, 'certain passages—or indications—in our justly—hitherto justly —respected sister which make me uneasy. They lead me to believe that her thoughts of late have been much occupied with things which do not become one of her advanced profession. Especially have I observed in her a weakness—let us call it a weakness, not a moral or a spiritual fall—which may be criticised. In a word, the same weakness which we have deplored in our two members who have rebelled—a Single Attachment.'

'I too,' said Sister Euphemia quickly, 'have observed this Single Attachment. It began when Brother Gilbert first came among us. She sat nearly opposite him at meals. I observed how she put chops and kidneys before him, because he won't eat pork and beans, which Brother Silas would eat all day long if he could.'

'And all night,' said Brother Silas readily, and not ashamed. 'And between meals.'

'She makes tea cakes for him in the kitchen—much better tea cakes than the rest of us get. She makes coffee on purpose for him, because he won't drink the muddy coffee that is good enough for us.'

'Oh! oh!' murmured three or four.

'And she makes tea for him in a special teapot—the best Oolong, because he doesn't like our strong family Ceylon. And she waylays him in the verandah, and follows him about with her eyes. And she's just spiteful about Cicely, whom the boy loves. Oh! and I've heard her, myself, tell him the kind of man she should like to marry, just describing himself. Oh! it's too bare-faced. And then for her to sit up and criticise that poor dear child because her nature told her that if she wanted Elevation she must get it through Love!'

Sister Phœbe sat bolt upright, with folded arms. She turned her head, but made no reply to these charges.

'I am not alone, then,' said the Master, 'in the painful suspicion that was awakened in me by her evident desire to marry Brother Gilbert. Yet I was considering that brother's case, and did not, till afterwards, understand what this eagerness might mean. Your own case, Sister Phœbe, must be seriously taken in hand.'

'It must be cured,' said Sister Euphemia, 'if we are ever to get that dear boy back again, or that sweet child.'

'I now leave, for a moment, our Sister Phœbe, and turn,' the Master continued, 'to Brother Silas.' The brother turned as red as one of his own turkeys. 'The eagerness which he displayed, in offering to cure Cicely of her Single Attachment by marrying her himself, should have opened my eyes to the fact that he is himself a young man and likely to be carried away by the loveliness of a woman.'

'And such loveliness, too!' said Sister Euphemia, again bursting in. 'You are quite right, dear Master. I've

seen it for months past. I know the signs. His
shoulder lurches when he passes her: his eyes turn after
her and follow her; he gets red when Gilbert talks to
her; he hates Gilbert——'

'He's an Englishman,' Silas explained.

'It's disgraceful ignorance to hate the poor man for
what he can't help. You might as well hate a man
because he's got a hump on his back. You hate him
because Cicely doesn't—that's your reason; and because
you can't please her fancy and he can. Pretty reasons,
all of them, for a member of this Community to nourish
in his soul! Where are you in Meditation? Going
down, Brother Silas, going down. I haven't met you,
up above, not for months.'

The Master resumed. 'Brother Silas, you are a good
worker; you obey the Rule of the House faithfully;
you stand very high in our esteem; you meditate
regularly and, I hope, profitably. It has been, however,
I doubt not, most injurious to your Elevation to be
always thinking about this young girl. It would have
been still more injurious in the years to come were you
hampered with a wife of whom you would be always
thinking, and concerning whom you would be always
anxious. I do not, Brother Silas, greatly blame you in
this matter. The girl has been to me as a daughter: I
doubt not that to you it has become, for the time, impossible for her to be as a sister. This must be seen to,
in your own interests.'

Brother Silas listened guiltily. He was, as you know,
one of the inarticulate. Every speech, however short,
troubled him. As has been seen, he had fallen so completely into the habit of silence that he was not only
unready but almost incapable of conversation. For the
moment, he could think of no reply whatever. Nor,
indeed, has he yet, after many months, been able to
think of a reply which would have been suitable. It
was quite true, you see, that he had, in an instinctive,
taurine fashion, entertained an amorous disposition

towards Cicely; and, also in an instinctive, taurine fashion, entertained a profound jealousy of Gilbert. But he made no reply.

'All earthly passions, brother,' said the Master, with the cheerfulness of one who at seventy-five has long since left these things behind him, 'all earthly passions, and especially Single Attachments, must here be cast aside: we rise alone; we must have no such distractions to turn us back, no such earthly affections to pull us down. Forget these distractions, Brother Silas. Forget them, Sister Phœbe. Cast them aside, as part of the forgotten Past, and press on, alone.

'But,' he added, after a pause, 'it must be remembered that these two have shown themselves peculiarly open to the temptation of the Single Attachment. My brothers and sisters, many of our Community are still in the age which feels this temptation. It is a most insidious temptation; it takes all kinds of forms; it suggests all kinds of excuses: we call it the worship of an ideal, but we ought to have no other ideal but a Perfect Self; we call it the sacrifice of self, but we do this when we work for each other, not when we fall in love, as it is called Outside: we call it the defence of the helpless—we defend the helpless here. The temptation presents itself, I say, in a thousand forms: behind the mask there stands the demon of self-gratification. We must guard against the Single Attachment. On account of this temptation we have just lost—I hope for a season only—a desirable brother and my own spiritual daughter. Let us lose no more. Above all, let the Committee set an example to the Community and show the members how to overcome their weakness. For which reason we will remove from the Committee, for the present, Sister Phœbe and Brother Silas.'

He looked around. They all murmured assent, except Sister Phœbe herself, whose cheek was flushed and whose hands trembled. They murmured assent. How easy it is for a committee, or for a chapter, to assent to the discipline of an erring brother or a sinful sister! Thus readily did the monks of Westminster assent to the discipline of a brother.

'The only way open to us,' the Master went on, 'is to make, for these two, Single Attachments henceforward impossible. I take it for granted that Brother Silas has no such feeling towards Sister Phœbe, nor she to him. If Brother Gilbert was Sister Phœbe's ideal husband it would be difficult to find any one more unlike that dream than Brother Silas. And certainly, in the appearance or the character of Sister Phœbe, Silas will never be reminded of Cicely. They shall be married, therefore, and that without the least delay, lest a worse thing happen to them.'

The bride and bridegroom elect looked at each other. Aversion and disgust were in their faces. Yes; they would certainly be cured for ever of any leaning towards the Single Attachment.

'Do you obey my ruling in this matter, Brother Silas?' the Master asked. 'If you do not, the doors are open for you, as for our late Brother Charles. You can leave the House and go away.'

Brother Silas grunted something meant for assent. Whither could he go? Where else could he find such a Home, with three square meals every day and the management of a farm fully provided with machinery and buildings and stock? Alas! there was no other place for him. He looked at his bride with eyes of disgust and loathing. He grunted huskily his acceptance of the terms, and hung his head.

'It is well,' said the Master. 'There will be no attachment to draw your thoughts out of yourself, Brother Silas. You will begin to ascend again. I hope that we may meet in higher worlds before long.'

He turned to the bride elect. 'Sister Phœbe, do you accept?'

She, too, reflected on the consequence of refusal. After eight years her place among her own people was filled up. She knew not even what had become of them. The New England farmers move West for the most part; 'West' is a very vague word, almost as vague and vast and uncertain as 'Outside.' Where would she get so many comforts and such little work and the care of so lovely a dairy? Nowhere. Life with Silas for a companion would be terrible, but not so terrible as starvation. With dry lips and burning cheeks she murmured her consent.

'You do well to obey,' said the Master, with more severity than the brethren generally observed in his manner. Then he began again to preach, and his voice rolled like music as he spoke. 'In the married state, Sister Phœbe, you will probably learn more than mere obedience to the Community. In obedience to your husband you will find a powerful assistance in subduing the rebellious spirit which we have of late observed in you. Be a good wife, and you will doubtless before long regain the levels which you have clearly lost. My dear friends'—the Master rose—'we have this day had a meeting, the like of which, for excitement and rebellion, I never remember since we first began. I trust it will not interfere too much with Meditation. The work of the Committee is completed.'

The Master walked away.

The Committee rose as well and slowly dissolved without speaking to the bridal pair. There were left at last only the bride, the bridegroom, and Sister Euphemia.

'I congratulate you both,' said Euphemia, with a cheerful brow. 'This is a joyful wedding ; a happy wedding; a most beautiful wedding. Oh, what a thing it is to have a wedding without an atom of love in it ! What a beautiful thing it is for bride and bridegroom to hate even looking at each other ! No nasty love to keep you on the earth when you ought to be soaring high in the heavens; no kissing and billing and cooing ; no interference of pretty things to do and say and think about for each other. My dear children, I've been in love myself. I know what Single Attachments mean. Oh, dear me! I know. And how they want always to be together—dragging each other down. But as for you—you—you! Why, the higher you fly upwards, both of you, the farther off from each other you'll get!—one more reason for getting as high up as you possibly can. Ah! what a beautiful thing is marriage in this House!'

The happy pair looked at each other guiltily, but they made no reply.

'Now, there's Gilbert, the best boy I ever saw and the handsomest: he's gone off with Cicely—the best and sweetest girl in the whole world—with Cicely. And he'll be in love with her all his life. Very likely there'll be children——'

'Don't be undelicate,' said Brother Silas, colouring.

'Children; and he'll love them, too. And so he'll stay in this very identical level world—the world that is—all his life, and he won't desire any better world, till death parts him and her. Poor Gilbert! poor lost Cicely! while as for you——' she chirruped, and ran out of the Hall.

Left alone, the man turned away his head and held out his hand.

'Phœbe!' he said.

She turned away her head as well, but gave him her hand.

'Silas!' she murmured.

And so they were man and wife, and all temptation to Single Attachments was removed once for all.

And this proves that sometimes the most solemn and serious of men will do the most humorous things.

CHAPTER XII.

REVOLUTION.

THE expulsion of a brother from the Monastery was an event so remarkable that one might imagine that it would be the subject of abiding comment. Brother

Charles was criticised; Brother Charles was ordered to depart on or before Saturday. As you will presently learn, he did depart. Yet, if you ask the Community about him now, you will find that the event and the man are both forgotten. If the erring brother is remembered at all it is on account of his very remarkable and aristocratic appearance—accounted for by the tradition of the British nobleman forced to leave his native country on account of profligacy. The reason of this speedy oblivion was that there followed upon his expulsion a series of epoch-making events.

What happened was nothing short of Revolution.

By those who delight in searching out the hidden causes of things it is always averred that the real originator of the rebellion was none other than Gilbert Maryon. For, they say, when that brother arrived, the House was fast drifting into an unquestioning spirit—a simple vacuity of mind—which would seem to be the frame most to be desired by those who meditate continually. If you neither talk, nor read, nor think, nor desire, nor hope, nor fear, vacuity is the result. In this most desirable frame of mind, Meditation is always possible, at any time of day or night—and if people believe that in Meditation they achieve heights and raptures of which they remember nothing when they return, then, of course, Meditation is the most desirable of all conditions, and therefore *à priori*, vacuity; and therefore—it is like a proposition in Euclid—total abstinence from all disturbing causes of every kind. To be sure, had the House gone too far in that respect, no one would have been able to do any work, and so they would all starve either into death or activity; in either case they would lose the power of Meditation; they would have to climb down. In other words, the logical end and result of the cultivation of trance would be clearly a choice between starvation or a return to earthly laws— which means work in return for food. The Master recognised this alternative when he enjoined daily work;

but he had not foreseen the danger of mental vacuity—which would render work impossible.

Gilbert startled them into wakefulness; he disturbed them; he broke the Rule about frivolous talk, and talked with all of them who were still capable of speech. He talked during Fatigue; during Recreation; during Restoration. He was curious about their reasons for joining the Community; he wanted to know why they had left Outside; he revived the Past, which many of them would willingly have seen buried and done with, and all had agreed to forget if they could. He wanted also to know what they remembered about Meditation.

Everybody knows that whenever two or three are gathered together with the avowed intention of seeing what nobody else can see, of hearing voices which nobody else can hear, and of receiving communications which advance nobody, there is an irresistible temptation to 'go one better.' Everyone wishes to be thought more richly endowed with spookishness than his neighbours. Hence whispers, mystery, affectation, and pretensions. It was admitted by all that the greatest achievements were those of the Master, who, as a true visionary, gave himself no airs at all. Now, by the simple process of cross-examination, Gilbert arrived at the discovery that nobody, except the Master and Cicely, ever remembered what they saw in Meditation. In sleep one sometimes gets dreams; there is some reason in going to sleep; in Meditation no one gets anything except oblivion for an hour.

Gilbert made this discovery public. That is to say, he communicated it to every one who still preserved the power of speech and thought. And it made them uneasy. Their pride was hurt—their pride in themselves, and their pride in each other. Those who pretended, and had succeeded in deceiving themselves, were angry and out of conceit with the whole business; those who were modest, and only hoped to arrive, some time or other, at the Elevation claimed by others, had their hopes dashed to the ground, on hearing that there was no proof of Elevation or Higher Plains. What is the use of soaring to the peaks of the Himalayas where dwell those philosophers whose wisdom compared with our wisdom is reported to be as Lombard Street compared with a China orange, if one remembers nothing on returning? These things, and such things as these, were whispered about. Except for the most vacuous, who could do no more than eat, drink, sleep, and meditate, the peace of the House was disturbed; an agitation went on below the surface; the members began to talk again, and with animation.

Then fell upon them suddenly the news of the morning's work. Everything was known. Sister Euphemia, indignant with the Committee, yet delighted with the discomfiture of the pair who had brought about the mischief, ran about and told everybody. Brother Gilbert and Sister Cicely had been criticised for entertaining a Single Attachment to the danger of their Elevation; they had been ordered to marry where they could not be expected to entertain any kind of Single Attachment; they had rebelled; Brother Gilbert had boldly carried off the girl, and they were now launched into Outside—an awful, perilous position for a pair so young and so singly attached. What terrible thing would happen to them? For they had all become like children in their dread of the Unknown and the Wild.

'Nothing,' said Sister Euphemia gloomily. 'That is, nothing bad will happen to *them*. The bad things will happen to us. For they are gone; they will never come back to us again. Love will make them too happy. Do you think that I should have come here twenty years ago if Love had made me as happy as I hoped? Certainly not. We may meditate, and rise to Heights—though nobody remembers anything about it—but we can't be happy without Love. No; it isn't in nature.'

'Happiness is not to be desired,' replied another

sister. 'There is nothing to be desired but Elevation. We all know that.'

'The question is how to get it,' said Sister Euphemia. 'The more I think about it, which is all day long, the more I feel that I'd rather get it through Love than through Meditation. At all events, that way you see what you've got. By Meditation you don't see anything, and so you don't know what you've got when you have got it!'

And then they heard that Sister Phœbe, that most rigid observer of the Rule, the first at Meditation, the first at Fatigue, the austere, the uncompromising, the manager of the Dairy, had been also criticised; and with her, Brother Silas, Silas the Silent, the champion Meditator, Silas, the Director of the Farm. Criticised! These two! If such things could be done to the chief among them, what might be done to the least? And these two, who had been willing to sacrifice their own inclinations for the good of others even so far as to marry the two rebels, had been actually ordered to marry each other!

All these things together caused a condition of restless excitement which spread from one to the other, and loosened tongues, and caused eager discussion. Yet there were some unmoved by these, or any other events, who sat apart in silent vacuity, with empty brains, happy, if that can be called happiness where there is nothing left but bodily pain and the physical satisfaction of food. These, his disciples, were to the Master a continual source of satisfaction: he thought that they were uplifted, even to the severance of soul and body; he thought they were soaring, like himself, upwards to other worlds peopled by men and women advanced to wisdom unattainable here and to enjoyment inconceivable. And all without the least aids of instruction, exhortation, reading, prayer, or praise, such as in every other religion have always been found necessary. Think, if you can, of the glorious conditions of that country in which, as in this House, the material wants of every man should be secured for him without any anxiety or trouble on his own part. Think, if you can, of the splendid spirit of enterprise which would grow up among a people who had already all that they desired. Think, if you can, of a community cut off from the outside world, forbidden to read, forbidden to speak except of things necessary, deprived of aims and ambitions.

They were not all reduced to the condition naturally resulting from these rules; many were still open to reason and to observation. With these the whispers grew into murmurs; the murmurs swelled; the verandah was crowded with fifty or sixty members, all talking at once and all talking loudly.

Then rang the supper bell, loud and discordant. They stopped talking, and all together as usual trooped into the Hall.

Sister Phœbe and Brother Silas occupied their customary places opposite each other; the bride's face was red and angry, the bridegroom's sullen and resentful. Brother Charles—he whom the Committee had ordered to leave the House—occupied his own place, taking his food in his usual cold and gloomy silence. The places of Brother Gilbert and Sister Cicely were empty—it was true, then, they had fled. In his chair sat the Master, but with hanging head and heavy looks; everybody knew that Cicely was to the old man as a daughter. Yet he had driven her away; so admirable was his faith in his own teaching. No one, to be sure, has ever heard of a crank who shrank from acting, even to his own injury and unhappiness, up to his own crankiness; and if the members of a crank's own household should refuse obedience, belief, and conformity, what must happen to them? The answer to this question is perfectly well understood by every woman who has a father or a husband in the tents of Crankiness. Wherefore, if women, instead of men, had framed the Liturgy, they would have added a special clause for protection against the crank; and above all against the religious crank.

Cicely was gone; the Master had himself driven her out; and now he sat in mourning which would last his life through, and beyond.

There was more than simple mourning in the Master's mind. He had lost the child. That was much. But he could not, as usual, send forth his soul into the unseen world for sweet commune with the child's mother; his spirit was heavy as lead within him; perhaps, he thought, the mother was angry with him. Had she not always loved her own husband, that pure and spotless saint? Yet he had acted on his own teaching, and in the spiritual interests of the child. Would the mother desert him? If he was to be deprived both of his spiritual sister and his spiritual daughter, what would become of him?

You have heard of the music with which, during supper, their souls were lifted up. The piano was played for them by a German, the only musician in the House. This evening the piano was closed. The musician took his place at the tables.

'No,' he said, with tears in his eyes, 'I cannot play no more. The little girl'—he called her 'Ze leedle curl,' but we must make allowance for emotion—'she has gone away. For five years have I played to make her dance when you have done what you call your dance—your crawl'—he called it 'grawl,' which one writes down, not in foolish ridicule, but because it really seems a word which very well describes the uncouth dance or shuffle of the members. It was not a crawl so much as a 'grawl.' 'For five years, to be rewarded every evening with her lovely dance at the end. Her dance was my joy. When she stopped I could feel my soul flying right out of my head and going up—right up, going up high—so high, that I don't know nosings where I am. No. I play no more. The little girl is gone.'

So he sat down, and began to drink coffee with as much avidity as if it had been Vienna beer.

They knew not what he meant by the little girl's dancing. They never saw her dance. Nobody had ever seen her dance. Their one walk-round, or double shuffle, or 'grawl,' that many of them performed for soothing purposes every night before going off, they knew, of course. But what did he mean by the joy of seeing the little girl dance? However, they sat down, and in unwonted excitement they broke the bread of the evening meal.

When supper was finished, the Englishman known as Brother Charles rose and went out, as he had done every evening since his arrival. The others assumed their usual position; leaning their backs against the table, with feet outstretched, with hands folded, and their heads leaning slightly down. Some of them—those who have been indicated as the most advanced in vacuity—went off instantly. Of the rest it was noticed that the Master was restless; as a rule he lost no time in getting his soul under weigh; this evening he fidgeted and changed his position; he crossed his legs, he laid his hand on the table, he supported his head on the other hand, he kept his eyes closed; but it was obvious to all that he was neither asleep nor in Meditation. Sister Phœbe and Brother Silas, in general most zealous in Meditation, were equally restless; and at least half the members fidgeted in their places, getting no nearer the point of absorption. Some of them, without the aid of the music, tried their shuffling dance, but it proved powerless to soothe anyone. In a word, for the first time the Community were unable to meditate; they remained wide awake; they became only more wide awake the longer they sat there.

Then Sister Euphemia arose and spoke. She made a great speech.

'Brothers and sisters,' she said, 'a very terrible and cruel thing has been done in the House this day.'

Sister Phœbe groaned. 'I mean to say what I think. Those of us who have gone off won't hear; those of us who can't go off may say what they please. I don't care what they say. A cruel thing it was. I was on the Committee, but I couldn't help it. They took Cicely, that sweet child, the only pretty thing in the House, and they took Gilbert, the only man in the place who's awake and real, and they drove them into rebellion. They've run away together. Will they come back again? I don't think so.'

Nobody answered her. She went on with what turned out to be a long sermon.

'Brothers and sisters, we're a frumpy lot. There's nothing interesting about any of us except those two. We pretend to forget our Past—we shut our eyes and pretend that it isn't there. Most of us have got a dismal Past—I have, for one—I've pretended to forget it for twenty years. But Gilbert showed me that I hadn't. A bad Past—some of us have got. But those two haven't got any Past at all. Some said that Gilbert was a British lord, and therefore a profligate. He isn't. He's only a well-behaved young gentleman, and he loves the girl, down to the very ground she walks upon.

'I've seen it growing with both of them. I've sat under the trees with my knitting, and watched them, timid and shy, and trying to explain. Oh! as if I didn't know what it means! As if I could ever forget the Past! It made me so happy that I can't tell you, only to look on, till I saw that they understood each other at last. And then they were criticised. Sakes alive! What for?

'They told the girl—that delicate, dainty flower—that she was to marry a man who's little better than a stable boy: his place is in the farmyard among the pigs and the straw—look at him! And they told the young man, who's just as sensitive as any lady, that he was to marry a woman ten years older than himself, with no more feelings than the cheese-press and no more manners than a dairymaid—look at her! So they've run away. And what those two poor lambs will do out in the wide world the good Lord only knows!

'They loved each other,' she went on, growing more eloquent. 'Oh! why did I come here out of the world? It was to forget the misery of lost love. Why did they run away? To escape the misery of lost love. What does the Committee know of love? Nothing. What does the Master know of love? Nothing. He tells us to avoid Single Attachments. I've been here twenty years, I'm the oldest member next to the Master, and I've never seen one person advanced an inch by keeping out of Single Attachments—not one inch. Only here and there a saint like the Master comes out perhaps—I don't know for sure—the stronger for being alone all the time. And even he, if you come to think of it, loved the girl. I've been looking on for twenty years. I've never spoken before, because I wanted to forget the Past, and all that I had to say depended on my own past experience. But I will say it now, if it's only just for once. I look round, I say, and I see that we are all of us, all together, except the Master, growing selfish more and more. The Master says we stand every one alone. So we do, I dare say, but we stand in a crowd as well, and we ought to help each other all we can, and to lean on each other, and to think more about each other than about ourselves. There is no support or encouragement to be got here from anybody: we are looking out, every one for himself. We are like pigs feeding in a trough, each helping himself; we have no thought, nor pity, nor care for any one but ourselves. Oh! my friends, this is the end of our beautiful community!

'Why, when Gilbert came — bless him!—we had almost through long silence lost the power of speech altogether. We had left off asking how it fared with the Soul. We were dropping into a deadly, dismal, selfish silence. Was that what we came here for?

'What do we see when we go off in Meditation?

Eh! I ask any of you what do we see? I have been here twenty years—all the time mistaking forgetfulness for Elevation—every evening I make that mistake—same as all of us. I don't want that any more. I want to remember, not to forget. What do we get out of Meditation but forgetfulness? Does anybody get anything else? Does any one,' she repeated earnestly—'any one in this room—any one who's awake and can answer—get anything else? Does any one remember anything that he saw, or heard, or felt in Meditation?'

'I remember,' said the musician, 'a little girl and a lovely dance. And now she's gone.'

'Hold up hands all of you who remember anything of last night's Meditation.'

Not a hand was held up.

'Why?' she asked triumphantly, feeling her own strength. 'Meditation is a lovely thing. The Master is carried up to the Heavens in Meditation. When he comes back, he remembers. Why do we remember nothing? Because we have been going down—down—down—getting more and more selfish, more silent, each for himself more and more. That is why.'

The company murmured. Then one of them, one of the younger women, yet a woman of thirty or so, rose and spoke in her turn.

'What Sister Euphemia says is true. I remember nothing—I have got nothing out of Meditation. But this is a Home to me, and there is no other Home in all the world except this—for me. I cannot forget the Past, because I know that if I go back again there is not one of all the people—the people—the dear people who loved me once——' her voice broke down—' who would take me in and love me again. I couldn't dare ask it.' She sat down and covered her face.

'Poor dear!' said Euphemia. 'She cannot forget the Past: can any one among us forget the Past?

'What are we to do, then?

'We must become brothers and sisters in reality.

We must love each other as much as we can. We must work for each other and help each other. We must make the younger members marry for love; we must have children among us; we must make our lives happier. Oh! I see a thousand ways. Leave it to me. You men, leave it to the sisters: they are brighter than you because they talk more. And you women, to-morrow we will talk.'

Then the musician arose and walked solemnly to the piano, which he opened with the air of an officiating clergyman. He looked round, and he said, 'Let us sing.'

He played a German folk-song, and began to sing it himself in a full powerful baritone. The Community had never before heard any singing, except the light voice of Cicely at her work. They listened. They knew no words; presently they began to join in one by one. At last they were all singing—a song literally without words; high up in the astonished rafters rolled and rang the voices of those who sang, one with another. There was no longer the least desire for Meditation; the vacuous expression went out of their faces; life and light returned.

The singing was at its height when the Master, who had not been meditating, but was absorbed in gloomy reflection and forebodings, became aware of something unusual. He looked round him, rose, and walked out of the Hall without remark.

At last they grew tired of singing.

'Now,' cried the leader, the deliverer, the new Joan of Arc, 'we have begun, and we will go on. To-morrow we must let them all know what we mean. There's going to be a change in our ways. Those who please may meditate. For my own part I have meditated for twenty long years, and nothing at all has come of it. I shall try for the Higher Life by talking and singing and helping the others.'

Thus simply and unexpectedly was struck the first blow of the great rebellion which transformed the House.

CHAPTER XIII.

WHAT IS HER NAME?

MEANTIME Gilbert had recovered his portmanteau from the House and was enabled once more to put himself into the sombre habiliments which represent evening dress. A pleasing discovery awaited him: on opening the portmanteau he found that his watch and chain, his rings, his seals, his studs, the silver topped toilet things, his silver cigarette case, his gold pencil case, his ivory brushes, and all the little costly things with which a young man loves to furnish his travelling gear and himself, had vanished. Everything that could be turned into money was gone. His purse, you remember, had already gone. He gazed at the gaps left in the portmanteau: and he laughed grimly, because he entertained no doubt at all as to the person who had conveyed away that valuable and saleable property.

'Good Heavens!' he said, in admiration. 'To him nothing is mean: nothing degrades: nothing is unworthy. He does these things and he preserves the manners of a Duke! He organizes villainous conspiracies: he invents villainous Long Firms: he concocts villainous frauds—all in the Noble, Stately, and Grand Style: and besides these schemes which mark his greatness, he does not disdain the humble practice of the area sneak. A wonderful man! A marvellous man! And to-day is Thursday: and on Saturday—we shall see—what shall we see?'

Then he remembered the message. 'What must be done shall be done, but not by your hands.'

'Why do I trust these words?' he asked himself. 'There is no reason at all: not the least reason. The thing is miraculous: it is supernatural: it haunts me: yet I trust it.'

At the customary hour he presented himself. In the

middle of the room stood Cicely, receiving, with colour a little heightened, the last touch from the maid.

'I think we have done very well,' said Lady Osterley, critically superintending. 'To-morrow we must get some more things for you, my dear child, if the shops of this town are equal to the occasion.'

Gilbert stepped forward. The maid withdrew, took the pin out of her mouth, and watched his astonishment, pleased as an artist at the result of her work.

Lady Osterley stepped aside with an expectant smile. Cicely stood revealed.

'Heavens!' cried Gilbert. 'What have they done to you, Cicely?'

She was transformed: not in face, because any change in that face would be a change for the worse; but she was glorified. She was no longer Sister Cicely of the House of Meditation, disguised with hair cut short, hanging over her ears, and in the most hideous costume possible to imagine. She was Cicely of the world: Cicely of Outside. The maid, recognising the splendid possibilities of face and figure, had kept that pin in her mouth all the afternoon while she brought to bear on the subject all the artistic feeling and craft that she possessed. The result was a really high-class work of Art. You know that artificial but extremely lovely product of the gardener's skill, the Moss rose; you also know the very humble but also lovely product of Nature, unaided, and left to the hedge and to the cold wind, the Briar rose. By what magic art can one transform the Briar rose into the Moss rose in a single afternoon? Gilbert stood staring in amazement. Then he went down on one knee, as to a queen, and took her hand and kissed it.

'My dear,' he said, 'you are always beautiful; now, for the first time, your dress sets off your face.'

'You are satisfied, Gilbert, with our afternoon's work?' asked Lady Osterley.

Satisfied? Good Heavens! He could not reply.

Cicely stood before him blushing and confused. Yet she held her head erect, as if these fine things actually belonged to her of right, and from the beginning. She had just been brought out of the dressing-room where the maid had been shut up with her all the afternoon with this result. Her hair was dressed in something like the mode—as near as its cruel shortness permitted; she wore one of Dorabyn's own white dresses, hurriedly altered for her, all covered with beautiful lace and embroidery; there was a touch of colour at the throat.

Gilbert saw the effect, but did not ask how it was produced: her slender neck was set off with a necklace of pearls and gold: her half bare arms were adorned with two bracelets: a white flower was in her hair: she looked more dainty, more exquisitely, delicately beautiful than even Gilbert, her lover, could have imagined possible—and she stood before him blushing, smiling, pleased to please her lover, wondering why she herself was so pleased with her new finery, she who had never in her life before had dreams of dress or yearnings after lovely things. Can you imagine, my dear young lady, the existence of a girl with no dreams of dress?

'Cicely,' said Gilbert, taking her hand, 'Dorabyn will make you as queenly as herself.'

The maid retired, well pleased with this homage to her powers. She knew, of course, to whom the credit was due; this assurance is too often the only reward of the artistic lady's-maid. 'As for her dress when she came'—this was what she told the nurse—'I assure you that I was ashamed—ashamed to look at it—I wouldn't dress a scullery maid so: and for a young lady—but there! I suppose they're just carried away with fads and fancies! I blushed; I really did: it was almost improper. Boots like a ploughboy's; stockings of wool; frock just a common serge: her hair short—the most beautiful soft and silky hair you ever saw, cut round her ears. Oh! I could have sat down and cried to see the Lord's gifts and graces thrown away in such a manner.

Well, my dear, I know a figure when I see one—there's not too many good figures to be found. My lady herself hasn't got a finer figure than Miss Cicely. All the afternoon I've been over the job. Now she's dressed like a countess. When you take in the boy for goodnight, look at her—you may well look at her, for you won't find a lovelier young lady anywhere. Lovely? She's like an angel in Heaven now she's dressed! And in white, like an angel!'

'Fine feathers,' said the nurse, 'make fine birds. Not but what my lady has got a figure.'

'Well, you look at the young lady. I suppose she *is* a lady born, otherwise Mr. Gilbert wouldn't have fallen in love with her. And my lady wouldn't otherwise take her in, even to oblige Mr. Gilbert. She'll make a lovely bride.'

'What's her name?' asked the nurse.

'I don't know. My lady only called her Cicely. And I called her Miss Cicely.'

The same question occurred to Lady Osterley. What was her name? You can get along very well with a girl in domestic matters even if you know only her Christian name, but for external affairs it is really necessary to know her surname.

It was close upon dinner-time. Mr. Annandale would probably dine with them, and Lady Osterley suddenly remembered that there must be a little ceremony of introduction.

'Before we go down, Gilbert, there is one thing—how could we forget it?—you have not told me Cicely's name.'

'Cicely's name? Did I forget to tell you Cicely's name? Why—I don't know her name. What is it, Cicely? Now I come to think about it, Dorabyn, she hasn't got any name.'

'Nonsense. She must have a name. Everybody has a name.'

WHAT IS HER NAME?

'Cicely hasn't then. She's the only person in the world who hasn't got a name. You see, she was born in the House; we all have Christian names only in the Community; we leave our surnames behind us when we leave the world. I have, in fact, already forgotten my own. Cicely never left the world, because this is the first time she has ever entered the world. You have no name, have you, Cicely?'

'I have never known any other name than Cicely.'

'Well—but what was your father's name?' asked Lady Osterley.

Cicely shook her head gravely.

'He never told me. I did not know that he had a name. In the House he was Brother Raymond.'

'Oh! but this is absurd. We can't introduce you about as Cicely, daughter of Brother Raymond, can we? Don't you really know your own father's name, my dear?'

Cicely shook her head again. She really did not know this elementary fact.

And then there happened a most wonderful thing: one of the things that are improbable in the highest degree: a thing so strange that Gilbert now believes it to be one link in a chain of events specially brought about by the Intelligence—the Soul—the Unseen Personality—which sent him the message so full of hope and reassurance. Well, you shall hear what happened.

'My father never told me his name,' Cicely repeated. 'He left his name behind him, I suppose, when he came over from England. All the members of the House leave their Past behind them, names and all, when they come in. I should have done so, but I have no Past to leave—and no name.'

'She is the daughter of the House, Dorabyn, I told you. Her mother died at her birth.'

'Poor girl! But what are we to do? Shall we invent a name for her—just for a little while, Gilbert, until——'

Gilbert's eyes fell on the desk which he had carried

away from the House. 'You have told me that you have some papers here, Cicely,' he said, laying his hand upon it. 'Do you think they might throw some light upon this vanished Past? It may become important to find out not only your name, but your people at home. Do you think you could search the papers for some clue to your own belongings?'

Cicely opened the desk. 'I have not looked into it,' she said, 'for some years—for a long time. Here are some letters'—she took out a bundle—'letters which my father wrote to my mother before they were married—and some written by her to him. He treasured them, and so I have always kept them.'

She took them out of the desk, and laid them on the table. 'Here is a book of drawings and paintings—my mother's book: here is a book full of verse which my mother wrote: here is a book of music which I think was written by my mother.'

'Will you look at your father's letters, Cicely?'

She untied the string and took out the letters. They were written in a handwriting most artistic, every letter being beautifully formed and finished as if it was an artistic effort of the greatest importance. But there was no signature except a single letter—'R.'

'I can find no name,' said Cicely. 'Will you look?'

'It seems like sacrilege to look at a dead man's letters —and his love letters. But the occasion justifies us, perhaps.'

Lady Osterley glanced at the letters. They were all written in the year 1873, and there were about twenty of them in all. 'They do not tell us,' said Lady Osterley, 'what we want to know. But they are very remarkable letters. Cicely, your father must have been a man of great elevation and some enthusiasm. These are the letters of a prophet, or a visionary. Was he a dreamer of dreams?'

'He belonged to the next world,' Cicely replied gravely, 'before he was permitted to go there.'

'They are all addressed "Dearest Alice"; and they are signed "R.," and nothing more. Let us see what else you have, Cicely.'

'Here is my mother's book of verses.'

Lady Osterley turned over the pages. 'Why,' she said, 'I have seen some of these verses. Where? I seem to know them. They are verses of aspiration. Your father, Cicely, seems to have been equally mated. Oh! but these are beautiful verses; they ought to be published. We must read in this book again, Cicely. Meantime there is no name or signature.'

'This is her book of paintings.'

They were water colours, representing angels singing in a divine rapture; souls borne upwards; souls reaching down to help those still in earthly bonds; Heavenly messengers flying from world to world; the lifting of the soul from the lowest depths.

'Cicely,' said Lady Osterley, 'it fills one with a kind of shame to feel how low one is lying. We must study this book again. Meantime, no name—no signature.'

It was the same with the book of music—no name.

'Here, then,' said Cicely, 'are two portraits taken when they were young—before they married, before they left England: the only pictures I have of them.'

Cicely took them out. They were cabinet photographs. One of them represented a young man with a high square forehead and limpid eyes—the forehead and eyes of an enthusiast—exactly the same forehead and the same kind of dreamy eyes that the Master had. His face was extremely handsome, but not strong: there was no fight in it: but there was the possibility of every Christian virtue—obedience, discipline, patience, faith, hope, and visions—yes, visions in plenty.

'A strange and beautiful face,' said Dorabyn, taking up the portraits. 'This other is your mother, I suppose. Why—I seem to know that face. Surely I know that face.' This too was the face of one who might become a visionary: Cicely resembled her mother in the sweetness of her face; in the purity of her face; in the seriousness of her face; she lacked, however, the mysterious depths that lay in her mother's eyes, which were like wells of light and faith. 'You curiously resemble her, Cicely—oh! you are so very much like her. But—but—but where have I seen this face? Where have I seen this face?'

She turned the portrait to the light and looked at it with a kind of bewilderment. 'I know the face,' she said. 'I am certain that I know the face. I have seen her somewhere. Where have I seen her?'

She handed it to Gilbert.

'It reminds me of someone,' he said. 'Like you, Dorabyn, I know the face. Whose is it?'

Just then the nurse brought in the boy to say goodnight. Gilbert looked up and caught the child's face as he held it up for his mother to kiss.

'Why, Dorabyn, it is like the boy. Look at it.'

She looked from boy to picture and from picture to boy. 'It *is* like him,' she said. 'It is strangely like him. Good-night, my son, good-night. Is it coincidence, Gilbert?'

'Good heavens!' he cried. 'It is like—oh! is it possible that I did not see it at once? And Cicely, too! Why, it is like her, too—it is stamped all over her face—Can't you see it, Dorabyn? Are we dreaming? Are we in a world of shadows? She must have been some close relation.'

These were incoherent words. He stopped and replaced the photograph in Dorabyn's hands. 'Is it possible?' he murmured. 'Does it still escape you? Cannot you see the resemblance?' And he turned away his face. For the person resembled was nothing less than Lady Osterley's husband, the man who had brought about all their misery.

The man's wife laid the picture, face downwards, on the table. 'I see the likeness,' she said in a hard voice.

Cicely looked from one to the other: Gilbert stood with guilty, hanging head, and face averted. Lady Osterley sat with contracted brow, and eyes in which nothing could be discerned but wrath implacable. Then Cicely's eyes grew large and full of light and gazed afar off.

'Oh!' she cried, returning, 'you must not: you must not. My mother says that you must not. "Forgive—forgive—forgive—now, if ever."'

'Child!' said her new friend, 'what do you mean? Your mother? Where is she?'

'She is dead. But I can go to her when I please. She says, "Forgive—forgive—forgive."'

'You don't understand, Dorabyn,' said Gilbert. 'The House is a House of spiritual connections and strange experiences. When Cicely tells you what her mother says, you may understand that her mother does say so.'

'I understand nothing, Gilbert—neither you, nor this child—nothing, except the likeness—and that I know now whose the portrait is.'

'Who is it?'

'Cicely's mother was that man's sister.'

Lady Osterley turned to Cicely. 'Your mother, my dear. I met her once only, many years ago, when I was a child. I knew—other members of her family more intimately, when I grew up. Your mother was the eldest of her family. It is strange! It is strange!'

'Oh! You knew my mother. Then listen when she says, "Forgive, forgive."'

Lady Osterley drew her closer, and kissed her on the forehead. 'Child!' she said, 'may you never learn how hard it is to forgive! There are some things which—pray, my dear, that you may never encounter such things. Let me look at one or two of her letters. Let me only look at their signature.'

Cicely gave her the bundle of letters tied up with ribbon. Lady Osterley turned to the end of the first letter and read the signature, which she showed to Gilbert.

'Is it not most strange?' she asked.

'It is more strange than you think. If you knew all——' but he stopped.

'Cicely'—Lady Osterley took her hands and held them closely—'you are the daughter of Alice Osterley, the sister of my husband. He was six years her junior.'

'Is my name Osterley, too?'

'No—no. Oh! I remember now. She married a man named Raymond Moulton: I have heard of it since, from her sister. He was a man with strange opinions—poetical and visionary. But he made her believe whatever he believed. Indeed, I think she was ready to believe everything that was saintly. They were married, and he gave away all his money and took his wife to America, and to this day no one knows what became of them. They came here, then. Strange, Cicely, that I should come across her daughter here! There was a preacher or minister of some kind who went away with them: he had been a Baptist, I believe; or a Bible Christian; or something humble: but he preferred to create a little revelation for himself. I have heard them talk about him, as well. They said he was a man of no education, but with gifts and graces: he had eloquence: he could move people; and he had a most splendid voice. Oh! it is all so wonderful! And you are her daughter—Alice's daughter—my husband's niece!'

'He has the splendid voice still,' said Gilbert. 'But if you only knew all!'

'My dear,' Lady Osterley went on, 'your mother, whom you so much resemble, was the most saintly woman in the whole wide world. She was a miracle of holiness and sweetness. She lived far above everybody else. In the Catholic Church they would have canonized her. She had the most exquisite dreams and visions: she put them into poetry: she put them into pictures: she sang them and she painted them. It is so strange

—oh! so strange—that I should have come here to meet her daughter!' She kept on repeating the words: 'The strangeness of it!'

'Yes,' said Gilbert again; 'and far, far stranger than you know.'

She paid no heed to these words, though they, too, were a repetition.

'You are my niece, child: my boy's first cousin. You must love me and your cousin, too.' She kissed the girl again, but with a little shudder, because the shadow of her husband stood between them. 'It is so strange!' she repeated; 'so very strange and wonderful! Yes—you have your mother's face—that sweet and serious face. My husband had the features—but there were reasons—yes, good reasons—why he could not have that face.'

'This precious desk!' said Gilbert. 'How lucky that we brought it along! Cicely Moulton—Moulton—Miss Moulton—do you like your new name just to wear for a little interval?'

'I like to think that I have a friend who knew my mother,' Cicely replied. 'What does it matter about a name?'

'Oh! I wish I had known all this before,' said Gilbert; 'and the likeness is so wonderful! I ought to have guessed it. Yet—likeness in unlikeness.'

'Only the lines of the face are like his, Gilbert. Let us abide by the unlikeness.'

'Yes—yet—if you only knew. However—you are Lady Osterley's niece, Cicely—only you must call her Dorabyn, because that is her name. And her boy is your cousin—and we will take you to England and find you plenty of cousins in addition—some of them most eligible cousins.'

'You must not wait for me if you are going in search of cousins, Cicely, because I shall not return to England for a long time.'

'My dear Dorabyn'—what did Gilbert mean? And

why did he look so strangely serious? 'To-day is Thursday. On Sunday—next Sunday—we shall leave this town and go to New York. On Monday or Tuesday we shall leave New York by the first steamer that sails. And a week later, Dorabyn, or eight days at the most, you shall be in your own country house, or in your own town house—which you choose.'

'You are for the moment deranged by your new happiness, my dear Gilbert. What does this mean?'

'I have, I assure you, this information on the very best possible authority. Cicely, in fact, gave it to me—by order of her mother.'

He spoke quite gravely and seriously.

'I do not pretend to understand you, Gilbert.'

'I do not pretend to understand myself; all I know is that Cicely, child of your sister-in-law, is here, unknown to you or anyone else: that I have been brought here: that you have been brought here: that you have been able to discover this dear girl's parentage: and that—there are other things.'

'Yes, I can see that there are other things. Well—I can wait. Come now, we must go to dinner. Mr. Annandale will be waiting for us.'

She was wrong. Mr. Annandale was not waiting for them. He was not there at all. They dined without him, a silent party, pleased to be silent. After dinner they sat on the balcony which overlooked the street.

It was the first time that Cicely had seen a street. It was a hot, still night and the street was crowded with people strolling up and down. The city of Aldermanbury contains eighty thousand people, of whom fifteen thousand are working girls. Obviously, therefore, the majority of the passengers were working girls taking the air after work: they walked arm in arm, two or three abreast: they chattered gaily: they looked happy. The young man was conspicuous by his absence. Where is the young man of Aldermanbury? He is away. He is out West. The girls do the work that he should have done. Therefore they get no love, and have neither husband nor children. Whereby the good old American stock is dying out, and there are grave doubts whether the great Cosmopolitan Blend — of German, Irish, Scandinavian, Italian, Russian, Polish, French blood—will possess virtues of its own sufficient to compensate for its loss.

'How they talk!' said Cicely, excited and interested. 'How they laugh! Oh! how pretty it is! Are they all wicked, Gilbert?'

'All alike, Cicely; desperately wicked. They like pretty things to put on—you understand that wickedness, don't you? And they like to talk about anything —you understand that temptation, too—and they would all of them—or nearly all—like someone to love them —you understand that form of wickedness, don't you?'

'You mean that they are not wicked at all, Gilbert.'

'Not a bit more than the people you have left behind. Rules cannot make people better.'

Cicely was silent, still gazing at the crowd below.

'They are all alone in space,' she murmured. 'The Master said so. All these people are alone, and they are all going up or down.'

'They are not quite alone. They are hand in hand. They go up or down together. You must not think so much of the going up or down, dear Cicely. You are in the world which has many interests of the day; so many that very few of us ever ask whether we are going up or down.'

'But we must. The Master says that there is nothing else.'

'Since he has cut you off from everything, he is right, I suppose. Certainly at the House it was much more wholesome for you to consider yourself than the people round you.'

'Tell me, Cicely,' said Lady Osterley, 'something more about your parents. Your mother died and you never saw her?'

'Oh, yes! I see her every day.'

'You think you do—yes—you think about her.'

'My father talked about her every day: he kept the place where she is buried covered with flowers: the place is in the coppice at the end of the lawn: between a lime tree and a maple. You know it, Gilbert?'

'Yes, Cicely, I know it well.'

'Brother Charles—who is a bad man—sits every afternoon on the bench there. Even the flowers droop when he sits there. But only her dust lies there. She herself is in a better world, and my father with her. They were never parted. Every day he went away to talk with her: every day she called him. Now they are both together, they do not forget me. Every day they call me.'

'Dear child, I understand nothing.'

For her face was full of light, as of one who looks upon a distant splendour. Lady Osterley looked and wondered, and shivered.

'I will tell her—I will ask her to make you understand. Something is to be done; and it is all in her hands: I know it is. Hush! she calls me!' Cicely sprang to her feet and listened. 'Hush! she calls me! I must be alone with her.' She walked out of the room, and shut her own door.

'What does she mean, Gilbert?' asked Lady Osterley. 'What does it all mean? What do you mean by what you kept saying about things being stranger still?'

'My dear Dorabyn, I am not mad. I am quite certain that my dear Cicely is not mad. But I do know that she has trances: in her trances she thinks that she is in communication with her mother. The Master—the Leader in the Community of Cranks, the Crankiest of all—has similar illusions, if they are illusions; Cicely's father had the same illusions. Cicely brings me messages which she cannot understand; but I can. Laugh at me, if you please. But, Dorabyn, I cannot choose but believe.'

'You, Gilbert, to believe in trances and spiritualism?'

'This is not stupid spiritualism. There are no pretences here. It is very certain to me that this girl communicates with her dead mother. Sometimes she remembers what her mother tells her—that is when the words concern herself: sometimes she forgets when she has uttered them. That is when the words are a message. I have received several messages from her mother in this way.'

'You, Gilbert? You? Messages from Alice?'

'As you say: from Alice. From that lofty and saintly soul who was allowed to remain on earth no longer than to give birth to Cicely. Then she went away. But still—Dorabyn, listen very seriously. It is Alice who is guiding things. She brought me here. She brought you here. She made me bring Cicely here. And, believe me, there are other things, greater things still, which she will accomplish for her daughter—and her sister-in-law.'

The time had been when words such as these from Gilbert would have been a mockery, or a parody. In fact, they would have been impossible. Lady Osterley listened with wonder and with that mixture of eagerness and doubt which falls upon one when the veil seems lifted if only a little.

'Come, Dorabyn,' Gilbert went on; 'Cicely has gone into her own room in order to fall into trance. If you are curious, you can go and look—you need not be afraid. Nothing could wake her, if it be as I think.'

Dorabyn opened the door. She came back in a moment, terrified.

'Gilbert! Come. It is dreadful. She is lying on the couch rigid, in a kind of catalepsy.'

Gilbert followed her. They stood over the unconscious girl.

'Do not be afraid,' he said. 'She will return presently. Is she not beautiful, Dorabyn?'

'She is very beautiful. Her beauty is ethereal, like her mother's.'

'Dorabyn, you remember those days when you used to write me long letters? Well, out of those letters there grew up in my mind an ideal woman. Not you, but like you. We could never have loved in that way. But she was like you—as noble—as——'

'Noble, Gilbert? And I married — for ambition, because I would be the wife of a great statesman—that man!'

'As good and as generous and as sweet, Dorabyn. And the ideal woman—is Cicely.'

He stooped and kissed her cold, white forehead; and his voice dropped, and his eyes grew humid.

CHAPTER XIV.

HUSBAND AND WIFE.

THE English traveller, Mr. Annandale, was one of that large class of moderns who spend a great part of their lives in travelling. They do not make voyages to Spitzbergen, nor do they explore Patagonia; nor are they found on the steppes of Siberia. Their travels are never beyond the modern hotel with its little comforts; they cease to journey where claret and champagne cease to be accessible: they look about for each other wherever they go. And they always find each other. Their knowledge of the world is limited to Clubland, which, although it is universal, is limited as to population. 'I never go anywhere,' said Mr. Annandale, 'without meeting someone I know.' The unexpected meeting and the unexpected greeting made up for this traveller the whole joy of strange lands.

It was a most amazing circumstance, had they reflected upon it, that Mr. Annandale did not appear at dinner. Never before had he been known to break such an engagement. What had happened? But there were other things to engage their attention and his defection passed almost unnoticed.

In the morning he appeared at breakfast. He looked embarrassed, a thing quite unusual in this man of the world. But there are things which may surprise even the most experienced man of the world.

'Why did you not dine with me yesterday?' Lady Osterley asked.

'I was—I was out on a drive and—in fact—I was unable to get back in time. I am really very sorry. I can only hope that you did not wait.'

'Not long. But let me introduce you to my niece, Miss Cicely Moulton. She is a niece of romance, only just discovered: a long lost niece: in fact, I think you may have known her mother, Mr. Annandale. She was my husband's sister, Alice, who married a man named Moulton.'

'Your husband's sister, Alice, who married Raymond Moulton? Really?'

'Alice died in a House or Monastery near here.' Mr. Annandale started. 'Cicely has been all her life a resident of the place—what is the matter, Mr. Annandale?' For the veteran who ought to have been equal to any kind of unexpectedness looked bewildered to an extent incapable of concealment.

'Nothing—only—in a House or Monastery near here? Is it a certain place called the House of Meditation?'

'That, I believe, is its name. Cicely only left it yesterday.'

'Only left it yesterday?' he repeated. 'Only yesterday? Why—I was over there yesterday. Then, of course, she knows—she knows all the people there——'

'Oh yes,' said Cicely. 'I know all the Brothers and Sisters.'

'All?' Mr. Annandale's face expressed more bewilderment.

'The House,' Lady Osterley went on, 'is, I understand, an embodiment of Raymond Moulton's dreams

—equality, brotherhood, work, and meditation. He died there some years after his wife. Gilbert found Cicely there, an orphan.'

'Oh!' he repeated stupidly. 'Gilbert found her there! Oh! Gilbert found her there!'

'Yes, and brought her to me. She will not go back again, I believe.'

'No,' said Gilbert, 'she will not go back.'

'I understand. Quite so. Gilbert goes back though, I suppose?'

'I think not.'

'Then how?—I mean, why? And here he stopped, and said nothing more.

Breakfast over, Gilbert and Cicely rose.

'Stay a moment, Lady Osterley,' said Mr. Annandale. 'I have something to tell you.'

'I perceive, in fact, my friend, that you have something on your mind.'

'It is this.' He dropped his voice mysteriously, because there were other people in the room. 'Yesterday afternoon I drove over to see this House or Community, or whatever you call it. I was curious to see what kind of place that was whose attractions were strong enough to convert Gilbert into a Brother and a costermonger. Of course, I supposed there was a woman. So there was. And yet——' He stopped abruptly.

'Yes? I was thinking of going over there myself. Did you find the place interesting?'

He looked at her in obvious expectancy. He observed no signs of any interest out of the ordinary in this communication of his. He cleared his throat, and proceeded to reveal all he had to tell.

'And there, Lady Osterley—I think I ought to tell you—in fact, I must tell you—I had no suspicion or thought of the thing, I assure you—God forbid that I should go about prying—but there—quite accidentally, I say—I discovered your great secret.'

'My great secret, Mr. Annandale?'

'Why,' thought the man, 'should she go on to pretend surprise?'

'Your secret. I discovered the one cardinal fact which explains all.'

'Mr. Annandale, will you please explain your explanation?'

'I will, if you wish it. I thought you would rather——'

'Still, if you will, kindly. We cannot be too explicit when we come to discovering secrets.'

'Well, of course you must be well aware of the way in which people talk about your silence and your husband's whereabouts. He must be alive, they say, because no announcement of his death has ever been made. Where is he, then? Where is Lady Osterley? She is reported as having been seen here and there. Why does she write to no one? Why is it that even her husband's friends cannot hear of his place of residence? That is what they say.'

'It is. I know all that perfectly well.'

'I can go home, if you permit me, with a complete answer to all these questions. I can say'—Lady Osterley took up her fan—'I can say—if you authorize me—that I have seen him. He lives in a Community. He is a crank, like his sister and his brother-in-law. He has gone to the Community which they founded. He has been converted to their crankiness. He is quite mad—and there he lives.'

Lady Osterley made no reply. She held the fan before her face to hide the change of colour and her startled look. Of all things in the world she least expected this. That her husband should become a gambler by profession: that he should go down in the world: this would not surprise her: that he should become capable of any depths would not surprise her. But that he should have become a religious crank—what *could* it mean?

Mr. Annandale went on: 'And now, of course, I understand why Gilbert is there, too.'

Lady Osterley shivered: for she understood, too, why Gilbert was there. 'I will set you free'—she remembered the words. How was she to be set free? She understood, too, what those words meant. There was but one way of freedom for her.

'Gilbert,' this intelligent person continued, 'is one of your oldest friends: you have sent him to look after your husband. He belongs to the Community in order to be with him and to watch over him. I declare, Lady Osterley, that I have never known a case of truer friendship than this of Gilbert's. When I understood what it meant, and thought of him selling strawberries in the street—out of a basket, mind you—I thought I was going to cry. I did, indeed. Gilbert, you know! I was never so amazed in all my life,' Mr. Annandale went on. 'I saw your husband sitting in the shade under some trees. I was so astonished that I did not believe my own senses. I asked one of the people who the man was. He told me it was Brother Charles—Brother Charles—Brother Charles—Brother! Think of Sir Charles Osterley being a Brother! Sir Charles Osterley —the proudest man in the whole world!'

Lady Osterley put down her fan and drank a little iced water.

'You say that you saw—with your own eyes—my husband—Sir Charles—my husband—in the House?'

'I did. And then, I say, I understood all. I called out to him. "You here, Sir Charles?" I cried. He wouldn't answer. Oh! he is stark, staring mad! He lifted his head and recognised me. I saw that he recognised me. But he wouldn't speak to me. He got up and walked away. I suppose he does not wish to see any of his old friends. He looks just the same—tall, austere, a devil of a fellow with his religious exercises, I should say—looks as if he wore a hair-shirt: the same old poker down his back—I beg your pardon, Lady

Osterley. His face is changed, though. I thought he looked savage—perhaps because I disturbed him. I wonder what made him take up this particular craze? Why did he go into the House of Meditation? I suppose because his sister was there before him.'

'Indeed, Mr. Annandale, there are so many strange things happening——'

'And you may understand my surprise this morning when you told me that this girl was his own niece—as like him as a girl can be to a man! And you say they were together in this House. Good Heavens! Fancy your finding your niece in the same House as your husband!'

'But they did not know the relationship. Cicely did not even know her own name.'

'And Gilbert came to look after him. Went so far as to sell strawberries along the street in a basket—carried a basket! Did it very well, too.'

'Mr. Annandale.' She had now entirely recovered her self-possession, and she went on acting her part. She sat up, laid aside the fan, and placed her hand upon his. 'Since you know so much, my friend, learn a little more. Gilbert has been in search of my husband for two years. The reason of my long silence was that I really did not know where he was. As for the reasons that brought him to the House of Meditation, I confess that I do not know them. Perhaps, as you suppose, he was influenced by his sister's example. Nor can I even guess what he hopes to find in the place, or how long he will stay there.'

'Is he, then, so hopelessly mad?'

'Hopelessly, I fear. There seems no hope at all for his kind of madness. And now, Mr. Annandale, for the next thing, please, for the moment, keep my secret to yourself. I do not wish his people, if I can help it, to learn anything about his mental condition. If it should happen that he is really settled down into a harmless visionary condition, I will tell them. Meanwhile, do not speak to anyone of what you have seen.'

'You have come here, of course, in order to see him?' She answered this very direct question evasively.

'I am going over this morning—immediately. Thank you for telling me—what you discovered—Mr. Annandale, and—if you please, do not again attempt to speak to him. You might waken old memories.'

'Poor Charles! What a change! What a break up! And when one thinks——'

Lady Osterley left him thinking. She had plenty to think about by herself. Her husband in this very place! And Gilbert with him! What was Gilbert doing? Looking after a madman? Had her husband really become an Enthusiast? Was he mad? Why was Gilbert here? Then, once more, the words of Gilbert echoed in her brain. She remembered them. 'I will set you free.' He was there in order to set her free. How? She trembled. The only way of freedom was, for one or the other, for the broken gamester, or for herself, to pass through the Gate of Death. One of the two must die for the freedom of the other. One must die. Gilbert would set her free. How? A mist rose before her eyes: a horrible deadly sickness seized her. Alone in her bedroom she sank into a chair and lost consciousness.

She came to herself after a little. Then—it was wonderful how, one after the other, the feeling of guidance by the dead hand seized and held each of them in turn—she looked up, and she whispered, 'Alice! Alice! If you can hear me, listen. If you can help us in this fearful trouble, help us now. It is your own daughter you must help: it is your own brother: it is your brother's wife: it is your brother's son: it is your daughter's lover. Alice, if you *can* hear me, as your daughter believes, tell me what to do.'

A man of science once developed a theory that prayer is often a great help to the man who prays, because it leads him, in some quite scientific way, to a clearer understanding of the situation, and of the right proportion of the events which lead up to it and affect its composition. This, he maintained, was the true function of prayer, and the only answer that ever comes to it. I give his opinion for what it is worth, and to enable those who agree with him to explain all that has gone before and all that follows. No answer came in words to the prayer: but Lady Osterley rose from her chair with decision in her mind. She felt no longer any hesitation nor any doubt.

She opened the door of her room. In one of the two sitting-rooms Gilbert and Cicely sat laughing and lovemaking, as happy as two young lovers can hope to be. How could Gilbert laugh and talk so light of heart if his purpose was—that way?

In the other room, all the doors were wide open; her boy was careering about the room, shouting and laughing. He should never know: he must never know.

She shut her door again: they should not be disturbed. She rang the bell, told her maid that she was going for a drive for an hour or two, put on her hat and went downstairs.

She understood now what Gilbert meant by hinting at other things. If it was strange that Gilbert and she herself, and Cicely, her niece, should all be brought together in the place where Alice died, it was still more strange that her husband, too, should be brought here. By this time she began to believe, as Gilbert himself believed, that they were brought here by one hand and for one purpose: it was the dead hand of Alice that brought them here, and the dead hand was to do more for them. What more?

It was about eleven in the forenoon when the carriage drove up at the porch and verandah of the House. Lady Osterley got down and told the driver to wait. No one was in the verandah: she looked in at the open door and saw a great, bare, ugly room with a permanent fragrance of fried steak, mingled with that of pork and beans, hanging about the place. At the head of the

central table sat an old man, a venerable old man. He
looked like one who was already dead : his hands were
folded : his head was leaning back : his eyes were open.
He, like Cicely, the evening before, was in a trance.
Dorabyn shuddered, and went out into the open air.

There were sounds of work : an engine of some kind
was throbbing and panting not far off : there was the
thumping and beating, the stumping about, the murmur
and humming and echoing which belong to work of all
kinds : before the House, and on either side of it, were
gardens, kitchen-gardens, market-gardens, melon-patches,
tomato-fields, vineyards, orchards : and about the garden
were men at work, very leisurely work it seemed. At
the end of the garden was a belt of wood.

'He was under the shade of the trees,' said Lady
Osterley. She walked across the lawn and reached the
coppice.

Yes. There, alone on a bench, his elbow on the
arm : his chin in his hand : his hat beside him : sat her
husband, the man who had done all the mischief. As
he sat there, in deep shade, with the pallor of his face,
and the austerity of his brow, he looked like an ideal
preacher or theologian : he might have sat for the portrait of the most uncompromising Puritan or Calvinistic
Divider of the Word : some Hammer of Heresy. Yet
there was no change in him. Such he looked when she
married him : so he looked in the House : thus he commanded the respect of the world, but never its affection.

As the wife gazed upon him, she remembered the
days, not so long past, when she awaited his coming,
the visits of the frigid lover, with a kind of awe ; when,
with the same pale cheek and cold eye, he seemed to her
more than a man in his wisdom and his austerity and his
freedom from the common weaknesses. She remembered
how nothing moved him : not injustice and wrong—they
were things which had to be removed out of the way :
not ambition even—high place—the highest—was the
certain end for such a man. Not any kind of sport,

game, recreation : not desire for literary fame : not any endeavour to move the populace; if plain, cold reason would not succeed, rhetoric should not. She saw in him a strong, able, cold man, one who never swerved from his high purpose, never lost his temper, and was a hero even to his valet. That time returned to her. And while she stood and looked upon him, she remembered the awakening : the sacrifice of half her fortune : her discovery of the truth : the sudden, tragic end of that Act.

No change ? Yes. Suddenly some thought crossed his mind. His face lost its austerity : it clouded over : the pallor remained, but it only brightened the terrible change that came upon him and revealed the devil within him. He sat up : he looked about him with sudden surprise : his face before had been hidden with a mask. Now, it was full of evil thoughts and evil memories : it was natural.

'He has gone down—down—deeper than I thought,' said his wife.

She stepped forward. He knew the footstep—turned his head and recognised her. Then he rose and bowed gravely, as if receiving a visitor, with the same calm and indifference with which he had treated Gilbert.

'Lady Osterley ?' he asked, showing in his voice no sign of any emotion whatever.

'I heard by accident, Sir Charles, that you were here. Mr. Annandale, whom you may remember—formerly an acquaintance of yours—saw you here and told me of your presence here. A strange place, but you have your reasons, no doubt.'

'Annandale ? Why not say at once that it was Mr. Gilbert Maryon who brought you here ?'

'Gilbert had not given me to understand that you were here. He does not know, as yet, that I have heard of your residence here. It is entirely by accident that I am at Aldermanbury.'

'Then he did not tell you why I am here ?'

'Certainly not. I have come partly to ask that question, if you choose to answer it. This is a very strange place for you to select as a home. There are other things I want to ask you—always supposing that you will answer these questions.'

'Will you sit down while you are asking these questions? You must allow me to exercise my own judgment as to answering any question.'

'Thank you, I will stand. Answer or not, as you please.'

'Then you will allow me? Thank you. The morning is hot. I will sit down. Now, Lady Osterley, if you please we will take your questions.' Again, as with Gilbert, the reverse of the true situation: the appearance of the Judge examining the accused.

'My position you will understand—to begin with—when I tell you that I have resolved on enduring banishment for life or anything else provided that I can save my son from the knowledge of his father's life. I have come abroad so that I may not be asked questions about you. I shall stay abroad so long as anybody remains who would be likely to inquire after you. You have been recognised here by an old acquaintance. I do not suppose that he will keep the secret, although I have asked him to do so. Such things as these get about. It will become known, sooner or later, that you are here. Your mother and sister, if they hear of your place of residence, will certainly come out to see you. They are continually imploring me to tell them where you are and how you are.'

'Please go on.'

'Do you wish them to see you?'

'I wish nothing; that is, I suppose that I am not anxious to see them.'

'Tell me, if you can, why you are here. I cannot believe it possible that you should be touched with the spirit of this Community, which is, I believe, one of religious Visionaries.'

'There is no reason why I should pretend—to you. Of course I am not touched by their religious nonsense. I came here because it is a convenient place for me. I have no money, to begin with. In this place, which is detestable in other respects, one wants no money. If you have any money with you give it to me.'

'Do you mean to stay here long?'

She evaded the question about money.

'They are going to turn me out. I leave the place to-morrow.'

'Where are you going, and what will you do?'

'I have no money. Therefore, of course, I do not know. I must be guided by what happens. Nobody knows what may happen.'

She drew out her purse, in which there was a roll of notes. She laid the roll on the bench beside him.

'There is some money to go on with. Two or three hundred dollars. Now, what shall you do?'

'I must get somewhere—out of this country—to Canada, I suppose. Perhaps it will be safer there.'

'Safer?'

'Yes. Safer. You don't know, perhaps, what that means. I will tell you, briefly.' He turned round on the seat and faced her—with the face of an evil spirit. 'I will tell you. It means that when a man is left without money he must devise some way of getting money. Do you see? He wants money to buy food, and he wants money to play with. How can a man play if he has no money? Without play one may as well be dead.' He took up the bundle of notes and counted them. 'One hundred—two hundred—three hundred and fifty dollars. I dare say I shall play a little with some of this—— Well, Lady Osterley, this necessity of getting money is one that has probably never struck you. To get money means to make somebody provide the money. There are many ways: some that society recognises— some that society does not. They all mean robbing your neighbour. I have been, like everybody else, preying on my neighbour: eating up the ignorant and deceiving the credulous. Now you begin to understand.'

'You mean that you are, in consequence, living in concealment? Be good enough to spare me details.'

'Exactly. The Law is in search of me.'

'On a charge of fraud, I suppose. Oh, my son! my son! if you should ever know!'

'There is something said about a commercial transaction in the nature of a conspiracy. All trade is fraud, to begin with. That, however, is not all.'

'Not all? Can there be anything worse?' She shuddered; then sat down on the opposite end of the long bench.

'Comparisons are deceitful: there is something, however, more dangerous. There was a gaming-house some time ago—and a little trouble arose, and some kind of fight—such things are not unusual—and next day there was a dead man found outside.'

'Oh!' Lady Osterley shivered and shook. 'You are —charged—with murder?'

'They call it murder, I believe. If they take me they will, I understand, try me for murder. I have to leave this place, as I told you, to-morrow. If they should arrest me there will be a trial and possibly a little experiment with an electric apparatus after it.'

Lady Osterley buried her face in her hands. The thing was too dreadful for indignation; it was too horrible for anything except blank despair.

'Oh!' she cried, springing to her feet again. 'How can you live—you—with what is behind you—and what is before you? How can you live? You ought to have killed yourself long, long ago!'

'There is a Rule in this House,' he replied, 'that we are to forget the Past. It is a Rule with which I very willingly complied. As for what is before, so long as I remain here there is nothing before. Nothing. The nothingness is intolerable. I have, in fact, sometimes considered whether it would not be better to face any dangers rather than go on living here in the House of Nothingness. At all events the danger will now have to be faced. To-morrow at latest.'

'You will be arrested, if you are caught: you will be tried for murder: you will be tried for fraud if you are acquitted of murder.'

'That is so. Put it more clearly. Say that my description is in the hands of the police of every town. Escape is only possible by keeping to the country roads and by travelling at night. I must make either for Canada or for the West. I must get out of the country somehow.'

'Oh! Will there never be any end of all this misery and shame?'

'So far as I can tell, Lady Osterley, no end at all until the natural end. We are not, however, a long-lived race, we who live by our wits. Sometimes our wits fail us: those who drop out can never get back again: sometimes there is a quarrel and a fight. Still, if I escape this danger, I may go on a great many years, long enough to make myself known some day, perhaps, to my son, who will be pleased, no doubt, to acknowledge his father.'

'Charles! At first I felt nothing but anger and shame. Now, it is too late for either. Anger will not help, and shame I must hide. There is nothing left for you but pity—oh, the sorrow of it! That such a man as you were once could by any temptation, or any madness, be brought so low! Oh! the Pity! and the Sorrow and the Shame of it! You! you! with your genius—your learning—your powers—your career stretching out clear and straight before you. Oh! Merciful GOD'— she threw up her arms—'do something—something—to make this man feel!'

'Heaven,' he said coldly, 'does not often, I believe, interfere in the case of a career *manqué*.'

'Charles, I am certain—I am quite certain—that

something terrible will happen, and that immediately. It has been arranged: we are all brought together for that purpose.'

'I think not, Lady Osterley. Thanks to you, I now have some money. I shall get away by night quietly. You will often hear of, or from me, in the years to come.'

Her eyes fell upon a place all covered with summer flowers, beyond the bench on which her husband was sitting. At first it looked like a garden bed of flowers— a long narrow bed: but as she looked she saw that it was raised in the middle: it became a grave: she remembered what Cicely said: 'My mother was buried in the coppice at the end of the lawn: there was a flower-bed— to mark her grave. Brother Charles, who was a bad man' —how did the girl know that he was a bad man?—' sat on the bench beside the grave and made the flowers wither by reason of his extreme badness.' Her mother held everything in her own hands: she guided all: something was going to happen that Alice would bring about. All this flashed across her mind in a moment.

'Charles!' she cried passionately, 'if this could move you—if anything could move *you*—who brought you to this place?'

'I heard about it from some paper.'

'Who brought you here?' she repeated. 'Who brought me here? In this House your sister Alice died'—the man started. 'In this House she is buried. Under the shade of the trees in this little wood she lies buried—at your very feet—your sister Alice—most saintly of women. She lies buried beneath those flowers.'

'My sister Alice? She died here?' The man was moved in spite of himself. The presence of Alice in this place, with him—there are some things too startling for even the most callous.

'In this House her child was born—the girl Cicely.'

'The girl Cicely is her daughter? Alice's daughter?'

He quickly recovered his emotion, and was now only curious.

'Is it accidental—think you—that we should all be brought together in this strange manner?'

'You mean that my sister Alice, being dead and buried, has been exerting her influence to bring about this agreeable reunion of friends and relations? Pardon me, Lady Osterley, I cannot follow you in this belief. The dead sleep well. They know nothing; they care nothing; they can do nothing.'

'Cannot even the memory of Alice move you?'

'What is the good of being moved by her memory? Why do you want me to be moved? I should be no better off by being moved. Am I to shed a tear over the memory of Alice? Will any such emotion make my escape the easier?'

'She has sent you messages, through her daughter.'

'Messages? Oh, you mean the foolishness with which the girl has been pestering me. She believes in the rubbish they pretend here. She is hysterical and thinks she has visions. Messages she brought me. Oh yes. I was to repent, I believe. She has threatened me, if I remember rightly. Do you really mean, Lady Osterley—do you wish me to believe—that Alice—who is dead and dust—sent me these messages?'

'They were her messages. I cannot choose but believe that they were messages. Since I have heard——'

'The girl is like her mother,' he went on. 'I ought to have perceived the likeness. But the dress reduces all the women here to hideousness. Still, I wonder that I did not observe the likeness. It is, I confess, somewhat bizarre that we should be all gathered together in this queer place: but to-morrow I am to go. So, you see, it all amounts to nothing, unless Alice has arranged that you shall witness my arrest, which will very likely take place to-morrow. It would be a delicate and thoughtful attention on the part of Alice. Not the kind of thing one would always expect of a dead sister—but then I never agreed with her ecstatic religion, and she could hardly agree with my morals. A delicate and thoughtful attention.'

'Oh!' His wife stepped back. 'I will waste no more words. You fly from us to hide your shameful head. And you cannot escape. We are here—we are all here—with you. Your wife—your son—your niece—your dead sister. Alice would save your life. I am sure she would, if you will turn from your evil ways.'

He laughed a metallic laugh without the least merriment in it.

'Lady Osterley, when I knew you some time ago you were incapable of talking such nonsense. It is the living hand, not the dead hand, that concerns us.'

'Oh, you are lost—lost—lost!' She wrung her hands in despair. 'Yet, Charles, there is one thing left. All is lost except your name—your father's name—your sister's—your son's. Oh, leave us that!' She threw herself upon her knees before him, weeping. 'For the sake of Alice; for the sake of your mother; for the sake of your son——'

He drew back coldly.

'It is for my own sake, Lady Osterley, believe me, not for your sake at all—I never considered you in the business at all—that I conceal my name. For that reason you may quite rely on a continuance of—of this concealment. And now this interview has perhaps been prolonged enough.'

He took off his hat. She inclined her head and left him. Yet she turned once more to look at him. It was a fine picture that she carried away in her memory—the last picture that she took of her husband. He was standing bareheaded, hat in hand, his face pale, his bearing erect, his expression proud and austere—a brave and honourable man, to look at. She remembered another picture—some old picture—which represented the execution of an officer. In this picture the officer about to die stood, firm and proud, before he received the shower of bullets. So stood Sir Charles. He must have known that the end was very near: he stood to meet his fate with the cold pride which never forsook him, though the last remains of honour and self-respect had long since disappeared.

CHAPTER XV.

BACK AGAIN.

THE Master was sitting in his own chair, the victim of extreme despondency. A great and terrible dread was upon him, in so much that his soul was stirred to the very depths. For he could no longer meditate. It was as if the gates of Heaven were closed to him: as if his whole life had been a failure. You have seen that in the evening the customary unconsciousness would not come to him: in the morning, save for a brief—a very brief and terrifying—spell, it was also impossible. Perhaps, he thought, this disquiet was caused by the departure of the child: perhaps it was a sign that he was now old, and that he was about to be transferred immediately to the next world, or the world after next, should he be worthy. Perhaps he was afflicted with this loss of power by his friends who were waiting for him, as a punishment for letting the child go. So he sat during the hot afternoon in the quiet Hall, an enthusiast with all the enthusiasm gone out of him; a Prophet who could no longer prophecy. Ever and anon he again attempted Meditation: it was like one afflicted with insomnia trying to sleep: after each attempt, he sat up again and looked about him with dismay.

It is hard on the young when their plans and schemes go wrong and their hopes are crushed. They, however, can invent new plans and work out new schemes. Think, however, what it means to the old, and above all

17

when such a scheme as this, practically a new religion, in good working order, seemingly, for twenty years, is suddenly threatened with collapse! A Prophet must not only believe in his own Prophecy, but he must believe in nothing else. Twenty-two years ago there came to this Prophet, a poor and despised preacher of a humble sect, preaching in a small chapel to a congregation of humble folk, a man who entered by accident; heard with surprise; and ended by becoming, he and his wife, ardent believers in a form of belief which they spiritualized, together with its Prophet, beyond his dreams. They gave him the power of living the life which he desired: they filled it, and himself, with hopes and endeavours which he by himself could never devise or attain to.

Well: he had given this life to a folk mostly of the common order of ill-educated enthusiasts: he thought it enough to turn them into the House as one turns sheep into a field: he gave them nothing to feed their minds or to stimulate their imagination: neither prayer; nor praise; nor holy times or seasons; nor singing: nor reading: nor exhortation. The machine went on, day by day; the wants of the body were supplied: they fell readily into the trance condition, which is, indeed, as contagious as fits: they were silent: they worked a little: they rested a great deal: they asked for nothing. The Master never taught or preached: the only corporate action was the criticism of the Committee. Upon all this fell a daily increasing terror of Outside: everyone believed that his neighbour soared to heights incredible while in Meditation: and everyone believed in the holiness of the House under the influence of its peculiar institution. No one believed in this more than the Master. In the rows of cataleptic brethren, he beheld the inanimate bodies of disciples whose souls, after his teaching and example, had flown upwards to realms beyond the skies.

We must never ask how far the Master was truthful

as regards the discourses which he held with Alice. That question must not be put. The vulgar pretender who writes on slates and unties knots must not be classed with such as the Master. He is neither a pretender nor a fraud. He has, to begin with, an ardent imagination: he sees things, actually, as they never exist: he believes so thoroughly that he realizes his own belief: if he believes in the spirit world, he goes into the spirit world and lives there.

And now the beautiful castle of cards lay fallen and scattered at his feet. The members were in revolt: his child had run away, and Alice refused to speak to him. At seventy-five such things are hard to endure.

All the morning he sat in the Hall, alone. Outside there were the customary sounds of work: engines throbbed: there was the clatter of pans from the dairy: hammering from the carpenters' and the blacksmiths' shops: the crowing of cocks: the rumbling of cart-wheels: for work must go on although revolution is in the air.

Presently the door was opened and a lady walked in: not a sister in the garb of the House, but a lady dressed in quite a different fashion: a fashion which in some dim and distant manner reminded him of Alice: she stood there for a moment curiously looking about her, and then went out again, closing the door softly behind her. This gentle treatment of the door, by some cryptic connection of ideas, took his thoughts back to England, the country where doors are never slammed: and again in imagination he saw Alice as he first met her walking on the lawn, a gracious, sweet, and gentle creature, in whose presence, Prophet as he was, he felt low and humble.

The bell rang—the discordant bell—for cessation of Fatigue. The trampling of footsteps in the verandah, on the stairs of the women's quarters, and about the House, recalled him to the present.

Sister Euphemia came in and sat down beside him just where the child used to sit.

'Master,' she said, ' there were strange things said and done last night. It was an upsetting and an awakening. Now there's going to be more things done, and if I don't mistake, Sister Phœbe's going to give trouble. But don't you mind. She'd like to put her husband in your place. Oh! she's deep. Then she thinks she'll rule the House through Silas. But she won't. Well, we're just tired of sitting still: Meditation is only good for such saints as you and that poor child. As for me, I've never, not for a single day, forgot the Past, nor the trouble that brought me here. But don't you mind, Master. Some among us will stand by you still. You shall have your Meditation, morning, noon, and night, just the same. We love you too much, dear Master, not to remember what we owe to you. Don't look like that, Master. It takes but little to set a woman crying. And you *shall* get back your child—you shall.'

The bell rang for Restoration. The men and women streamed in, and the feeding was conducted with a heartiness which almost forbade the idea of Revolution.

After Restoration the men went out into the verandah: the women divided into two parties: the larger of which, under Sister Euphemia, retired to the women's wing; the smaller, under the guidance of Sister Phœbe, went off to one of the workrooms.

The Master was left alone again. And still he sat in his armchair with heavy heart and dismal forebodings.

About three o'clock in the afternoon the doors flew open, and the child came running in—and, with her, Gilbert. But what a child! How transformed! She looked like nothing less than her own mother twenty years ago, before the dress of the House was invented. Her beauty, of which he had only been dimly conscious; her dress; her changed look, dazzled and bewildered him. Yet she was not changed. She sat down in her own place at the end of the bench beside his chair. She took his hands in hers—the old wrinkled hands in her warm and tender hands. 'Master,' she said, 'dear Master, I could not leave you here alone. I have come back to take you away with me.'

He only understood that she was come back. 'My dear,' he said, 'I fear I have done wrong: yet I meant well. Come closer: don't let go my hand. Cicely, your mother—your mother—is offended with me. The gates are shut:' he trembled and moaned. 'My dear, the gates are shut: the gates to the Upper World: I can no longer pass through them: I cannot meditate. Yet I did it for the best—for the best, my dear.' He spoke in the broken manner of the old, who understand slowly.

'Yes—yes! my mother knows that: she cannot be offended.'

So she bent over him and kissed him and patted his hand and consoled him.

'Of course, you did it for the best,' said Gilbert cheerfully. 'Why, we ran away partly in order that you should find out the strength of your own Single Attachment. If I cannot live without Cicely, how can you?'

The old man shook his head. He could not live without the child. Yet—to call it a Single Attachment!

'My dear'—he spoke to Cicely, not to Gilbert, because the reference to a Single Attachment perplexed and offended him—'I cannot live without you: it is true—and it was terrible to think that I had driven you out. What could I say to your mother? I was afraid to meet her. That was why she shut the gates. Perhaps I ought to have discerned things more clearly. I begin to understand that for some natures there must be exceptions. With the nobler soul a Single Attachment may be a help, not a hindrance. She should be your example as she has been my guide. And she loves her husband in the new world as much as in the old. But there were many examples, my dear, in this House, pointing the other way. There have been married people here: every one could see how they quarrelled and called names, and fell into tempers unseemly. I did not distinguish. It was not right to force the daughter of that pure and white Spirit, my Guide, who discourses daily with me, into union with a rustic—as I now understand—coarse and common. Let like mate with like.'

'That is finished, dear Master,' said Cicely. 'We have come to talk about other things. Gilbert will talk for me. You must listen to what he says. Come! Let us talk together, we three.'

The Master shook his head. He did not expect much to come out of the promised talk: indeed, he would rather have sat quite still and silent, looking at the child, until he might be permitted, as a penitent, to drop into Meditation. But Gilbert began, sitting on the opposite bench.

'First of all, Master,' he said, 'we are very glad, indeed, that you have now learned to distinguish. Marry one with the other, as much as you please; but like with like: not like with unlike. One does not marry a rose of June with a—with an onion of September.'

The Master inclined his head gravely. 'What do you mean,' he said, 'by saying that you have come to take me away? What are you going to do with Cicely?'

'Cicely is in good keeping, Master. Do not be in any anxiety about her.'

'Last night, Cicely,' he began again querulously, 'I could not meditate. For the first time during twenty years—yes, more than twenty years—I failed to meditate. Again, this morning—I failed. After dinner, just now, it is true I was borne upwards; but only to see that transparent soul clouded, and she said—what did she say? She held her husband by the hand and she rebuked me.' He laid his hand upon his head. 'She said, "Master, should we two be here but for the love we have borne to each other? Should we two have risen so high but for the comfort and stay of one towards the other? Nay: we should have been far lower—far lower—far more selfish—far more earthly. Go now." She told me to go. "We will discourse again when this has been set straight." So I see—at last—that there are natures to whom love is as the sunshine to the flowers—your flowers, Cicely.'

'Nay, Master, I am sure my mother knows that you acted for the best.'

'I have had a terrible time,' he repeated. 'You were gone, Gilbert was gone. Your mother would not receive me, and the members have rebelled against the Rule. I know not what they want: but I cannot fight against them: I am too old: they must go their own way. They no longer believe that we stand alone in space, every one alone.'

Gilbert laughed gently. 'My dear Master, you yourself have never been alone: you have always had your dead friend Alice to sustain you: and you have always entertained a most delightful Single Attachment for Cicely.'

'It is true,' he replied humbly. 'In that sense I have never seemed to be alone. Yet one must be alone. It is a fact which must be recognised. We are born alone: we die alone: we rise or fall alone.'

'Love removes the solitude: you acknowledge that you yourself have never been alone: you have always loved and been loved: and you have never felt alone.'

'Yet——'

'To ruder natures marriage may be a hindrance. To the rather rough and boorish people here marriage may present itself, when they consider it at all, as a condition of life which is a hindrance to the soul. In marriage they must be absorbed in the cares of the house: the husband working too hard every day: the wife working too hard every day: with sordid accompaniments, privations, quarrels, bad tempers and pinchings.'

'That is so,' the Master interrupted. 'To such persons love might seem a hindrance. Yet it might not be so, because it might possibly produce virtues such as the single life could never attain.'

'Yet, Brother Gilbert, Sister Phœbe was willing to marry you.'

'That excellent Sister,' Gilbert replied softly, ' was so very good as to be willing to take me, different as I am from her at every point. She is a zealous member of the Rule. Yet she was willing to enter upon a Single Attachment. It proves that the most orthodox member in the whole of this Community actually desires the companionship which is regarded with dislike by the Master.'

'Come back to us, Gilbert, and stay with us. You shall marry Cicely and make your Elevation in your own way.'

'No, Master; that is impossible. I will tell you directly what we propose.'

'Stay with us, Gilbert,' he repeated. 'The Community will be the richer for your presence. Besides, I can read your soul through and through. Like my dead friend Raymond you are true and loyal: you have no selfish purpose of your own to serve.'

'Nevertheless, I came here, five weeks ago, with a purpose which I did not confess to you.'

'It was some purpose connected with the man who calls himself Charles Lee. I know now. I do not know how I learned it: nor what your purpose was. It is now too late, because to-morrow he leaves the House. I have turned him out.'

'Oh! You have turned him out? Curious. Yes: I think he will go to-morrow.'

Gilbert's face grew hard. But only for a moment. He returned to the business before him.

'You tell me,' he said, ' that your members are in a state of rebellion. Frankly, I do not wonder. When I came here and began to look about and to talk to them it seemed to me as if they were all dropping slowly into a condition in which nothing would be left to them except a mouth for the reception of food. They were becoming like unto the common slug. I went about the workshops : only those members who felt that they must put forth a certain amount of bodily exertion and fatigue were turning out any real work. The Farm : the Dairy : the Garden : the Laundry—those do well because the bodily exertion keeps life in them : all the rest are shams. You have the account-books—is it not so ?'

'It is so.'

'You have taken from these people everything, except a little work and a great deal of food. You have left nothing that can occupy their minds. You discourage conversation because it may become frivolous. What is the consequence ? They cannot talk any longer : they never speak : many of them have almost forgotten how to frame a sentence—my friend Silas, for instance, is almost inarticulate. You think, from the heights on which you live, that everybody will be thinking of things high and sacred when you have left them nothing else.'

The Master inclined his head again. 'True. Their minds naturally turn in the direction of things high and sacred.'

'Do they ? Then you have not suffered them to read books, and they never leave this place. Therefore, they think about what you have left them. What is that ? Food, chiefly, and repose—vacuous repose. Do any of them meditate on higher things ? I do not know : I can see no sign of any such Meditation. Most of them appear to me to be exactly like the hogs in a sty : they feed : they sleep : they grunt. In the evening they fall into a state of catalepsy : when they recover they remember nothing. Of what good is their catalepsy, of which they remember nothing ?'

'It is hoped that in time they will remember. For my own part I do remember.'

'So does Cicely, sometimes. The rest—never. I have

asked them all. Each thinks that others remember: they believe in glimpses and glances, and flashes of light. They know only that they have been unconscious. I suppose that the dropping off is pleasant, and perhaps the recovery as well: otherwise they wouldn't do it at all. But as for the help they get from it, I can tell you, Master, speaking quite plainly, there is none at all. You and Cicely are the only two with whom the Hour of Meditation is more than an hour of catalepsy. You have restored, you say, the Eastern custom of Meditation to the West. Well—to all these people—your rank and file, the custom is a pretence and a sham.'

The Master groaned. He had not the strength to dispute the point. He could not in this hour of despondency stand up for his teaching or its results.

'It is not your fault. You imagined that these people were made of the same material as yourself and your earliest disciples. That is not so. They are a highly nervous and excitable people, because they are Americans. They have been brought up in a narrow and selfish religion, in which Individualism is carried to its extreme. They are easily reduced to the condition of trance by their nervous organization: and they are enabled to accept your teaching of the separate and lonely condition of the soul because it falls in with their own early religion. I dare say they honestly hope to penetrate by this way into the other world. Meantime, what are their habitual thoughts? They have none: they have lost the influences of their former life—their church, their singing, their religious exercises: and you have given them nothing in place of these things. They grow worse, therefore, every day, instead of better: more animal, and less intellectual; half a dozen, already, at least, have become pure imbeciles who can only eat and sleep and go into trance: they have gone back to the primeval prehistoric creature consisting of a bag to hold food and a mouth, and two hands to put food into it!'

'You are hard, Gilbert,' said Cicely. 'Spare the Master.'

'One person alone has kept her mind open and healthy. You gave Cicely, happily, the only work that could have kept her mentally awake. She has lived among the flowers. They are live things to her: they speak to her: and she has talked with you every day—about her dead parents—until she has grown to know them both, and believe that in trance she speaks with them——'

'Nay: not believes: she does speak with them every day.'

'It is well for her that she does, then. Now, Master, what do you think of my picture?'

'I cannot say what I think—I am an old man. If this is true, then have I spent my life in vain: and I have led these poor people after a will-o'-the-wisp.'

'Nay: at least, they have led in this place innocent and harmless lives. What would they be doing Outside? Cheating each other in trade, perhaps. Struggling, ignobly, to lead an ignoble life. You have done no harm to them. Don't think of it that way.'

'What way, then? Cicely, tell me how I am to think of it. You tell me this—and that'—he spoke in a wandering, helpless kind of fashion, his eyes unsteady —the Master, who had been always so alert and strong that one forgot his seventy-five years. 'You say that Cicely will not stay. How can I think at all without her? How can I live without the child?'

'You shall keep your child,' said Gilbert, moved to pity by his weakness and distress.

'We shall not part, dear Master,' said Cicely, 'believe me. Never again.'

'Tell him, Cicely, what we have planned for him.

Gilbert left them together in the Hall. He closed the door, and sat down in the verandah. Beyond the lane, under the shade of the trees, sat, as usual, the man whose fate was to be determined on the morrow.

He sat motionless—his legs crossed, his hands folded—hatless—his face white as of marble, his lips set—the man whom nothing could move.

The place—it was nearly five in the afternoon—was very silent: now and again there was heard the lowing of kine. The engines had ceased their throbbing, and there was no grinding of the wheels: the work of the day was over. Gilbert thought of the strange, apathetic people, who had no interests in life and cared for nothing, and believed that they were making straight for Heaven by going off into trance every night. 'Many and wonderful,' he thought, 'are the ways that lead to the narrow gate; but truly this of the nightly trance is the most wonderful. To do nothing except to become insensible. Heard one ever a more remarkable belief in the efficacy of annihilation?'

Presently the bell rang for supper, and the Community came flocking in to the Hall. First the men, with slow but resolute step, advancing to the chief event of the day. Even the most vacuous faces lit up when that discordant bell began to clash and clang. 'Pork and cabbage!' it cried aloud. 'Come! Pork and cabbage! Pork and beans! Come! Tender loin and tough! Beef and bacon! Come! Huckleberry and apple pie! Come! Coffee and iced water! Come! Supper first and Meditation after. Work finished. Recreation done. Come! come! come!'

They looked at Gilbert in curiosity as they passed: something had been said about running away: but it mattered nothing to them now. They wanted to eat, and then to sleep, and afterwards to become insensible. The women were not so punctual: they dropped in by twos and threes. Among them was Sister Euphemia.

'You, Gilbert?' she cried. 'You are back again?'

'I have brought Cicely to see the Master. They are both unhappy without each other. And you, Euphemia —why—what have you done to yourself?'

'Some of us have discarded the old costume—we've

been dressmaking all the afternoon—I hope you like my new dress. I made it myself this afternoon, from an old frock that I haven't worn for twenty years.'

She had tied up her hair with a ribbon; she wore lengthened skirts so that the horrible trouserette thing at the ankles had either vanished or been sent away: she had a coloured ribbon round her neck and a little bunch of flowers at her throat and a coloured silk sash: and her frock was in the fashion of the year 1875, when she left the Outside. Well, it is not so very long ago, but there was an old world look about it.

'I congratulate you, dear Euphemia. And what next?'

'Oh! a good deal next. But come in.'

The Hall was full by this time. The Master sat in his own chair, at the head of the middle table: but beside him was Cicely—and he held her hand in his, and his eyes dwelt upon her as if he could not bear to let anything else be seen at all.

Sister Euphemia took her place. Brother Charles did not appear at all.

'Cicely is with the Master,' said Euphemia. 'Oh! it would kill him to part with her. He loves her as much as an old man can love a girl. And yet he wouldn't allow a Single Attachment! That's going to be changed.'

Sister Euphemia's manner was quite altered. She had gone back, it seemed, to her old self, which was a cheerful, chattering self.

'I will take Cicely's place this evening.'

She did so. Gilbert took his old place as before. Opposite him sat Sister Phœbe. On his left was Brother Silas. Neither of them took the least notice of him, except by their shoulders, which were expressive.

'Oh, Brother Gilbert,' Euphemia went on, 'how nice it is to see you back again! You should have been in the Hall last night. Oh, but you don't know. Here are the Bride and Bridegroom—congratulate them.'

She indicated the blushing pair.

'What do you mean?' asked Gilbert.

'Why, after you went away, the Master ordered these two to marry each other, so's to cure them of Single Attachments. Brother Silas, you know, was singly attached to Cicely and Sister Phœbe was singly attached to you. Their condition was dangerous as regards Elevation.'

'Really!' Gilbert's face assumed quite a rosy wreath of smiles. 'Permit me, Sister Phœbe, to wish you every joy—and you—Brother Silas. Happy Dog!—I have been thinking, Sister Phœbe,' he said, with another smile, 'what could be designed to make you happier, if anything could be hit upon; and, truly, I do not think there is anyone in all this House more worthy for you in every respect—none able to meet every virtue and grace in yourself with one corresponding of his own—than Brother Silas. You will soar—happy, wingless spirits —together: and I am quite sure that you can neither of you mount so much as a single inch higher than the other.'

Sister Phœbe looked ominous, but she said nothing. She was quick enough to understand what was meant. Brother Silas was not: he only understood that something dangerous was said: something scornful.

'I hate an Englishman,' he replied doggedly.

'Why, then,' said Gilbert, 'what could more endear you to Sister Phœbe? How better could you hope to soar than on the wings of such a sentiment?'

'Don't make him mad,' whispered Euphemia. 'He's half mad already at losing Cicely. Let him be. He'll take it out in ill temper with his wife. I know that sort.'

'And you have had a mutiny, or a rebellion, I hear.'

'Yes: we only began last night. We are going on, though. Things have got to be changed a bit. Why, when you came here first it was like a great big tomb. I didn't mind. The Past was buried; there was no more joy left: I'd just as soon be buried in the tomb with all the rest. Nobody spoke, nobody laughed, nobody cared for anybody. We were all selfish logs. Then you came and broke us up. Oh, we are going to change a good many things! We are going to make things hum. Going to stay, Brother Gilbert? See you've got your store-clothes on. So's Cicely. My! Isn't she just too lovely?'

'I'm not going to stay, I fear.'

'And Cicely?'

'She will not stay either. She will come with me.'

'Then I tell you, young man, that the Master will just sit down and die. As for me, I don't know but what I'll go back again—Outside. There's Mamie and James—I don't know how they're doing, nor what children they've got. Since the Past came back—you brought it back—yet it never really left me—it's borne in upon me that I ought to go and see them. I've got a little money, so's not to be a burden upon anybody, and perhaps to be a help—and—and—I shall see. If the Master goes, and you, and Cicely—this will be a poor kind of place for such as me.'

'But your Meditations?'

'Bless you, my dear boy, with an apron over my head I can meditate anywhere. Besides'—she dropped her voice—'what's the good? I never remember anything. Sometimes there's a kind of a sort of a flash—just a gleam —but nothing comes of it. I shouldn't wonder if I went away and never came back here any more.'

Just then the shuffling of feet and the colliding of plates showed that the repast was concluded.

'Now for Meditation,' said Euphemia cheerfully.

CHAPTER XVI.

THE MASTER ABDICATES.

AT that moment, contrary to reasonable expectation, instead of stretching out his legs, folding his hands and going off into Meditation without any delay, the Master rose in his place, looked round the room, as every Master, Professor, or Lecturer does, to command attention, and held up his hand. Then those who were preparing to meditate recalled the soul just stepping out of its earthly tenement for its night ramble among undiscovered worlds, and sat upright with open eyes and great astonishment. And silence fell upon all: for the Master was going to speak. Great as had been the recent events in the House, this was the greatest event of all. The Master was going to address them.

He began to speak: at first, because he was out of practice, with hesitating words, and with half-forgotten phrases that he was seeking after and recovering. But as he went on, his old power came back to him: that magic touch by which oratory commands and holds an audience returned once more; and, as his rich full voice rolled about the walls and among the rafters, his hearers listened as much entranced as in Meditation itself. Some there were who heard the music of his voice but could no longer understand the meaning of his words—these were the vacuous members whose minds had been completely cleaned out and emptied: they understood nothing: and they presently, after a little uncomfortable patience under the unaccustomed, fell into their usual condition of temporary annihilation. The newly-married pair, also, received the preaching without any show of enthusiasm, because their minds were now naturally full of themselves. The honeymoon was cloudy, with promise of much rain and heaviness, which shows how Elevation is hindered by the wedded condition even without the distraction of the Single Attachment. As for the discourse itself, one cannot reproduce the whole of it. But the following is perhaps the more important part: the part which most concerns this narrative.

'My children, my brothers, my sisters,' said the Prophet, 'it is long since I have addressed the Community: it is many years since I have spoken on our common Life and on its objects. It is so long that most of you have never heard my voice at all and have never learned the reasons why I founded this House with Raymond, my first Brother, and Alice, my first Sister.

'It was our sole intention in founding this House to further Elevation—so, that, when the time for migration arrived, we should be enabled to take our places at once in an upper and a happier world. There are, as you know, endless worlds: we are always rising or always falling: man is never at rest: therefore there is always room for anxiety as regards the future: yet there has grown up in my mind a steadfast belief and consolation that, as man rises higher, descent becomes less easy for him: in other words, Elevation strengthens as well as raises. But the great mass of men and women, from generation to generation, hover about, now above, and now below: and the lower we fall, the more difficult it is to rise, the easier it is to fall lower still: and the pit is bottomless: for there is no depth but what there lies a deeper depth below. There may come a time when a man may cease altogether to discern good from evil, or to desire any good thing at all.

'I know these things, partly because they were revealed to me long ago: partly because I am confirmed in the knowledge by daily commune with the parents of Sister Cicely, whom we foolishly and wickedly drove from among us, the Daughter of the House. They are things which Outside knows not at all, thinking that this existence begins and ends everything, or else that it is the prelude to unearned happiness, or undeserved agonies to last for ever. Why did I not preach these things Outside? Because it would be useless. No one would listen: no one would believe, as I quickly learned. The prejudices and the early teaching and the poetry and the literature of Outside all alike maintain the old belief. I therefore refrained from further effort and withdrew, coming over here with my only two disciples to live the life of Meditation for which Outside is, as yet, unfitted.

'How did we propose to lead that life? First by seclusion: we would be quite alone with our own thoughts, undisturbed. We would have none of the temptations of Outside: there should be no desire at all to make money: there must be no anxieties about keeping the body alive and in health. These two main points we secured by resolving that everybody in the House should do every day a fair day's work of seven or eight hours: we had money enough with us to buy this land and to build a frame-house of three or four rooms to begin with: we lived simply, as we do now. Then, having made it possible to feed the body, we had to keep it well and strong and free from pain, because physical pain affects the mind. So we resolved, whether we wanted money or not, upon taking exercise, if not by our work, then in some other way—in the open air: this we called Fatigue: it was, as you know, followed by daily Restoration in the common Hall. It was necessary, we also thought, to keep the mind in health and strength: therefore we would have Recreation in the afternoon. And thus everything led up to the great work for which this House stands alone, namely, Elevation by Meditation. Yes: we introduced once more into the Western world the long forgotten practice of Meditation. It is peculiar to ourselves. We may boast, if we allowed ourselves to boast at all, that there is no other place, out of India, where Meditation is the chief end and aim of existence. We do not read—why should we? Reading is a distraction, not an aid: it leads the mind away: it suggests disturbing thoughts: it is a disquieting influence: it is full of Outside. What can reading teach us? Nothing, we thought, that is helpful. Nothing that elevates. We do not conduct services— why should we? Retired from man, we do not need the services of prayer and praise that are necessary— Outside—in order to withdraw their minds from their own work. We have no ambitions: we have no social distinctions: we have no cark or care about business: for us such services as the world desires would prove to be disturbing. We have no sermons. Why should we want a preacher? He can warn and admonish Outside, not ourselves: we need no such admonition, because there is no evil doing or evil thinking in this Community. Aids there are—music—dancing—the rhythmic motion of the body to the sound of music—these may help. Then we are, every one of us, alone in the vast universe: we do not therefore want any of the so-called alleviations of solitude—the illusions of love—the daily companionship of another—the mirage of the Single Attachment. Quite alone we live: quite alone we meditate: quite alone we climb. That is why in Retirement and in Repose we occupy each a solitary cell.'

There was a solemnity in the last utterance which made Gilbert, at least, think that in Outside most people slept six in a room.

The Master continued: 'One thing was necessary for the success of this endeavour—namely, a severance complete and absolute from the Past. We must forget the Past. It is our chief rule—forget the Past. Bring to Meditation a mind cleared of all that has gone before. Let there be no memory of it: no regret for it: no longing for it. Let it be dead—all the follies of the Past—all that made it pleasant or unhappy. This is our only Rule: the rest is practice or custom which has grown up. On that condition we admitted everybody —the greatest sinner—the greatest criminal—if he or she would forget the Past.' Here some of the Community hung their heads. 'I fondly hoped that all had forgotten the Past. There can be no true Meditation without it. I learn to-day, to my confusion and shame, that the Past has not been forgotten. You still remember it, some of you: you live in the Past: you think of the Past all day long. One among us whose

Past was very black, I have ordered to leave the House. How many more of you are there who still remember the Past?'

'Master,' it was Sister Euphemia who rose up and replied, 'I have never forgotten the Past. I lived in it as in a grave, till Brother Gilbert came and bade me think of the present. In Meditation there has never come even a gleam of light or a ray of hope.' She sat down.

Another woman rose—a woman who had once been beautiful.

'I have never forgotten the Past,' she said, 'except in Meditation, I see it always. There are the fingers of scorn and the cruel eyes. The Past can never be forgotten.'

And then a man arose. 'Master, why should we try to forget what follows us like our shadow? The Past cannot be forgotten. In Meditation we seem to forget it, because we are senseless. As for climbing into higher planes, I know nothing about any climbing at all. The Past is always before me. If I had continued in Outside I might have forgotten it. Things happen there to make one forget the Past: we must press onwards: we are driven on. But here? Nothing happens. The Past is always before me, like a ghost.'

An unhappy Past, this man's.

And another. And another. And another. All followed with the same story of the Past that they could not forget.

The Master bowed his head. 'My children,' he said, 'I have lived in a Fool's Paradise. I thought you were climbing high into other worlds, while you were only sinking into forgetfulness to escape the living Past. We must change all this. There have been other signs of discontent—the trouble about the women's dress. I never thought upon the subject. I wished you all to have the same dress so that there should be no rivalry in vanities. You wish that dress changed for some other—perhaps you wish to dress as you please. Well: remember only the main object of the Community. What else do you desire?'

'We want books to read,' said one; and a murmurous approval came from every voice. 'Books,' they said. 'Books to read.'

The Master bowed his head. 'If books will not distract you,' he said, 'read books.'

'And the newspapers,' said another. And from every man there came a shout: 'The newspapers! The newspapers!' They were Americans, and they had never seen a newspaper since they entered the House! The thirst for the newspapers came back to them like a flood or a mountain torrent after rain. 'The newspapers!' they repeated again and again.

'And we want,' said Sister Euphemia, 'a chapel and regular services and a choir to sing hymns.'

'Yes,' said another woman. 'And tea meetings.'

'And a Minister.'

'And Lectures.' They remembered, little by little, all the old life and the things that they used to love.

'And a Sunday School.'

'And a Literary Society.'

'And picnics and Surprise parties.'

'And not to work on Sabbath Day.'

'And concerts.'

'And prayer meetings.'

'And dramatic performances.'

'And missionary meetings.'

They cried one after the other.

'And SHOPPING,' said Sister Euphemia solemnly. Then all the women sighed and smiled and gasped as with a yearning after the long lost. 'Oh! how we could meditate,' Euphemia added, 'after a morning's shopping, and in a dress like Sister Cicely's!'

It seemed as if the last word had been spoken. What could be added?

But Sister Phœbe rose in her place and spoke. 'And

we want besides—we want—for incompatibility of temper—we want Divorce.'

Silas looked round him slowly. 'I can't talk much,' he said. 'I never could talk much. But I don't mind if we do have Divorce.'

'In short,' said the Master, 'you want in everything a return to Outside. So be it. For my own part, I am too old to change. I must continue till I die in the old lines. Well, I have made up my mind to hand over the charge of the House to others. Choose your own Master. As for me, I am going away with Cicely and Gilbert. I leave you in prosperity: the House has been largely blessed, the barns are overflowing: there is money at the Bank: the farm is stocked: the gardens are productive: the workshops are fitted with all that is wanted. Keep up the habit of daily Fatigue, and remember that the aim of the Community is Elevation not Degradation. Keep up the common Restoration: the Recreation: the Meditation. As for the rest, you will add to our simple life what you think best. In one thing I have been wrong. There are some to whom love—I mean the Single Attachment—is a necessity of their lives. It has been impressed upon me by recent events, and by the contemplation of Raymond and Alice always together, always thinking of each other first, always rising together—that the upward Way to some may lie through Single Attachment. I was led to think otherwise by inexperience: I have never in my life loved any woman in that way—the two women whom I love most are Alice, who is my sister: and Cicely, who is my child. Forget all that I have said about the Single Attachment: yet do not seek it, do not think of it, lest it prove unworthy, and so become a snare and a pitfall. Outside, I know, they write and think about the Single Attachment as if life had no other joy.

'I leave this place. I would have stayed on until the end, but I perceive very clearly that you will have change. Forgive me if I have injured or wounded anyone by criticism or in any other way. We have been for the most part a harmonious community. Until the last day or two there has been nothing to mar the peace of our home. Let me believe that it will be carried on, if not in the same way—the old believe there is no other way—then with the same ends in view. And now, dear friends, let me not think the work of my life has been a failure. Keep the same end in view. Let me die happy in the thought that though you may change the method, you preserve the truths that have brought us together. Think of the blessings that have fallen upon us all—the increased wealth—the easy life that has been granted to you. Where else would you find a life so easy or food so abundant, or work so light? Remember these things, and, if you would have them continued, observe the way of life; the industry: the Community: the Simplicity: which have given them to you. And now, dear brothers and sisters, I make an end. Farewell! farewell!'

He walked down the Hall slowly, his tall and venerable figure slightly bent, his soft and limpid eyes dim with tears. With him, one on each side, walked Cicely and Gilbert. Now, at the sight of this abdication, the members suddenly recollected all that the Master had done for them: they remembered, as he had reminded them, the peace and order, the abundance, the light work, the quiet of the life. The women wept and kissed his hands. 'Stay, Master, stay!' they cried. But he shook his head sadly. The men caught at his hands. 'Stay, Master, stay!' they cried. But he shook his head. His life-work was done. If there had been one—only one—to rise up and proclaim the blessing of Meditation, and how it had enabled his soul to soar aloft to heights ineffable, then, perhaps, he would have stayed. But there was none. They had not forgotten the Past, and they could not remember whither they went, or what they saw and heard, in Meditation. Not one to stand up for the Rule! What, think you, would have been the feelings of St. Francis of Assisi, if, at the close of his life, there had not been found one single brother or sister to soothe his soul with the assurance of one at least who had been raised by the Rule? Not one to declare the efficacy of Meditation! Yes: there were about a dozen. Gilbert remarked them. They proclaimed its efficacy, because at the beginning of this long speech they had 'gone off' as usual, and were now sitting, with outstretched feet, heads back and eyes open, in that trance which was become their passion—the desire of which was a yearning stronger than the yearning for drink, more irresistible than the yearning for the green table. They illustrated the efficacy of the Rule: they had neither past nor future: their minds and memories and brains were swept out and empty: not even a cobweb was left in them: they had nothing to think about except the regularly recurrent joy of Restoration and that of 'going off' into blankness and returning with a vague sense of glories witnessed and forgotten.

'Look!' Gilbert would have said, but refrained. 'There are the triumphs of your system! There are the people who have been elevated by Meditation!' In their places at the table, nearly opposite to each other, sat the newly-married pair. Their faces indicated the happiness of a honeymoon undertaken by order. They alone, except the Vacuous Ones, suffered the Master to depart without a word of regret. Their cheeks burned, their eyes showed the deepest resentment. Silas was inarticulate, but he gazed after Cicely with a strange and rather dangerous look of the wild animal ready to fight for his mate. It wanted but little for him to rise and fall upon his rival. But he wanted words in which to clothe that temptation. He could say nothing.

'Silas!' Phœbe said, 'you ought to have followed him and brought them both back. You are a coward —you are a coward. It's too late now.'

Said Silas: 'I hate an Englishman.'

'Here they come,' said Phœbe, loud enough to be

heard by the Master if he was listening, and by Gilbert, who did listen, pleased to observe the discomfiture of these zealous members. 'Here they come—with their Single Attachments against the rules. Let them go. We don't want Englishmen here. I hate an Englishmen, too, Silas—you great log—you great coward—do you hear? If there's law in the land we'll have a divorce!'

'I want it,' said Silas the Unready, after a pause, 'worsen you.'

'Here,' Gilbert would have said, but did not, 'are two more examples of the House. They are the most zealous to carry out the Rules. Have they been elevated in the least? One began as a Boor, and so remains, with the manners and the habits of a Boor: had he been taught instead of being left alone, he might have become a kind of gentleman. The other is a village shrew, with the tongue and the mind and the passion of her class.'

So they passed through the people and went out. There was waiting for them a carriage, and they put the Master in and drove away.

'I have brought you the Master, Dorabyn,' said Gilbert. 'He has made up his mind to resign his Mastership, and to live with Cicely wherever she may go.'

Lady Osterley gave the old man her most gracious welcome. He was a good deal worn by the fatigues and excitements of the day, and he looked old and shaken. It has been seen that the revolt of his people was trying after so many years of peaceful rule. Moreover, the strangeness and the newness of the place troubled him; and the aspect, even the gracious welcome, of the *grande dame* embarrassed him. Remember that for twenty years and more he had never stepped outside the House of his Community. He sat down and looked about the room as if he hardly understood what was happening. He was like a domestic cat taken to a strange house. His bewilderment became alarming.

'Master,' said Cicely, taking his hand, 'you know me, don't you? I am Cicely, your daughter.'

'Yes—yes—Cicely. I know you, but I do not know myself. Where is the Community?'

'Dear Master, if you will go and talk with my mother a little! Please play something,' she said. 'He wants his usual Meditation; then he will get better.'

Lady Osterley complied, playing things that soothe: things that float about the brain and allay all kinds of trouble. The old man sat quite still and silent, listening to the music. Then his head fell back: his feet stretched themselves out: his hands lay folded: and he became rigid like a dead man. He was once more in Meditation.

'Heavens!' Lady Osterley whispered. 'Does he do this every night?'

'Every night,' Gilbert replied. 'You need not whisper: you can talk as loud as you please, he will not hear you.'

'Why does he do it?'

'He believes that in trance he can transport his soul wherever he pleases. He goes to converse with his friend Alice—Cicely's mother. She sends messages by Cicely and by him to me, you know.'

'Gilbert! Again. This from you? I shall end by believing.'

'I assure you again, Dorabyn, that I cannot choose but believe. However, now that he is off, I should like——' He glanced at Cicely. She looked restless; her face was assuming the expression that fell upon the Community when they could not 'go off' so easily as was customary. 'Play something else—play a waltz—the best waltz that you know. I think that you will be rewarded for your trouble.'

Lady Osterley changed the music: she played a most lovely waltz: one of those that make old people remember their youth, and make them sick with yearning for the impossible return, and put life, and joy, and cadenced

motion into the feet of the young. And then she learned
why Gilbert asked for a waltz. For Cicely rose, her face
grave and serious, as one who begins some religious
function. She rose, as if unconscious of the presence
of any other person; she stepped into the middle of
the room, and then began one of those mystic, self-
taught dances of hers which had so moved Gilbert on
the first day of Meditation. It was a kind of skirt
dance, with movements of the arms, and bendings of
the body—a graceful dance, in which every limb played
its part, but without contortions, and quite seriously.
Dorabyn played and looked on in amazement. 'Faster!'
cried Gilbert. She played the waltz faster—faster.
Then the girl turned up her arms over her head, and
whirled round swiftly. Dorabyn brought the music to
an end with a crash of chords, and Cicely sank breathless, with closed eyes, into Gilbert's arms. He laid her
on a sofa, apparently lifeless.

Lady Osterley left the piano, and bent over the girl,
lying supine on the long, low couch.

'Strange!' she whispered. 'Last night I was ready
to call it Death. And this they have been doing every
night! Yes, Gilbert, such a wonderful, mysterious
power as this would be sure to attract the mystic
nature of Alice Osterley. Cicely, as I look at her,
grows more and more like her mother as I remember
her. A delicate creature, Gilbert. She will want all
the love and thought that you can give her if she is
really like her mother.'

'She will have all the love and thought that I can
give her.'

Gilbert stooped and kissed her forehead. It was very
cold, as in death. He lifted her hand and felt her
pulse. There was none perceptible, nor did she seem
to breathe. He sat down beside her, and they began
to talk in whispers.

'See,' he said, 'there is nothing of her left but the
shell. Life and thought have gone out of her. It is

a beautiful shell, Dorabyn. Did mortal maiden ever before have a face so delicate and so sweet?'

'She is very beautiful, Gilbert. I hope she will not become too saintly for this world's use. But I think not. Alice had a husband who was like herself. They encouraged each other. This girl will have a more earthly husband. You must not destroy the spiritual side of her. But you will not.'

'She has gone to see her mother. They are talking together now.'

'Gilbert!'

'I say, Dorabyn, that I cannot choose but believe. She has told me things that she could not otherwise know: as that her mother was in Lucknow when it was relieved—a little girl—and that my father, then a subaltern, took her up and kissed her. Well, my father was with his regiment at the Relief of Lucknow. How could Cicely know that fact?'

'It is difficult to answer that question. Still——'

'Still, I must believe these things because now, in a way that I cannot explain to you, the whole of this child's happiness, and that of—of other people as well—depends upon their truth.'

He spoke very seriously—more seriously than he had ever spoken before—this young man who mostly took things so lightly. And, indeed, there was something solemn in the presence of these two lifeless persons lying as if dead. Dorabyn whispered in reply, but what she whispered were no more than words of sympathy—such words as belong to a woman.

'If the messages are from Alice—really and truly from Alice—they must be true messages, for Alice is all truth and purity through and through, in death as in life.'

The Master was the first to return. He looked round; he remembered where he was and what had happened: he laid his hand on his forehead.

'My children,' he said, remembering. 'Have no fear. I am commanded to tell you—have no fear: for all is well—and all will continue well. Peace and love and union which shall never be destroyed. All is well.'

Then he rose and, as at the House, he retired after Meditation to Repose.

They sat beside the unconscious girl.

At last she, too, returned.

'You have come back, Cicely.'

'Yes, Gilbert. And oh! I am to dance no more.'

'To dance no more?'

'My mother tells me that I am to dance no more. And I am to have no more Meditation. And until she calls me, I am to have no more talk with her. Gilbert, she tells me to think of nothing now—not of her—or of the Master—or of the House—but only and always—all day and all night—of you!'

He stooped and kissed her forehead. And there was an unwonted dimness in his eyes and a strange choking at his throat.

'And I have a message for Brother Charles.' She looked about the room as if expecting to see him there.

CHAPTER XVII.

THE ORDEAL BY CARDS.

It was Saturday morning: the last day of the limit assigned: the day on which the hunted man was to be turned out to the hounds: the last day of grace to the criminal: the day of Death to one or other—perhaps to the avenger. Gilbert sat up in bed when he awoke—not a single minute before the usual time—and said this to himself over and over again. He said it over and over again while he was dressing. It would be a day of Death to one or two. Strange! The full certainty of the fact moved him not one whit. His nerves were perfectly steady, his pulse was quiet; he felt no anxiety or fear or doubt. Because, you see, he was by this time strangely persuaded of the reality of that message. Because in his brain the words rung and echoed over and over again: 'What must be done shall be done, but not by your hands.'

What should be done? How should it be done? Once more it was as if he ran his head against a brick wall. For there came no answer; none at all. It is impossible to believe certain things, especially certain things calling themselves supernatural. This was no silly nonsense about rapping tables and inverted baskets. It was as if to persons most incredulous as regards things supernatural there had come out of the very skies a message clear and unmistakable, with a promise equally clear and unmistakable. Should such a promise, such a prophecy, to be tested and proved in a few hours, be spoken by a person professing himself to be a medium, even those who are most incredulous would keep themselves from ridicule or judgment until the time of fulfilment. This was such a promise—Cicely, who delivered the message, declaring that she had received it, could know nothing about his own purpose, nothing about the past history of Brother Charles. Yet the message bade him wait for five weeks—how could the girl invent such a message?—and assured him that what had to be done would be done, but not by his hands. How should Cicely know that his father, of whom she could never have heard, had met her mother in Lucknow when she was a child?

He took up his revolver: he saw that it was loaded: he dropped it into his breast-pocket and descended to breakfast. 'Now we shall see,' he said. Meantime he marvelled that his mind was so calm and his hand so steady. Nothing short of Death faced him. That meant—to Dorabyn and to Cicely—what? He could not even think. It seemed as if it was some other man's business, not his own.

The others came into the *salle à manger* one by one,

Somehow all their faces—even Cicely's—were grave and serious. They took their breakfast almost in silence.

'Something is going to happen,' said Lady Osterley. 'I feel that something is going to happen.'

The touch of the supernatural in the trance of the Master and the girl probably caused this feeling. One cannot look into another world without being saddened. We never hear of mirth or laughter in any other world. It may be that the greatest happiness does not allow of laughter, which belongs to the unexpected and to the imperfect. This experience should be of itself quite enough to account for Dorabyn's shaky nerves. Yes. Something, she was sure, was certainly going to happen. And, besides, why should one try to account for nerves?

'I have known for some time,' said the Master, 'that something terrible will happen. I have not asked what kind of trouble it will be, or whom it will affect. It is enough for me to know that it will not bring sorrow on this child.'

He spoke in the deepest and most prophetic voice, insomuch that Lady Osterley, who was going to ask if he would take another cup of tea, feared to spoil the effect and held out her hand in silence for the cup.

'Well,' said Mr. Annandale cheerfully, 'since the terrible thing is not going to affect Cicely, it won't affect anybody here except me. And I don't feel the air heavy, not at all; it's a hot, bright stimulating air. I shall sit in the porch presently with a cigar, and I shall feel warm and good through and through.'

'There is Rebellion at the House,' said the Master. 'Perhaps it is that which was to happen. They may rebel; they may desire to change things, but they are sound at heart. I am old, and I see no longer so well as formerly the meaning and the forces of things. The young must reign over the world. It is the rule of the world.'

'You may trust them, Master,' said Gilbert. 'They have most of the things they want—they will only let in a little light from outside. Nowhere else could they continue to enjoy their three square meals a day even without the Meditation of the evening. They will all stay where they are.'

After breakfast Gilbert, without any explanation—without feeling impelled even to say farewell to Cicely—quietly ordered a carriage and drove to the House.

He arrived there about half-past ten, an hour when Fatigue is commonly in full swing. This morning no one was in the gardens; there was no sound of the engine from the workshops; there was no sign of any work at all. But from the Refectory came the clash and clang—as discordant as the sound of the bell—of many voices—yea, even of fifty speaking like one. The Revolt was going on. Speaking as a historian, they were in the middle of the second chapter.

So complete was the tranquillity of Gilbert's mind that even on this occasion, when his very life was hanging on a chance, he could postpone that business while he looked into the Hall for a few minutes upon this Parliament of rebels.

Everybody was there, and there were apparently divisions and dissensions—they were split up into knots and circles, all talking at once. And at one end of the Hall sat the company of the Vacuous who had too faithfully interpreted the Rule, and now had neither voice nor understanding left. They sat together, huddled like sheep, and they trembled.

Then Sister Phœbe sprang out from a knot of eager disputants, and jumped upon the Master's chair and spoke from that place as from a position of authority. Her shrill voice rang through the Hall like a prolonged shriek: her flushed cheek showed the excitement which possessed her.

'The Master has gone,' she cried. 'Why are we lamenting over what cannot be helped? He is gone. Well—we can do better without him. He was too old: he was held down by a Single Attachment. Let us have a younger Master. Let us select him at once, lest we fall into confusion. We must not wait a single hour. Why should we? Have we not a Brother—the only Brother who is fit to replace him? Has he not been the real Master for years? Who has provided Restoration for us? Brother Silas! Who finds us three regular meals a day? Brother Silas! The meals come out of the profits of the farm which he manages. Look at him! There is your true Master. He is the man you want.'

Brother Silas sat in his place quite silent, taking no part whatever in the discussion, even when it concerned himself.

'Look at him, I say! He is your farmer: on him depends everything—all your well-being. And he will sustain the Rule. Nothing but the Simple Rule. That must be maintained and obeyed. We won't have any new things to disturb us. The Simple Rule for us—the Simple Rule. Who is the man to elect for the Simple Rule? The man who manages your farm. No other. He will go on managing your farm and providing the three square meals a day. Nobody else can. Look at him! There is your Master!' She pointed again at Silas, who shook his head for want of words. 'What will you do for them, Silas?'

He made reply, shortly, 'Restoration.'

Gilbert, looking in at the door, marvelled at the change which a short twelve hours had accomplished. Last night the woman was glaring with thunder on her brow and lightnings in her eyes at the husband imposed upon her—call it the Alliance demanded by the Rule. She was crying out for divorce: she was calling her husband Log and Coward. This morning all was changed. She was crying out for her husband to be elected Master of the Community, with, apparently, no more thought or desire for divorce. A little later, when he was able to recall the scene, he remembered that marriage may very well become a partnership for purposes of ambition. As Dorabyn married the man who was certain to be Prime Minister for the sake of the position, so Phœbe was ready to remain the consort of Silas if he was to be Master—knowing full well who, in that case, would be the real Master of the Community.

'We will have no change,' she repeated, 'the Rule must not be altered.' She spoke as if it was the Ten Commandments or the American Constitution. 'There's Fatigue and Repose. There's Restoration and Recreation. There's Elevation and Meditation. No change. And there's Criticism. There's nothing more to desire. But we must all work harder. There have been slugs among us. We must put more heart into the work. Else there will be Criticism—and Expulsion.'

'We won't have Brother Silas,' cried little Sister Euphemia, jumping on the table; 'we'll have a man who can speak, not a dumb one who can only eat and work. And we're going to have lots of change. We're going to dress like decent people, and we shall have our Pastor and our Chapel and all—and we're going to town when we like. I'll be your Master. If you'll make me Master I'll see that Brother Silas goes on working. If he won't work, he shall go. Sister Phœbe, too. I'll look after your Restoration. You shan't have any more black mud for coffee—and the chops and the steaks shan't be fried together in the same pan. And——'

Then Sister Phœbe flew upon her and dragged her off the table. And then—where was Meditation? Where was Elevation? There was a fierce struggle among the sisters, who rushed one after the other tearing and dragging at arms and skirts—and in the middle Sister Phœbe and Sister Euphemia shook each other. It was the meeting of the two great principles, Reform and Conservatism. As for the men, they looked on, troubled and uncertain.

The floor was strewed with the fallen: it was even strewed with torn skirts and fragments of sleeves. The cries of the combatants might have been heard as far as Aldermanbury.

Then suddenly the Sisters desisted: they ceased pulling and dragging each other: they became ashamed of themselves, and they stood back, with panting chests and burning cheeks. Euphemia and Phœbe got up and pulled themselves straight and smoothed their hair with looks of war and determination, and again Euphemia the unconquered sprang upon the table.

'Make me the Master,' she said, 'and you shall have all that you have had already—and more—and more—and more. You shall have love if you like: you shall have books and newspapers: you shall have lectures and tea meetings. Make me your Master. Hold up your hands all who want me.'

A crowd of hands went up.

'All those who want the dumb man who can only eat and work hold up their hands.'

No one moved. The Community respected one who grew Pork so toothsome—beans so delicious: but Silas was inarticulate: and his wife's temper and her tongue they all knew. At this point Gilbert shut the door and left them.

In case my reader should find himself in Aldermanbury, and should wish to visit the House of Meditation, he will learn that the innovators have quite prevailed. It is only a year since the Rebellion. The Fraternity exists and flourishes. It is now a Community of men and women who lead the Common Life, many of them being married: they have bought more land; Brother Silas, who is not divorced, manages the farm with great skill and prudence, while his wife, who remains in all respects unchanged, manages the Dairy. Meditation survives; but it is no longer practised by the majority. The younger members doubt its efficacy: their Pastor—for they have now a Chapel of their own Persuasion—openly derides Meditation; they have a promising Literary Association: some of the associates have even proffered Poems to the Magazines: they were rejected, but the mere production proclaims a newly-born intellectual activity. They have built reading-rooms and writing-rooms. They take in the newspapers and the magazines: they have started a Library: they get wandering lecturers to discourse before them and country companies to play before them: they have dances and they have concerts of their own. In fact, it is a very comfortable Community: Restoration continues to be plentiful and admirable: and the Sisters dress just as they please.

Gilbert closed the door and stood on the verandah looking about him. At the end of the lawn where the trees stood thick, so that as you have seen there was coolness and shade on the very hottest mornings, he saw his enemy sitting on the bench beside his sister's grave. He walked across the grass to meet him. Gilbert was no braggart, nor was he reckless of life, or indifferent to life: on the contrary, he was as much attached to life as a young man in love should be. He knew that he was come to meet his fate: either to do what he had resolved to do: or to be himself destroyed: he knew and understood that very well. Yet he neither felt nor showed the least emotion. You have seen how he believed, with the strong faith of an early Christian, that things would in some way be made safe for him.

Sir Charles—we may give him his real name at last—rose and lifted his hat. He was no longer dressed in the uniform of the House, but in that of an English gentleman, with a long frock-coat, a white waistcoat, irreproachable linen, and a white flower in his buttonhole.

'I expected you,' he said.

'Have you anything to propose?' asked Gilbert.

'In one moment. We understand each other, I think. You came here with the intention of getting me out of the way—somehow.'

'You will admit that it is the only way of setting your wife free.'

'True. The only way. I have seen my wife and talked things over with her.'

'You have seen her? Lady Osterley came here? Who told her you were here?'

'You did—or perhaps Annandale, who came here; you sent him, too, I suppose—you would send half Piccadilly, if you could.'

'Your wife has been to see you! She told me nothing about it.'

'She even made me an offer—if I would live quietly. Women unfortunately do not understand. I cannot live quietly, as she calls it. Good Lord! man'—for one moment only he lost his external calm and showed emotion—'do you suppose it possible that I should have thrown away—what I have thrown away—if I could live quietly, as she calls it? My wife, I say, was good enough to wonder how a man can live under these conditions. For me, I confess, life has but one pursuit to be named or thought of.' He stopped for a moment. 'Cicely has been to see me, too. Cicely, who is, it appears, my sister's child. She is like her mother. She came yesterday, at night; she walked all the way over from the town.'

'Yesterday? In the evening? After we all went to bed? Cicely came here last night? She must have walked over in a dream.'

'She came at midnight. She came to my room. I was asleep. She said that her mother sent her—my sister. Curious! my sister Alice. She sent me word that she would meet me—this evening—this evening. If I was a superstitious man, I should believe that you would win. But we shall see.'

'Your sister will meet you—to-night,' Gilbert repeated. 'If she said this——'

'I used to think that you put her up to the messages. It seems ridiculous, but I cannot think so any longer. The Master yesterday morning came to offer me help—money. He said, very oddly, "I would offer you a hundred dollars, but it is useless. Five dollars will carry you on to Saturday evening. After that you will want no more."'

'The Master told you that?'

Gilbert observed that the man's look was changed. He had lost something from his iron face; the look that nothing could move. His eyes were restless: there was some kind of doubt—not fear—in them.

'You wish me to believe in these superstitions, I suppose. Well, sir, they shall not affect me in the least. Perhaps they were of your own devising?'

'No, they are not of my own devising.'

'Have you got any little message of the same kind for me?'

'None, I assure you.'

'Then, Mr. Maryon, we will proceed to business.'

'As you please.'

'I thought at first that we might use one of the workshops. There is no one at work this morning: they are all wrangling about something. But perhaps it is better to have things done in the open. I know a place up the stream a little way where we shall be undisturbed, and where you will be able to lie undiscovered for ever.'

'I follow you.'

Sir Charles rose from his seat: he was going to put his foot upon the flower-bed—his sister's grave—but remembered, and walked round it. He led the way across the lawn, past the workshops, to the stream. Then he turned to the left, where there was no path, but a narrow level way over grass up the bed of the stream.

Presently he turned sharply. 'Who is that with you?'

'There is no one.'

'I heard footsteps beside you.'

'Perhaps you hear the footsteps of Death. We have invited him.'

Sir Charles turned and went on without reply. Then he stopped.

'What are you whispering for?' He turned again.

'I am not whispering.'

'There is someone with you whispering.'

'I hear the rustle of the leaves and the babbling of the water over the stones. There is no whisper.'

'Look here! You have been trying to frighten me with your damned messages! You have set on that girl to worry me. You think at the last moment to shake my nerves with whispers and footsteps.'

'Have it as you please. I have sent you messages from your sister. Put it any way you please.'

Sir Charles made no reply, but turned and continued to lead the way. A few minutes brought them to the place where one of them might lie comfortably undiscovered for ever.

It was the same place where, under the disapproving eyes of Sister Phœbe, Gilbert had made love to Cicely. The same place, now sacred to the memory of Love and Life, soon, perhaps, to be sacred to the memory of Death and Murder. There rose the low cliff—a rock of shade and shelter; there lay the little green level between rock and stream: there were the overhanging wild vines: and there the projecting shelf of rock about four feet high and so many broad which Gilbert remembered: it would make a table fit for the Ordeal by Cards. On the other side of the stream was the forest, whose solitudes were never disturbed except by minx and snake. The place was perfectly silent save for the sough of the light summer breeze in the branches and the babbling of the brook. It was a place sacred to Love and Life, and these men were going to desecrate it by calling on Death to pollute it.

'Will this suit you?' Sir Charles asked.

'Perfectly.'

Sir Charles seated himself on one corner of the rock shelf. This again gave him an advantage over his adversary, who was standing. One who stands before another who sits is an inferior or an accused person or a servant.

'When we last discussed this matter,' he said, 'I mentioned a case similar to our own which was decided by a game of cards. It might be objected that the man who won had probably prepared the cards beforehand. As he understood perfectly how to prepare a pack of cards, it is very possible that he did do so. Few would blame him. Knowledge is power. But I propose, since we two are going to end our quarrel in the same manner, that there shall be no possibility of preparing the cards beforehand: no possibility even of a suspicion.'

'I accept.'

'We shall play *for the revolver*. That is understood. The stake is the possession of that revolver which I see is in your pocket. Take it out. So. Is it loaded? Very good. Lay it down on the rock between us. We will have the stake on the table. You may fully trust me, sir. On this occasion I will not touch the revolver or play you false in any particular. You shall be treated as a gentleman by—one who understands what that word means.'

Gilbert obeyed. He had no distrust of the man, who seemed to have become a man of honour once more: perhaps his appearance in the garb of an English gentleman helped him to this comfortable pretence.

The revolver, then, lay between them. They stood one on each side of the rock table. Gilbert listened to the music of the stream over the stones, and saw the fish darting to and fro in the shallows. Over his head hung the fresh green leaves and the branches of the wild vine. Perhaps he saw these things and felt the warmth of the air, and the splendour of the sun, and heard the rustle of the trees for the last time. Yet he was not afraid. He was neither anxious nor afraid. And as for the other man, he was like one who prepares to sit down at his club to play at whist for half-crown points—as cool and as undisturbed. When he held the cards in his hand his eyes lost their restless look: he became once more keen and cold and self-possessed.

'You have brought no cards with you, of course. I thought not. Here is a new and uncut pack—which I found in my portmanteau.' He drew the pack from his pocket. 'I wish you to examine the fastenings carefully, in order to satisfy yourself that it is a new and unopened pack. It is, in fact, an English pack which has been lying in my portmanteau for two years. You are satisfied? Very well. Cut the string yourself.' He gave his adversary the pack. 'Now—shuffle the cards yourself and cut them yourself; I do not suspect you—in fact, you don't know how to shuffle—and you shall have no cause for suspicion of me. So. Can you play écarté?'

'I can.'

'I probably play better than you, but I should have that advantage whatever game was proposed. Écarté is a short, quick game—much too short for such a stake as ours. I should like to play all night long for such a noble stake. All night long—to rise at six o'clock—the winner.'

'To make it longer, we will play for two games out of three.'

'Very good. Let us cut. Your deal, Mr. Maryon;' his eyes flashed: he became suddenly murderous; 'you understand quite well—if I win, it is my intention to kill you. I shall have no mercy upon you. It was to kill me out of the way that you came here. Very good. I shall kill you and bury you here in this quiet place, where no one will ever look for you or find you. I shall kill you, besides, because you have turned me out of my only refuge: because, I firmly believe, you have brought the police upon me. And because you have endeavoured to cover all up with hypocritical pretences about my dead sister. You quite understand?'

'Perfectly.'

Gilbert dealt.

Sir Charles took up his hand, and marked the king. 'I play.' He played: he took every trick. The next deal was his own.

'I propose,' said Gilbert.

'No;' and marked the king again.

They played the hand. The first game, quickly despatched, went to Sir Charles.

They began the second game. It was absurd. Again —twice—Sir Charles marked the king and took every trick. Never before, in any Ordeal on record, by cards, by fire, by water, was Judgment more clearly declared than in this. The second game was his, too. Two games out of three. And Gilbert had lost.

So strong was his faith in the messages that, even at that moment of defeat, he felt no fear.

Sir Charles collected and put up the cards in their wrapper and dropped the pack in his pocket, without the least hurry.

'We were playing,' he said quietly, 'for the revolver. It is, you will acknowledge, mine.'

'It is yours,' said Gilbert.

Sir Charles took it up and looked at it. 'A pretty thing,' he said; 'I know the make and the maker. Now, Mr. Maryon.' He was sitting on the rock; Gilbert was standing at the other side. Sir Charles raised his arm and pointed the revolver. Not even then did the bitterness of death assail him: the words of the message rang in his brain: 'What must be done shall be done.' And the words of the Master: 'Have no fear: for all is well.' The dark circle of the pistol's mouth by which was the way of death had no terrors for him.

Suddenly the hand that held the pistol dropped. Sir Charles started, looked round, and changed colour: and to his eyes there returned the look of doubt and anxiety. He laid down the pistol. He stood up and looked round again. He was bareheaded: the fingers of his right hand rested on the rock table, those of the left played with his watch-chain. Just so he had stood scores of times in the House of Commons amid a hailstorm of cries and questions. Just as he had looked then, just as austere, save for that look of perplexity, so he looked now, preparing for a murder in cold blood.

'The place is haunted,' he said. 'By what trickery did you knock down my hand? Who the devil have you brought with you?'

'I have brought nobody. As for the messages, they are true: you will not kill me. This evening, Sir Charles, you will meet your sister, as she warned you. I have only to say that I did not bring Lady Osterley here: that I did not send Annandale over here: that I did not invent any message: that I have not communicated with the police.'

Sir Charles made no reply whatever. He looked as if he had not heard. He took up the revolver again and looked at it. Was he going to raise the weapon once more?

'What must be done shall be done—but not by your hands.' Again the words went ringing through Gilbert's brain.

Sir Charles replaced the revolver on the table.

'Take it up,' said Gilbert.

'What do you mean?'

'Take the revolver. It is yours.

'Sir,' said Sir Charles, 'we played a fair game for life; I won. You have nothing to complain of. I am quite justified in killing you. It has been a fair duel.'

'A very fair duel. We played for the revolver, and I lost. It is yours.'

'Then you own that I am justified.' He took up the pistol.

'In killing yourself? Quite.'

'No, in killing you.'

'The revolver gives you the choice. You can kill either yourself or me.'

'Why should I kill myself?'

'I think I can make that clear.'

'You would have killed me if you had won.'

'I should not have been permitted to do so. You won, and the choice was not even left to me.'

'If you think to save your life by pretence and lies, you are mistaken.'

'You will not kill me.'

Sir Charles sat down again. 'Explain, if you please,' he said coldly.

'Sir Charles'—Gilbert spoke solemnly and slowly—'in the whole of this business I have been led. I cannot choose but believe that I have been led from the very beginning, and that by the dead hand of your sister Alice, who died in this place twenty years ago. She has led me through her daughter, and through her old friend the Master. You may scoff—but this is not a moment for scoffing. She has warned you. Had you shown any signs of repentance she would have preserved you. There were no such signs. The time has come when you will be permitted to work no more evil. I did not understand at first, but now she makes me understand every step.'

'She makes you understand? Are you mad? You are all gone mad, I think, about my sister Alice.'

'Consider, Sir Charles. You are in a position of deadly peril: you are a notorious criminal—we need not at this moment explain. If you step outside this place you will be very speedily arrested. Your identification is quite certain, because you cannot disguise yourself: once arrested, your photograph will be taken and published in every paper in the United States, so great is the interest taken in your remarkable career——'

'Pray go on, sir.' For Gilbert paused and hesitated.

'Only one thing is wanting, and your photograph will inform the world of your true name and your true career. Imagine, if you can, the delight of the Americans at having an ex-Minister of the British Cabinet in such a position. Now this is the danger which we are so anxious to avert. It affects the honour and the happiness of those at home, who are still in ignorance of your record—your mother and sister: it affects the whole future of your son: it affects your niece, Cicely Moulton. The danger has been provided for, but not by us: it exists, in fact, no longer, for you will meet your sister Alice this evening.'

Sir Charles stood with the pistol in his hand motionless: unmoved externally.

'Was it accident,' Gilbert went on, 'I ask you to consider, that brought you here to the house where your sister died and her child has lived? Was it accident that brought her here? Was it accident that brought your wife here? Was it accident that brought Annandale—your old friend—here to discover where you were hidden? Was it accident that determined this game of cards? You have the revolver: you know what use to make of it. If you use it rightly, you will die under a false name; nobody will know anything about you except the one or two who are certain not to talk. Is that accident? You have won the game and the revolver. If you use it wrongly, you will most certainly be arrested, put to a shameful death, and bring shame and suffering inconceivable upon your own people.'

Sir Charles stood up and looked round upon the sunshine and the hills. The most dreadful thing in Death, said the Greek, was to lose the sunshine and the light.

'I believe you are right,' he said. 'You stand for my wife and my people. They have cause for complaint, I suppose. For their sake, I ought not to face the publicity of the electric-machine. Well, sir, you have won. I don't acknowledge your theory of the leading, but—in fact, you have won. I will pay this debt of honour. But not by daylight. Let it be at night, and in the place that I shall choose.'

'Good. Let it be where you please—but some time to-day.'

'You mentioned my son—I have no desire, certainly, to bring upon him any kind of—social stigma—I hope that he may be led to believe in the outward respectability of his father. It is for his sake, and for no other reason, that I accept the award, and your reading of the oracle.' He dropped the pistol into his pocket. 'The revolver is mine; I promise you to discharge this debt in the course of the day.'

'Can I trust you?'

'I don't know why you should. If you do not—here is the revolver;' he took it from his pocket and offered it. 'Settle this business at once.'

'I do trust you, Sir Charles.'

'About my sister Alice,' he spoke with a strange hesitation; 'if it is really possible—I may learn the truth this evening — if she has brought about this termination—she would naturally be prejudiced against my way of life. . . . She was always proud of the family name — she may have designed this chain of accidents. . . . The family name—there was never a madman in it before. Well, I will actually leave it uninjured—after all.' His manner was changed: his eyes lost their hardness, and his very voice became soft. Yet he preserved his pride of carriage.

'And how shall I learn——?'

'I think that if you happen to be on the Quay of Aldermanbury at about eleven this evening, or perhaps at midnight—I have a few dollars to get rid of first— you will have an opportunity of proving my trustworthiness. And now, sir, we have said enough.' He assumed once more the manner of a Cabinet Minister granting an audience.

'May I bear any message to Lady Osterley?'

'None, sir, I thank you.' He bowed and gently waved his hand.

Gilbert, unable to meet his manner with corresponding dignity, bowed in his turn and walked away. At the next bend of the river, he looked round. The man was playing some game, or practising some trick, with the cards upon the shelf of rock.

CHAPTER XVIII.

FREEDOM.

GILBERT returned slowly to the House, where his carriage waited for him. Not then. Not till many days afterwards; not till something of the strength and reality in the message had died away in his heart, did he realize the danger he had run in losing that game. His mind for the moment was filled with a kind of awe and of pity for the austere man whose outward show of pride rose higher as his life grew more shameful. That the man would die he was perfectly certain; but why should he wait until the evening? And why should he appoint the Quay of Aldermanbury for the verification of his promise?

As he passed the door of the Hall he could hear the noise of the quarrelling community, but he was in no mood to interest himself further in their wrangle. He drove straight back to the city. Everything that day stood out in contrast. On the one side stood Death about to strike its victim, a tall pale man, proud and stern of face, who stood with folded hands and waited with no sign of fear. On the other side were the brethren and sisters of the monastery wrangling like ordinary mortals of the lower class, and showing the failure of Meditation, since, after all these years, it had left them all on so low a level. On the other side, too, he remembered the peace and rest and confidence in Cicely's eyes. He could not bear to look at them for thinking of the awful end awaiting the man to whom she had taken that message.

'What is the matter with you, Gilbert?' asked Lady Osterley. 'And why cannot you sit still?'

'I suppose it is the great heat of the day.'

'It is always hot here—I think I like the heat—and it certainly suits the boy. Cicely was telling me about the House, Gilbert, and about your first coming to it, only a few weeks ago.'

'Five weeks,' said Cicely—'five weeks to-day.'

She appeared to remember nothing about the message and the long and lonely walk of last night.

'Only five weeks ago?' Gilbert took her hand. 'And so much has happened to this dear child since then. The world was Outside then—a terrible, wicked, deadly world. The day was divided into portions like a Benedictine Monastery—only one day exactly like another. Fatigue and Repose: Meditation and Elevation: Restoration and Retirement. Then there was the dancing. You have seen her dance, Dorabyn, but only once. I have seen her every evening, and I never got tired of it.'

Cicely blushed. 'I must never dance again,' she said, 'because I am not to meditate any more. I began when I was quite a little girl. I danced because no one could see me—they were all in Meditation: and so—somehow—it helped me to fall into Meditation. So I kept on—and Gilbert saw me.'

'I should like to see you again,' said Lady Osterley. 'You will dance often to us—won't you?'

'No—I should be ashamed.'

'We have got a great deal to teach her, Dorabyn. We must teach her not to be ashamed of doing clever and graceful things. Dear me, Cicely, when we go home—which will be next week——'

Lady Osterley looked up. It was the second time that Gilbert had uttered that prediction.

'Next week,' he repeated, looking in her face. She saw something written on his face; she turned pale, and trembled.

Then she sprang to her feet. 'Come with me, Gilbert,' she said, and led the way into the inner room. 'Now'—she turned upon him almost fiercely—'what do you mean by saying that we may go home next week?'

'I mean that you may leave this place to-morrow: that you may leave New York by the first boat that sails: that you may go home, to your own country house, and see once more your friends and—yes—your husband's friends as well.'

'Tell me more.'

'I will tell you all—this evening.'

'Oh! this evening—not till then? This evening. There are hours to get through. Gilbert—there is but one way. Oh! tell me—how?—how? God forgive me for desiring his death, but it is the only way.'

'It is the only way. Therefore——'

'Not by your hands, Gilbert!' She caught those hands, and whispered: 'No—no! Not by your hands! Anything—anything but that!'

'No—not by my hands. Dorabyn, if you have ever doubted that the spirit of a good woman may protect and guide those whom she loves, doubt it no longer.'

'You mean Cicely's mother?'

'Yes, I seem to understand it all so well. It was Alice who led her brother to the House—it was the only place in the whole habitable globe where he could be safe from the hands of Justice. Once arrested, his portrait would have been taken and sent to all the papers: he would have been recognised: all the world would have known the truth: and your boy, Dorabyn—Alice's nephew—would have had a life-long disgrace to bear. I say that she led her brother to this place where her only daughter was living: she led me after him: she sent him a message urging him even at this late moment to change his manner of life: she sent me a message ordering me to put off my purpose for five weeks: she brought you here so that you might see him once more, and might offer him the means of living in

20

honesty. She even brought Annandale here, so that he might tell the world that he saw him, that he was quite mad, and that I was watching him for you. Mind, the whole thing is complete: the case hangs together perfectly. Two more messages were sent: one to me—namely, that what had to be done should be done, but not by my hands: and one to him—the last message—it was delivered to him by Cicely last night at midnight——'

'Why, I saw her in bed at ten.'

'At midnight: she must have got up and walked all the way there and back: a lonely walk for a girl: eight miles: but she was protected by her mother.'

'What was the message?'

'She must have been in a trance of some kind. The message was very serious. It was a warning that he would meet his sister next day—this day.'

'How did he take it?'

'At first he received it in his cold and superior way —you have seen him. It was part of my conspiracy against him: it was I who had brought about his expulsion: it was I who was bringing the police upon him. We played——'

'You played?'

'Life for life—with a pack of cards, Dorabyn, but I knew very well what would be the result if we played— and I won—that is to say, I lost the game, and he won —the revolver.'

'Well?'

'Then I told him, as solemnly as I could, how the spirit of his sister had been working for him—to save him and his family from disgrace. He broke down—so far as such a man can break down. He even spoke of the family name. He is, so far, broken, Dorabyn. He will save the name—and the boy—from disgrace. And oh!'—the tears crowded into his eyes—'the shame and the pity of it! Yet he will keep his word—I am sure of it—I know it—he will meet his sister this evening.'

'You left him to take his own life? Oh! it is horrible; and yet—yet——'

'He will take his own life with his own hand. Of that you may rest perfectly assured, Dorabyn. This evening you will be free, and your son will be safe, and your husband's name and fame and honour will remain unblemished in the eyes of the world.'

'Tell me no more, Gilbert. Leave me alone to think. I must find some pity for him, if I can. Oh, if it is in very truth the last day of this man's life, I must try to remember that once I respected him—once, for a brief week, I even thought I loved him. Leave me, Gilbert; take Cicely somewhere—I want to be alone all day. I must pray for him—and for myself—and for my boy.'

Her eyes were full of tears: her lips were trembling. Gilbert left her to her prayers, and softly closed the door.

There was a boat which called at Aldermanbury about one o'clock. Gilbert found that he could go down the river for three or four hours; land at a certain place forty miles down, and return by train. He took Cicely with him, and widened Outside for her, thus beguiling for himself the weary hours of waiting.

There were no more messages: Cicely looked for none: the final message had come: she knew that she must desire no more converse with her mother until another change: but she had begun to live in this world: the next had already lost some of its attractions: already the House was left behind, soon to be forgotten in new interests and with new friends, and there was something new to learn; something new to observe, every moment. She was like one who runs about on a newly-discovered island.

They steamed down the noble river: they heard the echoes in the mountains where Rip Van Winkle played at bowls; they marked the cliffs and rocks and the hanging woods: an impertinent band played a selection from Offenbach's operas; but even that did not spoil the woods and mountains, and the broad breadth of river: they sat under the awning and looked out upon the sunny hills: and with the bright and eager girl to ask questions continually, Gilbert almost forgot the Ordeal of the morning and the dreadful purpose of the winner.

It was ten o'clock when they reached the station on their return. Gilbert took Cicely back to the hotel, where the Master sat in the corner in his usual attitude —feet out, hands folded—head back—in his customary meditation. Annandale was looking on in a kind of stupor.

'Look here,' he whispered. 'He just sat down—put out his feet, and went off—like that. Thank God you have come back, Gilbert! What are we to do? Lady Osterley is in her own room with a headache. Shall I run for a doctor?'

'No—no—do nothing. He goes off like this every evening. It's the regular thing with him. Talk as loud as you like, Annandale, he won't hear. It is a strange custom, but it is the custom of his Fraternity.'

'It looks creepy. Does he say things? It would be like a voice from the Tombs.'

'We can leave him in charge of Cicely. You know the Master's ways, don't you, Cicely? As for you and me, Annandale, we will just go out and have a cigar on the Quay. The air from the river will be fresher than in the street—come.'

They went out: it is not far from the hotel to the Quay: two steamers lay alongside: the Quay was deserted save for two or three low saloons, of which we have already heard. There the lights were brilliant, and there the noise of voices showed that life, even on so hot a night, still has an animated side.

'They are gambling,' said Annandale, looking into one. 'Faugh! what an intolerable stink of bad whisky and bad gas! I wonder what they are playing. Why,

Gilbert—see! see!—there is Sir Charles Osterley—the man you have been looking after! Sir Charles himself! Oh, he must be awfully mad! How did you come to leave him?'

Gilbert looked in.

'Yes—it is Sir Charles.' In fact, the loser of the game was playing with eagerness at a dirty table among three or four common men. 'I suppose they let him out. I was not his keeper, you know. I agree with you. He must be very mad indeed to come to such a place as this.'

'I thought he was religious mad. There isn't much religion in this. Sir Charles Osterley, of all men, to be found in such a den! Why, the fellows look like stokers.'

'We had best not interfere, Annandale. I suppose that he fancies himself someone else. Come; he will be looked after, and it would be best for him not to see us.'

He drew Annandale away, and they resumed their walk up and down the Quay.

'I can think of nothing else,' said Annandale. 'That poor madman! I found him by accident. Of course I told Lady Osterley that I had discovered her secret. That explained everything: your presence here—you and your confounded strawberries; his presence here; her coming here—I thought it was to see you—and, of course, she knew all along; her silence about him—— Why, his own mother hasn't been told. And now to find him, after he'd been religious mad, in a low class gambling den like this! It's wonderful, Gilbert.'

'Yes,' said Gilbert sadly. 'Some things are too wonderful to be believed at all.'

'All the same, you're a good fellow to look after him. What are you going to do with him? Leave him?—stay with him?'

'I fear he cannot be left. We must wait—something may happen—he may recover—he may——'

He stopped, because just then, as the clock began to strike eleven, two shots in rapid succession struck upon his ear.

'What is that?' asked Annandale. 'The shots came from that place.'

The voices, which had been very noisy, quieted for a moment; then they began all over again.

Tramp—tramp came the footsteps of men bearing something; they came out of the saloon in the dark night, they laid their burden on the stones of the street, the face covered with a handkerchief.

'He's dead,' said one of the bearers. 'He'd lost all his money, every dollar, and he jest stood up and blew out his brains before anyone could say anything. He's quite dead.'

Gilbert stooped and lifted the handkerchief. Then with a shudder he placed it back. The man's eyes were wide open, and they seemed to say, 'I have kept my promise.'

And once more the words of the message rang through Gilbert's brain:

'That which must be done shall be done—but not by your hands.'

'Come,' he said, 'we can do nothing. The body will be looked after. Come home, I will tell Lady Osterley. And—Annandale—not a word to Cicely. She need not be alarmed.'

'Shall we tell these people who he is?'

'By no means—why should we parade the fact that Sir Charles Osterley blew out his brains in a vile gambling den? We must not proclaim abroad that this suicide was once an English statesman. This must be our secret, Annandale. Mad, you know he was—and in the House of Cranks. All the world may know that. But not the place or the manner of his end. Let us keep that secret, for the sake of Dorabyn, to ourselves, Annandale.'

They went back to the hotel. 'I am best out of the

way, Gilbert. I shall go to my own room,' said Annandale. 'Come presently, and we will talk.'

'Ask Dorabyn if I may speak to her, Cicely.'

The Master was still in Meditation. Cicely was sitting in the dark, waiting in her patient way. She had not yet acquired the Outside habit of always doing something—reading for instance—and I think she never will. The habit of Meditation will always remain with her in a milder form.

'Stay, Cicely—one moment. Have you any more messages for me?'

'Nothing, Gilbert. My mother has left off talking to me. She leaves me to you—oh! Gilbert—to you!'

He kissed her solemnly.

'Your mother has spoken again to-day, dear. She has spoken to me directly: she has guided me through a great and terrible danger. Now I must go to Dorabyn.'

She received him in the dark. It was best that such a message should be received in the dark.

'Tell me—tell me, Gilbert.'

'He is dead, Dorabyn.'

'How?'

'By his own hand. He died where he mostly loved to live—in a gambling den.'

'Is it known who he was?'

'Annandale saw him—I thought it well that Annandale, who saw him alive, should know that he is dead. Annandale is persuaded that he was mad. Now you can go home, Dorabyn. You can write to his people, truthfully, that he disappeared—truthfully, that you went in search of him—truthfully, that he was found by me in a religious community—truthfully, that he broke out, apparently, in a new place, and that he killed himself—if they want to know more—in a gambling den. It is a tale of madness, no worse. For the general world it will be enough to announce that Sir Charles Osterley died at Aldermanbury, New York State, on such and such a day.'

'Yes—yes—I shall understand better, perhaps, in a little while.'

'Meantime, Dorabyn—at last—you are free!'

THE END.

[Sept. 1897.

LIST OF BOOKS PUBLISHED BY

CHATTO & WINDUS
111 ST. MARTIN'S LANE, CHARING CROSS, LONDON, W.C.

About (Edmond).—The Fellah: An Egyptian Novel. Translated by Sir RANDAL ROBERTS. Post 8vo, illustrated boards, 2s.

Adams (W. Davenport), Works by.
A Dictionary of the Drama: being a comprehensive Guide to the Plays, Playwrights, Players, and Playhouses of the United Kingdom and America, from the Earliest Times to the Present Day. Crown 8vo, half-bound, 12s. 6d. [Preparing.
Quips and Quiddities. Selected by W. DAVENPORT ADAMS. Post 8vo, cloth limp, 2s. 6d.

Agony Column (The) of 'The Times,' from 1800 to 1870. Edited with an Introduction, by ALICE CLAY. Post 8vo, cloth limp, 2s. 6d.

Aidé (Hamilton), Novels by. Post 8vo, illustrated boards, 2s. each.
Carr of Carrlyon. | Confidences.

Albert (Mary).—Brooke Finchley's Daughter. Post 8vo, picture boards, 2s.; cloth limp, 2s. 6d.

Alden (W. L.).—A Lost Soul: Being the Confession and Defence of Charles Lindsay. Fcap. 8vo, cloth boards, 1s. 6d.

Alexander (Mrs.), Novels by. Post 8vo, illustrated boards, 2s. each.
Maid, Wife, or Widow? | Valerie's Fate. | Blind Fate.

Crown 8vo, cloth, 3s. 6d. each.
A Life Interest. | Mona's Choice. | By Woman's Wit.

Allen (F. M.).—Green as Grass. With a Frontispiece. Crown 8vo, cloth, 3s. 6d.

Allen (Grant), Works by.
The Evolutionist at Large. Crown 8vo, cloth extra, 6s.
Post-Prandial Philosophy. Crown 8vo, art linen, 3s. 6d.
Moorland Idylls. Crown 8vo, cloth decorated, 6s.

Crown 8vo, cloth extra, 3s. 6d. each; post 8vo, illustrated boards, 2s. each.
Babylon. 12 Illustrations. | The Devil's Die. | The Duchess of Powysland.
Strange Stories. Frontis. | This Mortal Coil. | Blood Royal.
The Beckoning Hand. | The Tents of Shem. Frontis. | Ivan Greet's Masterpiece.
For Maimie's Sake. | The Great Taboo. | The Scallywag. 24 Illusts.
Philistia. | In all Shades | Dumaresq's Daughter. | At Market Value.

Under Sealed Orders. Crown 8vo, cloth extra, 3s. 6d.
Dr. Palliser's Patient. Fcap. 8vo, cloth boards, 1s. 6d.

Anderson (Mary).—Othello's Occupation: A Novel. Crown 8vo, cloth, 3s. 6d.

Arnold (Edwin Lester), Stories by.
The Wonderful Adventures of Phra the Phœnician. Crown 8vo, cloth extra, with 12 Illustrations by H. M. PAGET, 3s. 6d.; post 8vo, illustrated boards, 2s.
The Constable of St. Nicholas. With Frontispiece by S. L. WOOD. Crown 8vo, cloth, 3s. 6d.

Artemus Ward's Works. With Portrait and Facsimile. Crown 8vo, cloth extra, 3s. 6d.—Also a POPULAR EDITION post 8vo, picture boards, 2s.

Ashton (John), Works by. Crown 8vo, cloth extra, 7s. 6d. each.
History of the Chap-Books of the 18th Century. With 334 Illustrations.
Humour, Wit, and Satire of the Seventeenth Century. With 82 Illustrations.
English Caricature and Satire on Napoleon the First. With 115 Illustrations.
Modern Street Ballads. With 57 Illustrations.
Social Life in the Reign of Queen Anne. With 85 Illustrations. Crown 8vo, cloth, 3s. 6d.

Bacteria, Yeast Fungi, and Allied Species, A Synopsis of. By W. B. GROVE, B.A. With 87 Illustrations. Crown 8vo, cloth extra, 3s. 6d.

Bardsley (Rev. C. Wareing, M.A.), Works by.
English Surnames: Their Sources and Significations. FIFTH EDITION, with a New Preface. Crown 8vo, cloth, 7s. 6d.
Curiosities of Puritan Nomenclature. Crown 8vo, cloth, 3s. 6d.

Baring Gould (Sabine, Author of 'John Herring,' &c.), **Novels by.**
Crown 8vo, cloth extra, 3s. 6d. each; post 8vo, illustrated boards, 2s. each.
Red Spider. | Eve.

Barr (Robert: Luke Sharp), Stories by. Cr. 8vo, cl., 3s. 6d. each.
In a Steamer Chair. With Frontispiece and Vignette by DEMAIN HAMMOND.
From Whose Bourne, &c. With 47 Illustrations by HAL HURST and others.
A Woman Intervenes. With 8 Illustrations by HAL HURST.
Revenge! With 12 Illustrations by LANCELOT SPEED and others.

Barrett (Frank), Novels by.
Post 8vo, illustrated boards, 2s. each; cloth, 2s. 6d. each.
Fettered for Life.
The Sin of Olga Zassoulich.
Between Life and Death.
Folly Morrison. | Honest Davie.
Little Lady Linton.
A Prodigal's Progress.
John Ford; and His Helpmate.
A Recoiling Vengeance.
Lieut. Barnabas. | Found Guilty.
For Love and Honour.
The Woman of the Iron Bracelets. Cr. 8vo, cloth, 3s. 6d.; post 8vo, boards, 2s.; cl. limp, 2s. 6d.
Crown 8vo, cloth extra, 3s. 6d. each.
The Harding Scandal. | A Missing Witness. With 8 Illustrations by W. H. MARGETSON.

Barrett (Joan).—Monte Carlo Stories. Fcap. 8vo, cloth, 1s. 6d.

Beaconsfield, Lord. By T. P. O'CONNOR, M.P. Cr. 8vo, cloth, 5s.

Beauchamp (Shelsley).—Grantley Grange. Post 8vo, boards, 2s.

Besant (Sir Walter) and James Rice, Novels by.
Crown 8vo, cloth extra, 3s. 6d. each; post 8vo, illustrated boards, 2s. each; cloth limp, 2s. 6d. each.
Ready-Money Mortiboy.
My Little Girl.
With Harp and Crown.
This Son of Vulcan.
The Golden Butterfly.
The Monks of Thelema.
By Celia's Arbour.
The Chaplain of the Fleet.
The Seamy Side.
The Case of Mr. Lucraft, &c.
'Twas in Trafalgar's Bay, &c.
The Ten Years' Tenant, &c.
** There is also a LIBRARY EDITION of the above Twelve Volumes, handsomely set in new type on a large crown 8vo page, and bound in cloth extra, 6s. each; and a POPULAR EDITION of **The Golden Butterfly**, medium 8vo, 6d.; cloth, 1s.

Besant (Sir Walter), Novels by.
Crown 8vo, cloth extra, 3s. 6d. each; post 8vo, illustrated boards, 2s. each; cloth limp, 2s. 6d. each.
All Sorts and Conditions of Men. With 12 Illustrations by FRED. BARNARD.
The Captains' Room, &c. With Frontispiece by E. J. WHEELER.
All in a Garden Fair. With 6 Illustrations by HARRY FURNISS.
Dorothy Forster. With Frontispiece by CHARLES GREEN.
Uncle Jack, and other Stories. | Children of Gibeon.
The World Went Very Well Then. With 12 Illustrations by A. FORESTIER.
Herr Paulus: His Rise, his Greatness, and his Fall. | The Bell of St. Paul's.
For Faith and Freedom. With Illustrations by A. FORESTIER and F. WADDY.
To Call Her Mine, &c. With 9 Illustrations by A. FORESTIER.
The Holy Rose, &c. With Frontispiece by F. BARNARD.
Armorel of Lyonesse: A Romance of To-day. With 12 Illustrations by F. BARNARD.
St. Katherine's by the Tower. With 12 Illustrations by C. GREEN.
Verbena Camellia Stephanotis, &c. With a Frontispiece by GORDON BROWNE.
The Ivory Gate. | The Rebel Queen.
Beyond the Dreams of Avarice. With 12 Illustrations by W. H. HYDE.
Crown 8vo, cloth extra, 3s. 6d. each.
In Deacon's Orders, &c. With Frontispiece by A. FORESTIER.
The Revolt of Man. | The Master Craftsman.
The City of Refuge. With a Frontispiece by F. S. WILSON.
All Sorts and Conditions of Men. CHEAP POPULAR EDITION. Medium 8vo, 6d.; cloth, 1s.
A Fountain Sealed. With Frontispiece by H. G. BURGESS. Crown 8vo, cloth, 6s.
The Charm, and other Drawing-room Plays. By Sir WALTER BESANT and WALTER H. POLLOCK. With 50 Illustrations by CHRIS HAMMOND and JULE GOODMAN. Crown 8vo, cloth, gilt edges, 6s.
Fifty Years Ago. With 144 Plates and Woodcuts. Crown 8vo, cloth extra, 5s.
The Eulogy of Richard Jefferies. With Portrait. Crown 8vo, cloth extra, 6s.
London. With 125 Illustrations. Demy 8vo, cloth, 7s. 6d.
Westminster. With Etched Frontispiece by F. S. WALKER, R.P.E., and 130 Illustrations by WILLIAM PATTEN and others. Demy 8vo, cloth, 7s. 6d.
Sir Richard Whittington. With Frontispiece. Crown 8vo, art linen, 3s. 6d.
Gaspard de Coligny. With a Portrait. Crown 8vo, art linen, 3s. 6d.

Beautiful Pictures by British Artists: A Gathering of Favourites from the Picture Galleries, engraved on Steel. Imperial 4to, cloth extra, gilt edges, 21s.

Bechstein (Ludwig).—As Pretty as Seven, and other German Stories. With Additional Tales by the Brothers GRIMM, and 98 Illustrations by RICHTER. Square 8vo, cloth extra, 6s. 6d.; gilt edges, 7s. 6d.

Bellew (Frank).—The Art of Amusing: A Collection of Graceful Arts, Games, Tricks, Puzzles, and Charades. With 300 Illustrations. Crown 8vo, cloth extra, 4s. 6d.

Bennett (W. C., LL.D.).—Songs for Sailors. Post 8vo, cl. limp, 2s.

Bewick (Thomas) and his Pupils. By AUSTIN DOBSON. With 95 Illustrations. Square 8vo, cloth extra, 6s.

Bierce (Ambrose).—In the Midst of Life: Tales of Soldiers and Civilians. Crown 8vo, cloth extra, 6s.; post 8vo, illustrated boards, 2s.

Bill Nye's History of the United States. With 146 Illustrations by F. OPPER. Crown 8vo, cloth extra, 3s. 6d.

Biré (Edmond).—Diary of a Citizen of Paris during 'The Terror.' Translated and Edited by JOHN DE VILLIERS. With 2 Photogravure Portraits. Two Vols., demy 8vo, cloth, 21s.

Blackburn's (Henry) Art Handbooks.
Academy Notes, 1897. 1s.
Academy Notes, 1875-79. Complete in One Vol., with 600 Illustrations. Cloth, 6s.
Academy Notes, 1880-84. Complete in One Vol., with 700 Illustrations. Cloth, 6s.
Academy Notes, 1890-94. Complete in One Vol., with 800 Illustrations. Cloth, 7s. 6d.
Grosvenor Notes, Vol. I., 1877-82. With 300 Illustrations. Demy 8vo, cloth, 6s.
Grosvenor Notes, Vol. II., 1883-87. With 300 Illustrations. Demy 8vo, cloth, 6s.
Grosvenor Notes, Vol. III., 1888-90. With 230 Illustrations. Demy 8vo, cloth, 3s. 6d.
The New Gallery, 1888-1892. With 250 Illustrations. Demy 8vo, cloth, 6s.
English Pictures at the National Gallery. With 114 Illustrations. 1s.
Old Masters at the National Gallery. With 128 Illustrations. 1s. 6d.
Illustrated Catalogue to the National Gallery. With 242 Illusts. Demy 8vo, cloth, 3s.

The Illustrated Catalogue of the Paris Salon, 1897. With 300 Sketches. 3s.

Blind (Mathilde), Poems by.
The Ascent of Man. Crown 8vo, cloth, 5s.
Dramas in Miniature. With a Frontispiece by F. MADOX BROWN. Crown 8vo, cloth, 5s.
Songs and Sonnets. Fcap. 8vo, vellum and gold, 5s.
Birds of Passage: Songs of the Orient and Occident. Second Edition. Crown 8vo, linen, 6s. net.

Bourget (Paul).—A Living Lie. Translated by JOHN DE VILLIERS. With special Preface for the English Edition. Crown 8vo, cloth, 3s. 6d.

Bourne (H. R. Fox), Books by.
English Merchants: Memoirs in Illustration of the Progress of British Commerce. With numerous Illustrations. Crown 8vo, cloth extra, 7s. 6d.
English Newspapers: Chapters in the History of Journalism. Two Vols., demy 8vo, cloth, 25s.
The Other Side of the Emin Pasha Relief Expedition. Crown 8vo, cloth, 6s.

Bowers (George).—Leaves from a Hunting Journal. Coloured Plates. Oblong folio, half-bound, 21s.

Boyle (Frederick), Works by. Post 8vo, illustrated bds., 2s. each.
Chronicles of No-Man's Land. | Camp Notes. | Savage Life.

Brand (John).—Observations on Popular Antiquities; chiefly illustrating the Origin of our Vulgar Customs, Ceremonies, and Superstitions. With the Additions of Sir HENRY ELLIS, and numerous Illustrations. Crown 8vo, cloth extra, 7s. 6d.

Brewer (Rev. Dr.), Works by.
The Reader's Handbook of Allusions, References, Plots, and Stories. Eighteenth Thousand. Crown 8vo, cloth extra, 7s. 6d.
Authors and their Works, with the Dates: Being the Appendices to 'The Reader's Handbook,' separately printed. Crown 8vo, cloth limp, 2s.
A Dictionary of Miracles: Imitative, Realistic, and Dogmatic. Crown 8vo, cloth, 3s. 6d.

Brewster (Sir David), Works by. Post 8vo, cloth, 4s. 6d. each.
More Worlds than One: Creed of the Philosopher and Hope of the Christian. With Plates.
The Martyrs of Science: GALILEO, TYCHO BRAHE, and KEPLER. With Portraits.
Letters on Natural Magic. With numerous Illustrations.

Brillat-Savarin.—Gastronomy as a Fine Art. Translated by R. E. ANDERSON, M.A. Post 8vo, half-bound, 2s.

Brydges (Harold).—Uncle Sam at Home. With 91 Illustrations. Post 8vo, illustrated boards, 2s.; cloth limp, 2s. 6d.

Buchanan (Robert), Novels, &c., by.
Crown 8vo, cloth extra, 3s. 6d. each; post 8vo, illustrated boards, 2s. each.

The Shadow of the Sword.
A Child of Nature. With Frontispiece.
God and the Man. With 11 Illustrations by FRED. BARNARD.
The Martyrdom of Madeline. With Frontispiece by A. W. COOPER.
Love Me for Ever. With Frontispiece.
Annan Water. | Foxglove Manor.
The New Abelard. | Rachel Dene.
Matt: A Story of a Caravan. With Frontispiece.
The Master of the Mine. With Frontispiece.
The Heir of Linne. | Woman and the Man.

Crown 8vo, cloth extra, 3s. 6d. each.
Red and White Heather. | Lady Kilpatrick.

The Wandering Jew: a Christmas Carol. Crown 8vo, cloth, 6s.

The Charlatan. By ROBERT BUCHANAN and HENRY MURRAY. Crown 8vo, cloth, with a Frontispiece by T. H. ROBINSON, 3s. 6d.; post 8vo, picture boards, 2s.

Burton (Richard F.).—The Book of the Sword. With over 400 Illustrations. Demy 4to, cloth extra, 32s.

Burton (Robert).—The Anatomy of Melancholy. With Translations of the Quotations. Demy 8vo, cloth extra, 7s. 6d.
Melancholy Anatomised: An Abridgment of BURTON'S ANATOMY. Post 8vo, half-bd., 2s. 6d.

Caine (T. Hall), Novels by. Crown 8vo, cloth extra, 3s. 6d. each; post 8vo, illustrated boards, 2s. each; cloth limp, 2s. 6d. each.
The Shadow of a Crime. | A Son of Hagar. | The Deemster.
Also a LIBRARY EDITION of The Deemster, set in new type, crown 8vo, cloth decorated, 6s.

Cameron (Commander V. Lovett).—The Cruise of the 'Black Prince' Privateer. Post 8vo, picture boards, 2s.

Cameron (Mrs. H. Lovett), Novels by. Post 8vo, illust. bds. 2s. ea.
Juliet's Guardian. | Deceivers Ever.

Captain Coignet, Soldier of the Empire: An Autobiography. Edited by LOREDAN LARCHEY. Translated by Mrs. CAREY. With 100 Illustrations. Crown 8vo, cloth, 3s. 6d.

Carlyle (Jane Welsh), Life of. By Mrs. ALEXANDER IRELAND. With Portrait and Facsimile Letter. Small demy 8vo, cloth extra, 7s. 6d.

Carlyle (Thomas).—On the Choice of Books. Post 8vo, cl., 1s. 6d.
Correspondence of Thomas Carlyle and R. W. Emerson, 1834-1872. Edited by C. E. NORTON. With Portraits. Two Vols., crown 8vo, cloth, 24s.

Carruth (Hayden).—The Adventures of Jones. With 17 Illustrations. Fcap. 8vo, cloth, 2s.

Chambers (Robert W.), Stories of Paris Life by. Long fcap. 8vo, cloth, 2s. 6d. each.
The King in Yellow. | In the Quarter.

Chapman's (George), Works. Vol. I., Plays Complete, including the Doubtful Ones.—Vol. II., Poems and Minor Translations, with Essay by A. C. SWINBURNE.—Vol. III., Translations of the Iliad and Odyssey. Three Vols., crown 8vo, cloth, 3s. 6d. each.

Chapple (J. Mitchell).—The Minor Chord: The Story of a Prima Donna. Crown 8vo, cloth, 3s. 6d.

Chatto (W. A.) and J. Jackson.—A Treatise on Wood Engraving, Historical and Practical. With Chapter by H. G. BOHN, and 450 fine Illusts. Large 4to, half-leather, 28s.

Chaucer for Children: A Golden Key. By Mrs. H. R. HAWEIS. With 8 Coloured Plates and 30 Woodcuts. Crown 4to, cloth extra, 3s. 6d.
Chaucer for Schools. By Mrs. H. R. HAWEIS. Demy 8vo, cloth limp, 2s. 6d.

Chess, The Laws and Practice of. With an Analysis of the Openings. By HOWARD STAUNTON. Edited by R. B. WORMALD. Crown 8vo, cloth, 5s.
The Minor Tactics of Chess: A Treatise on the Deployment of the Forces in obedience to Strategic Principle. By F. K. YOUNG and E. C. HOWELL. Long fcap. 8vo, cloth, 2s. 6d.
The Hastings Chess Tournament. Containing the Authorised Account of the 230 Games played Aug.-Sept., 1895. With Annotations by PILLSBURY, LASKER, TARRASCH, STEINITZ, SCHIFFERS, TEICHMANN, BARDELEBEN, BLACKBURNE, GUNSBERG, TINSLEY, MASON, and ALBIN; Biographical Sketches of the Chess Masters, and 22 Portraits. Edited by H. F. CHESHIRE. Crown 8vo, cloth, 7s. 6d.

Clare (Austin).—For the Love of a Lass. Post 8vo, 2s.; cl., 2s. 6d.

Clive (Mrs. Archer), Novels by. Post 8vo, illust. boards, 2s. each.
Paul Ferroll. | Why Paul Ferroll Killed his Wife.

Clodd (Edward, F.R.A.S.).—Myths and Dreams. Cr. 8vo, 3s. 6d.

Coates (Anne).—Rie's Diary. Crown 8vo, cloth, 3s. 6d.

Cobban (J. Maclaren), Novels by.
The Cure of Souls. Post 8vo, Illustrated boards, 2s.
The Red Sultan. Crown 8vo, cloth extra, 3s. 6d.; post 8vo, Illustrated boards, 2s.
The Burden of Isabel. Crown 8vo, cloth extra, 3s. 6d.

Coleman (John).—Curly: An Actor's Story. With 21 Illustrations by J. C. DOLLMAN. Crown 8vo, picture cover, 1s.

Coleridge (M. E.).—The Seven Sleepers of Ephesus. Cloth, 1s. 6d.

Collins (C. Allston).—The Bar Sinister. Post 8vo, boards, 2s.

Collins (John Churton, M.A.), Books by.
Illustrations of Tennyson. Crown 8vo, cloth extra, 6s.
Jonathan Swift: A Biographical and Critical Study. Crown 8vo, cloth extra, 8s.

Collins (Mortimer and Frances), Novels by.
Crown 8vo, cloth extra, 3s. 6d. each; post 8vo, illustrated boards, 2s. each.
From Midnight to Midnight. | Blacksmith and Scholar.
Transmigration. | You Play me False. | The Village Comedy.
Post 8vo, illustrated boards, 2s. each.
Sweet Anna Page. | A Fight with Fortune. | Sweet and Twenty. | Frances.

Collins (Wilkie), Novels by.
Crown 8vo, cloth extra, many Illustrated, 3s. 6d. each; post 8vo, picture boards, 2s. each; cloth limp, 2s. 6d. each.

*Antonina.	My Miscellanies.	Jezebel's Daughter.
*Basil.	Armadale.	The Black Robe.
*Hide and Seek.	Poor Miss Finch.	Heart and Science.
*The Woman in White.	Miss or Mrs.?	'I Say No.'
*The Moonstone.	The New Magdalen.	A Rogue's Life.
*Man and Wife.	The Frozen Deep.	The Evil Genius.
After Dark.	The Law and the Lady.	Little Novels.
The Dead Secret.	The Two Destinies.	The Legacy of Cain.
The Queen of Hearts.	The Haunted Hotel.	Blind Love.
No Name.	The Fallen Leaves.	

⁎ Marked * are the NEW LIBRARY EDITION at 3s. 6d., entirely reset and bound in new style.

POPULAR EDITIONS. Medium 8vo, 6d. each; cloth, 1s. each.
The Woman in White. | The Moonstone. | Antonina.

The Woman in White and The Moonstone in One Volume, medium 8vo, cloth, 2s.

Colman's (George) Humorous Works: 'Broad Grins,' 'My Nightgown and Slippers,' &c. With Life and Frontispiece. Crown 8vo, cloth extra, 7s. 6d.

Colquhoun (M. J.).—Every Inch a Soldier. Post 8vo, boards, 2s.

Colt-breaking, Hints on. By W. M. HUTCHISON. Cr. 8vo, cl., 3s. 6d.

Convalescent Cookery. By CATHERINE RYAN. Cr. 8vo, 1s.; cl., 1s. 6d.

Conway (Moncure D.), Works by.
Demonology and Devil-Lore. With 65 Illustrations. Two Vols., demy 8vo, cloth, 28s.
George Washington's Rules of Civility. Fcap. 8vo, Japanese vellum, 2s. 6d.

Cook (Dutton), Novels by.
Post 8vo, illustrated boards, 2s. each.
Leo. | Paul Foster's Daughter.

Cooper (Edward H.).—Geoffory Hamilton. Cr. 8vo, cloth, 3s. 6d.

Cornwall.—Popular Romances of the West of England; or, The Drolls, Traditions, and Superstitions of Old Cornwall. Collected by ROBERT HUNT, F.R.S. With two Steel Plates by GEORGE CRUIKSHANK. Crown 8vo, cloth, 7s. 6d.

Cotes (V. Cecil).—Two Girls on a Barge. With 44 Illustrations by F. H. TOWNSEND. Post 8vo, cloth, 2s. 6d.

Craddock (C. Egbert), Stories by.
The Prophet of the Great Smoky Mountains. Post 8vo, Illustrated boards, 2s.
His Vanished Star. Crown 8vo, cloth extra, 3s. 6d.

Cram (Ralph Adams).—Black Spirits and White. Fcap. 8vo, cloth, 1s. 6d.

CHATTO & WINDUS, 111 St. Martin's Lane, London, W.C.

Crellin (H. N.), Books by.
Romances of the Old Seraglio. With 28 Illustrations by S. L. WOOD. Crown 8vo, cloth, 3s. 6d.
Tales of the Caliph. Crown 8vo, cloth, 2s.
The Nazarenes: A Drama. Crown 8vo, 1s.

Crim (Matt.).—Adventures of a Fair Rebel. Crown 8vo, cloth extra, with a Frontispiece by DAN. BEARD, 3s. 6d.; post 8vo, illustrated boards, 2s.

Crockett (S. R.) and others.—Tales of Our Coast. By S. R. CROCKETT, GILBERT PARKER, HAROLD FREDERIC, 'Q.,' and W CLARK RUSSELL. With 12 Illustrations by FRANK BRANGWYN. Crown 8vo, cloth, 3s. 6d.

Croker (Mrs. B. M.), Novels by. Crown 8vo, cloth extra, 3s. 6d. each; post 8vo, illustrated boards, 2s. each; cloth limp, 2s. 6d. each.
Pretty Miss Neville. | Diana Barrington. | A Family Likeness.
A Bird of Passage. | Proper Pride. | 'To Let.'
Village Tales and Jungle Tragedies. | Two Masters. | Mr. Jervis.

Crown 8vo, cloth extra, 3s. 6d. each.
Married or Single? | In the Kingdom of Kerry.
The Real Lady Hilda. | Interference. | A Third Person.

Beyond the Pale. Crown 8vo, buckram, 6s.

Cruikshank's Comic Almanack. Complete in Two SERIES: The FIRST, from 1835 to 1843; the SECOND, from 1844 to 1853. A Gathering of the Best Humour of THACKERAY, HOOD, MAYHEW, ALBERT SMITH, A'BECKETT, ROBERT BROUGH, &c. With numerous Steel Engravings and Woodcuts by GEORGE CRUIKSHANK, HINE, LANDELLS, &c. Two Vols., crown 8vo, cloth gilt, 7s. 6d. each.
The Life of George Cruikshank. By BLANCHARD JERROLD. With 84 Illustrations and a Bibliography. Crown 8vo, cloth extra, 6s.

Cumming (C. F. Gordon), Works by. Demy 8vo, cl. ex., 8s. 6d. ea.
In the Hebrides. With an Autotype Frontispiece and 23 Illustrations.
In the Himalayas and on the Indian Plains. With 42 Illustrations.
Two Happy Years in Ceylon. With 29 Illustrations.

Via Cornwall to Egypt. With a Photogravure Frontispiece. Demy 8vo, cloth, 7s. 6d.

Cussans (John E.).—A Handbook of Heraldry; with Instructions for Tracing Pedigrees and Deciphering Ancient MSS., &c. Fourth Edition, revised, with 408 Woodcuts and 2 Coloured Plates. Crown 8vo, cloth extra, 6s.

Cyples (W.).—Hearts of Gold. Cr. 8vo, cl., 3s. 6d.; post 8vo, bds., 2s.

Daudet (Alphonse).—The Evangelist; or, Port Salvation. Crown 8vo, cloth extra, 3s. 6d.; post 8vo, illustrated boards, 2s.

Davenant (Francis, M.A.).—Hints for Parents on the Choice of a Profession for their Sons when Starting in Life. Crown 8vo, cloth, 1s. 6d.

Davidson (Hugh Coleman).—Mr. Sadler's Daughters. With a Frontispiece by STANLEY WOOD. Crown 8vo, cloth extra, 3s. 6d.

Davies (Dr. N. E. Yorke-), Works by. Cr. 8vo, 1s. ea.; cl., 1s. 6d. ea.
One Thousand Medical Maxims and Surgical Hints.
Nursery Hints: A Mother's Guide in Health and Disease.
Foods for the Fat: A Treatise on Corpulency, and a Dietary for its Cure.

Aids to Long Life. Crown 8vo, 2s.; cloth limp, 2s. 6d.

Davies' (Sir John) Complete Poetical Works. Collected and Edited, with Introduction and Notes, by Rev. A. B. GROSART, D.D. Two Vols., crown 8vo, cloth, 3s. 6d. each.

Dawson (Erasmus, M.B.).—The Fountain of Youth. Crown 8vo, cloth extra, with Two Illustrations by HUME NISBET, 3s. 6d.; post 8vo, illustrated boards, 2s.

De Guerin (Maurice), The Journal of. Edited by G. S. TREBUTIEN. With a Memoir by SAINTE-BEUVE. Translated from the 20th French Edition by JESSIE P. FROTHINGHAM. Fcap. 8vo, half-bound, 2s. 6d.

De Maistre (Xavier).—A Journey Round my Room. Translated by Sir HENRY ATTWELL. Post 8vo, cloth limp, 2s. 6d.

De Mille (James).—A Castle in Spain. Crown 8vo, cloth extra, with a Frontispiece, 3s. 6d.; post 8vo, illustrated boards, 2s.

Derby (The): The Blue Ribbon of the Turf. With Brief Accounts of THE OAKS. By LOUIS HENRY CURZON. Crown 8vo, cloth limp, 2s. 6d.

CHATTO & WINDUS, 111 St. Martin's Lane, London, W.C.

Derwent (Leith), Novels by. Cr. 8vo, cl., 3s. 6d. ea.; post 8vo, 2s. ea.
Our Lady of Tears. | Circe's Lovers.

Dewar (T. R.).—A Ramble Round the Globe. With 220 Illustrations. Crown 8vo, cloth extra, 7s. 6d.

Dickens (Charles).—Sketches by Boz. Post 8vo, illust. boards, 2s.
About England with Dickens. By ALFRED RIMMER. With 57 Illustrations by C. A. VANDERHOOF, ALFRED RIMMER, and others. Square 8vo, cloth extra, 7s. 6d.

Dictionaries.
The Reader's Handbook of Allusions, References, Plots, and Stories. By the Rev. E. C. BREWER, LL.D. With an ENGLISH BIBLIOGRAPHY. Crown 8vo, cloth extra, 7s. 6d.
Authors and their Works, with the Dates. Crown 8vo, cloth limp, 2s.
A Dictionary of Miracles: Imitative, Realistic, and Dogmatic. By the Rev. E. C. BREWER, LL.D. Crown 8vo, cloth, 3s. 6d.
Familiar Short Sayings of Great Men. With Historical and Explanatory Notes by SAMUEL A. BENT, A.M. Crown 8vo, cloth extra, 7s. 6d.
The Slang Dictionary: Etymological, Historical, and Anecdotal. Crown 8vo, cloth, 6s. 6d.
Words, Facts, and Phrases: A Dictionary of Curious, Quaint, and Out-of-the-Way Matters. By ELIEZER EDWARDS. Crown 8vo, cloth extra, 7s. 6d.

Diderot.—The Paradox of Acting. Translated, with Notes, by WALTER HERRIES POLLOCK. With Preface by Sir HENRY IRVING. Crown 8vo, parchment, 4s. 6d.

Dobson (Austin), Works by.
Thomas Bewick and his Pupils. With 95 Illustrations. Square 8vo, cloth, 6s.
Four Frenchwomen. With Four Portraits. Crown 8vo, buckram, gilt top, 6s.
Eighteenth Century Vignettes. IN THREE SERIES. Crown 8vo, buckram, 6s. each.

Dobson (W. T.).—Poetical Ingenuities and Eccentricities. Post 8vo, cloth limp, 2s. 6d.

Donovan (Dick), Detective Stories by.
Post 8vo, illustrated boards, 2s. each; cloth limp, 2s. 6d. each.
The Man-Hunter. | Wanted! | A Detective's Triumphs.
Caught at Last. | | In the Grip of the Law.
Tracked and Taken. | | From Information Received.
Who Poisoned Hetty Duncan? | Link by Link. | Dark Deeds.
Suspicion Aroused. | | Riddles Read.

Crown 8vo, cloth extra, 3s. 6d. each; post 8vo, illustrated boards, 2s. each; cloth, 2s. 6d. each.
The Man from Manchester. With 23 Illustrations.
Tracked to Doom. With Six full-page Illustrations by GORDON BROWNE.
The Mystery of Jamaica Terrace.
The Chronicles of Michael Danevitch, of the Russian Secret Service. Crown 8vo, cloth, 3s. 6d.

Dowling (Richard).—Old Corcoran's Money. Crown 8vo, cl., 3s. 6d.

Doyle (A. Conan).—The Firm of Girdlestone. Cr. 8vo, cl., 3s. 6d.

Dramatists, The Old. Cr. 8vo, cl. ex., with Portraits, 3s. 6d. per Vol.
Ben Jonson's Works. With Notes, Critical and Explanatory, and a Biographical Memoir by WILLIAM GIFFORD. Edited by Colonel CUNNINGHAM. Three Vols.
Chapman's Works. Three Vols. Vol. I. contains the Plays complete; Vol. II., Poems and Minor Translations, with an Essay by A. C. SWINBURNE; Vol. III., Translations of the Iliad and Odyssey.
Marlowe's Works. Edited, with Notes, by Colonel CUNNINGHAM. One Vol.
Massinger's Plays. From GIFFORD'S Text. Edited by Colonel CUNNINGHAM. One Vol.

Duncan (Sara Jeannette: Mrs. EVERARD COTES), Works by.
Crown 8vo, cloth extra, 7s. 6d. each.
A Social Departure. With 111 Illustrations by F. H. TOWNSEND.
An American Girl in London. With 80 Illustrations by F. H. TOWNSEND.
The Simple Adventures of a Memsahib. With 37 Illustrations by F. H. TOWNSEND.

Crown 8vo, cloth extra, 3s. 6d. each.
A Daughter of To-Day. | Vernon's Aunt. With 47 Illustrations by HAL HURST.

Dutt (Romesh C.).—England and India: A Record of Progress during One Hundred Years. Crown 8vo, cloth, 2s.

Dyer (T. F. Thiselton).—The Folk-Lore of Plants. Cr. 8vo, cl., 6s.

Early English Poets. Edited, with Introductions and Annotations, by Rev. A. B. GROSART, D.D. Crown 8vo, cloth boards, 3s. 6d. per Volume.
Fletcher's (Giles) Complete Poems. One Vol.
Davies' (Sir John) Complete Poetical Works. Two Vols.
Herrick's (Robert) Complete Collected Poems. Three Vols.
Sidney's (Sir Philip) Complete Poetical Works. Three Vols.

Edgcumbe (Sir E. R. Pearce).—Zephyrus: A Holiday in Brazil and on the River Plate. With 41 Illustrations. Crown 8vo, cloth extra, 5s.

Edwardes (Mrs. Annie), Novels by.
Archie Lovell. Post 8vo, illustrated boards, 2s. each.
A Point of Honour.

Edwards (Eliezer).—Words, Facts, and Phrases: A Dictionary of Curious, Quaint, and Out-of-the-Way Matters. Cheaper Edition. Crown 8vo, cloth, 3s. 6d.

Edwards (M. Betham-), Novels by.
Kitty. Post 8vo, boards, 2s.; cloth, 2s. 6d. | Felicia. Post 8vo, illustrated boards, 2s.

Egerton (Rev. J. C., M.A.).—Sussex Folk and Sussex Ways. With Introduction by Rev. Dr. H. WACE, and Four Illustrations. Crown 8vo, cloth extra, 5s.

Eggleston (Edward).—Roxy: A Novel. Post 8vo, illust. boards, 2s.

Englishman's House, The: A Practical Guide for Selecting or Building a House. By C. J. RICHARDSON. Coloured Frontispiece and 534 Illusts. Cr. 8vo, cloth, 7s. 6d.

Ewald (Alex. Charles, F.S.A.), Works by.
The Life and Times of Prince Charles Stuart, Count of Albany (THE YOUNG PRETENDER. With a Portrait. Crown 8vo, cloth extra, 7s. 6d.
Stories from the State Papers. With Autotype Frontispiece. Crown 8vo, cloth, 6s.

Eyes, Our: How to Preserve Them. By JOHN BROWNING. Cr. 8vo, 1s.

Familiar Short Sayings of Great Men. By SAMUEL ARTHUR BENT, A.M. Fifth Edition, Revised and Enlarged. Crown 8vo, cloth extra, 7s. 6d.

Faraday (Michael), Works by. Post 8vo, cloth extra, 4s. 6d. each.
The Chemical History of a Candle: Lectures delivered before a Juvenile Audience. Edited by WILLIAM CROOKES, F.C.S. With numerous Illustrations.
On the Various Forces of Nature, and their Relations to each other. Edited by WILLIAM CROOKES, F.C.S. With Illustrations.

Farrer (J. Anson), Works by.
Military Manners and Customs. Crown 8vo, cloth extra, 6s.
War: Three Essays, reprinted from 'Military Manners and Customs.' Crown 8vo, 1s.; cloth, 1s. 6d.

Fenn (G. Manville), Novels by.
Crown 8vo, cloth extra, 3s. 6d. each; post 8vo, illustrated boards, 2s. each.
The New Mistress. | Witness to the Deed. | The Tiger Lily. | The White Virgin.

Fin-Bec.—The Cupboard Papers: Observations on the Art of Living and Dining. Post 8vo, cloth limp, 2s. 6d.

Fireworks, The Complete Art of Making; or, The Pyrotechnist's Treasury. By THOMAS KENTISH. With 267 Illustrations. Crown 8vo, cloth, 5s.

First Book, My. By WALTER BESANT, JAMES PAYN, W. CLARK RUSSELL, GRANT ALLEN, HALL CAINE, GEORGE R. SIMS, RUDYARD KIPLING, A. CONAN DOYLE, M. E. BRADDON, F. W. ROBINSON, H. RIDER HAGGARD, R. M. BALLANTYNE, I. ZANGWILL, MORLEY ROBERTS, D. CHRISTIE MURRAY, MARY CORELLI, J. K. JEROME, JOHN STRANGE WINTER, BRET HARTE, 'Q.,' ROBERT BUCHANAN, and R. L. STEVENSON. With a Prefatory Story by JEROME K. JEROME, and 185 Illustrations. A New Edition. Small demy 8vo, art linen, 3s. 6d.

Fitzgerald (Percy), Works by.
Little Essays: Passages from the Letters of CHARLES LAMB. Post 8vo, cloth, 2s. 6d.
Fatal Zero. Crown 8vo, cloth extra, 3s. 6d.; post 8vo, illustrated boards, 2s.

Post 8vo, illustrated boards, 2s. each.
Bella Donna. | The Lady of Brantome. | The Second Mrs. Tillotson.
Polly. | Never Forgotten. | Seventy-five Brooke Street.

The Life of James Boswell (of Auchinleck). With Illusts. Two Vols., demy 8vo, cloth, 24s.
The Savoy Opera. With 60 Illustrations and Portraits. Crown 8vo, cloth, 3s. 6d.
Sir Henry Irving: Twenty Years at the Lyceum. With Portrait. Crown 8vo, 1s.; cloth, 1s. 6d.

Flammarion (Camille), Works by.
Popular Astronomy: A General Description of the Heavens. Translated by J. ELLARD GORE, F.R.A.S. With Three Plates and 288 Illustrations. Medium 8vo, cloth, 10s. 6d.
Urania: A Romance. With 87 Illustrations. Crown 8vo, cloth extra, 5s.

Fletcher's (Giles, B.D.) Complete Poems: Christ's Victorie in Heaven, Christ's Victorie on Earth, Christ's Triumph over Death, and Minor Poems. With Notes by Rev. A. B. GROSART, D.D. Crown 8vo, cloth extra, 3s. 6d.

Fonblanque (Albany).—Filthy Lucre. Post 8vo, illust. boards, 2s.

CHATTO & WINDUS, 111 St. Martin's Lane, London, W.C.

Forbes (Archibald).—The Life of Napoleon III. With Photogravure Frontispiece and Thirty-six full-page Illustrations. Demy 8vo, cloth, gilt top, 12s. [*Shortly.*

Francillon (R. E.), Novels by.
Crown 8vo, cloth extra, 3s. 6d. each; post 8vo, illustrated boards, 2s. each.
One by One. | A Real Queen. | A Dog and his Shadow.
Ropes of Sand. Illustrated.

Post 8vo, illustrated boards, 2s. each.
Queen Cophetua. | Olympia. | Romances of the Law. | King or Knave?
Jack Doyle's Daughter. Crown 8vo, cloth, 3s. 6d.

Frederic (Harold), Novels by. Post 8vo, illust. boards, 2s. each.
Seth's Brother's Wife. | The Lawton Girl.

French Literature, A History of. By HENRY VAN LAUN. Three Vols., demy 8vo, cloth boards, 7s. 6d. each.

Friswell (Hain).—One of Two: A Novel. Post 8vo, illust. bds., 2s.

Fry's (Herbert) Royal Guide to the London Charities. Edited by JOHN LANE. Published Annually. Crown 8vo, cloth, 1s. 6d.

Gardening Books. Post 8vo, 1s. each; cloth limp, 1s. 6d. each.
A Year's Work in Garden and Greenhouse. By GEORGE GLENNY.
Household Horticulture. By TOM and JANE JERROLD. Illustrated.
The Garden that Paid the Rent. By TOM JERROLD.
My Garden Wild. By FRANCIS G. HEATH. Crown 8vo, cloth, gilt edges, 6s.

Gardner (Mrs. Alan).—Rifle and Spear with the Rajpoots: Being the Narrative of a Winter's Travel and Sport in Northern India. With numerous Illustrations by the Author and F. H. TOWNSEND. Demy 4to, half-bound, 21s.

Garrett (Edward).—The Capel Girls: A Novel. Crown 8vo, cloth extra, with two Illustrations, 3s. 6d.; post 8vo, illustrated boards, 2s.

Gaulot (Paul).—The Red Shirts: A Story of the Revolution. Translated by JOHN DE VILLIERS. With a Frontispiece by STANLEY WOOD. Crown 8vo, cloth, 3s. 6d.

Gentleman's Magazine, The. 1s. Monthly. Contains Stories, Articles upon Literature, Science, Biography, and Art, and 'Table Talk' by SYLVANUS URBAN.
*** *Bound Volumes for recent years kept in stock, 8s. 6d. each. Cases for binding, 2s. each.*

Gentleman's Annual, The. Published Annually in November. 1s.
The Title of the 1897 ANNUAL is **The Secret of Wyvern Towers.** By T. W. SPEIGHT.

German Popular Stories. Collected by the Brothers GRIMM and Translated by EDGAR TAYLOR. With Introduction by JOHN RUSKIN, and 22 Steel Plates after GEORGE CRUIKSHANK. Square 8vo, cloth, 6s. 6d.; gilt edges, 7s. 6d.

Gibbon (Chas.), Novels by. Cr. 8vo, cl., 3s. 6d. ea.; post 8vo, bds., 2s. ea.
Robin Gray. With Frontispiece. | Loving a Dream.
The Golden Shaft. With Frontispiece. | Of High Degree.

Post 8vo, illustrated boards, 2s. each.
The Flower of the Forest. | In Love and War.
The Dead Heart. | A Heart's Problem.
For Lack of Gold. | By Mead and Stream.
What Will the World Say? | The Braes of Yarrow.
For the King. | A Hard Knot. | Fancy Free.
Queen of the Meadow. | In Honour Bound.
In Pastures Green. | Heart's Delight. | Blood-Money.

Gibney (Somerville).—Sentenced! Crown 8vo, cloth, 1s. 6d.

Gilbert (W. S.), Original Plays by. In Three Series, 2s. 6d. each.
The FIRST SERIES contains: The Wicked World—Pygmalion and Galatea—Charity—The Princess—The Palace of Truth—Trial by Jury.
The SECOND SERIES: Broken Hearts—Engaged—Sweethearts—Gretchen—Dan Druce—Tom Cobb—H.M.S. 'Pinafore'—The Sorcerer—The Pirates of Penzance.
The THIRD SERIES: Comedy and Tragedy—Foggerty's Fairy—Rosencrantz and Guildenstern—Patience—Princess Ida—The Mikado—Ruddigore—The Yeomen of the Guard—The Gondoliers—The Mountebanks—Utopia.

Eight Original Comic Operas written by W. S. GILBERT. In Two Series. Demy 8vo, cloth, 2s. 6d. each. The FIRST containing: The Sorcerer—H.M.S. 'Pinafore'—The Pirates of Penzance—Iolanthe—Patience—Princess Ida—The Mikado—Trial by Jury.
The SECOND SERIES containing: The Gondoliers—The Grand Duke—The Yeomen of the Guard—His Excellency—Utopia, Limited—Ruddigore—The Mountebanks—Haste to the Wedding.

The Gilbert and Sullivan Birthday Book: Quotations for Every Day in the Year, selected from Plays by W. S. GILBERT set to Music by Sir A. SULLIVAN. Compiled by ALEX. WATSON. Royal 16mo, Japanese leather, 2s. 6d.

CHATTO & WINDUS, 111 St. Martin's Lane, London, W.C.

Gilbert (William), Novels by. Post 8vo, illustrated bds., 2s. each.
Dr. Austin's Guests. | James Duke, Costermonger.
The Wizard of the Mountain.

Glanville (Ernest), Novels by.
Crown 8vo, cloth extra, 3s. 6d. each; post 8vo, illustrated boards, 2s. each.
The Lost Heiress: A Tale of Love, Battle, and Adventure. With Two Illustrations by H. NISBET.
The Fossicker: A Romance of Mashonaland. With Two Illustrations by HUME NISBET.
A Fair Colonist. With a Frontispiece by STANLEY WOOD.

The Golden Rock. With a Frontispiece by STANLEY WOOD. Crown 8vo, cloth extra, 3s. 6d.
Kloof Yarns. Crown 8vo, picture cover, 1s.; cloth, 1s. 6d.
Tales from the Veldt. With Twelve Illustrations by M. NISBET. Crown 8vo, cloth, 3s. 6d.

Glenny (George).—A Year's Work in Garden and Greenhouse:
Practical Advice as to the Management of the Flower, Fruit, and Frame Garden. Post 8vo, 1s.; cloth, 1s. 6d.

Godwin (William).—Lives of the Necromancers. Post 8vo, cl., 2s.

Golden Treasury of Thought, The: An Encyclopædia of QUOTATIONS. Edited by THEODORE TAYLOR. Crown 8vo, cloth gilt, 7s. 6d.

Gontaut, Memoirs of the Duchesse de (Gouvernante to the Children of France), 1773-1836. With Two Photogravures. Two Vols., demy 8vo, cloth extra, 21s.

Goodman (E. J.).—The Fate of Herbert Wayne. Cr. 8vo, 3s. 6d.

Greeks and Romans, The Life of the, described from Antique Monuments. By ERNST GUHL and W. KONER. Edited by Dr. F. HUEFFER. With 545 Illustrations. Large crown 8vo, cloth extra, 7s. 6d.

Greville (Henry), Novels by.
Post 8vo, illustrated boards, 2s. each.
Nikanor. Translated by ELIZA E. CHASE.
A Noble Woman. Translated by ALBERT D. VANDAM.

Griffith (Cecil).—Corinthia Marazion: A Novel. Crown 8vo, cloth extra, 3s. 6d.; post 8vo, illustrated boards, 2s.

Grundy (Sydney).—The Days of his Vanity: A Passage in the Life of a Young Man. Crown 8vo, cloth extra, 3s. 6d.; post 8vo, illustrated boards, 2s.

Habberton (John, Author of 'Helen's Babies'), **Novels by.**
Post 8vo, illustrated boards, 2s. each; cloth limp, 2s. 6d. each.
Brueton's Bayou. | Country Luck.

Hair, The: Its Treatment in Health, Weakness, and Disease. Translated from the German of Dr. J. PINCUS. Crown 8vo, 1s.; cloth, 1s. 6d.

Hake (Dr. Thomas Gordon), Poems by. Cr. 8vo, cl. ex., 6s. each.
New Symbols. | Legends of the Morrow. | The Serpent Play.
Maiden Ecstasy. Small 4to, cloth extra, 8s.

Halifax (C.).—Dr. Rumsey's Patient. By Mrs. L. T. MEADE and CLIFFORD HALIFAX, M.D. Crown 8vo, cloth, 6s.

Hall (Mrs. S. C.).—Sketches of Irish Character. With numerous Illustrations on Steel and Wood by MACLISE, GILBERT, HARVEY, and GEORGE CRUIKSHANK. Small demy 8vo, cloth extra, 7s. 6d.

Hall (Owen), Novels by.
The Track of a Storm. Cheaper Edition. Crown 8vo, cloth, 3s. 6d.
Jetsam. Crown 8vo, cloth, 3s. 6d.

Halliday (Andrew).—Every-day Papers. Post 8vo, boards, 2s.

Handwriting, The Philosophy of. With over 100 Facsimiles and Explanatory Text. By DON FELIX DE SALAMANCA. Post 8vo, cloth limp, 2s. 6d.

Hanky-Panky: Easy and Difficult Tricks, White Magic, Sleight of Hand, &c. Edited by W. H. CREMER. With 200 Illustrations. Crown 8vo, cloth extra, 4s. 6d.

Hardy (Lady Duffus).—Paul Wynter's Sacrifice. Post 8vo, bds., 2s.

Hardy (Thomas).—Under the Greenwood Tree. Crown 8vo, cloth extra, with Portrait and 15 Illustrations, 3s. 6d.; post 8vo, illustrated boards, 2s.; cloth limp, 2s. 6d.

Harwood (J. Berwick).—The Tenth Earl. Post 8vo, boards, 2s.

CHATTO & WINDUS, 111 St. Martin's Lane, London, W.C.

Harte's (Bret) Collected Works. Revised by the Author. LIBRARY EDITION, in Nine Volumes, crown 8vo, cloth extra, 6s. each.
  Vol. I. COMPLETE POETICAL AND DRAMATIC WORKS. With Steel-plate Portrait.
  „ II. THE LUCK OF ROARING CAMP—BOHEMIAN PAPERS—AMERICAN LEGEND.
  „ III. TALES OF THE ARGONAUTS—EASTERN SKETCHES.
  „ IV. GABRIEL CONROY. | Vol. V. STORIES—CONDENSED **NOVELS,** &c.
  „ VI. TALES OF THE PACIFIC SLOPE.
  „ VII. TALES OF THE PACIFIC SLOPE—II. With Portrait by JOHN PETTIE, R.A.
  „ VIII. TALES OF THE PINE AND THE CYPRESS.
  „ IX. BUCKEYE AND CHAPPAREL.

The Select Works of Bret Harte, in Prose and Poetry. With Introductory Essay by J. M. BELLEW, Portrait of the Author, and 50 Illustrations. Crown 8vo, cloth, 3s. 6d.
Bret Harte's Poetical Works. Printed on hand-made paper. Crown 8vo, buckram. 4s. 6d.
A New Volume of Poems. Crown 8vo, buckram, 5s. [*Preparing.*
The Queen of the Pirate Isle. With 28 Original Drawings by KATE GREENAWAY, reproduced in Colours by EDMUND EVANS. Small 4to, cloth, 5s.

Crown 8vo, cloth extra, 3s. 6d. each; post 8vo, picture boards, 2s. each.
A Waif of the Plains. With 60 Illustrations by STANLEY L. WOOD.
A Ward of the Golden Gate. With 59 Illustrations by STANLEY L. WOOD.

Crown 8vo, cloth extra, 3s. 6d. each.
A Sappho of Green Springs, &c. With Two Illustrations by HUME NISBET.
Colonel Starbottle's Client, and Some Other People. With a Frontispiece.
Susy: A Novel. With Frontispiece and Vignette by J. A. CHRISTIE.
Sally Dows, &c. With 47 Illustrations by W. D. ALMOND and others.
A Protegée of Jack Hamlin's, &c. With 26 Illustrations by W. SMALL and others.
The Bell-Ringer of Angel's, &c. With 39 Illustrations by DUDLEY HARDY and others.
Clarence: A Story of the American War. With Eight Illustrations by A. JULE GOODMAN.
Barker's Luck, &c. With 39 Illustrations by A. FORRESTIER, PAUL HARDY, &c.
Devil's Ford, &c. With a Frontispiece by W. H. OVEREND.
The Crusade of the "Excelsior." With a Frontispiece by J. BERNARD PARTRIDGE.
Three Partners; or, The Big Strike on Heavy Tree Hill. With 8 Illustrations by J. GULICH.

Post 8vo, illustrated boards, 2s. each.
Gabriel Conroy. | The Luck of Roaring Camp, &c.
An Heiress of Red Dog, &c. | Californian Stories.

Post 8vo, illustrated boards, 2s. each; cloth, 2s. 6d. each.
Flip. | Maruja. | A Phyllis of the Sierras.

Haweis (Mrs. H. R.), Books by.
The Art of Beauty. With Coloured Frontispiece and 91 Illustrations. Square 8vo, cloth bds., 6s.
The Art of Decoration. With Coloured Frontispiece and 74 Illustrations. Sq. 8vo, cloth bds., 6s.
The Art of Dress. With 32 Illustrations. Post 8vo, 1s.; cloth, 1s. 6d.
Chaucer for Schools. Demy 8vo, cloth limp, 2s. 6d.
Chaucer for Children. With 38 Illustrations (8 Coloured). Crown 4to, cloth extra, 3s. 6d.

Haweis (Rev. H. R., M.A.), Books by.
American Humorists: WASHINGTON IRVING, OLIVER WENDELL HOLMES, JAMES RUSSELL LOWELL, ARTEMUS WARD, MARK TWAIN, and BRET HARTE. Third Edition. Crown 8vo, cloth extra, 6s.
Travel and Talk, 1885-93-95: My Hundred Thousand Miles of Travel through America—Canada—New Zealand—Tasmania—Australia—Ceylon—The Paradises of the Pacific. With Photogravure Frontispieces. A New Edition. Two Vols., crown 8vo, cloth, 12s.

Hawthorne (Julian), Novels by.
Crown 8vo, cloth extra, 3s. 6d. each; post 8vo, illustrated boards, 2s. each.
Garth. | Ellice Quentin. | Beatrix Randolph. With Four Illusts.
Sebastian Strome. | | David Poindexter's Disappearance.
Fortune's Fool. | Dust. Four Illusts. | The Spectre of the Camera.

Post 8vo, illustrated boards, 2s. each.
Miss Cadogna. | Love—or a Name.

Hawthorne (Nathaniel).—Our Old Home. Annotated with Passages from the Author's Note-books, and Illustrated with 31 Photogravures. Two Vols., cr. 8vo, 15s.

Heath (Francis George).—My Garden Wild, and What I Grew There. Crown 8vo, cloth extra, gilt edges, 6s.

Helps (Sir Arthur), Works by. Post 8vo, cloth limp, 2s. 6d. each.
Animals and their Masters. | Social Pressure.
Ivan de Biron: A Novel. Crown 8vo, cloth extra, 3s. 6d.; post 8vo, illustrated boards, 2s.

Henderson (Isaac).—Agatha Page: A Novel. Cr. 8vo, cl., 3s. 6d.

Henty (G. A.), Novels by.
Rujub the Juggler. With Eight Illustrations by STANLEY L. WOOD. Crown 8vo, cloth, 3s. 6d.; post 8vo, illustrated boards, 2s.

Crown 8vo, cloth, 3s. 6d. each.
Dorothy's Double. | The Queen's Cup.

Herman (Henry).—A Leading Lady. Post 8vo, bds., 2s.; cl., 2s. 6d.

Herrick's (Robert) Hesperides, Noble Numbers, and Complete Collected Poems. With Memorial-Introduction and Notes by the Rev. A. B. GROSART, D.D. Steel Portrait, &c. Three Vols., crown 8vo, cloth boards, 3s. 6d. each.

Hertzka (Dr. Theodor).—Freeland: A Social Anticipation. Translated by ARTHUR RANSOM. Crown 8vo, cloth extra, 6s.

Hesse-Wartegg (Chevalier Ernst von).— Tunis: The Land and the People. With 22 Illustrations. Crown 8vo, cloth extra, 3s. 6d.

Hill (Headon).—Zambra the Detective. Crown 8vo, cloth, 3s. 6d.; post 8vo, picture boards, 2s.; cloth, 2s. 6d.

Hill (John), Works by.
Treason-Felony. Post 8vo, boards, 2s. | The Common Ancestor. Cr. 8vo, cloth, 3s. 6d.

Hoey (Mrs. Cashel).—The Lover's Creed. Post 8vo, boards, 2s.

Holiday, Where to go for a. By E. P. SHOLL, Sir H. MAXWELL, Bart., M.P., JOHN WATSON, JANE BARLOW, MARY LOVETT CAMERON, JUSTIN H. McCARTHY, PAUL LANGE, J. W. GRAHAM, J. H. SALTER, PHŒBE ALLEN, S. J. BECKETT, L. RIVERS VINE, and C. F. GORDON CUMMING. Crown 8vo, 1s.; cloth, 1s. 6d.

Hollingshead (John).—Niagara Spray. Crown 8vo, 1s.

Holmes (Gordon, M.D.)—The Science of Voice Production and Voice Preservation. Crown 8vo, 1s.; cloth, 1s. 6d.

Holmes (Oliver Wendell), Works by.
The Autocrat of the Breakfast-Table. Illustrated by J. GORDON THOMSON. Post 8vo, cloth limp, 2s. 6d.—Another Edition, post 8vo, cloth, 2s.
The Autocrat of the Breakfast-Table and The Professor at the Breakfast-Table. In One Vol. Post 8vo, half-bound, 2s.

Hood's (Thomas) Choice Works in Prose and Verse. With Life of the Author, Portrait, and 200 Illustrations. Crown 8vo, cloth, 3s. 6d.
Hood's Whims and Oddities. With 85 Illustrations. Post 8vo, half-bound, 2s.

Hood (Tom).—From Nowhere to the North Pole: A Noah's Arkæological Narrative. With 25 Illustrations by W. BRUNTON and E. C. BARNES. Cr. 8vo, cloth, 6s.

Hook's (Theodore) Choice Humorous Works; including his Ludicrous Adventures, Bons Mots, Puns, and Hoaxes. With Life of the Author, Portraits, Facsimiles, and Illustrations. Crown 8vo, cloth extra, 7s. 6d.

Hooper (Mrs. Geo.).—The House of Raby. Post 8vo, boards, 2s.

Hopkins (Tighe).—''Twixt Love and Duty.' Post 8vo, boards, 2s.

Horne (R. Hengist).—Orion: An Epic Poem. With Photograph Portrait by SUMMERS. Tenth Edition. Crown 8vo, cloth extra, 7s.

Hungerford (Mrs., Author of ' Molly Bawn '), **Novels by.**
Post 8vo, illustrated boards, 2s. each; cloth limp, 2s. 6d. each.
A Maiden All Forlorn. | A Modern Circe. | An Unsatisfactory Lover.
Marvel. | A Mental Struggle. | Lady Patty.
In Durance Vile.
Crown 8vo, cloth extra, 3s. 6d. each; post 8vo, illustrated boards, 2s. each; cloth limp, 2s. 6d. each.
Lady Verner's Flight. | The Red-House Mystery. | The Three Graces.
Crown 8vo, cloth extra, 3s. 6d. each.
The Professor's Experiment. With Frontispiece by E. J. WHEELER.
Nora Creina. | April's Lady. | Peter's Wife.
An Anxious Moment. | A Point of Conscience.
Lovice. Crown 8vo, cloth, 6s.

Hunt's (Leigh) Essays: A Tale for a Chimney Corner, &c. Edited by EDMUND OLLIER. Post 8vo, half-bound, 2s.

Hunt (Mrs. Alfred), Novels by.
Crown 8vo, cloth extra, 3s. 6d. each; post 8vo, illustrated boards, 2s. each.
The Leaden Casket. | Self-Condemned. | That Other Person.
Thornicroft's Model. Post 8vo, boards, 2s. | Mrs. Juliet. Crown 8vo, cloth extra, 3s. 6d.

Hutchison (W. M.).—Hints on Colt-breaking. With 25 Illustrations. Crown 8vo, cloth extra, 3s. 6d.

Hydrophobia: An Account of M. PASTEUR's System; The Technique of his Method, and Statistics. By RENAUD SUZOR, M.B. Crown 8vo, cloth extra, 6s.

Hyne (C. J. Cutcliffe).—Honour of Thieves. Cr. 8vo, cloth, 3s. 6d.

Idler (The): An Illustrated Monthly Magazine. Edited by J. K. JEROME. Nos. 1 to 48, 6d. each; No. 49 and following Numbers, 1s. each. The first EIGHT VOLS., cloth, 5s. each; Vol. IX. and after, 7s. 6d. each.—Cases for Binding, 1s. 6d. each.

CHATTO & WINDUS, 111 St. Martin's Lane, London, W.C.   13

Impressions (The) of Aureole. Cheaper Edition, with a New Preface. Post 8vo, blush-rose paper and cloth, 2s. 6d.

Indoor Paupers. By ONE OF THEM. Crown 8vo, cloth, 1s. 6d.

Ingelow (Jean).—Fated to be Free. Post 8vo, illustrated bds., 2s.

Innkeeper's Handbook (The) and Licensed Victualler's Manual. By J TREVOR-DAVIES. Crown 8vo, 1s.; cloth, 1s. 6d.

Irish Wit and Humour, Songs of. Collected and Edited by A. PERCEVAL GRAVES. Post 8vo, cloth limp, 2s. 6d.

Irving (Sir Henry): A Record of over Twenty Years at the Lyceum. By PERCY FITZGERALD. With Portrait. Crown 8vo, 1s.; cloth, 1s. 6d.

James (C. T. C.).—A Romance of the Queen's Hounds. Post 8vo, cloth limp, 1s. 6d.

Jameson (William).—My Dead Self. Post 8vo, bds., 2s.; cl., 2s. 6d.

Japp (Alex. H., LL.D.).—Dramatic Pictures, &c. Cr. 8vo, cloth, 5s.

Jay (Harriett), Novels by. Post 8vo, illustrated boards, 2s. each.
The Dark Colleen. | The Queen of Connaught.

Jefferies (Richard), Works by. Post 8vo, cloth limp, 2s. 6d. each.
Nature near London. | The Life of the Fields. | The Open Air.
*** Also the HAND-MADE PAPER EDITION, crown 8vo, buckram, gilt top, 6s. each.

The Eulogy of Richard Jefferies. By Sir WALTER BESANT. With a Photograph Portrait. Crown 8vo, cloth extra, 6s.

Jennings (Henry J.), Works by.
Curiosities of Criticism. Post 8vo, cloth limp, 2s. 6d.
Lord Tennyson: A Biographical Sketch. With Portrait. Post 8vo, 1s.; cloth, 1s. 6d.

Jerome (Jerome K.), Books by.
Stageland. With 64 Illustrations by J. BERNARD PARTRIDGE. Fcap. 4to, picture cover, 1s.
John Ingerfield, &c. With 9 Illusts. by A. S. BOYD and JOHN GULICH. Fcap. 8vo, pic. cov. 1s. 6d.
The Prude's Progress: A Comedy by J. K. JEROME and EDEN PHILLPOTTS. Cr. 8vo, 1s. 6d.

Jerrold (Douglas).—The Barber's Chair; and The Hedgehog Letters. Post 8vo, printed on laid paper and half-bound, 2s.

Jerrold (Tom), Works by. Post 8vo, 1s. ea.; cloth limp, 1s. 6d. each.
The Garden that Paid the Rent.
Household Horticulture: A Gossip about Flowers. Illustrated.

Jesse (Edward).—Scenes and Occupations of a Country Life. Post 8vo, cloth limp, 2s.

Jones (William, F.S.A.), Works by. Cr. 8vo, cl. extra, 7s. 6d. each.
Finger-Ring Lore: Historical, Legendary, and Anecdotal. With nearly 300 Illustrations. Second Edition, Revised and Enlarged.
Credulities, Past and Present. Including the Sea and Seamen, Miners, Talismans, Word and Letter Divination, Exorcising and Blessing of Animals, Birds, Eggs, Luck, &c. With Frontispiece.
Crowns and Coronations: A History of Regalia. With 100 Illustrations.

Jonson's (Ben) Works. With Notes Critical and Explanatory, and a Biographical Memoir by WILLIAM GIFFORD. Edited by Colonel CUNNINGHAM. Three Vols. crown 8vo, cloth extra, 3s. 6d. each.

Josephus, The Complete Works of. Translated by WHISTON. Containing 'The Antiquities of the Jews' and 'The Wars of the Jews.' With 52 Illustrations and Maps. Two Vols., demy 8vo, half-bound, 12s. 6d.

Kempt (Robert).—Pencil and Palette: Chapters on Art and Artists. Post 8vo, cloth limp, 2s. 6d.

Kershaw (Mark).—Colonial Facts and Fictions: Humorous Sketches. Post 8vo, illustrated boards, 2s.; cloth, 2s. 6d.

King (R. Ashe), Novels by.
A Drawn Game. Crown 8vo, cloth, 3s. 6d.; post 8vo, boards, 2s.
Post 8vo, illustrated boards, 2s. each.
'The Wearing of the Green.' | Passion's Slave. | Bell Barry.

Knight (William, M.R.C.S., and Edward, L.R.C.P.). — The Patient's Vade Mecum: How to Get Most Benefit from Medical Advice. Cr. 8vo, 1s.; cl., 1s. 6d.

Knights (The) of the Lion: A Romance of the Thirteenth Century. Edited, with an Introduction, by the MARQUESS OF LORNE, K.T. Crown 8vo, cloth extra, 6s.

Lamb's (Charles) Complete Works in Prose and Verse, including 'Poetry for Children' and 'Prince Dorus.' Edited, with Notes and Introduction, by R. H. SHEPHERD. With Two Portraits and Facsimile of the 'Essay on Roast Pig.' Crown 8vo, cloth, 3s. 6d.
The Essays of Elia. Post 8vo, printed on laid paper and half-bound, 2s.
Little Essays: Sketches and Characters by CHARLES LAMB, selected from his Letters by PERCY FITZGERALD. Post 8vo, cloth limp, 2s. 6d.
The Dramatic Essays of Charles Lamb. With Introduction and Notes by BRANDER MATTHEWS, and Steel-plate Portrait. Fcap. 8vo, half-bound, 2s. 6d.

Landor (Walter Savage). — Citation and Examination of William Shakspeare, &c., before Sir Thomas Lucy, touching Deer-stealing, 19th September, 1582. To which is added, **A Conference of Master Edmund Spenser** with the Earl of Essex, touching the State of Ireland, 1595. Fcap. 8vo, half-Roxburghe, 2s. 6d.

Lane (Edward William). — The Thousand and One Nights, commonly called in England The Arabian Nights' Entertainments. Translated from the Arabic, with Notes. Illustrated with many hundred Engravings from Designs by HARVEY. Edited by EDWARD STANLEY POOLE. With Preface by STANLEY LANE-POOLE. Three Vols., demy 8vo, cloth, 7s. 6d. ea.

Larwood (Jacob), Works by.
Anecdotes of the Clergy. Post 8vo, laid paper, half-bound, 2s.
Post 8vo, cloth limp, 2s. 6d. each.
Forensic Anecdotes. | **Theatrical Anecdotes.**

Lehmann (R. C.), Works by. Post 8vo, 1s. each; cloth, 1s. 6d. each.
Harry Fludyer at Cambridge.
Conversational Hints for Young Shooters: A Guide to Polite Talk.

Leigh (Henry S.). — Carols of Cockayne. Printed on hand-made paper, bound in buckram, 5s.

Leland (C. Godfrey). — A Manual of Mending and Repairing. With Diagrams. Crown 8vo, cloth, 5s.

Lepelletier (Edmond). — Madame Sans-Gêne. Translated from the French by JOHN DE VILLIERS. Crown 8vo, cloth, 3s. 6d.; post 8vo, picture boards, 2s.

Leys (John). — The Lindsays: A Romance. Post 8vo, illust. bds., 2s.

Lindsay (Harry). — Rhoda Roberts: A Welsh Mining Story. Crown 8vo, cloth, 3s. 6d.

Linton (E. Lynn), Works by.
Crown 8vo, cloth extra, 3s. 6d. each; post 8vo, illustrated boards, 2s. each.
Patricia Kemball. | **Ione.** | **Under which Lord?** With 12 Illustrations.
The Atonement of Leam Dundas. | **'My Love!'** | **Sowing the Wind.**
The World Well Lost. With 12 Illusts. | **Paston Carew,** Millionaire and Miser.
The One Too Many.

Post 8vo, illustrated boards, 2s. each.
The Rebel of the Family. | **With a Silken Thread.**

Post 8vo, cloth limp, 2s. 6d. each.
Witch Stories. | **Ourselves:** Essays on Women.
Freeshooting: Extracts from the Works of Mrs. LYNN LINTON.

Dulcie Everton. Crown 8vo, cloth extra, 3s. 6d.

Lucy (Henry W.). — Gideon Fleyce: A Novel. Crown 8vo, cloth extra, 3s. 6d.; post 8vo, illustrated boards, 2s.

Macalpine (Avery), Novels by.
Teresa Itasca. Crown 8vo, cloth extra, 1s.
Broken Wings. With Six Illustrations by W. J. HENNESSY. Crown 8vo, cloth extra, 6s.

MacColl (Hugh), Novels by.
Mr. Stranger's Sealed Packet. Post 8vo, Illustrated boards, 2s.
Ednor Whitlock. Crown 8vo, cloth extra, 6s.

Macdonell (Agnes). — Quaker Cousins. Post 8vo, boards, 2s.

MacGregor (Robert). — Pastimes and Players: Notes on Popular Games. Post 8vo, cloth limp, 2s. 6d.

Mackay (Charles, LL.D.). — Interludes and Undertones; or, Music at Twilight. Crown 8vo, cloth extra, 6s.

McCarthy (Justin, M.P.), Works by.

A History of Our Own Times, from the Accession of Queen Victoria to the General Election of 1880. LIBRARY EDITION. Four Vols., demy 8vo, cloth extra, 12s. each.—Also a POPULAR EDITION, in Four Vols., crown 8vo, cloth extra, 6s. each.—And the JUBILEE EDITION, with an Appendix of Events to the end of 1886, in Two Vols., large crown 8vo, cloth extra, 7s. 6d. each.
A History of Our Own Times, from 1880 to the Diamond Jubilee. Demy 8vo, cloth extra, 12s. LIBRARY EDITION, uniform with the previous Four Volumes.
A Short History of Our Own Times. One Vol., crown 8vo, cloth extra, 6s.—Also a CHEAP POPULAR EDITION, post 8vo, cloth limp, 2s. 6d.
A History of the Four Georges. Four Vols., demy 8vo, cl. ex., 12s. each. [Vols. I. & II. ready.

Crown 8vo, cloth extra, 3s. 6d. each ; post 8vo, illustrated boards, 2s. each ; cloth limp, 2s. 6d. each.

The Waterdale Neighbours.	**Donna Quixote.** With 12 Illustrations.
My Enemy's Daughter.	**The Comet of a Season.**
A Fair Saxon.	**Maid of Athens.** With 12 Illustrations.
Linley Rochford.	**Camiola :** A Girl with a Fortune.
Dear Lady Disdain.	**The Dictator.**
Miss Misanthrope. With 12 Illustrations.	**Red Diamonds.**

The Riddle Ring. Crown 8vo, cloth, 3s. 6d.
The Three Disgraces, and other Stories. Crown 8vo, cloth, 3s. 6d. [Oct. 28.
'**The Right Honourable.**' By JUSTIN MCCARTHY, M.P., and Mrs. CAMPBELL PRAED. Crown 8vo, cloth extra, 6s.

McCarthy (Justin Huntly), Works by.

The French Revolution. (Constituent Assembly, 1789-91). Four Vols., demy 8vo, cloth, 12s. each.
An Outline of the History of Ireland. Crown 8vo, 1s. ; cloth, 1s. 6d.
Ireland Since the Union : Sketches of Irish History, 1798-1886. Crown 8vo, cloth, 6s.
Hafiz in London : Poems. Small 8vo, gold cloth, 3s. 6d.
Our Sensation Novel. Crown 8vo, picture cover, 1s. ; cloth limp, 1s. 6d.
Doom : An Atlantic Episode. Crown 8vo, picture cover, 1s.
Dolly : A Sketch. Crown 8vo, picture cover, 1s. ; cloth limp, 1s. 6d.
Lily Lass : A Romance. Crown 8vo, picture cover, 1s. ; cloth limp, 1s. 6d.
The Thousand and One Days. With Two Photogravures. Two Vols., crown 8vo, half-bd., 12s.
A London Legend. Crown 8vo, cloth, 3s. 6d.
The Royal Christopher. Crown 8vo, cloth, 3s. 6d.

MacDonald (George, LL.D.), Books by.

Works of Fancy and Imagination. Ten Vols., 16mo, cloth, gilt edges, in cloth case, 21s. ; or the Volumes may be had separately, in Grolier cloth, at 2s. 6d. each.
 Vol. I. WITHIN AND WITHOUT.—THE HIDDEN LIFE.
 " II. THE DISCIPLE.—THE GOSPEL WOMEN.—BOOK OF SONNETS.—ORGAN SONGS.
 " III. VIOLIN SONGS.—SONGS OF THE DAYS AND NIGHTS.—A BOOK OF DREAMS.—ROADSIDE POEMS.—POEMS FOR CHILDREN.
 " IV. PARABLES.—BALLADS.—SCOTCH SONGS.
 " V. & VI. PHANTASTES : A Faerie Romance. | Vol. VII. THE PORTENT.
 " VIII. THE LIGHT PRINCESS.—THE GIANT'S HEART.—SHADOWS.
 " IX. CROSS PURPOSES.—THE GOLDEN KEY.—THE CARASOYN—LITTLE DAYLIGHT.
 " X. THE CRUEL PAINTER.—THE WOW O' RIVVEN.—THE CASTLE.—THE BROKEN SWORDS —THE GRAY WOLF.—UNCLE CORNELIUS.

Poetical Works of George MacDonald. Collected and Arranged by the Author. Two Vols., crown 8vo, buckram, 12s.
A Threefold Cord. Edited by GEORGE MACDONALD. Post 8vo, cloth, 5s.
Phantastes : A Faerie Romance. With 25 Illustrations by J. BELL. Crown 8vo, cloth extra, 3s. 6d.
Heather and Snow : A Novel. Crown 8vo, cloth extra, 3s. 6d. ; post 8vo, illustrated boards, 2s.
Lilith : A Romance. SECOND EDITION. Crown 8vo, cloth extra, 6s.

Maclise Portrait Gallery (The) of Illustrious Literary Characters : 85 Portraits by DANIEL MACLISE ; with Memoirs—Biographical, Critical, Bibliographical and Anecdotal—illustrative of the Literature of the former half of the Present Century, by WILLIAM BATES, B.A. Crown 8vo, cloth extra, 7s. 6d.

Macquoid (Mrs.), Works by. Square 8vo, cloth extra, 6s. each.

In the Ardennes. With 50 Illustrations by THOMAS R. MACQUOID.
Pictures and Legends from Normandy and Brittany. 34 Illusts. by T. R. MACQUOID.
Through Normandy. With 92 Illustrations by T. R. MACQUOID, and a Map.
Through Brittany. With 35 Illustrations by T. R. MACQUOID, and a Map.
About Yorkshire. With 67 Illustrations by T. R. MACQUOID.

Post 8vo, illustrated boards, 2s. each.
The Evil Eye, and other Stories. | **Lost Rose,** and other Stories.

Magician's Own Book, The : Performances with Eggs, Hats, &c. Edited by W. H. CREMER. With 200 Illustrations. Crown 8vo, cloth extra, 4s. 6d.

Magic Lantern, The, and its Management : Including full Practical Directions. By T. C. HEPWORTH. With 10 Illustrations. Crown 8vo, 1s. ; cloth, 1s. 6d.

Magna Charta : An Exact Facsimile of the Original in the British Museum, 3 feet by 2 feet, with Arms and Seals emblazoned in Gold and Colours, 5s.

Mallory (Sir Thomas). — Mort d'Arthur : The Stories of King Arthur and of the Knights of the Round Table. (A Selection.) Edited by B. MONTGOMERIE RANKING. Post 8vo, cloth limp, 2s.

Mallock (W. H.), Works by.
The New Republic. Post 8vo, picture cover, 2s.; cloth limp, 2s. 6d.
The New Paul & Virginia: Positivism on an Island. Post 8vo, cloth, 2s. 6d.
A Romance of the Nineteenth Century. Crown 8vo, cloth 6s.; post 8vo, illust. boards, 2s.
Poems. Small 4to, parchment, 8s.
Is Life Worth Living? Crown 8vo, cloth extra, 6s.

Marks (H. S., R.A.), Pen and Pencil Sketches by. With Four Photogravures and 126 Illustrations. Two Vols. demy 8vo, cloth, 32s.

Marlowe's Works. Including his Translations. Edited, with Notes and Introductions, by Colonel CUNNINGHAM. Crown 8vo, cloth extra, 3s. 6d.

Marryat (Florence), Novels by. Post 8vo, illust. boards, 2s. each.
A Harvest of Wild Oats.
Open! Sesame!
Fighting the Air.
Written in Fire.

Massinger's Plays. From the Text of WILLIAM GIFFORD. Edited by Col. CUNNINGHAM. Crown 8vo, cloth extra, 3s. 6d.

Masterman (J.).—Half-a-Dozen Daughters. Post 8vo, boards, 2s.

Matthews (Brander).—A Secret of the Sea, &c. Post 8vo, illustrated boards, 2s.; cloth limp, 2s. 6d.

Meade (L. T.), Novels by.
A Soldier of Fortune. Crown 8vo, cloth, 3s. 6d.; post 8vo, illustrated boards, 2s.
Crown 8vo, cloth, 3s. 6d. each.
In an Iron Grip.
Dr. Rumsey's Patient. By L. T. MEADE and CLIFFORD HALIFAX, M.D.
The Voice of the Charmer. With 8 Illustrations.

Merrick (Leonard), Stories by.
The Man who was Good. Post 8vo, picture boards, 2s.
Crown 8vo, cloth, 3s. 6d. each.
This Stage of Fools.
Cynthia: A Daughter of the Philistines.

Mexican Mustang (On a), through Texas to the Rio Grande. By A. E. SWEET and J. ARMOY KNOX. With 265 Illustrations. Crown 8vo, cloth extra, 7s. 6d.

Middlemass (Jean), Novels by. Post 8vo, illust. boards, 2s. each.
Touch and Go.
Mr. Dorillion.

Miller (Mrs. F. Fenwick).—Physiology for the Young; or, The House of Life. With numerous Illustrations. Post 8vo, cloth limp, 2s. 6d.

Milton (J. L.), Works by. Post 8vo, 1s. each; cloth, 1s. 6d. each.
The Hygiene of the Skin. With Directions for Diet, Soaps, Baths, Wines, &c.
The Bath in Diseases of the Skin.
The Laws of Life, and their Relation to Diseases of the Skin.

Minto (Wm.).—Was She Good or Bad? Cr. 8vo, 1s.; cloth, 1s. 6d.

Mitford (Bertram), Novels by. Crown 8vo, cloth extra, 3s. 6d. each.
The Gun-Runner: A Romance of Zululand. With a Frontispiece by STANLEY L. WOOD.
The Luck of Gerard Ridgeley. With a Frontispiece by STANLEY L. WOOD.
The King's Assegai. With Six full-page Illustrations by STANLEY L. WOOD.
Renshaw Fanning's Quest. With a Frontispiece by STANLEY L. WOOD.

Molesworth (Mrs.), Novels by.
Hathercourt Rectory. Post 8vo, illustrated boards, 2s.
That Girl in Black. Crown 8vo, cloth, 1s. 6d.

Moncrieff (W. D. Scott-).—The Abdication: An Historical Drama. With Seven Etchings by JOHN PETTIE, W. Q. ORCHARDSON, J. MACWHIRTER, COLIN HUNTER, R. MACBETH and TOM GRAHAM. Imperial 4to, buckram, 21s.

Moore (Thomas), Works by.
The Epicurean; and Alciphron. Post 8vo, half-bound, 2s.
Prose and Verse; including Suppressed Passages from the MEMOIRS OF LORD BYRON. Edited by R. H. SHEPHERD. With Portrait. Crown 8vo, cloth extra, 7s. 6d.

Muddock (J. E.) Stories by.
Crown 8vo, cloth extra, 3s. 6d. each.
Maid Marian and Robin Hood. With 12 Illustrations by STANLEY WOOD.
Basile the Jester. With Frontispiece by STANLEY WOOD.
Young Lochinvar.
Post 8vo, illustrated boards, 2s. each.
The Dead Man's Secret.
From the Bosom of the Deep.
Stories Weird and Wonderful. Post 8vo, illustrated boards, 2s.; cloth, 2s. 6d.

CHATTO & WINDUS, 111 St. Martin's Lane, London, W.C.

Murray (D. Christie), Novels by.
Crown 8vo, cloth extra, 3s. 6d. each; post 8vo, illustrated boards, 2s. each.
A Life's Atonement. | A Model Father. | Bob Martin's Little Girl.
Joseph's Coat. 12 Illusts. | Old Blazer's Hero. | Time's Revenges.
Coals of Fire. 3 Illusts. | Cynic Fortune. Frontisp. | A Wasted Crime.
Val Strange. | By the Gate of the Sea. | In Direst Peril.
Hearts. | A Bit of Human Nature. | Mount Despair.
The Way of the World. | First Person Singular.

The Making of a Novelist: An Experiment in Autobiography. With Portrait. Cr. 8vo, linen, 6s.
My Contemporaries in Fiction. Crown 8vo, buckram, 3s. 6d.
A Capful o' Nails. Crown 8vo, cloth, 3s. 6d.
This Little World. Crown 8vo, cloth, gilt top, 6s.
Tales and Poems. Crown 8vo, cloth, 3s. 6d.
[Preparing.

Murray (D. Christie) and Henry Herman, Novels by.
Crown 8vo, cloth extra, 3s. 6d. each; post 8vo, illustrated boards, 2s. each.
One Traveller Returns. | The Bishops' Bible.
Paul Jones's Alias, &c. With Illustrations by A. FORESTIER and G. NICOLET.

Murray (Henry), Novels by.
Post 8vo, illustrated boards, 2s. each; cloth, 2s. 6d. each.
A Game of Bluff. | A Song of Sixpence.

Newbolt (Henry).—Taken from the Enemy. Fcp. 8vo, cloth, 1s. 6d.

Nisbet (Hume), Books by.
'Bail Up.' Crown 8vo, cloth extra, 3s. 6d.; post 8vo, illustrated boards, 2s.
Dr. Bernard St. Vincent. Post 8vo, illustrated boards, 2s.
Lessons in Art. With 21 Illustrations. Crown 8vo, cloth extra, 2s. 6d.

Norris (W. E.), Novels by.
Saint Ann's. Crown 8vo, cloth, 3s. 6d.; post 8vo, picture boards, 2s.
Billy Bellew. With a Frontispiece by F. H. TOWNSEND. Crown 8vo, cloth, 3s. 6d.

O'Hanlon (Alice), Novels by. Post 8vo, illustrated boards, 2s. each.
The Unforeseen. | Chance? or Fate?

Ohnet (Georges), Novels by. Post 8vo, illustrated boards, 2s. each.
Doctor Rameau. | A Last Love.
A Weird Gift. Crown 8vo, cloth, 3s. 6d.; post 8vo, picture boards, 2s.

Oliphant (Mrs.), Novels by. Post 8vo, illustrated boards, 2s. each.
The Primrose Path. | Whiteladies.
The Greatest Heiress in England.
The Sorceress. Crown 8vo, cloth, 3s. 6d.

O'Reilly (Mrs.).—Phœbe's Fortunes. Post 8vo, illust. boards, 2s.

O'Shaughnessy (Arthur), Poems by:
Fcap. 8vo, cloth extra, 7s. 6d. each.
Music and Moonlight. | Songs of a Worker.
Lays of France. Crown 8vo, cloth extra, 10s. 6d.

Ouida, Novels by. Cr. 8vo, cl., 3s. 6d. ea.; post 8vo, illust. bds., 2s. ea.
Held in Bondage. | Folle-Farine. | Moths. | Pipistrello.
Tricotrin. | A Dog of Flanders. | In Maremma. | Wanda.
Strathmore. | Pascarel. | Signa. | Bimbi. | Syrlin.
Chandos. | Two Wooden Shoes. | Frescoes. | Othmar.
Cecil Castlemaine's Gage | In a Winter City. | Princess Napraxine.
Under Two Flags. | Ariadne. | Friendship. | Guilderoy. | Ruffino.
Puck. | Idalia. | A Village Commune. | Two Offenders.

Square 8vo, cloth extra, 5s. each.
Bimbi. With Nine Illustrations by EDMUND H. GARRETT.
A Dog of Flanders, &c. With Six Illustrations by EDMUND H. GARRETT.
Santa Barbara, &c. Square 8vo, cloth, 6s.; crown 8vo, cloth, 3s. 6d.; post 8vo, illustrated boards, 2s.
POPULAR EDITIONS. Medium 8vo, 6d. each; cloth, 1s. each.
Under Two Flags. | Moths.
Wisdom, Wit, and Pathos, selected from the Works of OUIDA by F. SYDNEY MORRIS. Post 8vo, cloth extra, 5s.—CHEAP EDITION, illustrated boards, 2s.

Page (H. A.).—Thoreau: His Life and Aims. With Portrait. Post 8vo, cloth, 2s. 6d.

Pandurang Hari; or, Memoirs of a Hindoo. With Preface by Sir BARTLE FRERE. Crown 8vo, cloth, 3s. 6d.; post 8vo, illustrated boards, 2s.

Parker (Rev. Joseph, D.D.).—Might Have Been; some Life Notes. Crown 8vo, cloth, 6s.

Pascal's Provincial Letters. A New Translation, with Historical Introduction and Notes by T. M'CRIE, D.D. Post 8vo, cloth limp, 2s.

Paul (Margaret A.).—Gentle and Simple. Crown 8vo, cloth, with Frontispiece by HELEN PATERSON, 3s. 6d.; post 8vo, illustrated boards, 2s.

Payn (James), Novels by.
Crown 8vo, cloth extra, 3s. 6d. each; post 8vo, illustrated boards, 2s. each.

Lost Sir Massingberd.
Walter's Word. | A County Family.
Less Black than We're Painted.
By Proxy. | For Cash Only.
High Spirits.
Under One Roof.
A Confidential Agent. With 12 Illusts.
A Grape from a Thorn. With 12 Illusts.
Holiday Tasks.
The Canon's Ward. With Portrait.
The Talk of the Town. With 12 Illusts.
Glow-Worm Tales.
The Mystery of Mirbridge.
The Word and the Will.
The Burnt Million.
Sunny Stories. | A Trying Patient.

Post 8vo illustrated boards, 2s. each.

Humorous Stories. | From Exile.
The Foster Brothers.
The Family Scapegrace.
Married Beneath Him.
Bentinck's Tutor.
A Perfect Treasure.
Like Father, Like Son.
A Woman's Vengeance.
Carlyon's Year. | Cecil's Tryst.
Murphy's Master. | At Her Mercy.
The Clyffards of Clyffe.
Found Dead. | Gwendoline's Harvest.
Mirk Abbey. | A Marine Residence.
Some Private Views.
Not Wooed, But Won.
Two Hundred Pounds Reward.
The Best of Husbands.
Halves. | What He Cost Her.
Fallen Fortunes. | Kit: A Memory.
A Prince of the Blood.

In Peril and Privation. With 17 Illustrations. Crown 8vo, cloth, 3s. 6d.
Notes from the 'News.' Crown 8vo, portrait cover, 1s.; cloth, 1s. 6d.

Payne (Will).—Jerry the Dreamer. Crown 8vo, cloth, 3s. 6d.

Pennell (H. Cholmondeley), Works by. Post 8vo, cloth, 2s. 6d. ea.
Puck on Pegasus. With Illustrations.
Pegasus Re-Saddled. With Ten full-page Illustrations by G. DU MAURIER.
The Muses of Mayfair: Vers de Société. Selected by H. C. PENNELL.

Phelps (E. Stuart), Works by. Post 8vo, 1s. ea.; cloth, 1s. 6d. ea.
Beyond the Gates. | An Old Maid's Paradise. | Burglars in Paradise.
Jack the Fisherman. Illustrated by C. W. REED. Crown 8vo, cloth, 1s. 6d.

Phil May's Sketch-Book. Containing 54 Humorous Cartoons. A New Edition. Crown folio, cloth, 2s. 6d.

Phipson (Dr. T. L.).—Famous Violinists and Fine Violins: Historical Notes, Anecdotes, and Reminiscences. Crown 8vo, cloth, 5s.

Pirkis (C. L.).—Lady Lovelace. Post 8vo, illustrated boards, 2s.

Planche (J. R.), Works by.
The Pursuivant of Arms. With Six Plates and 209 Illustrations. Crown 8vo, cloth, 7s. 6d.
Songs and Poems, 1819-1879. With Introduction by Mrs. MACKARNESS. Crown 8vo, cloth, 6s.

Plutarch's Lives of Illustrious Men. With Notes and a Life of Plutarch by JOHN and WM. LANGHORNE, and Portraits. Two Vols., demy 8vo, half-bound 10s. 6d.

Poe's (Edgar Allan) Choice Works in Prose and Poetry. With Introduction by CHARLES BAUDELAIRE. Portrait and Facsimiles. Crown 8vo, cloth, 7s. 6d.
The Mystery of Marie Roget, &c. Post 8vo, illustrated boards, 2s.

Pollock (W. H.).—The Charm, and other Drawing-room Plays. By Sir WALTER BESANT and WALTER H. POLLOCK. With 50 Illustrations. Crown 8vo, cloth gilt, 6s.

Pollock (Wilfred).—War and a Wheel: The Græco-Turkish War as Seen from a Bicycle. With a Map. Crown 8vo, picture cover, 1s.

Pope's Poetical Works. Post 8vo, cloth limp, 2s.

Porter (John).—Kingsclere. Edited by BYRON WEBBER. With 19 full-page and many smaller Illustrations. Second Edition. Demy 8vo, cloth decorated, 18s.

Praed (Mrs. Campbell), Novels by. Post 8vo, illust. bds., 2s. each.
The Romance of a Station. | The Soul of Countess Adrian.

Crown 8vo, cloth, 3s. 6d. each; post 8vo, boards, 2s. each.
Outlaw and Lawmaker. | Christina Chard. With Frontispiece by W. PAGET.
Mrs. Tregaskiss. With 8 Illustrations by ROBERT SAUBER. Crown 8vo, cloth extra, 3s. 6d.
Nulma: An Anglo-Australian Romance. Crown 8vo, cloth, 6s.

Price (E. C.), Novels by.
Crown 8vo, cloth extra, 3s. 6d. each; post 8vo, illustrated boards, 2s. each.
Valentina. | The Foreigners. | Mrs. Lancaster's Rival.
Gerald. Post 8vo, illustrated boards, 2s.

Princess Olga.—Radna: A Novel. Crown 8vo, cloth extra, 6s.

Proctor (Richard A.), Works by.
Flowers of the Sky. With 55 Illustrations. Small crown 8vo, cloth extra, 3s. 6d.
Easy Star Lessons. With Star Maps for every Night in the Year. Crown 8vo, cloth, 6s.
Familiar Science Studies. Crown 8vo, cloth extra, 6s.
Saturn and its System. With 13 Steel Plates. Demy 8vo, cloth extra, 10s. 6d.
Mysteries of Time and Space. With numerous Illustrations. Crown 8vo, cloth extra, 6s.
The Universe of Suns, &c. With numerous Illustrations. Crown 8vo, cloth extra, 6s.
Wages and Wants of Science Workers. Crown 8vo, 1s. 6d.

Pryce (Richard).—Miss Maxwell's Affections. Crown 8vo, cloth, with Frontispiece by HAL LUDLOW, 3s. 6d.; post 8vo, illustrated boards, 2s.

Rambosson (J.).—Popular Astronomy. Translated by C. B. PITMAN. With Coloured Frontispiece and numerous Illustrations. Crown 8vo, cloth extra, 7s. 6d.

Randolph (Lieut.-Col. George, U.S.A.).—Aunt Abigail Dykes: A Novel. Crown 8vo, cloth extra, 7s. 6d.

Read (General Meredith).—Historic Studies in Vaud, Berne, and Savoy. With 31 full-page Illustrations. Two Vols., demy 8vo, cloth, 28s.

Reade's (Charles) Novels.
The New Collected LIBRARY EDITION, complete in Seventeen Volumes, set in new long primer type, printed on laid paper, and elegantly bound in cloth, price 3s. 6d. each.

1. Peg Woffington; and Christie Johnstone.
2. Hard Cash.
3. The Cloister and the Hearth. With a Preface by Sir WALTER BESANT.
4. 'It is Never Too Late to Mend.'
5. The Course of True Love Never Did Run Smooth; and Singleheart and Doubleface.
6. The Autobiography of a Thief; Jack of all Trades; A Hero and a Martyr; and The Wandering Heir.
7. Love Me Little, Love me Long.
8. The Double Marriage.
9. Griffith Gaunt.
10. Foul Play.
11. Put Yourself in His Place.
12. A Terrible Temptation.
13. A Simpleton.
14. A Woman-Hater.
15. The Jilt, and other Stories; and Good Stories of Man and other Animals.
16. A Perilous Secret.
17. Readiana; and Bible Characters.

In Twenty-one Volumes, post 8vo, illustrated boards, 2s. each.

Peg Woffington. | Christie Johnstone.
'It is Never Too Late to Mend.'
The Course of True Love Never Did Run Smooth.
The Autobiography of a Thief; Jack of all Trades; and James Lambert.
Love Me Little, Love Me Long.
The Double Marriage.
The Cloister and the Hearth.
Hard Cash. | Griffith Gaunt.
Foul Play. | Put Yourself in His Place.
A Terrible Temptation.
A Simpleton. | The Wandering Heir
A Woman-Hater.
Singleheart and Doubleface.
Good Stories of Man and other Animals.
The Jilt, and other Stories.
A Perilous Secret. | Readiana.

POPULAR EDITIONS, medium 8vo, 6d. each : cloth, 1s. each.
'**It is Never Too Late to Mend.**' | **The Cloister and the Hearth.**
Peg Woffington; and Christie Johnstone.

It is Never Too Late to Mend' and **The Cloister and the Hearth** in One Volume, medium 8vo, cloth, 2s.
Christie Johnstone. With Frontispiece. Choicely printed in Elzevir style. Fcap. 8vo, half-Roxb. 2s. 6d.
Peg Woffington. Choicely printed in Elzevir style. Fcap. 8vo, half-Roxburghe, 2s. 6d.
The Cloister and the Hearth. In Four Vols., post 8vo, with an Introduction by Sir WALTER BESANT, and a Frontispiece to each Vol., 14s. the set; and the ILLUSTRATED LIBRARY EDITION, with Illustrations on every page, Two Vols., crown 8vo, cloth gilt, 42s. net.
Bible Characters. Fcap. 8vo, leatherette, 1s.
Selections from the Works of Charles Reade. With an Introduction by Mrs. ALEX. IRELAND. Crown 8vo, buckram, with Portrait, 6s.; CHEAP EDITION, post 8vo, cloth limp, 2s. 6d.

Riddell (Mrs. J. H.), Novels by.
Weird Stories. Crown 8vo, cloth extra, 3s. 6d.; post 8vo, illustrated boards, 2s.

Post 8vo, illustrated boards, 2s. each.
The Uninhabited House.
The Prince of Wales's Garden Party.
The Mystery in Palace Gardens.
Fairy Water.
Her Mother's Darling.
The Nun's Curse. | Idle Tales.

Rimmer (Alfred), Works by. Square 8vo, cloth gilt, 7s. 6d. each.
Our Old Country Towns. With 55 Illustrations by the Author.
Rambles Round Eton and Harrow. With 50 Illustrations by the Author.
About England with Dickens. With 58 Illustrations by C. A. VANDERHOOP and A. RIMMER.

Rives (Amelie).—Barbara Dering. Crown 8vo, cloth extra, 3s. 6d. post 8vo, illustrated boards, 2s.

Robinson Crusoe. By DANIEL DEFOE. With 37 Illustrations by GEORGE CRUIKSHANK. Post 8vo, half-cloth, 2s.; cloth extra, gilt edges, 2s. 6d.

Robinson (F. W.), Novels by.
Women are Strange. Post 8vo, illustrated boards, 2s.
The Hands of Justice. Crown 8vo, cloth extra, 3s. 6d.; post 8vo, illustrated boards, 2s.
The Woman in the Dark. Crown 8vo, cloth, 3s. 6d.

Robinson (Phil), Works by. Crown 8vo, cloth extra, 6s. each.
The Poets' Birds. | The Poets' Beasts.
The Poets and Nature: Reptiles, Fishes, and Insects.

Rochefoucauld's Maxims and Moral Reflections. With Notes and an Introductory Essay by SAINTE-BEUVE. Post 8vo, cloth limp, 2s.

Roll of Battle Abbey, The: A List of the Principal Warriors who came from Normandy with William the Conqueror, 1066. Printed in Gold and Colours, 5s.

Rosengarten (A.).—A Handbook of Architectural Styles. Translated by W. COLLETT-SANDARS. With 630 Illustrations. Crown 8vo, cloth extra, 7s. 6d.

Rowley (Hon. Hugh), Works by. Post 8vo, cloth, 2s. 6d. each.
Puniana: Riddles and Jokes. With numerous Illustrations.
More Puniana. Profusely Illustrated.

Runciman (James), Stories by. Post 8vo, bds., 2s. ea.; cl., 2s. 6d. ea.
Skippers & Shellbacks. | Grace Balmaign's Sweetheart. | Schools & Scholars.

Russell (Dora), Novels by.
A Country Sweetheart. Crown 8vo, cloth, 3s. 6d.; post 8vo, picture boards, 2s.
The Drift of Fate. Crown 8vo, cloth, 3s. 6d.

Russell (W. Clark), Novels, &c., by.
Crown 8vo, cloth extra, 3s. 6d. each; post 8vo, illustrated boards, 2s. each; cloth limp, 2s. 6d. each.
Round the Galley-Fire.
In the Middle Watch.
On the Fo'k'sle Head.
A Voyage to the Cape.
A Book for the Hammock.
The Mystery of the 'Ocean Star.'
The Romance of Jenny Harlowe.
An Ocean Tragedy.
My Shipmate Louise.
Alone on a Wide Wide Sea.
The Good Ship 'Mohock.'
The Phantom Death.

Crown 8vo, cloth, 3s. 6d. each.
The Tale of the Ten. With 12 Illustrations by G. MONTBARD.
Is He the Man? | The Convict Ship.
Heart of Oak. | The Last Entry.

Saint Aubyn (Alan), Novels by.
Crown 8vo, cloth extra, 3s. 6d. each; post 8vo, illustrated boards, 2s. each.
A Fellow of Trinity. With a Note by OLIVER WENDELL HOLMES and a Frontispiece.
The Junior Dean. | The Master of St. Benedict's. | To His Own Master.
Orchard Damerel. | In the Face of the World.

Fcap. 8vo, cloth boards, 1s. 6d. each.
The Old Maid's Sweetheart. | Modest Little Sara.

The Tremlett Diamonds. Crown 8vo, cloth extra, 3s. 6d.

Saint John (Bayle).—A Levantine Family. A New Edition.
Crown 8vo, cloth, 3s. 6d.

Sala (George A.).—Gaslight and Daylight. Post 8vo, boards, 2s.

Saunders (John), Novels by.
Crown 8vo, cloth extra, 3s. 6d. each; post 8vo, illustrated boards, 2s. each.
Guy Waterman. | The Lion in the Path. | The Two Dreamers.
Bound to the Wheel. Crown 8vo, cloth extra, 3s. 6d.

Saunders (Katharine), Novels by.
Crown 8vo, cloth extra, 3s. 6d. each; post 8vo, illustrated boards, 2s. each.
Margaret and Elizabeth. | Heart Salvage.
The High Mills. | Sebastian.

Joan Merryweather. Post 8vo, illustrated boards, 2s.
Gideon's Rock. Crown 8vo, cloth extra, 3s. 6d.

Scotland Yard, Past and Present: Experiences of Thirty-seven Years.
By Ex-Chief-Inspector CAVANAGH. Post 8vo, illustrated boards, 2s.; cloth, 2s. 6d.

Secret Out, The: One Thousand Tricks with Cards; with Entertaining Experiments in Drawing-room or 'White' Magic. By W. H. CREMER. With 300 Illustrations. Crown 8vo, cloth extra, 4s. 6d.

Seguin (L. G.), Works by.
The Country of the Passion Play (Oberammergau) and the Highlands of Bavaria. With Map and 37 Illustrations. Crown 8vo, cloth extra, 3s. 6d.
Walks in Algiers. With Two Maps and 16 Illustrations. Crown 8vo, cloth extra, 6s.

Senior (Wm.).—By Stream and Sea. Post 8vo, cloth, 2s. 6d.

Sergeant (Adeline).—Dr. Endicott's Experiment. Cr. 8vo, 3s. 6d.

Shakespeare for Children: Lamb's Tales from Shakespeare.
With Illustrations, coloured and plain, by J. MOYR SMITH. Crown 4to, cloth gilt, 3s. 6d.

Shakespeare the Boy. With Sketches of the Home and School Life, the Games and Sports, the Manners, Customs, and Folk-lore of the Time. By WILLIAM J. ROLFE, Litt.D. With 42 Illustrations. Crown 8vo, cloth gilt, 3s. 6d.

Sharp (William).—Children of To-morrow. Crown 8vo, cloth, 6s.

Shelley's (Percy Bysshe) Complete Works in Verse and Prose.
Edited, Prefaced, and Annotated by R. HERNE SHEPHERD. Five Vols., crown 8vo, cloth, 3s. 6d. each.
Poetical Works, in Three Vols.:
Vol. I. Introduction by the Editor; Posthumous Fragments of Margaret Nicholson; Shelley's Correspondence with Stockdale; The Wandering Jew; Queen Mab, with the Notes; Alastor, and other Poems; Rosalind and Helen; Prometheus Unbound; Adonais, &c.
„ II. Laon and Cythna; The Cenci; Julian and Maddalo; Swellfoot the Tyrant; The Witch of Atlas; Epipsychidion; Hellas.
„ III. Posthumous Poems; The Masque of Anarchy; and other Pieces.
Prose Works, in Two Vols.:
Vol. I. The Two Romances of Zastrozzi and St. Irvyne; the Dublin and Marlow Pamphlets; A Refutation of Deism; Letters to Leigh Hunt, and some Minor Writings and Fragments.
„ II. The Essays; Letters from Abroad; Translations and Fragments, edited by Mrs. SHELLEY. With a Biography of Shelley, and an Index of the Prose Works.
*** Also a few copies of a LARGE-PAPER EDITION, 5 vols., cloth, £2 12s. 6d.

Sherard (R. H.).—Rogues: A Novel. Crown 8vo, cloth, 1s. 6d.

Sheridan (General P. H.), Personal Memoirs of. With Portraits, Maps, and Facsimiles. Two Vols., demy 8vo, cloth, 24s.

Sheridan's (Richard Brinsley) Complete Works, with Life and Anecdotes. Including his Dramatic Writings, his Works in Prose and Poetry, Translations, Speeches, and Jokes. With 10 Illustrations. Crown 8vo, cloth, 3s. 6d.
The Rivals, The School for Scandal, and other Plays. Post 8vo, half-bound, 2s.
Sheridan's Comedies: The Rivals and The School for Scandal. Edited, with an Introduction and Notes to each Play, and a Biographical Sketch, by BRANDER MATTHEWS. With Illustrations. Demy 8vo, half-parchment, 12s. 6d.

Sidney's (Sir Philip) Complete Poetical Works, including all those in 'Arcadia.' With Portrait, Memorial-Introduction, Notes, &c., by the Rev. A. B. GROSART, D.D. Three Vols., crown 8vo, cloth boards, 3s. 6d. each.

Signboards: Their History, including Anecdotes of Famous Taverns and Remarkable Characters. By JACOB LARWOOD and JOHN CAMDEN HOTTEN. With Coloured Frontispiece and 94 Illustrations. Crown 8vo, cloth extra, 7s. 6d.

Sims (George R.), Works by.
Post 8vo, illustrated boards, 2s. each; cloth limp, 2s. 6d. each.

The Ring o' Bells.
Mary Jane's Memoirs.
Mary Jane Married.
Tinkletop's Crime.
Zeph: A Circus Story, &c.
Tales of To-day.
Dramas of Life. With 60 Illustrations.
Memoirs of a Landlady.
My Two Wives.
Scenes from the Show.
The Ten Commandments: Stories.

Crown 8vo, picture cover, 1s. each; cloth, 1s. 6d. each.
The Dagonet Reciter and Reader: Being Readings and Recitations in Prose and Verse selected from his own Works by GEORGE R. SIMS.
The Case of George Candlemas. | **Dagonet Ditties.** (From *The Referee*.)

Rogues and Vagabonds. A New Edition. Crown 8vo, cloth, 3s. 6d.
How the Poor Live; and Horrible London. Crown 8vo, picture cover, 1s.
Dagonet Abroad. Crown 8vo, cloth, 3s. 6d.; post 8vo, picture boards, 2s.

Sister Dora: A Biography. By MARGARET LONSDALE. With Four Illustrations. Demy 8vo, picture cover, 4d.; cloth, 6d.

Sketchley (Arthur).—A Match in the Dark. Post 8vo, boards, 2s.

Slang Dictionary (The): Etymological, Historical, and Anecdotal. Crown 8vo, cloth extra, 6s. 6d.

Smart (Hawley), Novels by.
Crown 8vo, cloth, 3s. 6d. each; post 8vo, picture boards, 2s. each.
Beatrice and Benedick. | Without Love or Licence.

Crown 8vo, cloth, 3s. 6d. each.
Long Odds. | The Master of Rathkelly. | The Outsider. | A Racing Rubber.
The Plunger. Post 8vo, picture boards, 2s.

Smith (J. Moyr), Works by.
The Prince of Argolis. With 130 Illustrations. Post 8vo, cloth extra, 3s. 6d.
The Wooing of the Water Witch. With numerous Illustrations. Post 8vo, cloth, 6s.

Society in London. Crown 8vo, 1s.; cloth, 1s. 6d.

Society in Paris: The Upper Ten Thousand. A Series of Letters from Count PAUL VASILI to a Young French Diplomat. Crown 8vo, cloth, 6s.

Somerset (Lord Henry).—Songs of Adieu. Small 4to, Jap. vel., 6s.

Spalding (T. A., LL.B.).—Elizabethan Demonology: An Essay on the Belief in the Existence of Devils. Crown 8vo, cloth extra, 5s.

Speight (T. W.), Novels by.
Post 8vo, illustrated boards, 2s. each.

The Mysteries of Heron Dyke. | The Loudwater Tragedy.
By Devious Ways, &c. | Burgo's Romance.
Hoodwinked; & Sandycroft Mystery. | Quittance in Full.
The Golden Hoop. | A Husband from the Sea.
Back to Life.

Post 8vo, cloth limp, 1s. 6d. each.

A Barren Title. | Wife or No Wife?

Crown 8vo, cloth extra, 3s. 6d. each.

A Secret of the Sea. | The Grey Monk. | The Master of Trenance.
A Minion of the Moon: A Romance of the King's Highway.

Spenser for Children. By M. H. TOWRY. With Coloured Illustrations by WALTER J. MORGAN. Crown 4to, cloth extra, 3s. 6d.

Stafford (John), Novels by.
Doris and I. Crown 8vo, cloth, 3s. 6d.
Carlton Priors. Crown 8vo, cloth, gilt top, 6s.

Starry Heavens (The): A POETICAL BIRTHDAY BOOK. Royal 16mo, cloth extra, 2s. 6d.

Stedman (E. C.), Works by. Crown 8vo, cloth extra, 9s. each.
Victorian Poets. | The Poets of America.

Stephens (Riccardo, M.B.).—The Cruciform Mark: The Strange Story of RICHARD TREGENNA, Bachelor of Medicine (Univ. Edinb.) Crown 8vo, cloth, 3s. 6d.

Sterndale (R. Armitage).—The Afghan Knife: A Novel. Crown 8vo, cloth extra, 3s. 6d.; post 8vo, illustrated boards, 2s.

Stevenson (R. Louis), Works by. Post 8vo, cloth limp, 2s. 6d. ea.
Travels with a Donkey. With a Frontispiece by WALTER CRANE.
An Inland Voyage. With a Frontispiece by WALTER CRANE.

Crown 8vo, buckram, gilt top, 6s. each.

Familiar Studies of Men and Books.
The Silverado Squatters. With Frontispiece by J. D. STRONG.
The Merry Men. | Underwoods: Poems.
Memories and Portraits.
Virginibus Puerisque, and other Papers. | Ballads. | Prince Otto.
Across the Plains, with other Memories and Essays
Weir of Hermiston. (R. L. STEVENSON'S LAST WORK.)

Songs of Travel. Crown 8vo, buckram, 5s.
New Arabian Nights. Crown 8vo, buckram, gilt top, 6s.; post 8vo, illustrated boards, 2s.
The Suicide Club; and The Rajah's Diamond. (From NEW ARABIAN NIGHTS.) With Eight Illustrations by W. J. HENNESSY. Crown 8vo, cloth, 3s. 6d.
The Edinburgh Edition of the Works of Robert Louis Stevenson. Twenty-seven Vols., demy 8vo. This Edition (which is limited to 1,000 copies) is sold in Sets only, the price of which may be learned from the Booksellers. The First Volume was published Nov., 1894.

Stories from Foreign Novelists. With Notices by HELEN and ALICE ZIMMERN. Crown 8vo, cloth extra, 3s. 6d.; post 8vo, illustrated boards, 2s.

Strange Manuscript (A) Found in a Copper Cylinder. Crown 8vo, cloth extra, with 19 Illustrations by GILBERT GAUL, 5s.; post 8vo, illustrated boards, 2s.

Strange Secrets. Told by PERCY FITZGERALD, CONAN DOYLE, FLORENCE MARRYAT, &c. Post 8vo, illustrated boards, 2s.

Strutt (Joseph).—The Sports and Pastimes of the People of England; including the Rural and Domestic Recreations, May Games, Mummeries, Shows, &c., from the Earliest Period to the Present Time. Edited by WILLIAM HONE. With 140 Illustrations. Crown 8vo, cloth extra, 7s. 6d.

Swift's (Dean) Choice Works, in Prose and Verse. With Memoir, Portrait, and Facsimiles of the Maps in 'Gulliver's Travels.' Crown 8vo, cloth, 3s. 6d.
Gulliver's Travels, and A Tale of a Tub. Post 8vo, half-bound, 2s.
Jonathan Swift: A Study. By J. CHURTON COLLINS. Crown 8vo, cloth extra, 8s.

Swinburne (Algernon C.), Works by.

Selections from the Poetical Works of A. C. Swinburne. Fcap. 8vo, 6s.
Atalanta in Calydon. Crown 8vo, 6s.
Chastelard: A Tragedy. Crown 8vo, 7s.
Poems and Ballads. FIRST SERIES. Crown 8vo, or fcap. 8vo, 9s.
Poems and Ballads. SECOND SERIES. Crown 8vo, 9s.
Poems & Ballads. THIRD SERIES. Cr. 8vo, 7s.
Songs before Sunrise. Crown 8vo, 10s. 6d.
Bothwell: A Tragedy. Crown 8vo, 12s. 6d.
Songs of Two Nations. Crown 8vo, 6s.
George Chapman. (See Vol. II. of G. CHAPMAN'S Works.) Crown 8vo, 3s. 6d.
Essays and Studies. Crown 8vo, 12s.
Erechtheus: A Tragedy. Crown 8vo, 6s.
A Note on Charlotte Bronte. Cr. 8vo, 6s.
A Study of Shakespeare. Crown 8vo, 8s.
Songs of the Springtides. Crown 8vo, 6s.
Studies in Song. Crown 8vo, 7s.
Mary Stuart: A Tragedy. Crown 8vo, 8s.
Tristram of Lyonesse. Crown 8vo, 9s.
A Century of Roundels. Small 4to, 8s.
A Midsummer Holiday. Crown 8vo, 7s.
Marino Faliero: A Tragedy. Crown 8vo, 6s.
A Study of Victor Hugo. Crown 8vo, 6s.
Miscellanies. Crown 8vo, 12s.
Locrine: A Tragedy. Crown 8vo, 6s.
A Study of Ben Jonson. Crown 8vo, 7s.
The Sisters: A Tragedy. Crown 8vo, 6s.
Astrophel, &c. Crown 8vo, 7s.
Studies in Prose and Poetry. Cr. 8vo, 9s.
The Tale of Balen. Crown 8vo, 7s.

Syntax's (Dr.) Three Tours: In Search of the Picturesque, in Search of Consolation, and in Search of a Wife. With ROWLANDSON'S Coloured Illustrations, and Life of the Author by J. C. HOTTEN. Crown 8vo, cloth extra, 7s. 6d.

Taine's History of English Literature. Translated by HENRY VAN LAUN. Four Vols., small demy 8vo, cloth boards, 30s.—POPULAR EDITION, Two Vols., large crown 8vo, cloth extra, 15s.

Taylor (Bayard). — **Diversions of the Echo Club:** Burlesques of Modern Writers. Post 8vo, cloth limp, 2s.

Taylor (Tom). — **Historical Dramas.** Containing 'Clancarty,' 'Jeanne Darc,' ''Twixt Axe and Crown,' 'The Fool's Revenge,' 'Arkwright's Wife,' 'Anne Boleyn,' 'Plot and Passion. Crown 8vo, cloth extra, 7s. 6d.
*** The Plays may also be had separately, at 1s. each.

Tennyson (Lord): A Biographical Sketch. By H. J. JENNINGS. Post 8vo, portrait cover, 1s.; cloth, 1s. 6d.

Thackerayana: Notes and Anecdotes. With Coloured Frontispiece and Hundreds of Sketches by WILLIAM MAKEPEACE THACKERAY. Crown 8vo, cloth extra, 7s. 6d.

Thames, A New Pictorial History of the. By A. S. KRAUSSE. With 340 Illustrations. Post 8vo, picture cover, 1s.

Thiers (Adolphe). — **History of the Consulate and Empire of** France under Napoleon. Translated by D. FORBES CAMPBELL and JOHN STEBBING. With 36 Steel Plates. 12 Vols., demy 8vo, cloth extra, 12s. each.

Thomas (Bertha), Novels by. Cr. 8vo, cl., 3s. 6d. ea.; post 8vo, 2s. ea.
The Violin-Player. | Proud Maisie.
Cressida. Post 8vo, Illustrated boards, 2s.

Thomson's Seasons, and The Castle of Indolence. With Introduction by ALLAN CUNNINGHAM, and 48 Illustrations. Post 8vo, half-bound, 2s.

Thornbury (Walter), Books by.
The Life and Correspondence of J. M. W. Turner. With Eight Illustrations in Colours and Two Woodcuts. New and Revised Edition. Crown 8vo, cloth, 3s. 6d.

Post 8vo, illustrated boards, 2s. each.
Old Stories Re-told. | Tales for the Marines.

Timbs (John), Works by. Crown 8vo, cloth extra, 7s. 6d. each.
The History of Clubs and Club Life in London: Anecdotes of its Famous Coffee-houses, Hostelries, and Taverns. With 42 Illustrations.
English Eccentrics and Eccentricities: Stories of Delusions, Impostures, Sporting Scenes, Eccentric Artists, Theatrical Folk, &c. With 48 Illustrations.

Transvaal (The). By JOHN DE VILLIERS. With Map. Crown 8vo, 1s.

Trollope (Anthony), Novels by.
Crown 8vo, cloth extra, 3s. 6d. each; post 8vo, Illustrated boards, 2s. each.
The Way We Live Now. | Mr. Scarborough's Family.
Frau Frohmann. | The Land-Leaguers.

Post 8vo, illustrated boards, 2s. each.
Kept in the Dark. | The American Senator.
The Golden Lion of Granpere. | John Caldigate. | Marion Fay.

Trollope (Frances E.), Novels by.
Crown 8vo, cloth extra, 3s. 6d. each; post 8vo, illustrated boards, 2s. each.
Like Ships Upon the Sea. | Mabel's Progress. | Anne Furness.

Trollope (T. A.).—Diamond Cut Diamond. Post 8vo, illust. bds., 2s.

Trowbridge (J. T.).—Farnell's Folly. Post 8vo, illust. boards, 2s.

Twain's (Mark) Books.
Crown 8vo, cloth extra, 3s. 6d. each.
The Choice Works of Mark Twain. Revised and Corrected throughout by the Author. With Life, Portrait, and numerous Illustrations.
Roughing It; and The Innocents at Home. With 200 Illustrations by F. A. FRASER.
The American Claimant. With 81 Illustrations by HAL HURST and others.
Tom Sawyer Abroad. With 26 Illustrations by DAN BEARD.
Tom Sawyer, Detective, &c. With Photogravure Portrait.
Pudd'nhead Wilson. With Portrait and Six Illlustrations by LOUIS LOEB.
Mark Twain's Library of Humour. With 197 Illustrations by E. W. KEMBLE.

Crown 8vo, cloth extra, 3s. 6d. each; post 8vo, picture boards, 2s. each.
A Tramp Abroad. With 314 Illustrations.
The Innocents Abroad; or, The New Pilgrim's Progress. With 234 Illustrations. (The Two Shilling Edition is entitled **Mark Twain's Pleasure Trip.**)
The Gilded Age. By MARK TWAIN and C. D. WARNER. With 212 Illustrations.
The Adventures of Tom Sawyer. With 111 Illustrations.
The Prince and the Pauper. With 190 Illustrations.
Life on the Mississippi. With 300 Illustrations.
The Adventures of Huckleberry Finn. With 174 Illustrations by E. W. KEMBLE.
A Yankee at the Court of King Arthur. With 220 Illustrations by DAN BEARD.
The Stolen White Elephant.
The £1,000,000 Bank-Note.

Mark Twain's Sketches. Post 8vo, illustrated boards, 2s.
Personal Recollections of Joan of Arc. With Twelve Illustrations by F. V. DU MOND. Crown 8vo, cloth, 6s.
More Tramps Abroad. Crown 8vo, cloth, gilt top, 6s. [*Now.*

Tytler (C. C. Fraser-).—Mistress Judith: A Novel. Crown 8vo, cloth extra, 3s. 6d.; post 8vo, illustrated boards, 2s.

Tytler (Sarah), Novels by.
Crown 8vo, cloth extra, 3s. 6d. each; post 8vo, illustrated boards, 2s. each
Lady Bell. | **Buried Diamonds.** | **The Blackhall Ghosts.**

Post 8vo, illustrated boards, 2s. each.
What She Came Through. | **The Huguenot Family.**
Citoyenne Jacqueline. | **Noblesse Oblige.**
The Bride's Pass. | **Beauty and the Beast.**
Saint Mungo's City. | **Disappeared.**

The Macdonald Lass. With Frontispiece. Crown 8vo, cloth, 3s. 6d.
The Witch-Wife. Crown 8vo, cloth, 3s. 6d. [*Shortly.*

Upward (Allen), Novels by.
A Crown of Straw. Crown 8vo, cloth, 6s.

Crown 8vo, cloth, 3s. 6d. each; post 8vo, picture boards, 2s. each.
The Queen Against Owen. | **The Prince of Balkistan.**
'God Save the Queen!' a Tale of '37. Crown 8vo, decorated cover, 1s.; cloth, 2s.

Vashti and Esther. By 'Belle' of *The World.* Cr. 8vo, cloth, 3s. 6d.

Vizetelly (Ernest A.).—The Scorpion: A Romance of Spain. With a Frontispiece. Crown 8vo, cloth extra, 3s. 6d.

Walford (Edward, M.A.), Works by.
Walford's County Families of the United Kingdom (1898). Containing the Descent, Birth, Marriage, Education, &c., of 12,000 Heads of Families, their Heirs, Offices, Addresses, Clubs, &c. Royal 8vo, cloth gilt, 50s.
Walford's Shilling Peerage (1898). Containing a List of the House of Lords, Scotch and Irish Peers, &c. 32mo, cloth, 1s.
Walford's Shilling Baronetage (1898). Containing a List of the Baronets of the United Kingdom, Biographical Notices, Addresses, &c. 32mo, cloth, 1s.
Walford's Shilling Knightage (1898). Containing a List of the Knights of the United Kingdom, Biographical Notices, Addresses, &c. 32mo, cloth, 1s.
Walford's Shilling House of Commons (1898). Containing a List of all the Members of the New Parliament, their Addresses, Clubs, &c. 32mo, cloth, 1s.
Walford's Complete Peerage, Baronetage, Knightage, and House of Commons (1898). Royal 32mo, cloth, gilt edges, 5s. [*In the press.*

Waller (S. E.).—Sebastiani's Secret. With Nine full-page Illustrations by the Author. Crown 8vo, cloth, 6s.

Walton and Cotton's Complete Angler; or, The Contemplative Man's Recreation, by IZAAK WALTON; and Instructions How to Angle, for a Trout or Grayling in a clear Stream, by CHARLES COTTON. With Memoirs and Notes by Sir HARRIS NICOLAS, and 61 Illustrations. Crown 8vo, cloth antique, 7s. 6d.

Walt Whitman, Poems by. Edited, with Introduction, by WILLIAM M. ROSSETTI. With Portrait. Crown 8vo, hand-made paper and buckram, 6s.

Ward (Herbert), Books by.
Five Years with the Congo Cannibals. With 92 Illustrations. Royal 8vo, cloth, 14s.
My Life with Stanley's Rear Guard. With Map. Post 8vo, 1s.; cloth, 1s. 6d.

Warner (Charles Dudley).—A Roundabout Journey. Crown 8vo, cloth extra, 6s.

Warrant to Execute Charles I. A Facsimile, with the 59 Signatures and Seals. Printed on paper 22 in. by 14 in. 2s.
Warrant to Execute Mary Queen of Scots. A Facsimile, including Queen Elizabeth's Signature and the Great Seal. 2s.

Washington's (George) Rules of Civility Traced to their Sources and Restored by MONCURE D. CONWAY. Fcap. 8vo, Japanese vellum, 2s. 6d.

Wassermann (Lillias) and Aaron Watson.—The Marquis of Carabas. Post 8vo, illustrated boards, 2s.

Weather, How to Foretell the, with the Pocket Spectroscope. By F. W. CORY. With Ten Illustrations. Crown 8vo, 1s.; cloth, 1s. 6d.

Westall (William), Novels by.
Trust-Money. Post 8vo, illustrated boards, 2s.; cloth, 2s. 6d.
Sons of Belial. Crown 8vo, cloth extra, 3s. 6d.
With the Red Eagle: A Romance of the Tyrol. Crown 8vo, cloth, 6s.

Westbury (Atha).—The Shadow of Hilton Fernbrook: A Romance of Maoriland. Crown 8vo, cloth, 3s. 6d.

White (Gilbert).—The Natural History of Selborne. Post 8vo, printed on laid paper and half-bound, 2s.

Williams (W. Mattieu, F.R.A.S.), Works by.
Science in Short Chapters. Crown 8vo, cloth extra, 7s. 6d.
A Simple Treatise on Heat. With Illustrations. Crown 8vo, cloth, 2s. 6d.
The Chemistry of Cookery. Crown 8vo, cloth extra, 6s.
The Chemistry of Iron and Steel Making. Crown 8vo, cloth extra, 9s.
A Vindication of Phrenology. With Portrait and 43 Illusts. Demy 8vo, cloth extra, 12s. 6d.

Williamson (Mrs. F. H.).—A Child Widow. Post 8vo, bds., 2s.

Wills (C. J.), Novels by.
An Easy-going Fellow. Crown 8vo, cloth, 3s. 6d.
His Dead Past. Crown 8vo, cloth, 6s.

Wilson (Dr. Andrew, F.R.S.E.), Works by.
Chapters on Evolution. With 259 Illustrations. Crown 8vo, cloth extra, 7s. 6d.
Leaves from a Naturalist's Note-Book. Post 8vo, cloth limp, 2s. 6d.
Leisure-Time Studies. With Illustrations. Crown 8vo, cloth extra, 6s.
Studies in Life and Sense. With numerous Illustrations. Crown 8vo, cloth extra, 6s.
Common Accidents: How to Treat Them. With Illustrations. Crown 8vo, 1s.; cloth, 1s. 6d.
Glimpses of Nature. With 35 Illustrations. Crown 8vo, cloth extra, 3s. 6d.

Winter (John Strange), Stories by. Post 8vo, illustrated boards, 2s. each; cloth limp, 2s. 6d. each.
Cavalry Life. | Regimental Legends.
Cavalry Life and Regimental Legends. LIBRARY EDITION, set in new type and handsomely bound. Crown 8vo, cloth, 3s. 6d.
A Soldier's Children. With 34 Illustrations by E. G. THOMSON and E. STUART HARDY. Crown 8vo, cloth extra, 3s. 6d.

Wissmann (Hermann von).—My Second Journey through Equatorial Africa. With 92 Illustrations. Demy 8vo, cloth, 16s.

Wood (H. F.), Detective Stories by. Post 8vo, boards, 2s. each.
The Passenger from Scotland Yard. | The Englishman of the Rue Cain.

Wood (Lady).—Sabina: A Novel. Post 8vo, illustrated boards, 2s.

Woolley (Celia Parker).—Rachel Armstrong; or, Love and Theology. Post 8vo, illustrated boards, 2s.; cloth, 2s. 6d.

Wright (Thomas), Works by. Crown 8vo, cloth extra, 7s. 6d. each.
The Caricature History of the Georges. With 400 Caricatures, Squibs, &c.
History of Caricature and of the Grotesque in Art, Literature, Sculpture, and Painting. Illustrated by F. W. FAIRHOLT, F.S.A.

Wynman (Margaret).—My Flirtations. With 13 Illustrations by J. BERNARD PARTRIDGE. Post 8vo, cloth limp, 2s.

Yates (Edmund), Novels by. Post 8vo, illustrated boards, 2s. each.
Land at Last. | The Forlorn Hope. | Castaway.

Zangwill (I.).— Ghetto Tragedies. With Three Illustrations by A. S. BOYD. Fcap. 8vo, cloth, 2s. net.

'Z. Z.' (Louis Zangwill).—A Nineteenth Century Miracle. Cr. 8vo, cloth, 3s. 6d.

Zola (Emile), Novels by. Crown 8vo, cloth extra, 3s. 6d. each.
His Excellency (Eugene Rougon). With an Introduction by ERNEST A. VIZETELLY.
The Dram-Shop (L'Assommoir). Edited by E. A. VIZETELLY.
The Fat and the Thin. Translated by ERNEST A. VIZETELLY.
Money. Translated by ERNEST A. VIZETELLY.
The Downfall. Translated by E. A. VIZETELLY.
The Dream. Translated by ELIZA CHASE. With Eight Illustrations by JEANNIOT.
Doctor Pascal. Translated by E. A. VIZETELLY. With Portrait of the Author.
Lourdes. Translated by ERNEST A. VIZETELLY.
Rome. Translated by ERNEST A. VIZETELLY.
Paris. Translated by ERNEST A. VIZETELLY. [In preparation.

SOME BOOKS CLASSIFIED IN SERIES.
₊ For fuller cataloguing, see alphabetical arrangement, pp. 1–26.

The Mayfair Library. Post 8vo, cloth limp, 2s. 6d. per Volume.
A Journey Round My Room. By X. DE MAISTRE. Translated by Sir HENRY ATTWELL.
Quips and Quiddities. By W. D. ADAMS.
The Agony Column of 'The Times.'
Melancholy Anatomised: Abridgment of BURTON.
Poetical Ingenuities. By W. T. DOBSON.
The Cupboard Papers. By FIN-BEC.
W. S. Gilbert's Plays. Three Series.
Songs of Irish Wit and Humour.
Animals and their Masters. By Sir A. HELPS.
Social Pressure. By Sir A. HELPS.
Curiosities of Criticism. By H. J. JENNINGS.
The Autocrat of the Breakfast-Table. By OLIVER WENDELL HOLMES.
Pencil and Palette. By R. KEMPT.
Little Essays: from LAMB'S LETTERS.
Forensic Anecdotes. By JACOB LARWOOD.
Theatrical Anecdotes. By JACOB LARWOOD.
Witch Stories. By E. LYNN LINTON.
Ourselves. By E. LYNN LINTON.
Pastimes and Players. By R. MACGREGOR.
New Paul and Virginia. By W. H. MALLOCK.
The New Republic. By W. H. MALLOCK.
Puck on Pegasus. By H. C. PENNELL.
Pegasus Re-saddled. By H. C. PENNELL.
Muses of Mayfair. Edited by H. C. PENNELL.
Thoreau: His Life and Aims. By H. A. PAGE.
Puniana. By Hon. HUGH ROWLEY.
More Puniana. By Hon. HUGH ROWLEY.
The Philosophy of Handwriting.
By Stream and Sea. By WILLIAM SENIOR.
Leaves from a Naturalist's Note-Book. By Dr. ANDREW WILSON.

The Golden Library. Post 8vo, cloth limp, 2s. per Volume.
Diversions of the Echo Club. BAYARD TAYLOR.
Songs for Sailors. By W. C. BENNETT.
Lives of the Necromancers. By W. GODWIN.
The Poetical Works of Alexander Pope.
Scenes of Country Life. By EDWARD JESSE.
Tale for a Chimney Corner. By LEIGH HUNT.
The Autocrat of the Breakfast Table. By OLIVER WENDELL HOLMES.
La Mort d'Arthur: Selections from MALLORY.
Provincial Letters of Blaise Pascal.
Maxims and Reflections of Rochefoucauld.

Handy Novels. Fcap. 8vo, cloth boards, 1s. 6d. each.
The Old Maid's Sweetheart. By A. ST. AUBYN.
Modest Little Sara. By ALAN ST. AUBYN.
Seven Sleepers of Ephesus. M. E. COLERIDGE.
Taken from the Enemy. By H. NEWBOLT.
A Lost Soul. By W. L. ALDEN.
Dr. Palliser's Patient. By GRANT ALLEN.
Monte Carlo Stories. By JOAN BARRETT.
Black Spirits and White. By R. A. CRAM.

My Library. Printed on laid paper, post 8vo, half-Roxburghe, 2s. 6d. each.
Citation and Examination of William Shakspeare. By W. S. LANDOR.
The Journal of Maurice de Guerin.
Christie Johnstone. By CHARLES READE.
Peg Woffington. By CHARLES READE.
The Dramatic Essays of Charles Lamb.

The Pocket Library. Post 8vo, printed on laid paper and hf.-bd., 2s. each.
The Essays of Elia. By CHARLES LAMB.
Robinson Crusoe. Illustrated by G. CRUIKSHANK.
Whims and Oddities. By THOMAS HOOD.
The Barber's Chair. By DOUGLAS JERROLD.
Gastronomy. By BRILLAT-SAVARIN.
The Epicurean, &c. By THOMAS MOORE.
Leigh Hunt's Essays. Edited by E. OLLIER.
White's Natural History of Selborne.
Gulliver's Travels, &c. By Dean SWIFT.
Plays by RICHARD BRINSLEY SHERIDAN.
Anecdotes of the Clergy. By JACOB LARWOOD.
Thomson's Seasons. Illustrated.
Autocrat of the Breakfast-Table and The Professor at the Breakfast-Table. By O. W. HOLMES.

CHATTO & WINDUS, 111 St. Martin's Lane, London, W.C.

THE PICCADILLY NOVELS.

LIBRARY EDITIONS OF NOVELS, many Illustrated, crown 8vo, cloth extra, 3s. 6d. each.

By Mrs. ALEXANDER.
A Life Interest | Mona's Choice | By Woman's Wit

By F. M. ALLEN.
Green as Grass.

By GRANT ALLEN.
Philistia.
Strange Stories.
Babylon.
For Maimie's Sake.
In all Shades.
The Beckoning Hand.
The Devil's Die.
This Mortal Coil.
The Tents of Shem.
The Great Taboo.
Dumaresq's Daughter.
Duchess of Powysland.
Blood Royal.
Ivan Greet's Masterpiece.
The Scallywag.
At Market Value.
Under Sealed Orders

By MARY ANDERSON.
Othello's Occupation.

By EDWIN L. ARNOLD.
Phra the Phoenician. | Constable of St. Nicholas.

By ROBERT BARR.
In a Steamer Chair. | A Woman Intervenes.
From Whose Bourne. | Revenge!

By FRANK BARRETT.
The Woman of the Iron Bracelets.
The Harding Scandal. | A Missing Witness.

By 'BELLE.'
Vashti and Esther.

By Sir W. BESANT and J. RICE.
Ready-Money Mortiboy.
My Little Girl.
With Harp and Crown.
This Son of Vulcan.
The Golden Butterfly
The Monks of Thelema.
By Celia's Arbour.
Chaplain of the Fleet.
The Seamy Side.
The Case of Mr. Lucraft.
In Trafalgar's Bay.
The Ten Years' Tenant.

By Sir WALTER BESANT.
All Sorts and Conditions of Men.
The Captains' Room.
All in a Garden Fair.
Dorothy Forster.
Uncle Jack.
The World Went Very Well Then.
Children of Gibeon.
Herr Paulus.
For Faith and Freedom.
To Call Her Mine.
The Revolt of Man.
The Bell of St. Paul's.
The Holy Rose.
Armorel of Lyonesse.
S.Katherine's by Tower
Verbena Camellia Stephanotis.
The Ivory Gate.
The Rebel Queen.
Beyond the Dreams of Avarice.
The Master Craftsman.
The City of Refuge.

By PAUL BOURGET.
A Living Lie.

By ROBERT BUCHANAN.
Shadow of the Sword.
A Child of Nature.
God and the Man.
Martyrdom of Madeline
Love Me for Ever.
Annan Water.
Foxglove Manor.
The New Abelard.
Matt. | Rachel Dene.
Master of the Mine.
The Heir of Linne.
Woman and the Man.
Red and White Heather.
Lady Kilpatrick.

ROB. BUCHANAN & HY. MURRAY.
The Charlatan.

By J. MITCHELL CHAPPLE.
The Minor Chord.

By HALL CAINE.
The Shadow of a Crime. | The Deemster.
A Son of Hagar.

By ANNE COATES.
Rie's Diary.

By MACLAREN COBBAN.
The Red Sultan. | The Burden of Isabel.

By WILKIE COLLINS.
Armadale. | AfterDark.
No Name. | Antonina
Basil. | Hide and Seek.
The Dead Secret.
Queen of Hearts.
My Miscellanies.
The Woman in White.
The Moonstone.
Man and Wife.
Poor Miss Finch.
Miss or Mrs.?
The New Magdalen.
The Frozen Deep.
The Two Destinies.
The Law and the Lady.
The Haunted Hotel.
The Fallen Leaves.
Jezebel's Daughter.
The Black Robe.
Heart and Science.
'I Say No.'
Little Novels.
The Evil Genius.
The Legacy of Cain.
A Rogue's Life.
Blind Love.

By MORT. & FRANCES COLLINS.
Transmigration.
Blacksmith & Scholar.
The Village Comedy.
From Midnight to Midnight.
You Play me False.

By E. H. COOPER.
Geoffory Hamilton.

By V. CECIL COTES.
Two Girls on a Barge.

By C. EGBERT CRADDOCK.
His Vanished Star.

By H. N. CRELLIN.
Romances of the Old Seraglio.

By MATT CRIM.
The Adventures of a Fair Rebel.

By S. R. CROCKETT and others.
Tales of Our Coast.

By B. M. CROKER.
Diana Barrington.
Proper Pride.
A Family Likeness.
Pretty Miss Neville.
A Bird of Passage.
'To Let.' | Mr. Jervis.
Village Tales & Jungle Tragedies.
The Real Lady Hilda.
Married or Single?
Two Masters.
In the Kingdom of Kerry
Interference.
A Third Person.

By WILLIAM CYPLES.
Hearts of Gold.

By ALPHONSE DAUDET.
The Evangelist; or, Port Salvation.

By H. COLEMAN DAVIDSON.
Mr. Sadler's Daughters.

By ERASMUS DAWSON.
The Fountain of Youth.

By JAMES DE MILLE.
A Castle in Spain.

By J. LEITH DERWENT.
Our Lady of Tears. | Circe's Lovers.

By DICK DONOVAN.
Tracked to Doom. | The Mystery of Jamaica
Man from Manchester. | Terrace.
The Chronicles of Michael Danevitch.

By RICHARD DOWLING.
Old Corcoran's Money.

By A. CONAN DOYLE.
The Firm of Girdlestone.

By S. JEANNETTE DUNCAN.
A Daughter of To-day. | Vernon's Aunt.

By G. MANVILLE FENN.
The New Mistress. | The Tiger Lily.
Witness to the Deed. | The White Virgin.

By PERCY FITZGERALD.
Fatal Zero.

By R. E. FRANCILLON.
One by One.
A Dog and his Shadow.
A Real Queen.
Ropes of Sand.
Jack Doyle's Daughter.

Prefaced by Sir BARTLE FRERE.
Pandurang Hari.

By EDWARD GARRETT.
The Capel Girls.

By PAUL GAULOT.
The Red Shirts.

By CHARLES GIBBON.
Robin Gray.
Loving a Dream.
Of High Degree.
The Golden Shaft.

By E. GLANVILLE.
The Lost Heiress.
A Fair Colonist.
The Fossicker.
The Golden Rock.
Tales from the Veldt

By E. J. GOODMAN.
The Fate of Herbert Wayne.

By Rev. S. BARING GOULD.
Red Spider. | Eve.

By CECIL GRIFFITH.
Corinthia Marazion.

THE PICCADILLY (3/6) NOVELS—*continued*.

By SYDNEY GRUNDY.
The Days of his Vanity.

By OWEN HALL.
The Track of a Storm. | Jetsam.

By THOMAS HARDY.
Under the Greenwood Tree.

By BRET HARTE.
A Waif of the Plains. | A Protégée of Jack Hamlin's.
A Ward of the Golden Gate. | (Springs.) Clarence.
A Sappho of Green | Barker's Luck.
Col. Starbottle's Client. | Devil's Ford. (celstor.'
Susy. | Sally Dows. | The Crusade of the 'Ex
Bell-Ringer of Angel's. | Three Partners.

By JULIAN HAWTHORNE.
Garth. | Beatrix Randolph.
Ellice Quentin. | David Poindexter's Disappearance.
Sebastian Strome.
Dust. | The Spectre of the Camera.
Fortune's Fool.

By Sir A. HELPS.
Ivan de Biron.

By I. HENDERSON.
Agatha Page.

By G. A. HENTY.
Rujub the Juggler. | The Queen's Cup.
Dorothy's Double.

By JOHN HILL.
The Common Ancestor.

By Mrs. HUNGERFORD.
Lady Verner's Flight. | Nora Creina.
The Red-House Mystery | An Anxious Moment.
The Three Graces. | April's Lady.
Professor's Experiment. | Peter's Wife.
A Point of Conscience.

By Mrs. ALFRED HUNT.
The Leaden Casket. | Self-Condemned.
That Other Person. | Mrs. Juliet.

By C. J. CUTCLIFFE HYNE.
Honour of Thieves.

By R. ASHE KING.
A Drawn Game.

By EDMOND LEPELLETIER.
Madame Sans Gene.

By HARRY LINDSAY.
Rhoda Roberts.

By HENRY W. LUCY.
Gideon Fleyce.

By E. LYNN LINTON.
Patricia Kemball. | The Atonement of Leam Dundas.
Under which Lord ?
'My Love!' | Ione. | The World Well Lost.
Paston Carew. | The One Too Many.
Sowing the Wind. | Dulcie Everton.

By JUSTIN McCARTHY.
A Fair Saxon. | Donna Quixote.
Linley Rochford. | Maid of Athens.
Dear Lady Disdain. | The Comet of a Season.
Camiola. | The Dictator.
Waterdale Neighbours. | Red Diamonds.
My Enemy's Daughter. | The Riddle Ring.
Miss Misanthrope. | The Three Disgraces.

By JUSTIN H. McCARTHY.
A London Legend. | The Royal Christopher.

By GEORGE MACDONALD.
Heather and Snow. | Phantastes.

By L. T. MEADE.
A Soldier of Fortune. | The Voice of the Charmer.
In an Iron Grip.

By L. T. MEADE and CLIFFORD HALIFAX, M.D.
Dr. Rumsey's Patient.

By LEONARD MERRICK.
This Stage of Fools. | Cynthia.

By BERTRAM MITFORD.
The Gun Runner. | The King's Assegai.
The Luck of Gerard Ridgeley. | Renshaw Fanning's Quest.

By J. E. MUDDOCK.
Maid Marian and Robin Hood.
Basile the Jester. | Young Lochinvar.

By D. CHRISTIE MURRAY.
A Life's Atonement. | Cynic Fortune.
Joseph's Coat. | The Way of the World.
Coals of Fire. | BobMartin's Little Girl.
Old Blazer's Hero. | Time's Revenges.
Val Strange. | Hearts. | A Wasted Crime.
A Model Father. | In Direst Peril.
By the Gate of the Sea. | Mount Despair.
A Bit of Human Nature. | A Capful of Nails.
First Person Singular. | Tales and Poems.

By MURRAY and HERMAN.
The Bishops' Bible. | Paul Jones's Alias.
One Traveller Returns.

By HUME NISBET.
'Bail Up!'

By W. E. NORRIS.
Saint Ann's. | Billy Bellew.

By G. OHNET.
A Weird Gift.

By Mrs. OLIPHANT.
The Sorceress.

By OUIDA.
Held in Bondage. | Two Little Wooden Shoes
Strathmore. | In a Winter City.
Chandos. | Friendship.
Under Two Flags. | Moths. | Ruffino.
Idalia. | (Gage.) | Pipistrello.
Cecil Castlemaine's | A Village Commune.
Tricotrin. | Puck. | Bimbi. | Wanda.
Folle Farine. | Frescoes. | Othmar.
A Dog of Flanders. | In Maremma.
Pascarel. | Signa. | Syrlin. | Guilderoy.
Princess Napraxine. | Santa Barbara.
Ariadne. | Two Offenders.

By MARGARET A. PAUL.
Gentle and Simple.

By JAMES PAYN.
Lost Sir Massingberd. | High Spirits.
Less Black than We're | Under One Roof.
Painted. | Glow-worm Tales.
A Confidential Agent. | The Talk of the Town.
A Grape from a Thorn. | Holiday Tasks.
In Peril and Privation. | For Cash Only.
The Mystery of Mir- | The Burnt Million.
By Proxy. | (bridge. | The Word and the Will.
The Canon's Ward. | Sunny Stories.
Walter's Word. | A Trying Patient.

By WILL PAYNE.
Jerry the Dreamer.

By Mrs. CAMPBELL PRAED.
Outlaw and Lawmaker. | Mrs. Tregaskiss.
Christina Chard.

By E. C. PRICE.
Valentina. | Foreigners. | Mrs. Lancaster's Rival.

By RICHARD PRYCE.
Miss Maxwell's Affections.

By CHARLES READE.
Peg Woffington; and | Love Me Little, Love
Christie Johnstone. | Me Long.
Hard Cash. | The Double Marriage.
Cloister & the Hearth. | Foul Play.
Never Too Late to Mend | Put Yourself in His
The Course of True | Place.
Love Never Did Run | A Terrible Temptation.
Smooth ; and Single- | A Simpleton.
heart andDoubleface. | A Woman-Hater.
Autobiography of a | The Jilt, & otherStories;
Thief; Jack of all | & Good Stories of Man
Trades; A Hero and | and other Animals.
a Martyr; and The | A Perilous Secret.
Wandering Heir. | Readiana; and Bible
Griffith Gaunt. | Characters.

By Mrs. J. H. RIDDELL.
Weird Stories.

By AMELIE RIVES.
Barbara Dering.

By F. W. ROBINSON.
The Hands of Justice. | Woman in the Dark.

By DORA RUSSELL.
A Country Sweetheart. | The Drift of Fate.

CHATTO & WINDUS, 111 St. Martin's Lane, London, W.C. 29

THE PICCADILLY (3/6) NOVELS—continued.

By W. CLARK RUSSELL.
Round the Galley-Fire.
In the Middle Watch.
On the Fo'k'sle Head.
A Voyage to the Cape.
Book for the Hammock.
Mystery of 'Ocean Star'
The Romance of Jenny Harlowe.
An Ocean Tragedy.
My Shipmate Louise.
Alone on Wide Wide Sea.
The Phantom Death.
Is He the Man?
Good Ship 'Mohock.'
The Convict Ship.
Heart of Oak.
The Tale of the Ten.
The Last Entry.

By BAYLE ST. JOHN.
A Levantine Family.

By JOHN SAUNDERS.
Guy Waterman.
Bound to the Wheel.
The Two Dreamers.
The Lion in the Path.

By KATHARINE SAUNDERS.
Margaret and Elizabeth
Gideon's Rock.
The High Mills.
Heart Salvage.
Sebastian.

By ADELINE SERGEANT.
Dr. Endicott's Experiment.

By HAWLEY SMART.
Without Love or Licence.
The Master of Rathkelly.
Long Odds.
The Outsider.
Beatrice & Benedick.
A Racing Rubber.

By T. W. SPEIGHT.
A Secret of the Sea.
The Grey Monk.
The Master of Trenance.
A Minion of the Moon.

By ALAN ST. AUBYN.
A Fellow of Trinity.
The Junior Dean.
Master of St. Benedict's.
To his Own Master.
In Face of the World.
Orchard Damerel.
The Tremlett Diamonds.

By JOHN STAFFORD.
Doris and I.

By RICCARDO STEPHENS.
The Cruciform Mark.

By R. A. STERNDALE.
The Afghan Knife.

By R. LOUIS STEVENSON.
The Suicide Club.

By BERTHA THOMAS.
Proud Maisie. | The Violin-Player.

By ANTHONY TROLLOPE.
The Way we Live Now.
Frau Frohmann.
Scarborough's Family.
The Land-Leaguers.

By FRANCES E. TROLLOPE.
Like Ships upon the Sea.
Anne Furness.
Mabel's Progress.

By IVAN TURGENIEFF, &c.
Stories from Foreign Novelists.

By MARK TWAIN.
Mark Twain's Choice Works.
Mark Twain's Library of Humour.
The Innocents Abroad.
Roughing It; and The Innocents at Home.
A Tramp Abroad.
The American Claimant.
Adventures Tom Sawyer
Tom Sawyer Abroad.
Tom Sawyer, Detective.
Pudd'nhead Wilson.
The Gilded Age.
Prince and the Pauper.
Life on the Mississippi.
The Adventures of Huckleberry Finn.
A Yankee at the Court of King Arthur.
Stolen White Elephant.
£1,000,000 Banknote.

By C. C. FRASER-TYTLER.
Mistress Judith.

By SARAH TYTLER.
Lady Bell.
Buried Diamonds.
The Blackhall Ghosts.
The Macdonald Lass.
The Witch-Wife.

By ALLEN UPWARD.
The Queen against Owen | The Prince of Balkistan.

By E. A. VIZETELLY.
The Scorpion: A Romance of Spain.

By WILLIAM WESTALL.
Sons of Belial.

By ATHA WESTBURY.
The Shadow of Hilton Fernbrook.

By C. J. WILLS.
An Easy-going Fellow.

By JOHN STRANGE WINTER.
Cavalry Life and Regimental Legends.
A Soldier's Children.

By MARGARET WYNMAN.
My Flirtations.

By E. ZOLA.
The Downfall.
The Dream.
Dr. Pascal.
Money. | Lourdes.
The Fat and the Thin.
His Excellency.
The Dram-Shop.
Rome. | Paris.

By 'Z. Z.'
A Nineteenth Century Miracle.

CHEAP EDITIONS OF POPULAR NOVELS.
Post 8vo, Illustrated boards, 2s. each.

By ARTEMUS WARD.
Artemus Ward Complete.

By EDMOND ABOUT.
The Fellah.

By HAMILTON AÏDÉ.
Carr of Carrlyon. | Confidences.

By MARY ALBERT.
Brooke Finchley's Daughter.

By Mrs. ALEXANDER.
Maid, Wife or Widow? | Valerie's Fate.
Blind Fate.

By GRANT ALLEN.
Philistia.
Strange Stories.
Babylon.
For Maimie's Sake.
In all Shades.
The Beckoning Hand.
The Devil's Die.
The Tents of Shem.
The Great Taboo.
Dumaresq's Daughter.
Duchess of Powysland.
Blood Royal. [piece.
Ivan Greet's Master.
The Scallywag.
This Mortal Coil.
At Market Value.

By E. LESTER ARNOLD.
Phra the Phoenician.

BY FRANK BARRETT.
Fettered for Life.
Little Lady Linton.
Between Life & Death.
The Sin of Olga Zassou-lich.
Folly Morrison.
Lieut. Barnabas.
Honest Davie.
A Prodigal's Progress.
Found Guilty.
A Recoiling Vengeance.
For Love and Honour.
John Ford; and His Helpmate.
The Woman of the Iron Bracelets.

By SHELSLEY BEAUCHAMP.
Grantley Grange.

By Sir W. BESANT and J. RICE.
Ready-Money Mortiboy
My Little Girl.
With Harp and Crown.
This Son of Vulcan.
The Golden Butterfly.
The Monks of Thelema.
By Celia's Arbour.
Chaplain of the Fleet.
The Seamy Side.
The Case of Mr. Lucraft.
In Trafalgar's Bay.
The Ten Years' Tenant.

By Sir WALTER BESANT.
All Sorts and Conditions of Men.
The Captains' Room.
All in a Garden Fair.
Dorothy Forster.
Uncle Jack.
The World Went Very Well Then.
Children of Gibeon.
Herr Paulus.
For Faith and Freedom.
To Call Her Mine.
The Bell of St. Paul's.
The Holy Rose.
Armorel of Lyonesse.
S. Katherine's by Tower.
Verbena Camellia Stephanotis.
The Ivory Gate.
The Rebel Queen.
Beyond the Dreams of Avarice.

By AMBROSE BIERCE.
In the Midst of Life.

By FREDERICK BOYLE.
Camp Notes.
Savage Life.
Chronicles of No man's Land.

BY BRET HARTE.
Californian Stories.
Gabriel Conroy.
The Luck of Roaring Camp.
An Heiress of Red Dog.
Flip. | Maruja.
A Phyllis of the Sierras.
A Waif of the Plains.
A Ward of the Golden Gate.

Two-Shilling Novels—*continued*.

By HAROLD BRYDGES.
Uncle Sam at Home.

By ROBERT BUCHANAN.
Shadow of the Sword. | The Martyrdom of Madeline.
A Child of Nature. |
God and the Man. | The New Abelard.
Love Me for Ever. | Matt.
Foxglove Manor. | The Heir of Linne.
The Master of the Mine. | Woman and the Man.
Annan Water. | Rachel Dene.

By BUCHANAN and MURRAY.
The Charlatan.

By HALL CAINE.
The Shadow of a Crime. | The Deemster.
A Son of Hagar. |

By Commander CAMERON.
The Cruise of the 'Black Prince.'

By Mrs. LOVETT CAMERON.
Deceivers Ever. | Juliet's Guardian.

By HAYDEN CARRUTH.
The Adventures of Jones.

By AUSTIN CLARE.
For the Love of a Lass.

By Mrs. ARCHER CLIVE.
Paul Ferroll.
Why Paul Ferroll Killed his Wife.

By MACLAREN COBBAN.
The Cure of Souls. | The Red Sultan.

By C. ALLSTON COLLINS.
The Bar Sinister.

By MORT. & FRANCES COLLINS.
Sweet Anne Page. | Sweet and Twenty.
Transmigration. | The Village Comedy.
From Midnight to Midnight. | You Play me False.
| Blacksmith and Scholar
A Fight with Fortune. | Frances.

By WILKIE COLLINS.
Armadale. | AfterDark. | My Miscellanies.
No Name. | The Woman in White.
Antonina. | The Moonstone.
Basil. | Man and Wife.
Hide and Seek. | Poor Miss Finch.
The Dead Secret. | The Fallen Leaves.
Queen of Hearts. | Jezebel's Daughter.
Miss or Mrs.? | The Black Robe.
The New Magdalen. | Heart and Science.
The Frozen Deep. | 'I Say No!'
The Law and the Lady | The Evil Genius.
The Two Destinies. | Little Novels.
The Haunted Hotel. | Legacy of Cain.
A Rogue's Life. | Blind Love.

By M. J. COLQUHOUN.
Every Inch a Soldier.

By DUTTON COOK.
Leo. | Paul Foster's Daughter.

By C. EGBERT CRADDOCK.
The Prophet of the Great Smoky Mountains.

By MATT CRIM.
The Adventures of a Fair Rebel.

By B. M. CROKER.
Pretty Miss Neville. | A Family Likeness.
Diana Barrington. | Village Tales and Jungle
'To Let.' | Tragedies.
A Bird of Passage. | Two Masters.
Proper Pride. | Mr. Jervis.

By W. CYPLES.
Hearts of Gold.

By ALPHONSE DAUDET.
The Evangelist; or, Port Salvation.

By ERASMUS DAWSON.
The Fountain of Youth.

By JAMES DE MILLE.
A Castle in Spain.

By J. LEITH DERWENT.
Our Lady of Tears. | Circe's Lovers.

By CHARLES DICKENS.
Sketches by Boz.

By DICK DONOVAN.
The Man-Hunter. | In the Grip of the Law.
Tracked and Taken. | From Information Received.
Caught at Last! |
Wanted! | Tracked to Doom.
Who Poisoned Hetty | Link by Link
  Duncan? | Suspicion Aroused.
Man from Manchester. | Dark Deeds.
A Detective's Triumphs | Riddles Read.
The Mystery of Jamaica Terrace.

By Mrs. ANNIE EDWARDES.
A Point of Honour. | Archie Lovell.

By M. BETHAM-EDWARDS.
Felicia. | Kitty.

By EDWARD EGGLESTON.
Roxy.

By G. MANVILLE FENN.
The New Mistress. | The Tiger Lily.
Witness to the Deed. | The White Virgin.

By PERCY FITZGERALD.
Bella Donna. | Second Mrs. Tillotson.
Never Forgotten. | Seventy-five Brooke
Polly. | Street.
Fatal Zero. | The Lady of Brantome

By P. FITZGERALD and others.
Strange Secrets.

By ALBANY DE FONBLANQUE.
Filthy Lucre.

By R. E. FRANCILLON.
Olympia. | King or Knave?
One by One. | Romances of the Law.
A Real Queen. | Ropes of Sand.
Queen Cophetua. | A Dog and his Shadow.

By HAROLD FREDERIC.
Seth's Brother's Wife. | The Lawton Girl.

Prefaced by **Sir BARTLE FRERE.**
Pandurang Hari.

By HAIN FRISWELL.
One of Two.

By EDWARD GARRETT.
The Capel Girls.

By GILBERT GAUL.
A Strange Manuscript.

By CHARLES GIBBON.
Robin Gray. | In Honour Bound.
Fancy Free. | Flower of the Forest
For Lack of Gold. | The Braes of Yarrow.
What will World Say? | The Golden Shaft.
In Love and War. | Of High Degree.
For the King. | By Mead and Stream.
In Pastures Green. | Loving a Dream.
Queen of the Meadow. | A Hard Knot.
A Heart's Problem. | Heart's Delight.
The Dead Heart. | Blood-Money.

By WILLIAM GILBERT.
Dr. Austin's Guests. | The Wizard of the
James Duke. | Mountain.

By ERNEST GLANVILLE.
The Lost Heiress. | The Fossicker.
A Fair Colonist. |

By Rev. S. BARING GOULD.
Red Spider. | Eve.

By HENRY GREVILLE.
A Noble Woman. | Nikanor.

By CECIL GRIFFITH.
Corinthia Marazion.

By SYDNEY GRUNDY.
The Days of his Vanity.

By JOHN HABBERTON.
Brueton's Bayou. | Country Luck.

By ANDREW HALLIDAY.
Every-day Papers.

By Lady DUFFUS HARDY.
Paul Wynter's Sacrifice.

By THOMAS HARDY.
Under the Greenwood Tree.

By J. BERWICK HARWOOD.
The Tenth Earl.

Two-Shilling Novels—continued.

By JULIAN HAWTHORNE.
Garth.
Ellice Quentin.
Fortune's Fool.
Miss Cadogna.
Sebastian Strome.
Dust.
Beatrix Randolph.
Love—or a Name.
David Poindexter's Disappearance.
The Spectre of the Camera.

By Sir ARTHUR HELPS.
Ivan de Biron.

By G. A. HENTY.
Rujub the Juggler.

By HENRY HERMAN.
A Leading Lady

By HEADON HILL.
Zambra the Detective.

By JOHN HILL.
Treason Felony.

By Mrs. CASHEL HOEY.
The Lover's Creed.

By Mrs. GEORGE HOOPER.
The House of Raby.

By TIGHE HOPKINS.
Twixt Love and Duty.

By Mrs. HUNGERFORD.
A Maiden all Forlorn.
In Durance Vile.
Marvel.
A Mental Struggle.
A Modern Circe.
Lady Verner's Flight
The Red House Mystery
The Three Graces
Unsatisfactory Lover.
Lady Patty.

By Mrs. ALFRED HUNT.
Thornicroft's Model.
That Other Person.
Self-Condemned.
The Leaden Casket.

By JEAN INGELOW.
Fated to be Free.

By WM. JAMESON.
My Dead Self.

By HARRIETT JAY.
The Dark Colleen. | Queen of Connaught.

By MARK KERSHAW.
Colonial Facts and Fictions.

By R. ASHE KING.
A Drawn Game.
'The Wearing of the Green.'
Passion's Slave.
Bell Barry.

By EDMOND LEPELLETIER.
Madame Sans-Gene.

By JOHN LEYS.
The Lindsays.

By E. LYNN LINTON.
Patricia Kemball.
The World Well Lost.
Under which Lord?
Paston Carew.
'My Love!'
Ione.
The Atonement of Leam Dundas.
With a Silken Thread.
Rebel of the Family.
Sowing the Wind.
The One Too Many.

By HENRY W. LUCY.
Gideon Fleyce.

By JUSTIN McCARTHY.
Dear Lady Disdain.
Waterdale Neighbours.
My Enemy's Daughter.
A Fair Saxon.
Linley Rochford.
Miss Misanthrope.
Camiola.
Donna Quixote.
Maid of Athens.
The Comet of a Season.
The Dictator.
Red Diamonds.

By HUGH MACCOLL.
Mr. Stranger's Sealed Packet.

By GEORGE MACDONALD.
Heather and Snow.

By AGNES MACDONELL.
Quaker Cousins.

By KATHARINE S. MACQUOID.
The Evil Eye. | Lost Rose.

By W. H. MALLOCK.
A Romance of the Nineteenth Century. | The New Republic.

By FLORENCE MARRYAT.
Open! Sesame!
Fighting the Air.
A Harvest of Wild Oats.
Written in Fire.

By J. MASTERMAN.
Half-a-dozen Daughters.

By BRANDER MATTHEWS.
A Secret of the Sea.

By L. T. MEADE.
A Soldier of Fortune.

By LEONARD MERRICK.
The Man who was Good.

By JEAN MIDDLEMASS.
Touch and Go. | Mr. Dorillion.

By Mrs. MOLESWORTH.
Hathercourt Rectory.

By J. E. MUDDOCK.
Stories Weird and Wonderful.
The Dead Man's Secret.
From the Bosom of the Deep.

By D. CHRISTIE MURRAY.
A Model Father.
Joseph's Coat.
Coals of Fire.
Val Strange. | Hearts.
Old Blazer's Hero.
The Way of the World.
Cynic Fortune.
A Life's Atonement.
By the Gate of the Sea.
A Bit of Human Nature.
First Person Singular.
Bob Martin's Little Girl
Time's Revenges.
A Wasted Crime.
In Direst Peril.
Mount Despair.

By MURRAY and HERMAN.
One Traveller Returns. | The Bishops' Bible.
Paul Jones's Alias.

By HENRY MURRAY.
A Game of Bluff. | A Song of Sixpence.

By HUME NISBET.
'Bail Up!' | Dr. Bernard St. Vincent.

By W. E. NORRIS.
Saint Ann's.

By ALICE O'HANLON.
The Unforeseen. | Chance? or Fate?

By GEORGES OHNET.
Dr. Rameau.
A Last Love.
A Weird Gift.

By Mrs. OLIPHANT.
Whiteladies.
The Primrose Path.
The Greatest Heiress in England.

By Mrs. ROBERT O'REILLY.
Phœbe's Fortunes.

By OUIDA.
Held in Bondage.
Strathmore.
Chandos.
Idalia.
Under Two Flags.
Cecil Castlemaine's Gage
Tricotrin.
Puck.
Folle Farine.
A Dog of Flanders.
Pascarel.
Signa.
Princess Napraxine.
In a Winter City.
Ariadne.
Friendship.
Two Lit. Wooden Shoes.
Moths.
Bimbi.
Pipistrello.
A Village Commune.
Wanda.
Othmar.
Frescoes.
In Maremma.
Guilderoy.
Ruffino.
Syrlin.
Santa Barbara.
Two Offenders.
Ouida's Wisdom, Wit, and Pathos.

By MARGARET AGNES PAUL.
Gentle and Simple.

By C. L. PIRKIS.
Lady Lovelace.

By EDGAR A. POE.
The Mystery of Marie Roget.

By Mrs. CAMPBELL PRAED.
The Romance of a Station.
The Soul of Countess Adrian.
Outlaw and Lawmaker.
Christina Chard.

By E. C. PRICE.
Valentina.
The Foreigners.
Mrs. Lancaster's Rival.
Gerald.

By RICHARD PRYCE.
Miss Maxwell's Affections.

TWO-SHILLING NOVELS—*continued.*

By JAMES PAYN.
Bentinck's Tutor.
Murphy's Master.
A County Family.
At Her Mercy.
Cecil's Tryst.
The Clyffards of Clyffe.
The Foster Brothers.
Found Dead.
The Best of Husbands.
Walter's Word
Halves.
Fallen Fortunes.
Humorous Stories.
£200 Reward.
A Marine Residence.
Mirk Abbey
By Proxy.
Under One Roof.
High Spirits.
Carlyon's Year.
From Exile.
For Cash Only.
Kit.
The Canon's Ward.
The Talk of the Town.
Holiday Tasks.
A Perfect Treasure.
What He Cost Her.
A Confidential Agent.
Glow-worm Tales.
The Burnt Million.
Sunny Stories.
Lost Sir Massingberd.
A Woman's Vengeance.
The Family Scapegrace.
Gwendoline's Harvest.
Like Father, Like Son.
Married Beneath Him.
Not Wooed, but Won.
Less Black than We're Painted.
Some Private Views.
A Grape from a Thorn.
The Mystery of Mirbridge.
The Word and the Will.
A Prince of the Blood.
A Trying Patient.

By CHARLES READE.
It is Never Too Late to Mend.
Christie Johnstone.
The Double Marriage.
Put Yourself in His Place
Love Me Little, Love Me Long.
The Cloister and the Hearth.
The Course of True Love.
The Jilt.
The Autobiography of a Thief.
A Terrible Temptation.
Foul Play.
The Wandering Heir.
Hard Cash.
Singleheart and Doubleface.
Good Stories of Man and other Animals.
Peg Woffington.
Griffith Gaunt.
A Perilous Secret.
A Simpleton.
Readiana.
A Woman-Hater.

By Mrs. J. H. RIDDELL.
Weird Stories.
Fairy Water.
Her Mother's Darling.
The Prince of Wales's Garden Party.
The Uninhabited House.
The Mystery in Palace Gardens.
The Nun's Curse.
Idle Tales.

By AMELIE RIVES.
Barbara Dering.

By F. W. ROBINSON.
Women are Strange. | The Hands of Justice.

By JAMES RUNCIMAN.
Skippers and Shellbacks. | Schools and Scholars.
Grace Balmaign's Sweetheart.

By W. CLARK RUSSELL.
Round the Galley Fire.
On the Fo'k'sle Head.
In the Middle Watch.
A Voyage to the Cape.
A Book for the Hammock.
The Mystery of the 'Ocean Star.'
The Romance of Jenny Harlowe.
An Ocean Tragedy.
My Shipmate Louise.
Alone on Wide Wide Sea.
The Good Ship 'Mohock.'
The Phantom Death.

By DORA RUSSELL.
A Country Sweetheart.

By GEORGE AUGUSTUS SALA.
Gaslight and Daylight.

By JOHN SAUNDERS.
Guy Waterman. | The Lion in the Path.
The Two Dreamers.

By KATHARINE SAUNDERS.
Joan Merryweather.
The High Mills.
Heart Salvage.
Sebastian.
Margaret and Elizabeth.

By GEORGE R. SIMS.
The Ring o' Bells.
Mary Jane's Memoirs.
Mary Jane Married.
Tales of To-day.
Dramas of Life.
Tinkletop's Crime.
My Two Wives.
Zeph.
Memoirs of a Landlady.
Scenes from the Show.
The 10 Commandments.
Dagonet Abroad.

By ARTHUR SKETCHLEY.
A Match in the Dark.

By HAWLEY SMART.
Without Love or Licence.
The Plunger.
Beatrice and Benedick.

By T. W. SPEIGHT.
The Mysteries of Heron Dyke.
The Golden Hoop.
Hoodwinked.
By Devious Ways.
Back to Life.
The Loudwater Tragedy.
Burgo's Romance.
Quittance in Full.
A Husband from the Sea

By ALAN ST. AUBYN.
A Fellow of Trinity.
The Junior Dean.
Master of St. Benedict's
To His Own Master.
Orchard Damerel.
In the Face of the World.

By R. A. STERNDALE.
The Afghan Knife.

By R. LOUIS STEVENSON.
New Arabian Nights.

By BERTHA THOMAS.
Cressida. | The Violin-Player.
Proud Maisie.

By WALTER THORNBURY.
Tales for the Marines. | Old Stories Retold.

By T. ADOLPHUS TROLLOPE.
Diamond Cut Diamond.

By F. ELEANOR TROLLOPE.
Like Ships upon the Sea.
Anne Furness.
Mabel's Progress.

By ANTHONY TROLLOPE.
Frau Frohmann.
Marion Fay.
Kept in the Dark.
John Caldigate.
The Way We Live Now.
The Land-Leaguers.
The American Senator.
Mr. Scarborough's Family.
Golden Lion of Granpere

By J. T. TROWBRIDGE.
Farnell's Folly.

By IVAN TURGENIEFF, &c.
Stories from Foreign Novelists.

By MARK TWAIN.
A Pleasure Trip on the Continent.
The Gilded Age.
Huckleberry Finn.
Mark Twain's Sketches.
Tom Sawyer.
A Tramp Abroad.
Stolen White Elephant.
Life on the Mississippi.
The Prince and the Pauper.
A Yankee at the Court of King Arthur.
The £1,000,000 Bank-Note.

By C. C. FRASER-TYTLER.
Mistress Judith.

By SARAH TYTLER.
The Bride's Pass.
Buried Diamonds.
St. Mungo's City.
Lady Bell.
Noblesse Oblige.
Disappeared.
The Huguenot Family.
The Blackhall Ghosts.
What She Came Through
Beauty and the Beast.
Citoyenne Jaqueline.

By ALLEN UPWARD.
The Queen against Owen. | Prince of Balkistan.
'God Save the Queen!'

By AARON WATSON and LILLIAS WASSERMANN.
The Marquis of Carabas.

By WILLIAM WESTALL.
Trust-Money.

By Mrs. F. H. WILLIAMSON.
A Child Widow.

By J. S. WINTER.
Cavalry Life. | Regimental Legends.

By H. F. WOOD.
The Passenger from Scotland Yard.
The Englishman of the Rue Cain.

By Lady WOOD.
Sabina.

By CELIA PARKER WOOLLEY.
Rachel Armstrong; or, Love and Theology.

By EDMUND YATES.
The Forlorn Hope. | Castaway.
Land at Last.

By I. ZANGWILL.
Ghetto Tragedies.

www.ingramcontent.com/pod-product-compliance
Lightning Source LLC
Chambersburg PA
CBHW032357230426
43672CB00007B/735